The RHS Encyclopedia of Practical Gardening

GARDEN PLANNING

ROBIN WILLIAMS

Robin Williams is a founder member of the Society of Garden Designers and has exhibited at the Chelsea Flower Show since 1969, winning 11 medals for constructed gardens. He has also contributed to numerous publications and books on garden design.

MITCHELL BEAZLEY

First published in 1996
Reprinted 1998, 1999
New edition 1999 Reprinted 2000, 2001, 2003, 2004

ISBN 1 84000160 7

Edited and designed by Mitchell Beazley, an imprint of Octopus Publishing Group Ltd
2-4 Heron Quays, London E14 4JP
Produced by Toppan Printing Co (HK) Ltd.
Printed and bound in Hong Kong

Contents

Introduction

Gardening is one of the world's most popular pastimes. It can be practised on many different levels: from tending a window box to working a garden of many acres, and this accounts for its almost universal appeal. Enjoyment may be a passive or active involvement, for gardens can be as stimulating, fascinating, restful and recreational to spend time in, as they are to create and work.

The response to and appreciation of a particular garden is, of course, highly subjective and each individual will draw on it emotionally and aesthetically according to his or her tastes. Gardens are very personal and frequently become an outward expression of their owners' characters. This is surely one of the reasons why designing one's own garden and watching it grow and develop can be one of life's most enduring pleasures.

The style of gardens has, over the centuries, reflected prevailing social conditions and developed in parallel with other forms of culture, and this remains true today. Because gardens normally take many years to establish they have been protected from the more extreme, often short-lived, trends. Garden fashions change, but relatively slowly, and there is still a place for traditional and modern design. Currently, there is much debate regarding the way forward in garden design but, in the final analysis, individuals will always design gardens according to their own needs and preferences.

There are as many reasons for wishing to create a garden as there are gardeners and the degree of involvement can range from an occasional weekend dabble through to almost fanatical devotion. So broad and diverse is the subject that there is something in it for everyone, whatever your level of interest, but it is important that the garden is appropriate for the level of use to which it is to be put and the interest of the gardener who is to develop and maintain it.

This book has been written for those who wish to develop their gardens into functional and beautiful places which fulfil their own desires and expectations. Anyone with sufficient enthusiasm is capable of designing a garden: the practical step-by-step approach adopted here should enable the reader to achieve a satisfactory and reasonably professional result.

The design process

With the many layers of detailed information that have to be synthesized, garden design is not a process that can be rushed. It must be approached methodically so that every aspect is considered before a final decision is made. This book goes through the critical stages of information gathering, measuring, plot and site assessment that contribute to the drawing up of a successful measurement plan.

Taking account of the owners' individual requirements and using them to draw up a function and outline plan will help to ensure that the design is truly individual and "tailor made". And a clear explanation of the principles of design will allow a schematic plan to be drawn up in an appropriate style and with features that will make the most of the plot.

Implementing the plan is the final step and with a methodical list of actions and the order in which they should be undertaken, the new design can be realized with confidence.

Glossary

Aggregates The sand and gravel that is mixed with cement and water to make concrete.
Arbour A shelter originally made by bending and weaving branches of trees or shrubs overhead – latterly a steel or cut timber structure.
Alpines Plants, usually of small stature or growing prostately, indigenous to high mountain terrain. Also applied, in gardening terms, to those plants suitable for a rock garden.
Axes Notional or actual sight lines around which a garden is designed.
Batter A backward slope at the face of a wall or embankment.
Bearer Used in a pergola, for example, to support lateral, overhead cross-beams. Another term for bearer is "joist".
Bond The pattern or arrangement that brick or stones have in paving or walling. In the case of walling, to give it strength.
Bull-nosed bricks Bricks used at the corner of the top of a wall which have been rounded off at the ends or edges.
Bund A mound of soil grassed or planted over, usually to appear naturalistic.
Butt-jointed Paving bricks or stones which touch, with no mortar or sand between them.
Butyl A waterproof, chemically transformed latex compound sheet used in pond making, valued for its strength and flexibility.
Calibration Inscribed or printed markings at regular intervals on measuring instruments, eg 1 m, 1 in.
Chevron A "V"-shaped pattern or design, for example, pointing upwards or downwards in a board fence, or to or from in a brick path.
Coping The weatherproofing layer at the top of a wall – usually extending beyond the wall a little at each side, ie "oversailing".
Course The individual horizontal layers that go to make up a wall, eg brick, stone, concrete blocks, etc.
Creasing course A course often of a different material to the main wall – tile, for example. Used for decorative and waterproofing purposes, usually projecting slightly beyond the wallface.
Cross-beams Part of an overhead structure – a pergola, for example (see Bearer).
Cross-fall Where the ground, lawn, or paving slopes from side to side – often deliberately introduced to shed rainwater.
Cross-section A drawing showing the changes in level, internal nature or workings of a design or structure.
DPC Damp-proof course – an impervious layer or sheet built into or applied to the bottom,top and, in retaining walls, the rear to prevent damaging water penetration.
Datum The point from which changes in levels are made or gauged. Usually expressed as 0.0. Subsequent comparative readings are expressed as plus or minus quantities.
Datum pole Usually a coloured, banded pole (eg red and white) stuck into the ground as a clearly visible indicator of the position of the datum.
Decking A popular reference to an area "paved" with timber boards as opposed to stone, brick, etc.
Directional compass A compass showing the position of magnetic north and consequently south, east, west, etc.
Dry-stone wall A wall built without any mortar between its joints, relying on its weight and structure for stability.
Elevation A scaled, two-dimensional drawing of any vertical element, eg a wall or gazebo (ie not drawn in perspective but as a plan), or one side of the element itself, eg the north elevation (facing) wall of a house.
Flexible curve A bendable plastic rule that can be used to achieve smooth curves when drawing.
Focal point The termination of a view that utilizes a distinctive artifact, sculpture, tree, etc. Focal points usually lie at the end of, or on, an axis, as in the case of an intermediate focal point.
French curve Drawing instrument possessing a varying curve at its edges used to achieve smooth curves when drawing.
Gazebo A structure or building from which views can be enjoyed.
Geotextile A spun polymer/mineral membrane used to stabilize ground and protect flexible pool liners from external or internal damage.
Grid line Notional lines, usually forming "squares" when at 90 degrees (as on graph paper), used in marking out and for recording changes in level – eg at the points where the grid lines intersect at 90 degrees.
Grotto Latterly, a man-made "cave", sometimes formal but having water within it in some form or another.

Groundfall Where or how the ground changes in level by becoming lower.
Hardwood Mostly timber derived from deciduous trees such as oak, elm, chestnut, mahogany, etc.
"Head" of water The point at which water issues from the ground, as in a high "spring", or at which a stream, cascade or waterfall starts.
Lime mortar Originally mortar made from builders' lime and sand or stone dust. Latterly a mix which contains lime but some cement to give more stability and durability, eg 1:2:8 – a typical paving bedding mortar where there is one proportion of cement, two of lime, and eight of sand.
Low-grade liner Polythene or other plastic used below impervious clay in pond lining, for example, to separate the clay from the soil beneath, or a material used to make a temporary pond.
Micro-climate A localized area where the prevailing climatic conditions are modified in some way, eg where the ambient temperature is higher due to the shelter provided by a wall or windbreak.
Mulch A layer of material placed upon the ground to reduce water-loss by evaporation, to inhibit weed growth and to moderate soil temperatures – eg organic materials, gravel, plastic sheeting, etc.
Offset A measurement taken at 90 degrees off a main base line measurement,
Overlay A means of testing ideas or modifications to an existing plan or photograph by drawing on a sheet of tracing paper laid over it.
Palisade In gardening terms a series of slender trees that have had their upper branches woven, tied or grafted together to appear as a series of arches. The main trunks are normally pruned of branches.
Pergola An open, overhead structure supported by posts or columns and usually carrying climbing plants.
pH The degree of alkalinity or acidity.
Pier The thickening of a wall at the ends or intermediately in order to give it added strength and stability.
Pleached hedge One that has been allowed to grow high and has then had its lateral branches woven along horizontal lines. Occasionally the lower part of the hedge is allowed to grow too and is clipped formally to create, with the bare trunks between, a series of "windows". Limes are the most popular trees for this type of hedge.
PVC Poly Vinyl Chloride – a vinyl plastic sheet used for pool lining and as a damp-proofing course in walls.
Range pole Calibrated (see Calibration) red/white colour-banded poles used in threes to aid the measurement of garden sites marking the conjunction of base lines.
Retaining wall Any wall that supports material pressures from the side – eg soil, water, paving bases, etc.
Roving pole A range pole which is moved around the garden during level-finding and against which changes in height can be gauged, when used in conjunction with a datum, or fixed pole and hand-held level.
Scale rule A special rule where the calibrations conform to specific scales reducing the true measurement to one more convenient to the designer for planning purposes, eg 1/50 represents one fiftieth of the actual size (approximately equivalent to one quarter inch to one foot). Each scale rule may have a variety of different scales upon it.
Scree The smaller broken rocks and gravel at the bottom of a rock face or cliff, resulting from natural weathering processes.
Sett A cube or block of hard stone used for paving or edging, eg granite.
Shuttering Vertical timber boarding or metal sheeting behind which concrete is poured to mould it to desired shapes and forms.
Triangulation A system for measuring a plot of land where it is divided into a series of notionally linked triangles.
Trompe l'oeil Literally "to deceive the eye". Devices used in garden design to, for example, create an illusion of greater space or create a focal point. Mirrors and altered perspective trellis are commonly used as *trompe l'oeil.*
Wearing layer The uppermost layer in a paving system that protects the base or supporting layers beneath from the wear and tear of vehicular and pedestrian traffic. In gardens, wearing layers are usually made attractive to make them visually acceptable as part of the design.
Xerophytic plants Plants tolerant of very dry habitats and able to withstand drought.
Xeroscaping Landscaping that utilizes xerophytic plants (xerophytes) in hot and/or dry climates or situations.

Where to begin

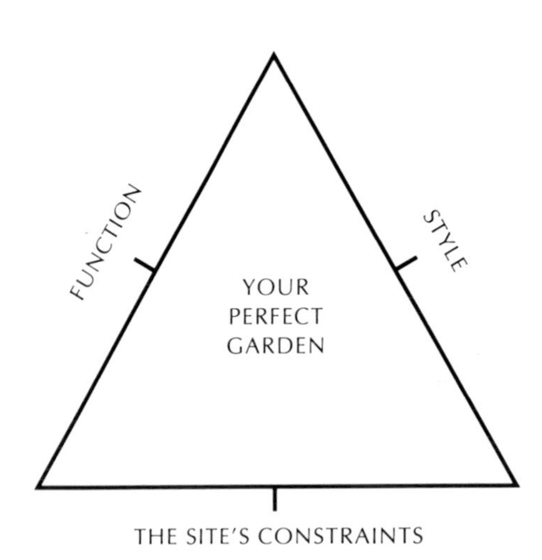

Think about your perfect garden in terms of an analogous design triangle. To begin with, the garden must be functional and fulfil all the needs of the owners. This suggests that it must also be feasible. Think also about the style of garden you prefer, not only in terms of your own expectations, but in terms of how it will harmonize with the site and associated architecture. Finally, consider how the functionality and style of the garden might be affected by the constraints set by the site – its shape, size, aspect, climate and so on. Bringing these three design factors together harmoniously should result in your perfect formula for success.

Some designers, both professional and amateur, design "on the ground", that is to say, without actually recording their design or thoughts on paper. This approach can work, but it calls for a great deal of skill and a good memory. Mistakes are much more expensive and difficult to rectify on the ground than on paper and, more to the point, to a budding designer even a modest plot can be intimidating. The importance of a drawn plan cannot, therefore, be emphasized too strongly.

Making a photographic record

When starting to assess your garden, it is helpful to make a full photographic record of the plot in all directions. The prints can then be pinned to a large board, preferably as a panoramic view. This can be especially helpful if the move to a new house and garden has not yet taken place and you are trying to prepare the garden plan in advance. Later on in the design process photographs can allow you to test the visual effects of your ideas. By overlaying them with tracing paper you can sketch in various options such as different tree shapes, path routes or an arch or pergola and decide which look best. Photographs are best taken from a normal standing or sitting position, since this is the height from which you will most frequently view and appreciate the garden. Photographs also provide the most accurate record of the garden features' relative positions.

The importance of a survey

It is vital to have an accurate record of the size and shape of the plot and of the features in it. Always start by taking measurements of the plot. This will ensure that every nook and cranny is recorded and, in the process, every view seen and remembered, for it is important to get to know the garden intimately.

Always check first to see if a measurement or survey plan exists before doing your own. If the site is fairly new or extensive alterations have been made recently, there may well be a survey of the house and its plot held by the architect or developer involved. If this is the case, and if the survey is sufficiently detailed, you can use this plan instead of making your own. Check the scale and at least a few of the measurements before using an existing plan, for it may have been enlarged or reduced, making the stated scale false. If this is the case, use a photocopier to reduce or enlarge the copy of the survey until it is to the correct scale.

Calling in a professional

If your garden is particularly large, or if the plot is very steep or complex in shape, it may be too difficult to measure by yourself. Calling in a professional surveyor will probably be more cost-effective and accurate in gardens of over about 1 acre (2½ hectares). Lazer instruments and computerized plotters can make light work of problems that would be almost insurmountable to the amateur surveyor.

On sites of several acres or more, an aerial survey undertaken by a professional is an option, although a costly one. This will give you a detailed analysis of your site and will even show, if requested, changes of level.

Tools and equipment

To survey your garden and draw up the measurement plan, you will need certain items of equipment, most of which are available from DIY shops, large stationer's or art shops.

1 Directional compass This is needed during the measuring and drawing up of a survey as the orientation of a garden determines the positioning of many of its features. Keep the directional compass away from strong electrical or magnetic fields as there is a risk of reversing the polarity. During the survey, avoid using the directional compass near any steel or iron objects, including the table if a metal one is being used, as these can distort the reading.

2 A 3 m (10 ft) retractable steel tape A tape of this kind is used for taking short measurements and, because of its comparative rigidity, it can be used for some vertical measurements. It can also be pushed through or beneath shrubs and hedges to take measurements in a way that would not be possible with a flexible tape measure. Retractable tapes are pulled out by hand to the appropriate length but retraction is usually automatic. The calibration on a 3 m (10 ft) tape is usually finer than that of a flexible tape measure, down to 1 mm or 1/16 in, and this is useful for taking precise details for construction projects.

3 Graph paper and masking tape Use graph paper rather than plain paper for survey plans because the squares will be a constant reminder of the scale and also help when it comes to drawing straight lines. Choose the size of graph paper most appropriate to the area you are surveying: the larger the plot, the larger the sheet of paper you need. A1 is perhaps the most popular size at 594 x 840 mm (23½ x 33 in), but for larger projects AO may be more appropriate at 840 x 1188 mm (33 x 47 in). For small projects, use A3 at 297 x 420 mm (11¾ x 16½ in). Graph paper is available in either an imperial or a metric scale; use whichever you favour but remember that metric measurements are easier to scale down. Buy paper with feint rather than bold rules so that your own pencil marks show up clearly. Use masking tape to

1 Directional compass
2 Retractable steel rule
3 Graph paper
4 Range poles
5 and **6** Tape measures
7 Folding table

Tools and equipment 2

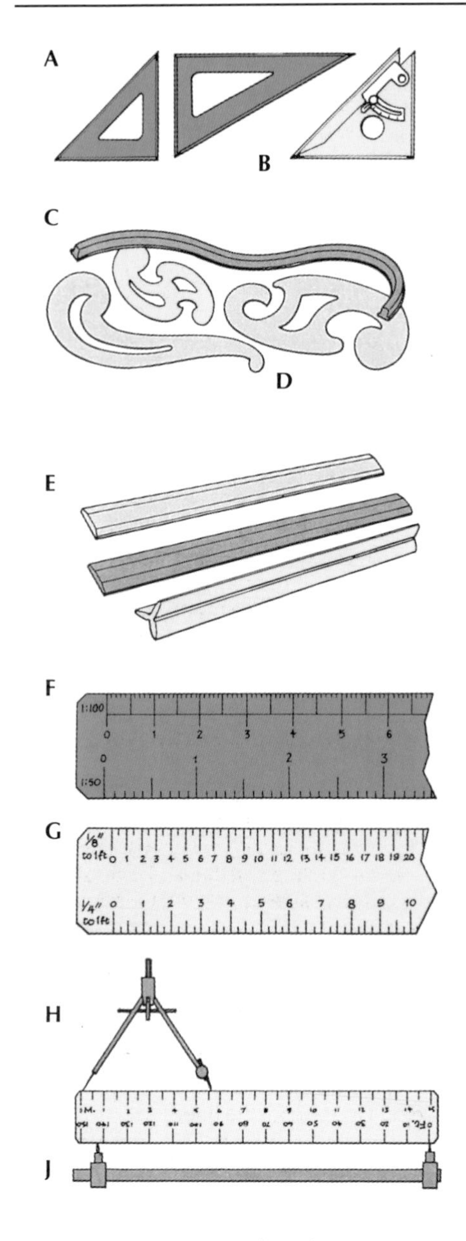

A Set squares (45° and 30°/60°)
B Adjustable set square
C Flexicurve
D French curves
E Scale rules: **F** Imperial; **G** Metric
H Pair of compasses
J Beam compass

stick the graph paper to the table, or you risk losing it in a gust of wind.

4 Range poles These are useful for surveying larger plots, especially those with no obvious boundaries. Range poles can be purchased from architectural suppliers or can be made at home. Available in wood or hard plastic and approximately 2 m (6 ft 6 in) tall and 2.5 cm (1 in) in diameter, range poles have a metal spike at one end to allow them to be stuck vertically into the ground and are painted in alternating bands of red and white some 20 cm (8 in) deep. Poles can be improvized from broom handles with a steel dibber (planting spike) fixed to the end, then painted as described above. Stout canes 1.5 m (5 ft) tall, calibrated using coloured electricians vinyl tape, are a convenient option.

5 and 6 Tape measures For general use a 30 m (100 ft) or 50 m (160 ft) tape measure is convenient and accurate over long distances. Two main styles are available: in the first the tape is enclosed in a plastic or plastic-covered circular steel case; in the second the tape is held in a frame. This second type is preferable since, if the tape becomes tangled or jammed, it can be freed easily. With the enclosed type the two halves of the case may have to be unscrewed and separated to untangle the tape.

Sprung steel and reinforced plastic tapes are available. Unless steel tapes are kept scrupulously clean and dry they may, with frequent use, start to rust; parts of the tape can eventually rust together, making it unusable. Reinforced plastic tapes must also be cleaned and dried after use. Choose imperial or metric calibration, or keep your options open with a tape calibrated in imperial on one side and metric on the other.

Using tape measures Always keep measuring tapes as close to the ground as possible, preferably on the ground. This way they will not be disturbed by the wind, nor can they sag in the middle, thereby giving a false reading.

When in use, a tape should be pulled taut for the sake of accuracy, but not excessively so since this may stretch or break it. When measuring through thorny plants or shrubs, extra care is needed. Sharp thorns can easily penetrate a plastic tape and might split it when you wind it up.

7 Table This serves as a mobile centre of operations. It should be portable, light and stable.

Set squares A 45° or 30°/60° set square is useful during the site assessment for plotting 90 degree offsets (see page 12) and later at the drawing board. It should not be smaller than about 20 cm (8 in) on the longest side. An adjustable set square, with a calibrated degree register and a fixing screw, can be used to plot practically any angle accurately.

French curves and flexicurves Transparent plastic French curves are available in sets of three or four units. They are moved around the paper until the desired curve can be traced. The process continues until the curve is complete. The flexible curve is available in lengths ranging from 30 cm (12 in) to 60 cm (24 in). The strip of tough, malleable plastic has a flat bottom surface to rest on the paper. To fix the curve temporarily, two vertical and parallel strips of sprung steel are embedded within the plastic. After use, the flexicurve must be turned on its side and straightened out against a flat surface.

Scale rule This allows measurements to be reduced to a given fraction of the full size so that they can be recorded, and helps to ensure that subsequent measurements are reduced at the same rate. Scale rules are also useful for reading a scaled-down plan to establish the real area that the plan represents. Scale rules are supplied in imperial or metric versions but rarely with both on the same rule. The formats vary: one scale rule might have a selection of larger scales while another has a selection of smaller scales.

Using a scale rule Ascertain the range of scales needed before making a purchase. Most scale rules are about 33 cm (1 ft) long and in cross-section they are usually thicker in the centre than at the edge. Different scales are printed on both sides of each long edge and their shape allows them to be rocked to place the calibrations directly against a drawing. Another type of scale rule has a cross-section in the form of a tri-star with concave sides and, again, the scales are printed along the outward edges. With the majority of scale rules two "related" scales are printed at each edge, for example 1:20 and 1:200.

Scale rules help to represent the scaled-down measurements as fractions. For example, the metric scale of 1:100 can be thought of as being 1/100 of the actual size, 1:50 as 1/50 and so on. On the 1:100 scale it will be seen that 1 m is represented by 1 cm as 1 cm is 1/100 of 1 m. The principle is the same for an imperial scale rule, but it is less obvious than with the metric scale. The scale of 1/8 in :12 in, for example, really represents a scale of 1:96 since 1/8 in is 1/96 of 12 in.

Transparent rule Most transparent non-scale rules are calibrated with centimetres on one edge and inches on the other. The types which have a series of parallel lines running horizontally are useful when lining up with other lines on the survey or plan drawing.

Pair of compasses These should have as wide a radius span as possible. For preference buy an extendible pair of compasses with an attachment to hold a propelling pencil or a pen. For particularly large radii a beam compass may be required. Both the beam compass point and the pencil-holding attachment can be moved along the beam to achieve the desired radius and then fixed in position with a pair of knurled screws.

Pencils and erasers Propelling pencils are useful for recording measurements and general designing work as they do not need to be sharpened and the thickness of the lead is consistent. The most useful size of lead is 0.3 mm or 0.5 mm lead in HB or B hardness. For surveying, choose an ordinary pencil in a bright colour that would be easy to spot should it be dropped onto grass or soil. A brightly coloured pencil eraser should always be on hand. If the eraser is too hard, it may damage the surface of the paper, especially if the paper is damp; too soft an eraser will smudge the line.

THE MOST POPULAR AND USEFUL SCALES

Metric / imperial (approximate equivalents)

1:200 / 1/16 in:1 ft (gardens of several acres)
1:100 / 1/8 in:1 ft (gardens of up to 1 acre)
1:50 / 1/4 in:1 ft (smaller or terrace gardens)
1:20 / 1/2 in:1 ft (very small gardens and construction detail)

The measurement plan

Starting to take measurements

The information to be collected forms the basis of the measurement plan and of the final design, so it is essential to work methodically and carefully. Do not be tempted to hurry this stage. A fine, still day will afford the best conditions for recording your findings.

With the table erected, graph paper stuck down firmly with masking tape and the rest of the equipment assembled, start by pacing out the garden or plot with approximately 1 m (3 ft) strides, roughly measuring the longest distances lengthways and across the garden. This will help you to decide on an appropriate scale for your plan so that the measurements to be drawn up can be accommodated on the graph paper. The larger the scale the better, since this will allow you to record more detail. Remember that 1:50 is a larger scale than 1:100.

Once you have decided on the scale, record it immediately in pencil at the side of the paper as it is surprisingly easy to forget.

Plotting the house

Again by pacing, determine the approximate size of the house and fix its position on the site, then pencil it in on the graph paper. For the next stage, start measuring the house using the tape measure and, using the scale rule, draw it in on the graph paper. Do not take too many measurements at a time before recording them.

Many of your subsequent measurements will be taken from the house, using the walls as "base lines", so be as accurate as you can. Include items such as drainpipes, windows and doors (noting whether they open inward or outward). If there are deep eaves, indicate with a dotted line how far they project beyond the house wall as they will create "rain shadows", resulting in dry areas underneath. This will have to be taken into consideration when choosing plants.

Measuring

A garden of half an acre or less can certainly be measured by one person. If you are working alone, you will have to secure the end of the tape each time you take a measurement, though most tape measures have a metal loop at the end that can be passed over a cane to hold it in place. If you can enlist help, it should speed up the process.

Triangulation

After measuring the house and plotting it on the graph paper, give each house corner a code letter, as shown opposite, and write the letters clearly on the plan. Next, establish and plot the corner points of the garden, then join them with lines to represent the garden boundary. The most convenient way of measuring the corners is to use a method called triangulation. This involves drawing a series of triangles on the plan using a scale rule and a pair of compasses or a beam compass. It is based on measurements taken on the ground using a 30 m (100 ft) tape and a 3 m (10 ft) steel retractable tape.

In the example shown opposite, a physical measurement is taken from house corner A to the boundary corner, in this case corner 1. The measurement is read from the tape and converted at the chosen scale using the scale rule, then plotted on the graph paper plan using the compasses, opened so that the radius (the distance between the compass point and the point of the pencil) accords with the scaled-down measurement. The compass point is placed on the plan on house corner A and a generous arc is drawn in the general location of the boundary corner 1 using the pencil in the compasses. Following the same process a second measurement is taken, this time from house corner B to boundary point 1 again. The true measurement is scaled down to give a radius for the compasses and, with the compass point at house corner B, a second arc is drawn, bisecting the first. The point at which the two arcs cross gives the precise position of boundary corner 1.

On your plan, establish and record each boundary corner in this way, using the appropriate house corners as points of reference. As each boundary corner is fixed, draw lines to join them. Check that your work is accurate by taking a physical measurement between the points of the boundary corners, scaling it down and comparing it with the distance you have plotted on the measurement plan.

Taking the time to do this as each corner point is established will make it easy to spot any errors and correct them immediately.

Occasionally a corner or object may be out of sight of the house, as is the case with corner 6 in the diagram. To establish its position, the position of the garage must be fixed, then the garage corners used as the reference points.

The measurement plan

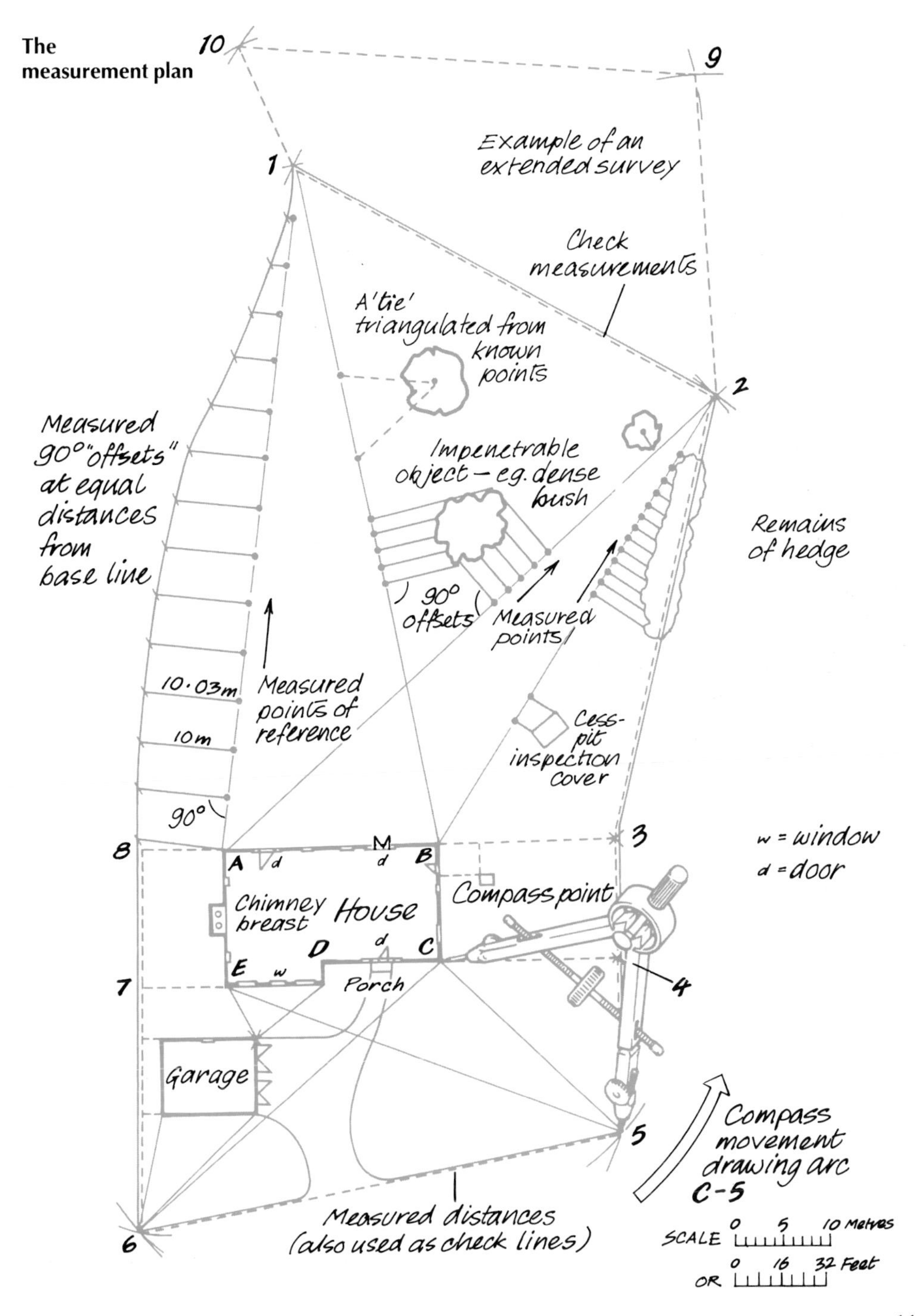

The measurement plan 2

In a very large garden with distances well beyond the scope of a 30 m (100 ft) or even 50 m (150 ft) tape measure, or where there are areas partly or wholly hidden from view, triangulation can still be achieved using a "leap frog" method. In the example shown on page 11, an established distant line 1–2 is used as a base line for the next section of the measurement plan. In the extended survey, further triangles have been constructed to fix the hypothetical corners 9 and 10.

Offsets

To plot curved boundaries or features, "offsets" are taken. Offsets are measured lines running at 90 degrees to the base line, usually at regularly spaced intervals, say 1 m (3 ft 3 in), 2 m (6 ft 6 in) or 3 m (10 ft). The more complicated the curve, the closer the offsets need to be.

In the measurement plan on page 11, the boundary line 1–8 is plotted by taking offsets from A–1, the nearest base line, but if there is no convenient line on which to base the offsets, you may have to establish one for the purpose.

A dot or cross is drawn on the graph paper to represent the end of each offset line drawn away from the base line. These dots or crosses are then joined with a pencil line to represent the curved boundary.

You can plot other features in this way, including thick bushes or areas of water, starting the measurements from the edges of the feature and moving toward the middle. It is important to ensure that the tape for measuring the offsets is at 90 degrees to the base line: this can be done by laying a second tape along the base line on the ground, making sure it is flat and taut. Then use a large set square or a builder's square to check that the offsets are perpendicular to it.

An alternative method of checking that the tapes are at right angles to each other is to lay the offset tape over the base line tape with its edge along the printed calibrations on the base

Positioning tapes for offset measurements

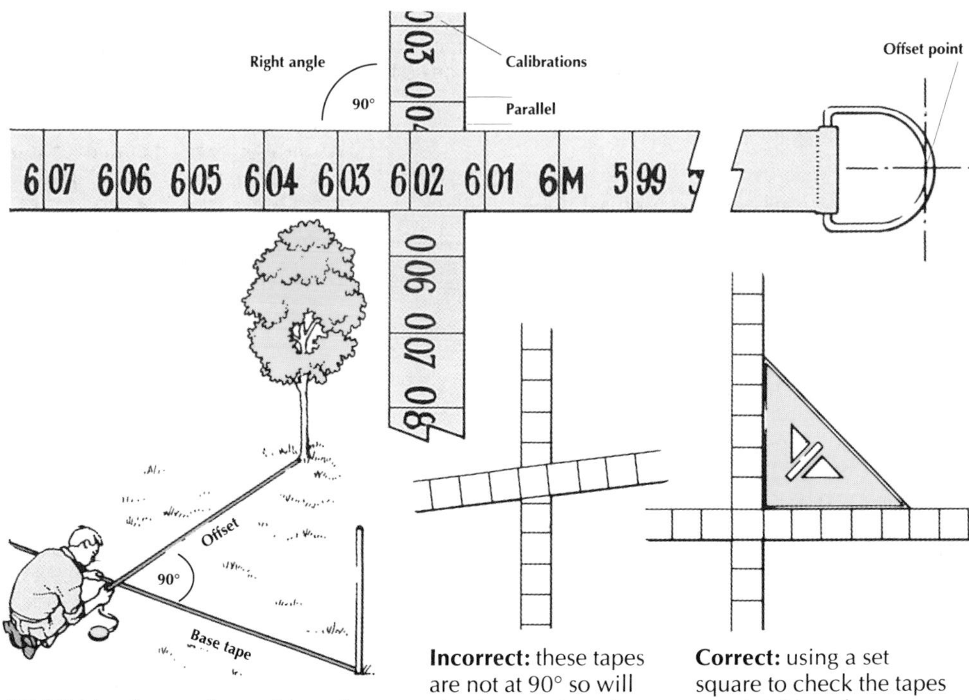

Establishing the precise position of a tree.

Incorrect: these tapes are not at 90° so will give incorrect readings.

Correct: using a set square to check the tapes are at right angles.

line tape. It will be apparent if the offset tape is not at 90 degrees as the tape and printed calibration lines will not line up.

Offsets are fairly accurate for distances of up to 10 m (30 ft) from the base line tape and can be used in conjunction with triangulation to establish the precise positions on the measurement plan of, in the example on page 12, a tree. When recording the positions of trees, it is as well to measure and record their approximate canopies or spreads at the same time, as the shade they cast will have a bearing on future planting plans.

Sighting off

If the plot is square or rectangular with the house sited squarely on it, and the boundaries or other features are close to the house, you may not need to use triangulation to establish their positions. A method known as "sighting off" is adequate, but two people are needed. One person looks along the appropriate house wall until it appears as a single vertical line while the second person, under instruction from the first, places a range pole or cane against the object or boundary to be plotted. The second person pushes the pole or cane into the ground at a point where it and the line of the house wall appear to align, then measurements can be taken between the two.

Range poles

Range poles or canes can be used as mobile points of reference and are especially useful if there are no other physical reference points in the plot being measured.

When using range poles for triangulation, however, remember to position the poles or canes forming the triangle so that they are clearly visible and the space between them is clear. Remember also to stretch the tape measure straight between the points being measured since the results will be inaccurate if the tape is curved or bent.

Adding detail

The "flat" measurement plan, giving a bird's eye view of the plot and the features in it, is important, but there are many other pieces of information that may have a bearing on your approach to garden design. This extra data can be recorded either on the measurement plan, or separately. One of the most important details you need to measure and record is any rise and fall in ground levels.

Changes of level

Whatever the style of garden you intend to design, you must take account of any changes of level in the plot, although if it is to consist mostly of grass, trees and shrubs, perhaps arranged in a naturalistic and informal way, you need only approximate information on the ground contours.

If you are designing a sloping garden along formal lines, perhaps with terraces, walls and steps, for example, then you need more precise information on the degree of slope. For example, if you intend to create a flat area upon an existing slope there will have to be an increase in the degree of the slopes immediately to the front and the rear of the flattened area. If you propose to build steps up the slope, you will have to calculate the number needed, their dimensions and the angle of ascent and descent. Without accurate measurements it would be easy to make some serious and expensive mistakes (see Structure, space and movement: Coping with sloping gardens, page 64).

Plotting cross-sections

If slopes are badly sited either naturally or as a result of poor planning, they can obliterate an attractive view from a house window or terrace.

Once the information about the slope has been gathered, sketch a simple cross-section or two of the garden (see Design principles: Cross-sections, page 42) to assess how they fit into the proposed design.

Establishing changes in level

Changes in level can be measured using simple equipment. This is especially so if only "spot" level measurements are required, indicating the relative levels of specific points in the garden: for example, the patio door relative to an inspection cover or to the base of a tree, or the four corners of a garden relative to each other.

Professionals use the "grid system", which calls for a comprehensive set of readings taken and recorded at the points of intersection of a series of equally spaced, notional parallel lines running at right angles to form squares over the

Site assessment

Using structures to establish ground levels

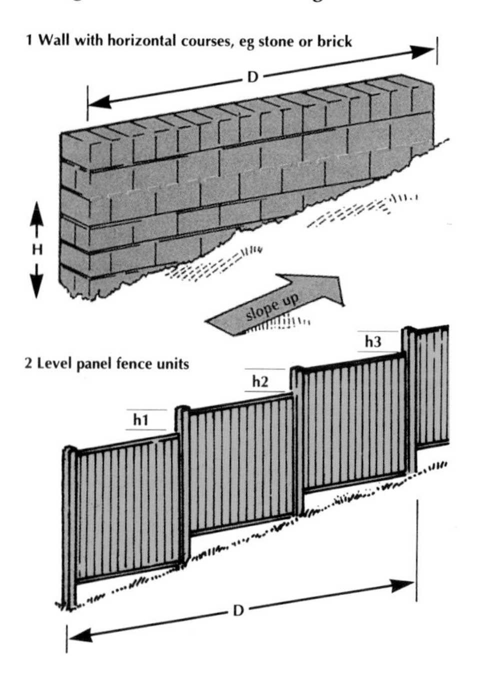

Wall:
H1 = height gained over distance D
Fence:
h1 + h2 + h3 = height gained over distance D

site (the grid). A measurement plan like this would probably have to be carried out professionally, whereas a spot measurement plan is much easier to achieve.

Using a wall or buildings to establish ground levels

In order to be appropriate for this technique, a wall must be constructed with its courses and mortar joints level and clearly visible, so brick and regular stone walls are most suitable. Where the ground is at its highest relative to the wall, make a note of the brick or stone horizontal mortar joint it reaches. Run your finger along this horizontal joint to the end of the wall and mark it, perhaps with a chalk line. Measure vertically down to the soil at this point, (H in the diagram). The reading indicates by how much the ground has sloped relative to the starting point. The distance over which the slope has occurred is equal to the length of the wall.

If the ground slopes fairly evenly beyond the wall, you can work out the approximate slope over the whole garden. Divide the length of the wall section into the overall length of the garden and multiply the result by the groundfall you have measured along the length of the wall. If the ground slopes by 450 mm (18 in) over the length of the wall, say 16 m (52 ft 6 in), and the entire garden length is 70 m (265 ft), the overall fall would be approximately 2.19 m (7 ft 2 in).

EQUATION

$$\frac{\text{Length of garden: 78 m (256 ft)}}{\text{Length of wall: 16 m (52 ft)}} \times \frac{\text{groundfall}}{\text{wall length: 0.45 m (18 in)}}$$

= fall over entire garden: 2.19 m (7 ft 2 in)

78 (256) ÷ 16 (52) = 4.87 (4.92)

4.87 (4.92) x 450 mm (18 in) = 2.19 m (7 ft 2 in)

Using panel fencing

There are countless gardens with ready-made fencing panels forming their boundaries. These are rectangular and are erected using vertical posts, so the tops of the panels should be level. This means that the rise or fall in the ground level of the garden can be calculated by adding together the measured steps h1 + h2 + h3 and so on (see diagram left). Base the measurements on relative tops of panels rather than on the posts since they often project unevenly and may have caps or finials attached.

Where the fence does not run the whole length of the garden, but the ground seems to slope more or less evenly beyond it, use the same principle as for the wall. Calculate the approximate overall slope by dividing the length of the fence into the length of the garden and multiply the result by the fall measured over the length of the fence.

Using a spirit level and straightedge

Choose a timber or metal straightedge about 2 m (6 ft 6 in) long. Check that it is straight by looking along its length with one eye; any bows will be apparent immediately. Lay the spirit level on top of the straightedge, then, resting one end of the straightedge on the ground at the highest level, lift the other until the bubble in the spirit level shows that it is horizontal.

Drive a stake into the ground just under the lifted or raised end of the straightedge. When you can place the raised end on top of the stake and the spirit level shows the straightedge to be horizontal, measure from the top of the stake to the ground. This indicates the fall over the entire length of the straightedge. Repeat the process, working down the slope, placing the end of the straightedge hard up against the base of the vertical stake. The entire slope can then be measured.

As an alternative to a timber straightedge, a 25mm square length of steel box shelving can be utilized. This will not warp as timber might; however, if the distance between the pegs is much over the recommended 2 m (6 ft 6 in), even this could sag a little and give a false level reading. Make the length of the straightedge an even measurement such as the 2 m (6 ft 6in) suggested. This will act as a distance gauge in the spacing of pegs and make the subsequent calculation simpler.

EQUATION

Calculate as follows:
Total length of the garden divided by the multiple of the length of the straightedge, multiplied by the sum of the heights, straight edge measured to ground.

Example:
The garden's length is 72 m (234 ft) approximately. The length of the straightedge is 2 m (6 ft 6in). Therefore, the length of the garden requires 36 separate straightedge readings.

The total fall measured from beneath the straightedge to the ground adds up to 4.15 m (13 ft 6 in approximately). The groundfall may vary a little down the slope so the 4.15 m (13ft 6 in), when divided by 36 straightedge lengths, shows an average fall of 12.5 cm (5 in) every 2 m (6 ft 6 in) equivalent to 6.25 cm (2½ in) every metre (3 ft 3 in).

Using a spirit level and straightedge to determine groundfall

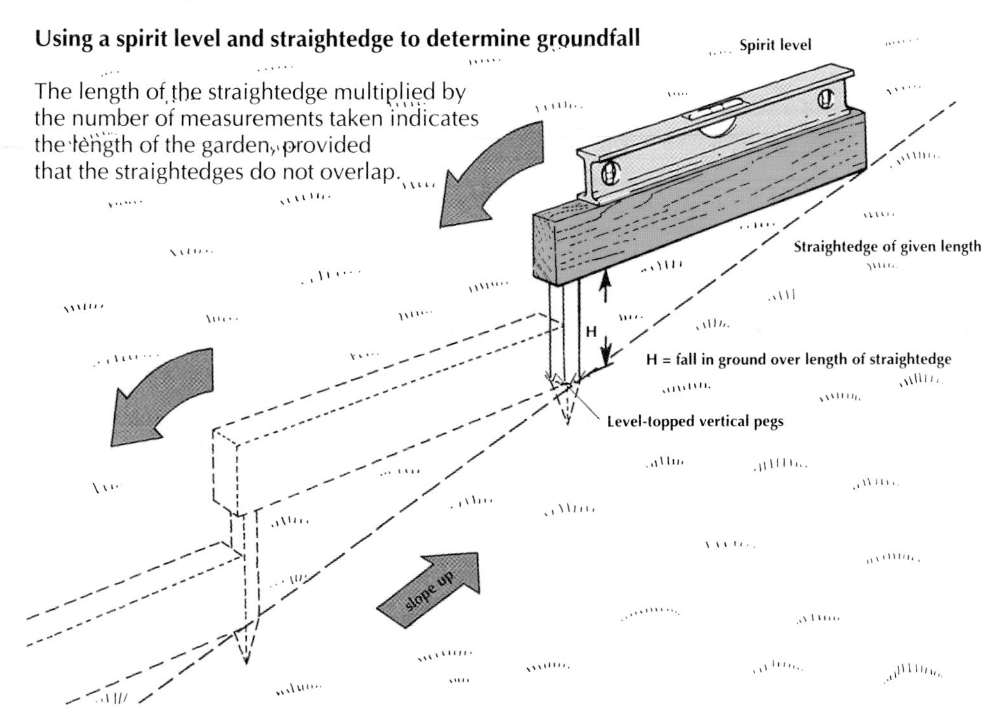

The length of the straightedge multiplied by the number of measurements taken indicates the length of the garden, provided that the straightedges do not overlap.

Site assessment 2

Using a garden hosepipe and two funnels

Start by inserting transparent funnels into each end of a garden hose. The hosepipe must be at least as long as the distance over which the fall is to be measured. Drive a stake vertically into the ground and attach one end of the hose with the funnel attached to it. Ask someone to hold the other end of the hosepipe with its funnel or, if the slope is particularly steep, it is better to attach the funnel to a hand-held pole (see diagram below).

Using a watering can or a second hose, slowly pour water into the fixed upper funnel A until the lower funnel B overflows. Move the lower funnel B up and down, carefully, and slowly add more water until in both funnels it is brimming but not overflowing. At this stage the funnels are at the same level. Now ask a third person to measure from the top lip of the "lower" funnel B to the ground using a steel tape. Subtract the height of funnel A from the height of funnel B to establish the groundfall between the two. One advantage of this method is that the hosepipe need not be straight and this makes it possible to measure around corners. In addition, the two people handling funnels A and B do not need to be able to see each other provided that they are within shouting distance. The method will not work properly, however, if there is a kink in the hosepipe or if any section of the hose is higher than the funnels, since either situation would affect the flow of water.

Using a hand-held level

The hand-held level is an inexpensive optical instrument which, with a little practice, can be used without an assistant. It comprises a horizontally mounted spirit level which is reflected in such a way as to appear vertical to the operator when looked at through the viewfinder. At the side is an opening affording a view of what lies beyond in the garden. Running horizontally across the centre of this "view" is a fine black line. By gently tilting the hand-held level up and down, the black line will eventually coincide with the bubble of the reflected spirit level. This will indicate that the instrument is

Using a hosepipe and two funnels to establish ground levels

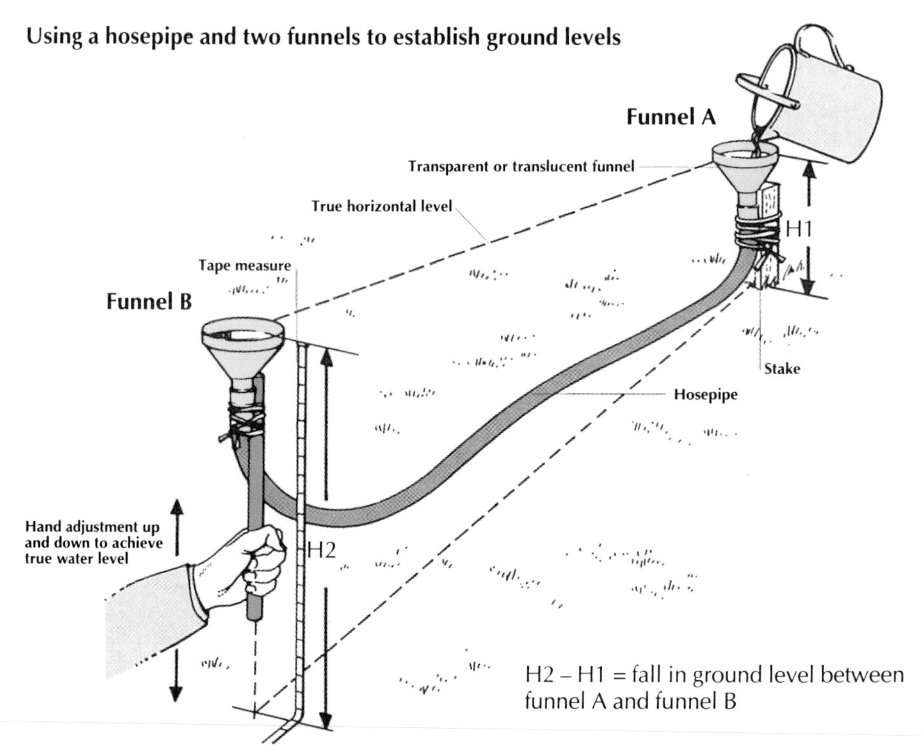

level and can be used in conjunction with a couple of range poles to detect changes in level.

The range poles must be the same height, preferably about 1.5 m (5 ft) rather than 2 m (6 ft 6 in) and calibrated identically. One is pushed into the ground at the lowest point to represent datum and remains there while all the measurements are taken.

Note by how much the datum pole is driven into the ground. Then drive the other pole, known as the "rover", into the ground by the same amount as the point where the increase in ground height is to be measured. Rest the hand-held level on top of the datum pole and look into the viewfinder. Move the level gently up and down until the horizontal line within the instrument bisects the bubble. Now look beyond the line and bubble to see where the horizontal line appears to coincide with the calibrations of the rover pole. You can estimate the change in level by noting how many calibrations appear above the horizontal line of the hand-held level and record this on the measurement plan as a plus quantity, such as +450 mm (18 in) or +750 mm (2 ft 6 in).

Reposition the rover in any part of the garden to establish spot levels, but make sure it is clearly visible from the datum pole. You may occasionally need to measure levels that are lower than the datum. Under these circumstances, position the rover in the lower spot and take the reading from there back to the datum pole, but record these measurements on the plan as minus quantities, such as -300 mm (1 ft) or -900 mm (3 ft), since they are lower than the datum.

Assessing a mature garden

If you inherit a mature garden and intend to make changes to meet your own requirements, do not make any immediate decisions because at any time of year there are bound to be plants that are dormant and features and effects that are not immediately apparent. If you assess a garden in winter, there may be no evidence of bulbs or herbaceous plants. Similarly, in summer, paths, paving and ornaments may be lost under luxuriant plant growth or grass. It is wise simply to observe the garden for a year before making plans and to note information for plotting on the site assessment.

In the meantime, you can clear any obviously overgrown plants, shrubs and grass, along with paths. Even so it is wise to exercise restraint as

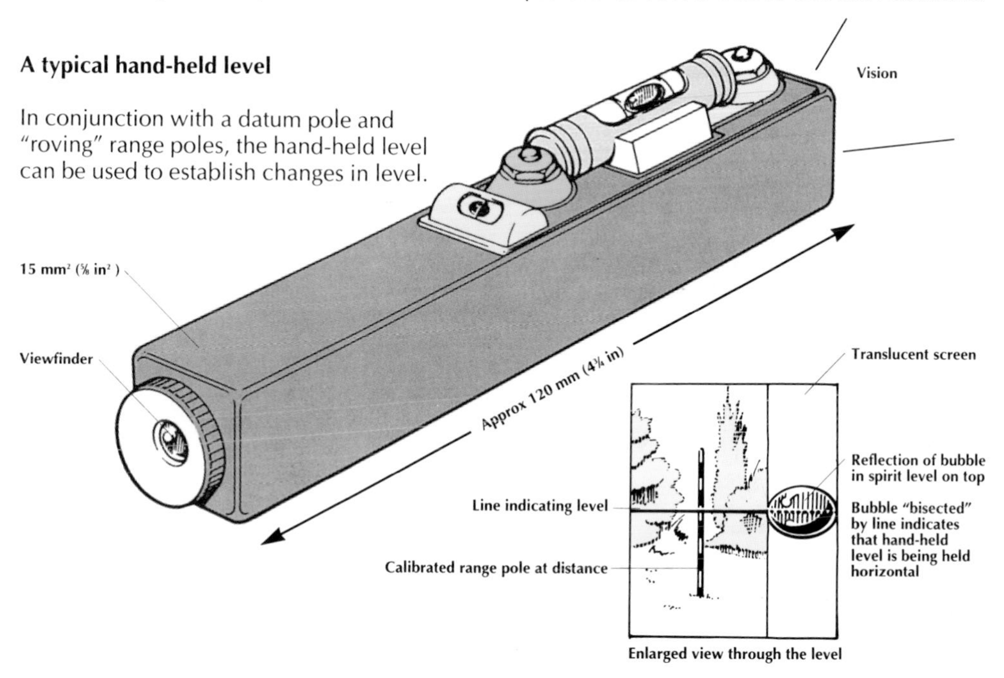

A typical hand-held level

In conjunction with a datum pole and "roving" range poles, the hand-held level can be used to establish changes in level.

Site assessment 3

Using a hand-held level and range poles

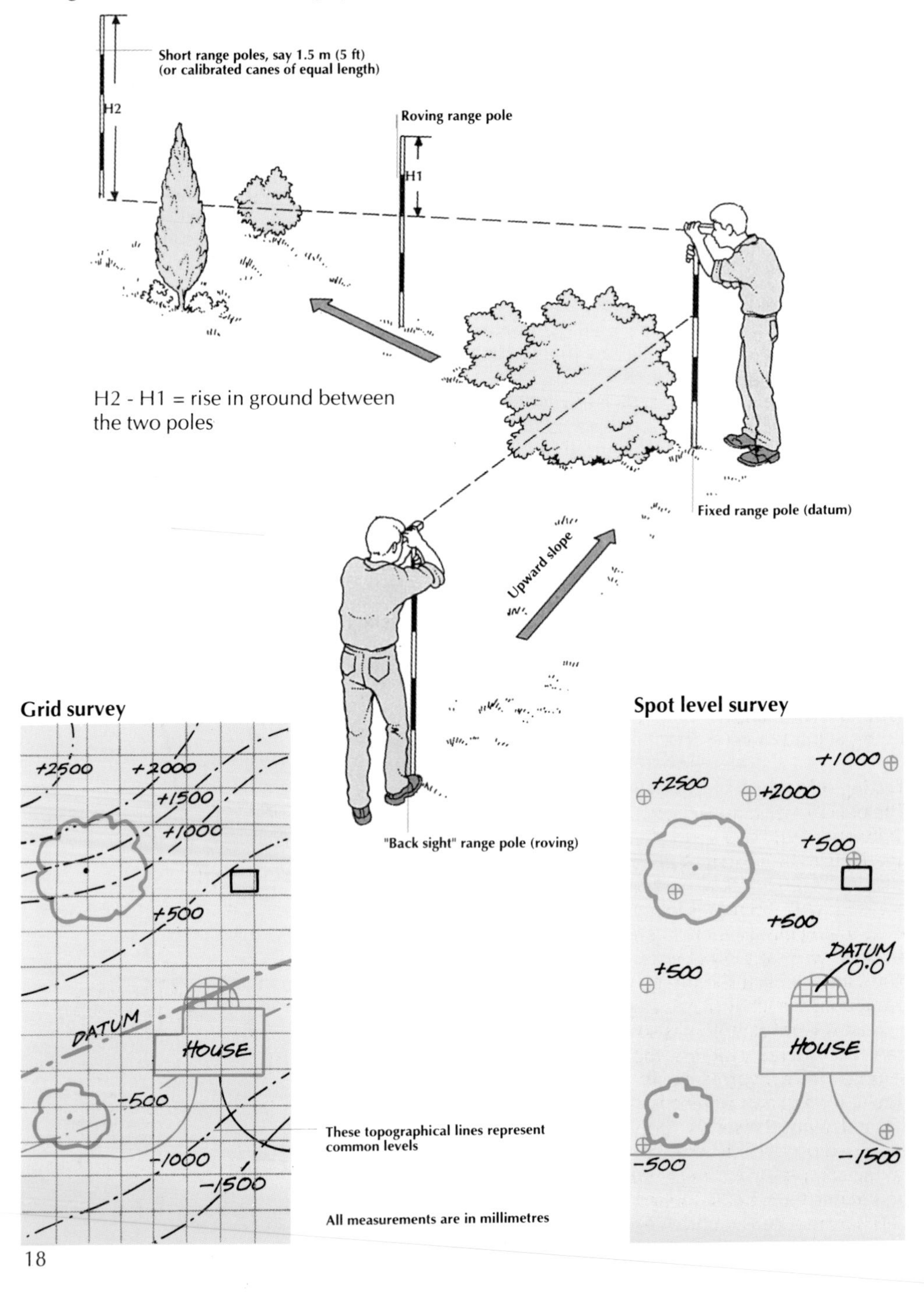

some of the existing features may contribute to the new scheme and it may be possible to move established plants around in your new design. This will help to reduce costs, and incorporating existing plants and features into a new design will give an instant sense of maturity which might otherwise take years to achieve.

Testing soil type

The best garden design is useless if no attention is paid to the soil, as the soil must be in good condition if the plants specified in the design are to thrive. In general, plants should be chosen to suit the local soil type, but it is not unknown within new housing developments for the native soil to have been removed and replaced with a token layer of soil from elsewhere, or soil of poor quality. A conscientious developer will put the top soil back in sufficient quantity to allow a garden to be established.

In any new garden make a proper check of the soil rather than relying on superficial observations. First check the soil structure. There are books in this series (see back cover for details) describing how checks can be made to identify the clay, sand, silt and organic material content, together with advice on correcting any deficiencies and methods of soil improvement. Then assess its texture and, if necessary, take steps to bring it closer to the ideal open crumb structure that allows optimal movement of water, air and roots.

Testing soil pH

The pH is a measurement of soil acidity or alkalinity and it will dictate the types of plants that are likely to thrive in it. A pH of 7.5 or higher is alkaline, 7 is neutral, while figures lower than 7 are acid, with 4.5 representing a very acid soil. Acid-loving plants, such as rhododendrons and azaleas, will simply not grow in alkaline soil. You can establish the pH of your garden soil using a simple kit available at garden centres.

Take several samples, as soil conditions can vary considerably across the plot. Take the samples from approximately 150 mm (6 in) down, then carry out the test as soon as possible, as leaving the soil in a polythene bag for an extended period may alter its condition. Avoid taking samples from areas where fertilizers or herbicides have been applied as these chemicals may result in an unrepresentative reading.

pH "test tube" testing kit

Soil testing with pH meter

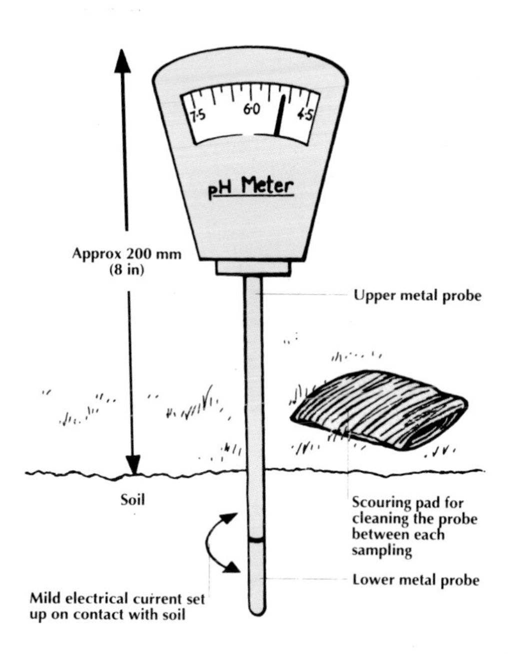

Plotting the site assessment

Plotting the information gained from the site assessment helps to assemble the design jigsaw. The site assessment plan shown opposite has been drawn up separately from the measurement plan, but it would be just as easy to combine the two. The garden site assessment plan adds a great deal of information to the "flat" measurement plan of the same plot, including changes in level, areas of shade, the direction of the prevailing wind, hot spots, dry spots, soil pH and type and routes of underground and overground services wherever possible. Make a note of any old garden structures, such as paths, concrete bases and greenhouses, as occasionally items can be recycled in the new design. Most of the features on it will be within the garden, but also record any that are outside the garden which affect the design, such as a neighbour's trees. There is no point including any features that will definitely not be retained in the new design, unless they are required as reference points to help with the measuring process. If in doubt about whether or not to keep an item, include it at this early stage of the design process.

Example of site assessment plan

In the example opposite, the datum point has been chosen at the level immediately to the rear of the house and changes in level are recorded as plus or minus (+ or -) quantities relative to datum. Datum could be established anywhere in the garden and it is usual to choose a low point, but it is generally easier to appreciate changes in level in relation to the house. Here, the level at the front door is precisely the same as that at the rear but this is often not the case, especially when gardens are steeply sloping.

The example shows that the garden level is higher at the front boundary in the left corner – +600 mm (24 in) with a cross-fall to +300 mm (12 in) in the right corner, viewed from the road. In other words, the ground falls between the two corners by 300 mm (12 in). From the front door at datum 0.0, the drive rises to the road by some 475 mm (18½ in). This signals a potential problem with water drainage near the front door. At the rear of the house the ground falls unevenly and a cross-fall remains from left to right, again viewed from the road.

The cesspit cover is 300 mm (12 in) lower than datum while the level about halfway down the rear garden is -150 mm (6 in). The lowest point, however, is far centre left, where -500 mm (-19½ in) is recorded relative to datum. Water collects at this point in winter. Almost immediately behind this the ground begins to rise in a small hillock to +600 mm (24 in).

The soil type is clay to loam with a pH range from the front to the rear of the garden of pH 6.5 to pH 7.5 (from slightly acid to alkaline).

Using information from the site assessment

Use the information gathered in the site assessment to make informed decisions about planting. Remember to mark north and south on the assessment plan so that the aspect of the garden is clear. The passage of the sun relative to the garden affects which part of the garden is allocated to which function. This is especially relevant when there are tall objects inside or outside the garden, as the shadows they cast are significant and will differ in size and intensity through the seasons. Cold winds not only cause personal discomfort but can damage tender plants, so position appropriate screening or choose hardier plants for windy areas. Tackle the problem of overlooking buildings or unsightly objects by introducing screening structures or plantings, or choose more secluded areas for leisure pursuits.

Structural safety

Check the routes of underground utilities and services wherever possible in order to avoid, for example, constructing garden wall foundations over sewer pipes. Lift inspection (man-hole) covers to see how far down any pipe junctions are. This may be a limiting factor on any plans you have to reduce ground levels in the immediate area. Carefully dig test holes to check the extent of wall or house foundations which might lie near to the ground surface and always avoid planning beds or borders requiring deep cultivation at the front of an existing retaining wall, since this might compromise the stability of the wall. Never plant "thirsty" trees like willows and poplars near to drains, as they can cause damage to the drains, even causing them to collapse. It is worth checking the drain routes in advance. Electronic detectors can establish the routes of underground metal pipes and electrical circuits more safely and conveniently than accidental discovery with a spade or fork.

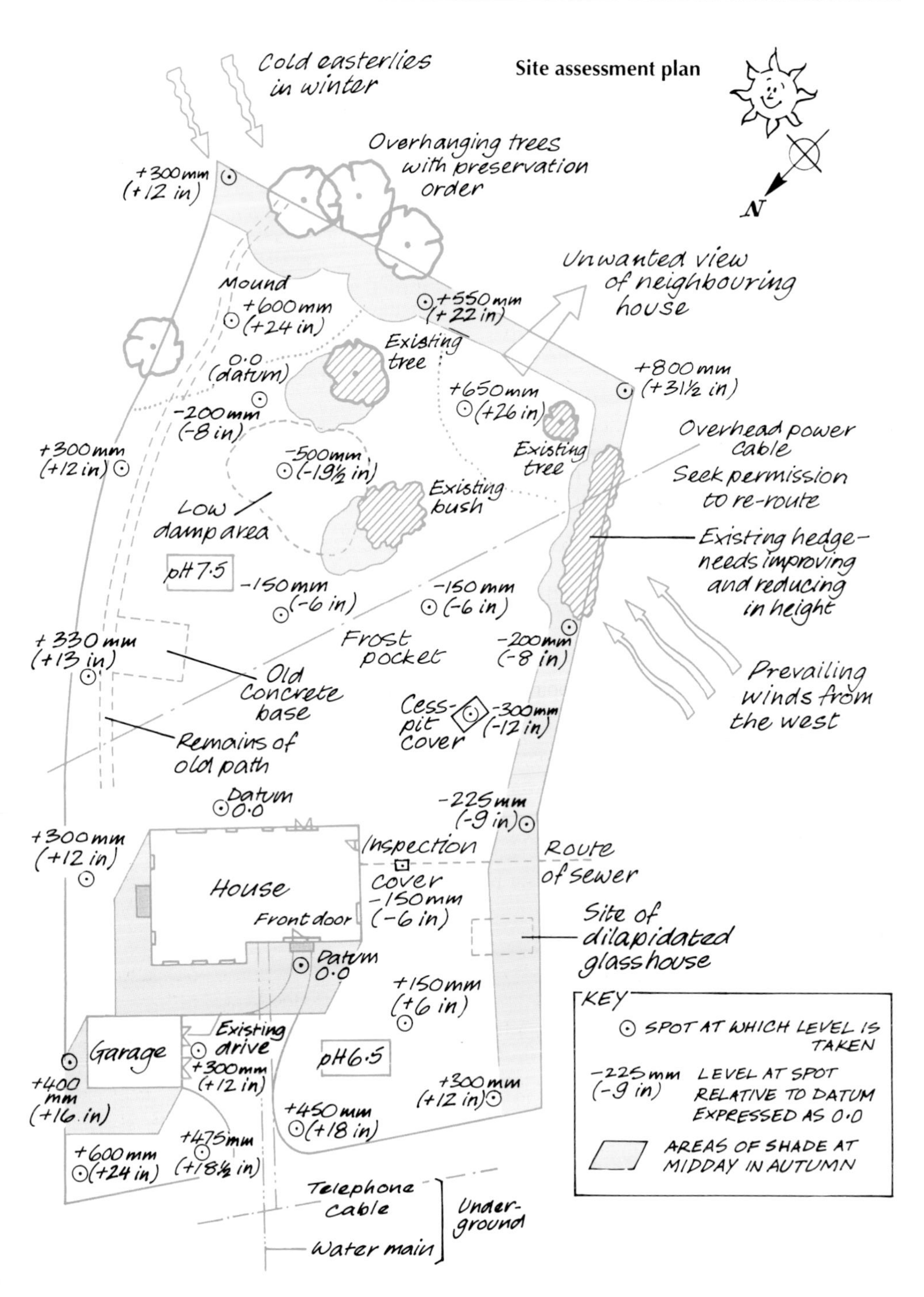

Site assessment plan
Cold easterlies in winter
Overhanging trees with preservation order
N
Unwanted view of neighbouring house
+300 mm (+12 in)
Mound +600 mm (+24 in)
+550 mm (+22 in)
Existing tree
0.0 (datum)
+650 mm (+26 in)
+800 mm (+31½ in)
-200 mm (-8 in)
Existing tree
Overhead power cable
Seek permission to re-route
+300 mm (+12 in)
-500 mm (-19½ in)
Existing bush
Low damp area
Existing hedge- needs improving and reducing in height
pH 7.5
-150 mm (-6 in)
-150 mm (-6 in)
+330 mm (+13 in)
Frost pocket
-200 mm (-8 in)
Prevailing winds from the west
Old Concrete base
Cess-pit cover
-300 mm (-12 in)
Remains of old path
Datum 0.0
-225 mm (-9 in)
+300 mm (+12 in)
Inspection cover
-150 mm (-6 in)
Route of sewer
House
Front door
Site of dilapidated glasshouse
Datum 0.0
+150 mm (+6 in)
Garage
Existing drive
+300 mm (+12 in)
pH 6.5
+400 mm (+16 in)
+300 mm (+12 in)
+450 mm (+18 in)
+600 mm (+24 in)
+475 mm (+18½ in)
Telephone cable
Water main
Under-ground
KEY
SPOT AT WHICH LEVEL IS TAKEN
-225 mm (-9 in) LEVEL AT SPOT RELATIVE TO DATUM EXPRESSED AS 0.0
AREAS OF SHADE AT MIDDAY IN AUTUMN

Garden function

Estimating costs

When designing a garden, it is important to consider the costs involved as you go along. Try to form at least an idea of the costs of plants, materials and services as the design develops, by visiting builders' merchants, garden centres and nurseries at an early stage to gauge current prices. You must decide how much of the work you are prepared or able to do yourself. DIY is obviously the least expensive option but you may decide to consult a professional garden contractor for at least some of the work. The contractor will need to be fully briefed in order to estimate accurately, so provide as much information as possible.

Materials and labour

As a rough guide, the cost of implementation is approximately the same as the cost of the materials. For example, a tree costs about the same to plant, stake and tie as it does to buy. Similarly, the cost of paving units per square metre will be about the same as the cost per square metre of having them laid.

Try to set a realistic overall budget at the outset; then, as the design develops, research the cost of implementing each area. Certain details of the design may have to be trimmed or adjusted as work advances to ensure that the work stays within budget, but this is better than having to abandon the project halfway through because funds have run out.

For a larger garden and an ambitious design, it might be better to organize the development programme so that it spans several years, in which case it is even more important to draw up a detailed budget forecast.

Needs and requirements

Each garden is unique. Even if the layout is originally identical to that of a neighbouring plot, the respective owners soon begin to express their individual ideas and tastes. A garden serves a purpose unique to its owner and family. Start by making a list of everything that is required from the garden.

Such a list can become complicated: it must include but distinguish between what is needed, what is desired and what is expected. What is truly needed must take top priority: for example, a means of approaching the front door or garage safely and directly and service paths linking the doors around the house. A "self sufficient" family might consider a vegetable garden or goat paddock an absolute necessity, and so on. What is desired might include a rose garden, a pool, a rock garden or a velvety lawn, while it is somewhat more difficult to define what is expected, and this is where style, atmosphere and aesthetics come into the equation.

A garden for everyone

Bringing the needs, desires and expectations of all the family members together into an harmonious whole is one of the most difficult parts of garden design. Almost inevitably the opinions or requirements of some members will be unacceptable to others. If the family circle includes younger children it is important that their needs are given equal consideration. However, since the needs and expectations of children alter dramatically almost from year to year, it is better to design a children's area to allow for change rather than to build it into the permanent structure of the garden.

To begin with, the drawing up of a family requirement list should be a "free for all" session. In the final analysis the list may not be entirely feasible or indeed affordable, but without it (and a degree of democracy) there is little chance of satisfying even one individual, let alone the whole family. The resulting list is unlikely to be exhaustive and a professional designer's list might be more formally constructed, but what matters is that the list is made. The needs, desires and expectations will migrate from one heading to another according to a particular family's priorities. When planning something as personal as a garden, individual tastes and wishes will dictate the general as well as the particular requirements.

Spend plenty of time studying the requirements list with the function plan (see page 25), then take a sheet of tracing paper, lay it over the site assessment plan and, using a pencil, start to allocate various areas on the plan that would best suit the proposed facilities. For example, set aside the sunniest, most sheltered spot for sunbathing and site the terrace for dining out and general use near the house for convenience. If the terrace occupies a sunny position, it can accommodate sun-worshippers and thereby perform a dual role.

THE SMITHS' GARDEN DESIGN PROJECT

Needs

1. Front door position to be more obvious
2. Drive to be enlarged and re-surfaced
3. Additional paths needed to link the front door with rear doors
4. Vegetable garden
5. A large tool shed (the garage now houses two cars)
6. Dog run and kennels for Jumbo and Myrtle
7. The existing pond to be fenced off for safety of the twins
8. The dilapidated fence on the road side to be replaced for safety and security
9. More space for the children, including a larger terrace for play following wet weather

Desires

1. Bed for cut flowers
2. Fine green lawn
3. Summer house
4. Plants to encourage birds and butterflies
5. Larger terrace for sunbathing and alfresco meals
6. Roses
7. Herbaceous border
8. Winter interest
9. Greenhouse
10. Secret area or den for the children
11. Sunken garden
12. Ferns, hostas, hellebores and other shade-loving plants
13. Pergola
14. Swing and climbing frame
15. Colourful flowers, tubs and planters
16. Lawn space for badminton

Expectations

1. General informality
2. A sense of security, privacy and mystery
3. The garden to "live" comfortably on the site and with surrounds
4. A series of linked sub-gardens
5. Changing views from the house windows
6. A welcoming front garden to set off the house
7. A sense of peace and tranquillity

Don't hesitate to move things around on paper. Take as much time as you need to get them exactly in their right place in functional terms as far as you are concerned. You will only get one opportunity to get it right. It might be too late after installation. Think of this very important, and, yes, exciting stage of the design as a dynamic jigsaw puzzle. The function of the garden, is, after all, its very reason for being.

Always ensure that each "functional" area is of an appropriate size, proportion or shape. As with the proportions of vertical elements, certain functions cannot be performed without a reasonable amount of space. Cardboard cut-outs made to scale, of seats, tables, ornamental and swimming pools – not forgetting their surrounds – are invaluable indications of how much space will be needed to accommodate them. These will help you to make sure that there is not only enough space to be functional, but, also, that there is not too much space where the feature could appear insignificant, or out of proportion with the surroundings. At this stage we are not concerned with form (this is the next stage in design), simply where and how things are going to happen.

The logic of garden function

When designing rear and side gardens, many professional designers commence drawing their function plan from the house, perhaps starting at the main point of access. The most important view of a rear garden will probably be from the house doors, windows or terrace, so this is the logical place to begin. Even though we know that particular functions have their most appropriate places within the garden and therefore their own "natural" order, starting here, and moving outwards, introduces a degree of logic to the process. This is helpful on two counts: firstly, each different function and new idea is given continuity, and secondly, it is more likely to result in a pleasing composition.

The same principle can, of course, be applied to the front garden, but here it is a good idea to start at the entrance to the drive and work towards the house. You will be aware from the start of the differing roles of the front and rear gardens: the front as an entrance, and house-setting versus the more generally recreational and horticultural function of the rear garden.

Garden function 2

This, then, is the value of the function plan: it allows ideas to be explored and activity areas or features to be moved around on paper until they are allotted their most appropriate place in the general scheme of things.

Example of a function plan

The example of a function plan (opposite) was produced by overlaying the assessment plan with tracing paper and drawing over it. This is where garden designing really begins.

Front garden

Starting at the front of the house, the owners have agreed that the drive needs upgrading and even enlarging to accommodate extra car parking or a turning area (the space needed for this is often underestimated).

The garage is not particularly attractive and the idea is that it should be visually softened from the direction of the road. The opposite side of the drive could be planted simply with grass and trees, or a formal treatment could incorporate something for the rose enthusiast. In either case, the garden should be cheery and welcoming. The trees and grass option would have the effect of "framing" the house, while a rose garden would become a feature in its own right, needing sensitive design in order to contribute to the composition as a whole and not be in conflict with it.

Improving access

Good access is called for at each side of the house, as is a general separation between front and rear areas.

The shady side of the house provides an opportunity to grow ferns and other shade-loving plants, but when such areas are situated at a distance from a house they risk becoming neglected and should be made as accessible and inviting as possible.

The sunny side of the house is generally agreed to be the best place for growing vegetables and herbs, especially as it is close to the kitchen door.

Placing the terrace

The area immediately to the rear of the house, being in full sun until well into the afternoon, is designated the centre of family recreational activities, including sitting, dining, sunbathing and children's wet weather play. The area needs to be large to accommodate this. Even a simple item such as a table 900 mm (3 ft) in diameter with four chairs, requires a surprisingly large space to permit ease of use: you should set aside an area of up to 4 m (12 ft) in diameter. This allows for sitting down and getting up and easy circulation all around.

Away from the house

Beyond the terrace is an open area of lawn with the other features arranged at its periphery. The left side of the grassed area is reserved for children's play, while to the left of that the wisteria-clad pergola has been positioned. The dip in the ground (see Site assessment plan, page 21) is the obvious place for the "wildlife" pool, although it will not be constructed until the children are old enough to enjoy it safely.

Trees and shrubs have been planted in the far corner to link with those in the neighbouring plot. The idea is to create the effect of light woodland while concealing the boundary fence, making the garden appear larger than it actually is as it will seem to extend into the adjacent area. Functionally, this planting will also create an effective barrier to the cold winter winds.

On the far right more trees will be needed to screen the neighbour's house from view. This same general area will accommodate a second sitting area for those members of the family who prefer shade to sun. Those seeking peace and quiet will also be heading in this direction.

Dealing with problem features

The existing cess-pit is not ideally placed as far as the new owner is concerned, but it is considered too costly an exercise to relocate it. Such unsightly but necessary features frequently have to be incorporated into gardens; the skill of the designer involves including them as unobtrusively as possible.

In addition to the specifications of the function plan, access routes around the garden must be planned with care. These form the "skeleton" of a garden design and, while being primarily practical, they are a valuable means of linking the various areas of a garden. At the function planning stage, access routes can only be approximated, but at the next stage routes will need to be precise.

The basic garden's function plan (on tracing paper)

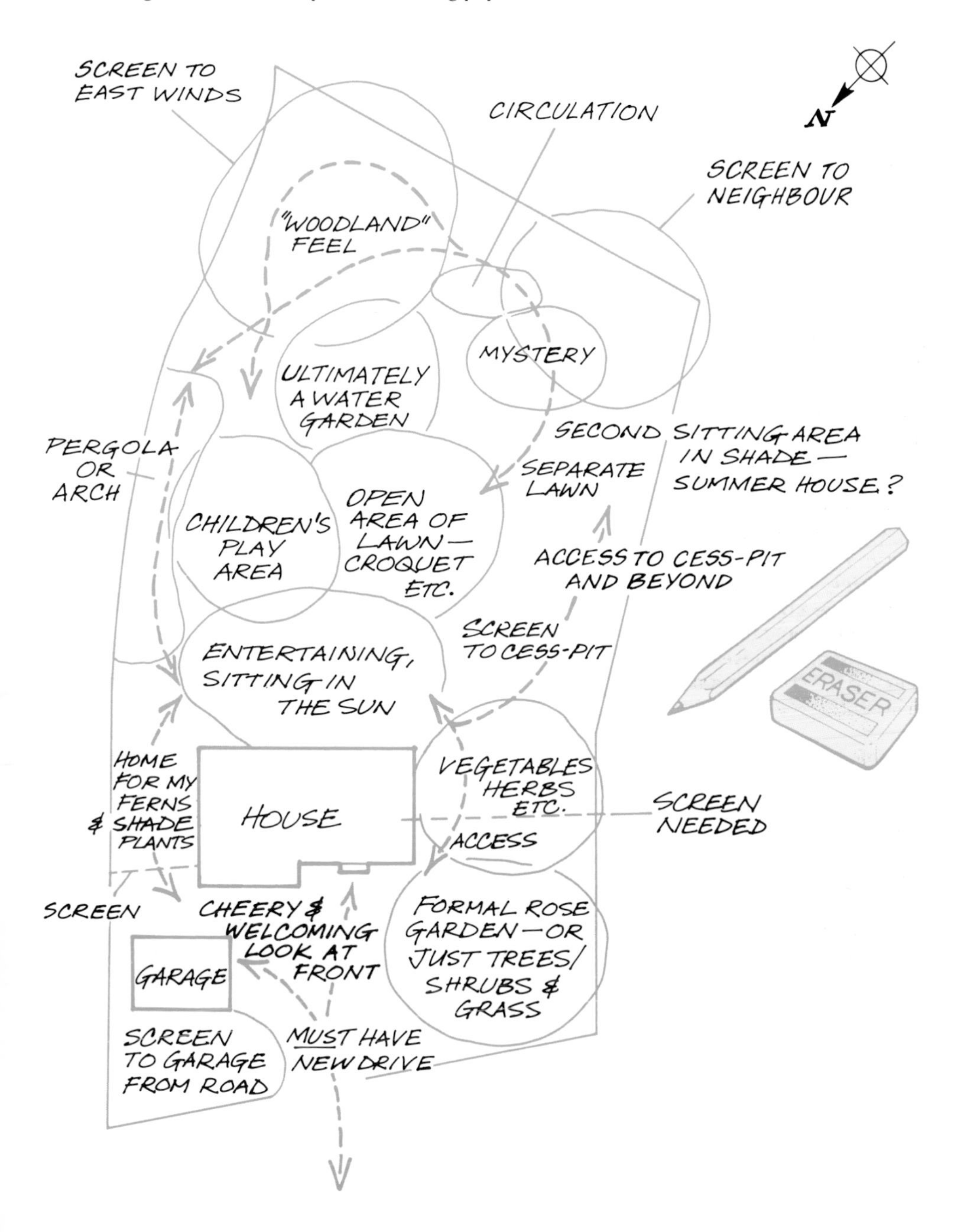

Theory and technique

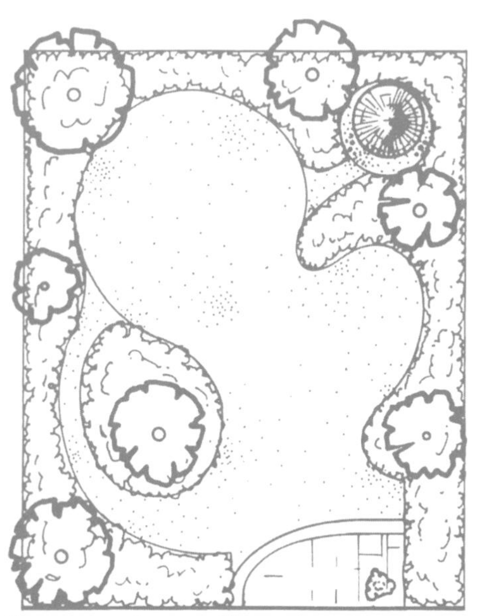

Harmony using curvilinear shapes in a large garden.

Harmony using rectangular and polygonal shapes in a small garden.

To develop the function plan into a successful and pleasing outline or schematic plan you need to appreciate the basic principles of garden design. These, along with your list of needs and expectations, will determine the structure of the garden and consequently the shapes and sizes of the spaces within it.

When drawing up an outline plan, always bear in mind that garden design must be practical, otherwise it will amount to nothing more than a drawing exercise.

Continuity

Individual garden spaces or rooms should never be designed to be totally independent of each other, even though their functions or reasons for existing are different. Continuity is essential within the garden, even when one space may be hidden from another. It helps to form a pleasing structure and, paradoxically, the more informal the garden, the greater the need for this kind of coherence as, without it, a garden will lack harmony.

Harmony

Perhaps the most important and intangible of garden design principles is harmony. To some this suggests a garden composed of flowing lines and curves, to others it is one possessing symmetry, but as a concept harmony is more encompassing. It is a just and balanced adaptation of all parts one to another, forming an agreeable whole. Sometimes it may arise from symmetry, sometimes not; sometimes from rectangular or polygonal shapes – but it can be achieved equally well with curving forms.

The creation of harmony in a garden, particularly a new one, can be slow. Paved surfaces and constructed vertical elements produce more or less instant effects but trees and plants generally take years to mature and gain their full stature and mass. Meanwhile the garden remains in a state of some disharmony. This must be accepted and calls for the more philosophical outlook which, fortunately, most gardeners develop. There are short-cuts involving planting mature or semi-mature trees and shrubs, but this is expensive and to some extent less satisfying. Though harmony may take a long time to achieve, the designer must have it in mind from the outset.

Different types of harmony For many gardeners, harmony of colour is paramount, but there are many other types: harmony should exist not only between one plant and another, but also between the plants and the constructed elements and, indeed, between the constructed elements themselves.

The concept of harmonious design also extends to textures and forms. This does not mean that the colours, textures and forms introduced into the design need to be "safe" or "uneventful". Quite the opposite can be true. Schemes using exciting, stimulating colours, textures or forms can be brought together harmoniously. Harmony is not synonymous with conventionality. Breaking with convention has often resulted in innovative, yet wholly satisfying, design.

Unity

Unity can be thought of as a thread or theme running through a garden, drawing its disparate parts into a whole, where architecture, hard and soft landscaping, planting and features come together to form a single coherent entity. Unity is a facet of harmony.

Balance

Balance must be present in all aspects of a garden design. It is one of those qualities that often goes unrecognized when it does exist, but when it doesn't, it is all too obvious. A simple example of balance would be a matching pair of conifers marking the entrance to a pathway, or two identical flights of steps at each end of a formal retaining wall.

Practical balancing

Balance is virtually intrinsic to symmetrical designs, but it can be harder to see how to achieve it in asymmetrical or informal design. This is where the hidden laws of balance come into play. For example, large masses can be balanced against smaller but "weightier" elements; in a garden context this may mean planting some large "frothy" trees at one side to strike an aesthetic balance with a "heavier" building at the other, the trees in this instance being the "mass" and the building the "weight".

A garden with a slope across the main view can be disconcerting, as the garden seems about to slide into the next property. This type of imbalance can usually be rectified by placing a much greater mass on the lower side than on the higher. Tree and shrub plantings are particularly useful for solving this sort of problem.

"Mass" and "weight" in balance

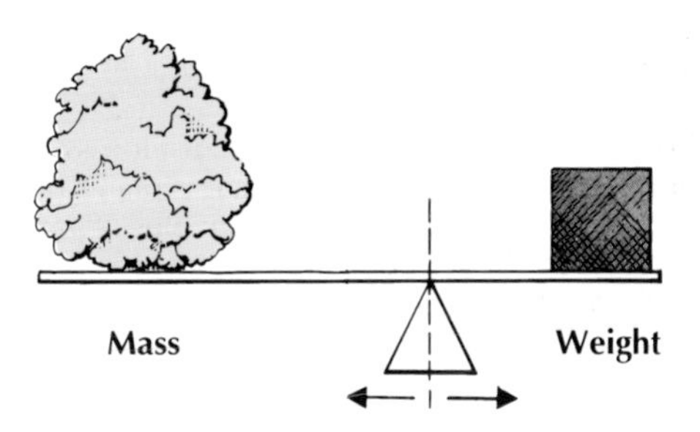

The balance of symmetry

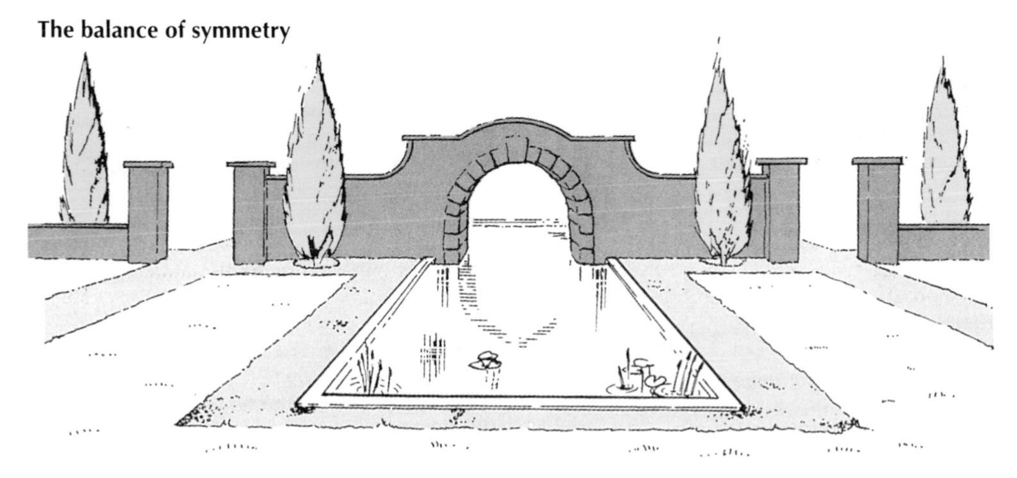

Theory and technique 2

Planning for balance

Where plants and trees are concerned, a rough sketch of the proposed arrangement in vertical form indicating ultimate height, form and, if possible, texture will give at least an idea of how a balance will eventually be achieved. As with harmony, balance is often lacking in the formative years of a garden, but it is important to plan ahead for it.

There is an unwritten law stating that groups of trees planted in odd numbers achieve balance. This does generally work, but rules of this type need not be followed slavishly; there are often occasions when an even number is more appropriate. Always follow your own design instincts rather than those of others – it is your garden after all and is being designed to satisfy what you want.

Balance in planting design

Before embarking on your own design make a point of visiting as many gardens as possible. Study those which, in your opinion, are well balanced and try to analyse why you feel that they are. When you have come to a conclusion, use what you have observed to apply the same techniques in your own garden.

Photographs are invaluable in helping you to remember and study at leisure any pleasing arrangements you saw.

Colour balance is not easy to achieve and it certainly cannot be sustained unless a proper planting plan has been prepared. Buying plants in flower on impulse is not recommended. It does not help to achieve any lasting balance or harmony of colour.

Drawing up a detailed planting plan allows you to consider each subject individually and in the context of the whole planting.

Make notes of foliage and flower colours, including shades and tones, stature, form, habit, cultural requirements and flowering season. This last characteristic is especially important since a scheme based on flower colour alone will lack harmony if the plants selected to complement each other bloom at different times of the year.

Since flowering periods can be relatively short it is also important to take into account other characteristics of a plant or tree. Make sure that the plants still combine well together when flowering is over.

An obvious cross-fall. The imbalance is emphasized by insufficient mass at the lower side of the garden.

A lack of balance, emphasized by the constructed elements and the immature planting which provides little "mass".

Balance restored now that the cross-fall has been camouflaged with mass provided in the form of plants added at the lower side.

Balance now achieved between planted and constructed elements. The mature plants provide stature and mass.

Scale and proportion

Good scale and proportion within a garden is dependent on several factors, including the size of the plot relative to the house and to the surroundings or environment and the proportional relationship between the garden and the elements within it.

Constructed elements

At a practical level too, constructed elements can suffer from being wrongly proportioned. For example, a summer house must be large enough to accommodate the maximum number of people likely to use it and the supports and beams of a pergola must be in proportion to its overall size. Such features would not function below a certain size, so they might have to be excluded from a very small plot.

Take plenty of time to make sure that everything fits well into the plan. Rough sketches of the features on tracing paper can be laid over photographs of the area or areas concerned and give an indication of how they will look.

Vertical proportions

Any single oversized element will make part of or even the entire garden appear smaller. For instance, a large tree growing in a relatively small plot apparently diminishes the area. (Another reason for not growing large trees in small spaces is the risk of structural damage to the house or to other nearby buildings.) Oversized hedges, fences and walls can also adversely affect the sense of space and movement within a garden.

Horizontal proportions

Horizontal surfaces should also be designed in proportion, not only to the area but to their function. Wherever possible a path should be a comfortable width with an allowance made for any adjacent plant overgrowth. The main pathways of a garden should be wide enough to accommodate the passage of garden equipment and to allow at least two people to walk side by side. The dimensions of a patio or terrace should be as generous as possible not only for practical purposes but to provide a satisfying visual foundation to the house. Any paved area must be constructed using paving units of a size proportional to its overall dimensions. Paving units which are too small make a large area appear fussy, while units which are too large make a limited area appear smaller (see Structure, space and movement, page 52).

An inappropriately large subject dwarfing its host house and garden.

Inappropriate planting in a small patio garden exemplifies how oversized plants and trees dominate a small area and make it appear even smaller and more cramped.

Proportion in a small garden

In pursuit of good proportion, certain compromises may have to be made in a small garden between the size of the paved areas, lawn and borders relative to plot size.

A horizontal surface which is too large relative to the overall size of the site will draw attention to the lack of space. Lawn and paving areas made deliberately large to increase the sense of space will often have the reverse effect, leaving little or no opportunity to screen or camouflage the boundary with planting. Where boundaries are obvious the sense of enclosure is increased.

Undersized elements are as unwelcome as those which are oversized. For example, a small flower bed in a large expanse of lawn will look incongruous and a small piece of sculpture at the end of a long vista will fail as a focal point because it looks insignificant.

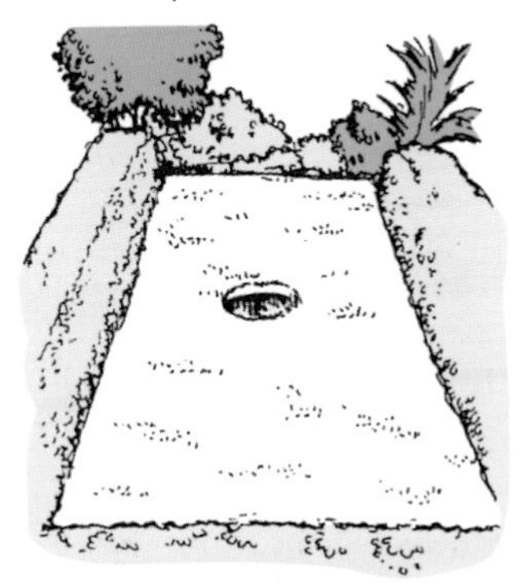

A round pool which is too small for its surroundings.

A round pool in proportion.

This pool is too large, both practically and visually.

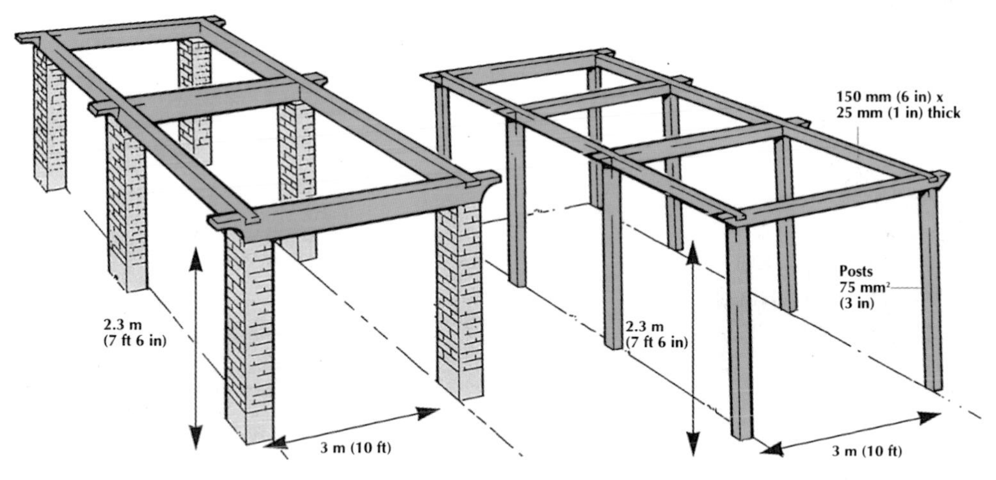

Pergolas and other structures need to be of an appropriate proportion for their environment, function and appearance. A pergola may be structurally and visually too flimsy for its site, size and function. The first example (left) looks purposeful, sturdy and strong, with proportions more appropriate to its function than those of the second, though some may prefer its airier appearance. Pergola arches should be high enough to accommodate people walking beneath, allowing space for plants and flowers to hang down. They should preferably be wide enough for two people to walk side by side.

Scale and proportion 2

Simplicity

A common fault with gardens is that they are too fussy or complicated. There are several possible reasons for this, the most common being that no proper plan was made in the first place, resulting in a collection of disjointed ideas, often following impulse-buying at the garden centre. The other reason is that the garden may have been over-designed, with too many features each competing for individual attention. Indecision or a lack of direction could be the cause, as there is often a compulsion to fill every available space.

Try to resist this, as simplicity is an essential part of good garden design and especially so if an atmosphere of calm and repose is desired.

Restraint in planning

When aiming for simplicity, be decisive and design your plan along simple lines in the style you prefer, resisting the temptation to cram in too many different plants and materials from the vast range available. Simplicity should be applied at all levels of design from the basic layout to the final choice of building materials and plants. All gardens benefit from simplicity, but small gardens particularly so.

Interest

What is interesting to one individual may not be of interest to another, but this is one of the joys of designing your own garden. A garden may be multi-functional, providing a space for relaxation and play and for accommodating a particular hobby or interest.

The purpose of your design is to create an environment in which specialized interests can be integrated with the overall scheme while satisfying aesthetic and practical needs. This can stretch the imagination but is attainable only if the specialists and enthusiasts, as well as other family members, are involved at the initial planning stage.

Creating suspense

Every garden should be interesting in its own right. Gardens which can be seen in their entirety and at one glance will inevitably

Paving/
sitting area
UP
UP
Lawn
Pool at
ground
level
Sculpture
Paving

An asymmetrical formal design based upon strict geometric shapes. Many permutations are possible.

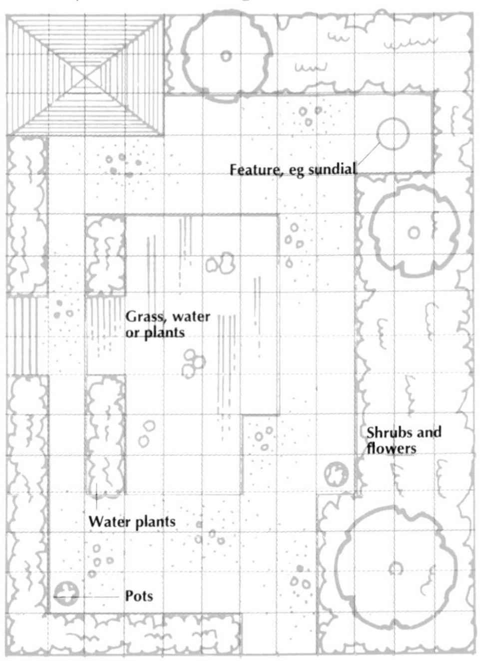

A garden based on the "grid" system. A useful early route to harmonious and unified design.

become boring – and quickly so, offering no surprises. Of course the family will know perfectly well what lies behind the screen or at the end of a curving path – but the sense of intrigue will remain.

Try to create certain areas which are not so readily seen or places which have to be visited – making sure of course that they are worth visiting. In the smallest of gardens, low walls, disappearing paths or planting can suggest hidden spaces even though, in reality, they may be non-existent.

Focal points

Focal points play an important role in providing garden interest. An attractive focal point, glimpsed at a distance, will have the effect of drawing the visitor from one area to another. Some designers position focal points especially for this purpose.

If the garden is large and contains several focal points, arrange them in such a way that, having arrived at one, another can be glimpsed further on. It is unacceptable in terms of good design for more than one focal point to be plainly visible at the same time as this will cause confusion, leading to a lack of balance and harmony (see page 63, below right).

A focal point need not necessarily be an artifact. A distinctive tree, an area of water or a composition of natural or naturalistic elements can be equally entrancing. A beautiful view lying outside the garden will almost inevitably become the principal focal point, reducing any others in the same field of vision to mere interruptions (see Structure, space and Movement: Partitions and focal points, page 59).

Functionality and feasibility

A garden may look attractive and exciting in plan form but if it is not feasible or does not function properly then it cannot be deemed to have been well designed. Keep in mind the old adage "form follows function". Research every element of the plan thoroughly, including the cost not only of creating the garden but also of maintaining it. The cost of the latter can quickly outrun the former.

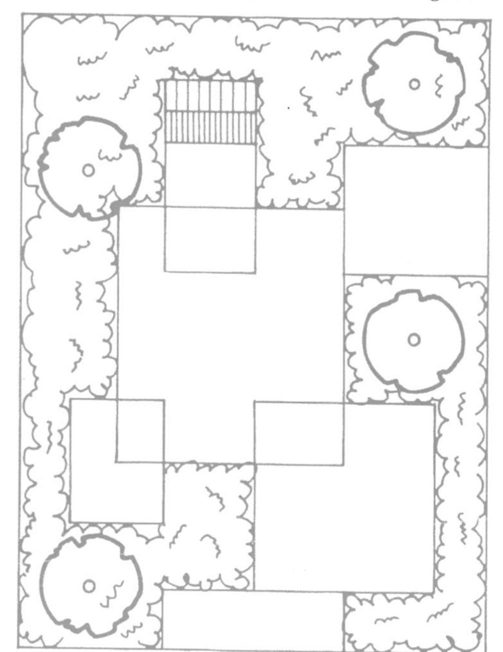

Overlapping squares and rectangles. The example does not designate the areas for specific purposes, but your own ideas can.

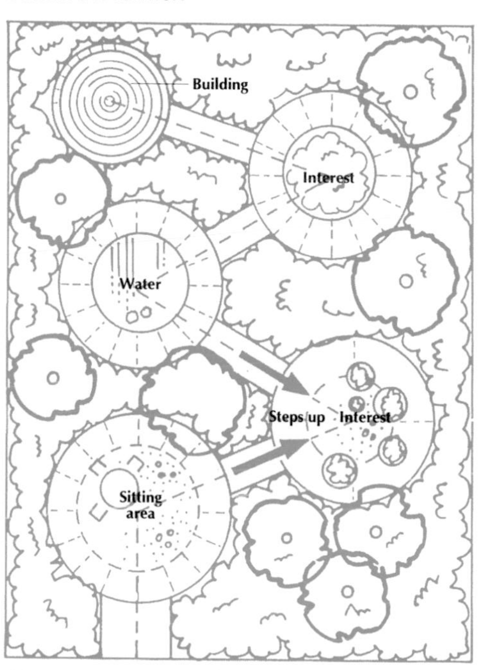

Circles are popular, although, if touching, they can create awkward shapes between them. Here each circular area has its own function.

Shaping open spaces

When shaping open spaces in the garden never allow them to be formed by accident or to be "leftovers" from adjacent features. The open spaces are at least as important as the other elements of the garden, being a vital part of its horizontal structure. Beds and borders, therefore, should not be shaped only for their own sake but for the contribution they make in shaping the open spaces with which they are associated.

Proportion and space

The scale and proportion of open spaces should always be relative to the size of the plot. Be prepared for a dramatic change of this proportion from that seen on the plan to the reality at ground level. In this regard plans are misleading as they give no impression of the effects of perspective: the way features appear from a normal standing or sitting position (see Structure, space and movement: Proportion and perspective, page 54). A rectangle in plan, for example (see diagram right), changes dramatically when viewed from an upper window, from a standing position or from a sitting position. In informal shapes, the gentlest of plan curves becomes quite exaggerated when viewed in perspective.

When deciding on horizontal proportions, consider from which level the area or feature will usually be viewed. The higher the viewpoint relative to the garden, the more the shapes will resemble the plan. Looking across the drawing from an appropriate height "to scale" should help.

Colour and space

Colour plays an important part in the perceived proportions of a garden's horizontal shapes and spaces. Bright, vibrant or "hot" colours such as pure whites, reds and yellows will, at a distance, make an area appear smaller or a boundary closer. Viewed at a distance, "cool" colours, such as blues, mauves, dark green and "off" or pastel whites, will make an area appear larger or a boundary further away. To make a small area appear larger or to give the impression of distance, place the hot, vibrant colours in the foreground and the cool colours in the background. Pastel colours occupying the middle ground will reinforce the illusion and link the two extremes.

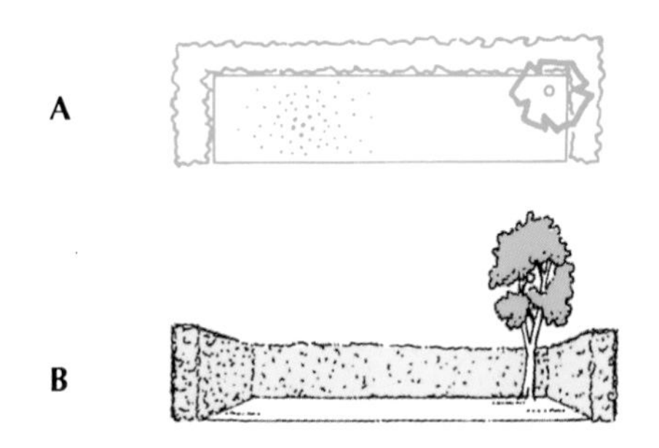

A shallow rectangle seen in plan (A) may have to be deepened to make it visible in perspective (B).

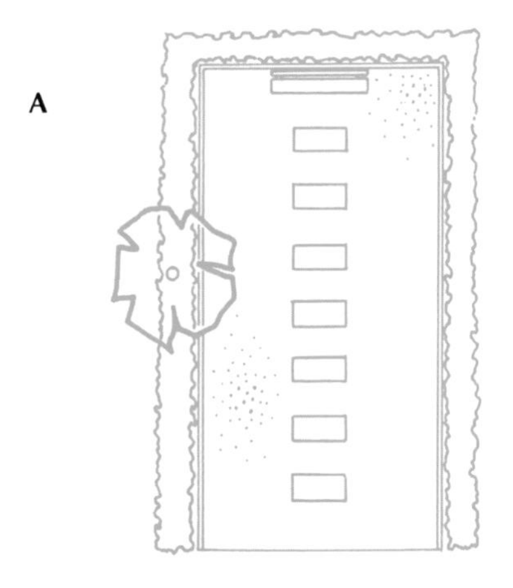

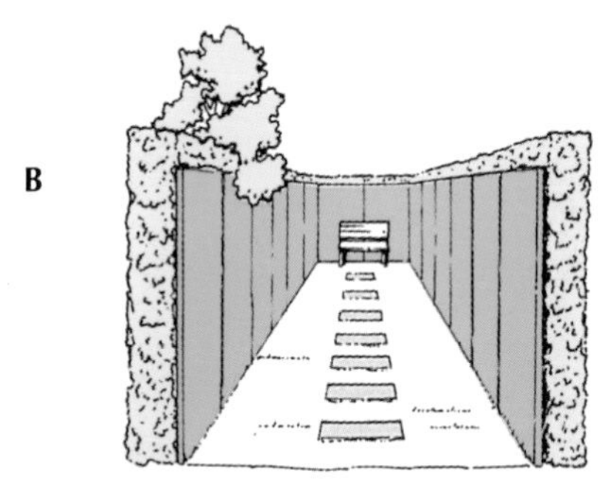

A rectangle in plan (A) takes on different proportions depending on the viewpoint (B).

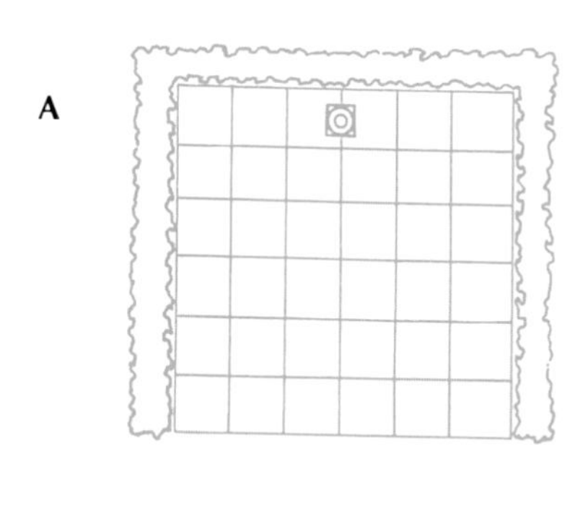

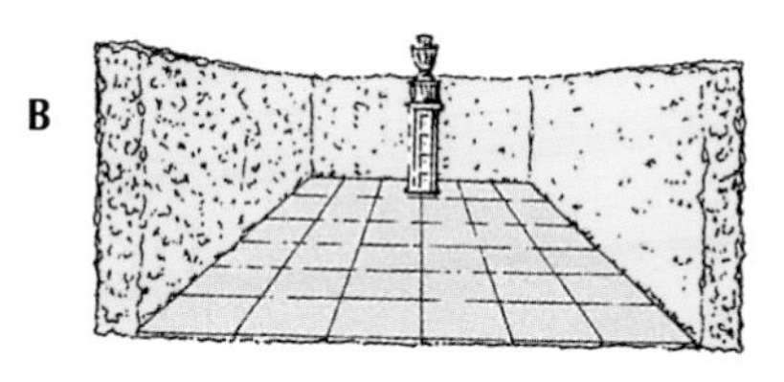

The plan square (A) appears to change its shape when viewed in perspective (B).

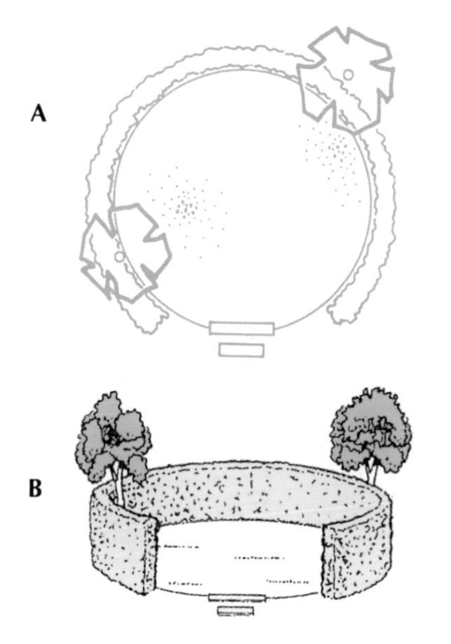

A plan circle (A) appears to contract from back to front to become an ellipse when viewed from standing (B).

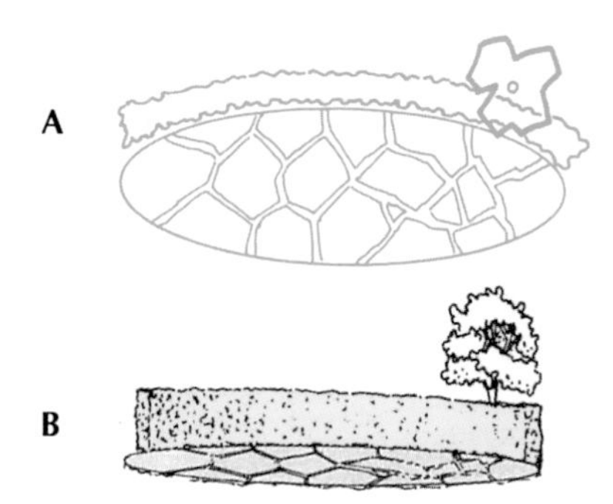

An ellipse (A), if it is too shallow, may disappear from view especially when seen from a sitting position.

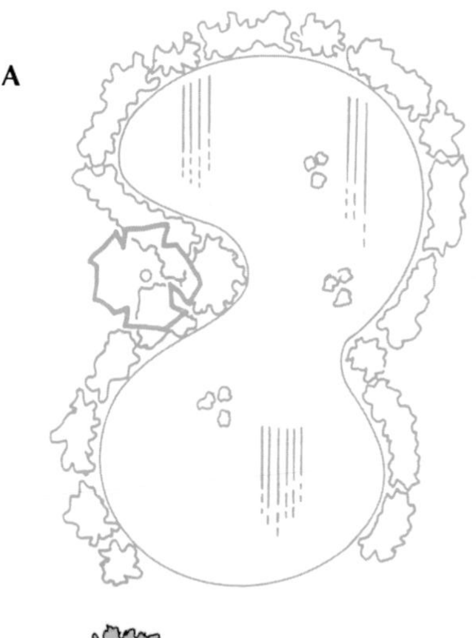

Informal shapes like the pool (plan A above) can be more difficult to predict in perspective (B) than their formal counterparts.

Drawing up the outline plan

The outline plan represents the penultimate stage in the planning process. It must take into account the information derived from the site measurement and assessment, the requirements list and the function plan and be based on the principles of functional and aesthetically pleasing design. Precise details such as construction materials and branded products, plant types and so on, can be decided later. The priority is to finalize the garden's structure.

How to set up for plan drawing

From now on, all versions of the plan need to be drawn with a greater degree of precision. Remember that the plan is not only a means of recording and illustrating your thoughts but will be useful for later calculations and for the quantification of plants and materials. It is important to draw the plan in a form that can be photocopied or duplicated in some way: on tracing paper, for example. The original is unlikely to last the entire period of the garden's construction, particularly if it is regularly used outdoors or if the development lasts several years.

The preparation of a garden plan is always time-consuming, but to what degree depends on its complexity, size and the amount of detail involved. Because of this it is necessary to set up a centre of operations. This could be based around a professional drawing board or simply a rectangle of smooth hardboard.

Looking after the plan

Drawings left attached to the boards should be covered with a sheet of thick paper, plastic or a blanket when not in use. Dust, grease and frequent handling adversely affect the surface of the tracing paper, making any subsequent drawing or modification difficult. This is especially so if drawing pens are used since the ink will not "take".

For the plan, use a piece of feint ruled graph paper, although plain tracing paper is most suitable for sketching initial thoughts in pencil. The survey drawing itself can be used for preliminary ideas but then any subsequent "rubbings out" may result in the loss of survey detail as well. To avoid this, place a separate piece of plain or graph tracing paper over the survey. The survey beneath can still be read through the tracing paper and various ideas can be explored on separate sheets of tracing paper.

Using a drawing board

Drawing boards are usually tilted when in use as this makes drawing easier and means that

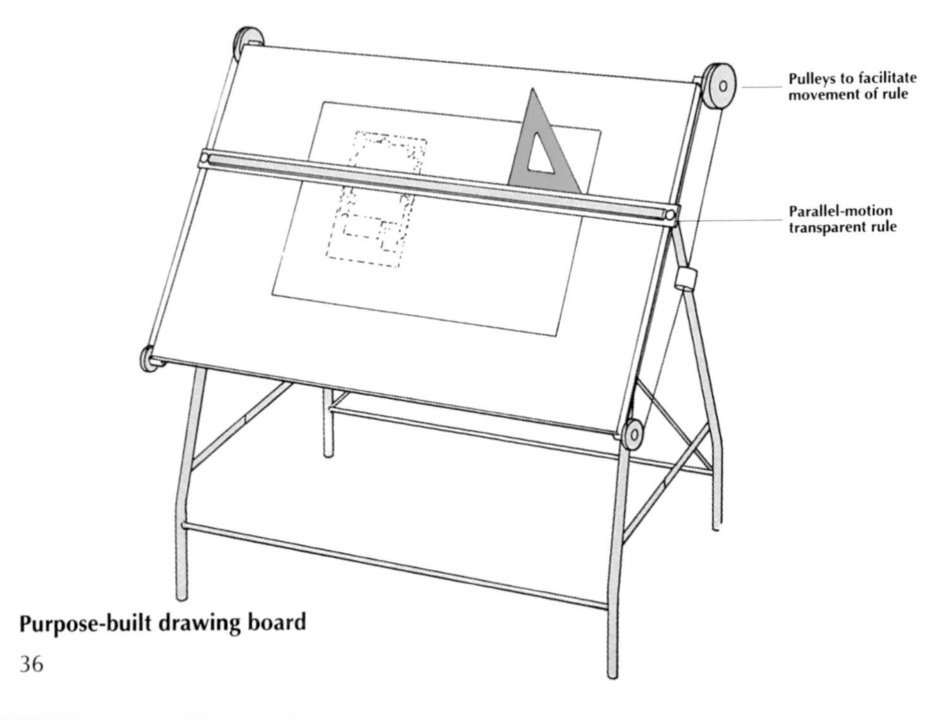

Purpose-built drawing board

more of the plan is visible. The degree of tilt is a matter of individual preference. Some drawing boards are intended for use on flat tables, although there is then a limit to the slope that can be achieved. Others have special stands with height-adjustable supports beneath. When using a flat, table-top drawing board or one made from a piece of hardboard, place a length of square or rectangular timber beneath the farthest side to tilt it. To prevent it from scratching the table, either wrap the timber in cloth or cover the entire table surface.

Drawing boards used by professionals incorporate adjustable parallel rules, but with simple table-top models, a T-square will do just as well. For the smallest plans, use graph paper so that the printed squares will give guidance, making even a T-square unnecessary.

Paper sizes

Drawing board sizes are made to accommodate particular sizes of paper: A0, A1, A2 or A3. An A0 paper sheet is 840 x 1188 mm (33 x 47 in); an A0 board is approximately 870 x 1270 mm (36 x 50 in). An A1 paper sheet is 594 x 840 mm (23½ x 33 in); an A1 board is approximately 650 x 900 mm (25½ x 35½ in). An A2 paper sheet is 420 x 594 mm (16½ x 23½ in); an A2 board is 470 x 660 mm (18½ x 26 in). An A3 paper sheet is 297 x 420 mm (11¾ x 16½ in). Sheet sizes A0–A1–A2–A3 are progressively smaller by one half.

Choosing a pen

Much of the equipment used for drawing up the survey plan can be used for general plan drawing later. Pencils are adequate for outlining and drafting but to make lines more permanent and precise on the final plan, use drawing pens. These are either disposable, re-fillable or use cartridges. All re-fillable or cartridge drawing pens must use specially formulated inks or they quickly become blocked and unusable.

There are many pen systems available and they vary considerably in price. A single pen size is sufficient, but if you are prepared to invest in one or two more to provide a selection of thicknesses, you can vary the line produced, perhaps to emphasize one garden element over another. For general purposes use a nib size of about 0.5 mm and for variation use 0.2 mm (thinner) and 0.7 mm (thicker).

Drawing pen nibs range in thickness from 0.1 mm up to 1.0 mm diameter. Re-fillable or cartridge pens are superior to disposable pens because the nib of a re-fillable pen is precisely

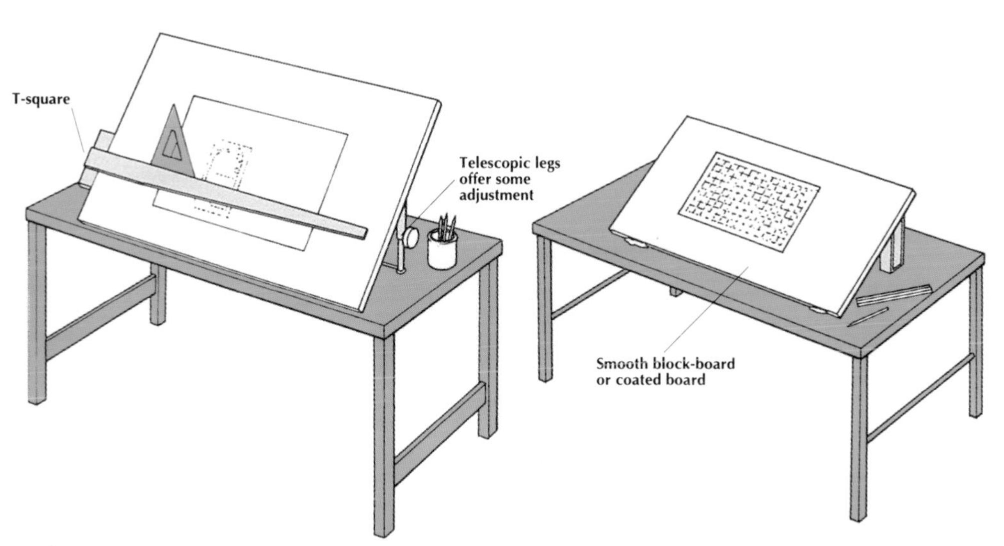

Desk- or table-mounted drawing board. A T-square and set square provide adjustable parallel and perpendicular lines.

Printed squares on graph paper obviate the necessity for T-squares and set squares.

Drawing up the outline plan 2

made to ensure that the lines drawn are always of uniform thickness. Most disposable types have internal ink reservoirs linked to writing tips which can become "blunt" with use, producing lines of inconsistent thickness. Disposable pens are, however, adequate for short-term use.

Drawing symbols

A garden plan is obviously more meaningful if the various elements have their own distinct symbols. You will probably develop your own graphic style but the symbol examples shown right may help at first.

If the drawing is intended not only as a working plan but also as a visual realization, then make the graphics more realistic, perhaps introducing colour.

Adding detail

To make the plan even clearer, give existing shrubs or trees a different symbol from proposed additions. Always draw the symbols for proposed trees to scale, with outlines representing their estimated spread at a reasonable stage of maturity, say in five to ten years. A good nursery catalogue contains such information and its inclusion in the plan provides an accurate indication of how the tree or trees will eventually fit into the scheme.

Draw existing mature trees to scale so that their true spread is represented – this is especially important if plants are to be placed under the canopy as the plant choice will be influenced by the availability of light and moisture.

Shrubs and herbaceous plants can also be represented in various ways according to the stage the plan has reached. At the earlier stages, use a general symbol simply to indicate how a bed or border will appear in size and shape. Later, when deciding precisely what plants are needed, their exact location, their estimated size on maturity and consequently their spacing and numbers, draw in labelled symbols indicating each plant group or tree.

Do the same for other structural details: show the vertical features and surface materials drawn to scale to give an accurate idea of intended sizes.

When inventing symbols of your own, begin by imagining the bird's eye view of the particular object or element and keep the symbols as simple as possible.

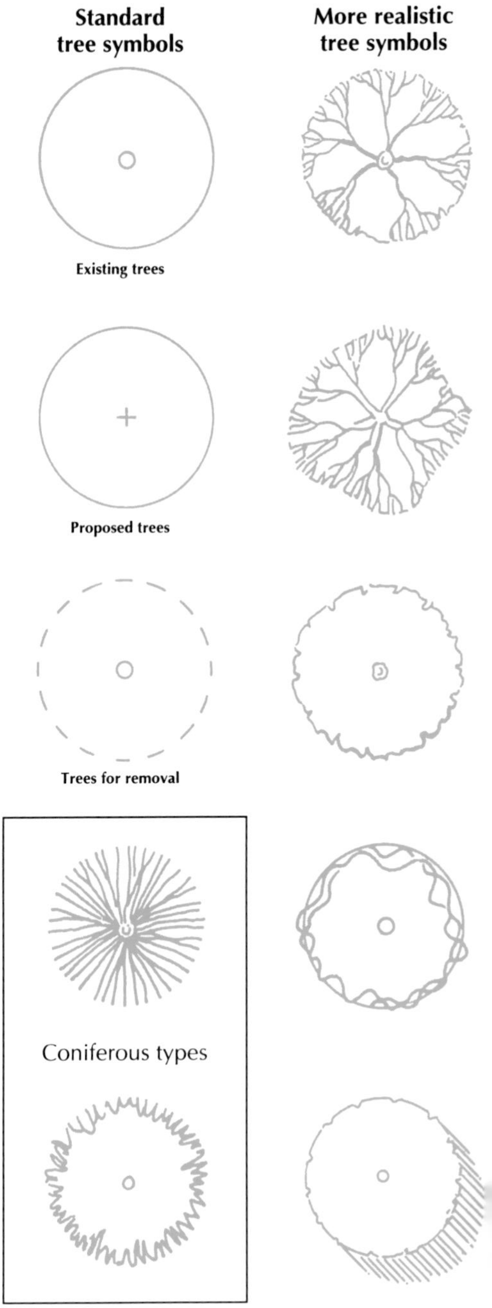

Standard tree symbols

More realistic tree symbols

Existing trees

Proposed trees

Trees for removal

Coniferous types

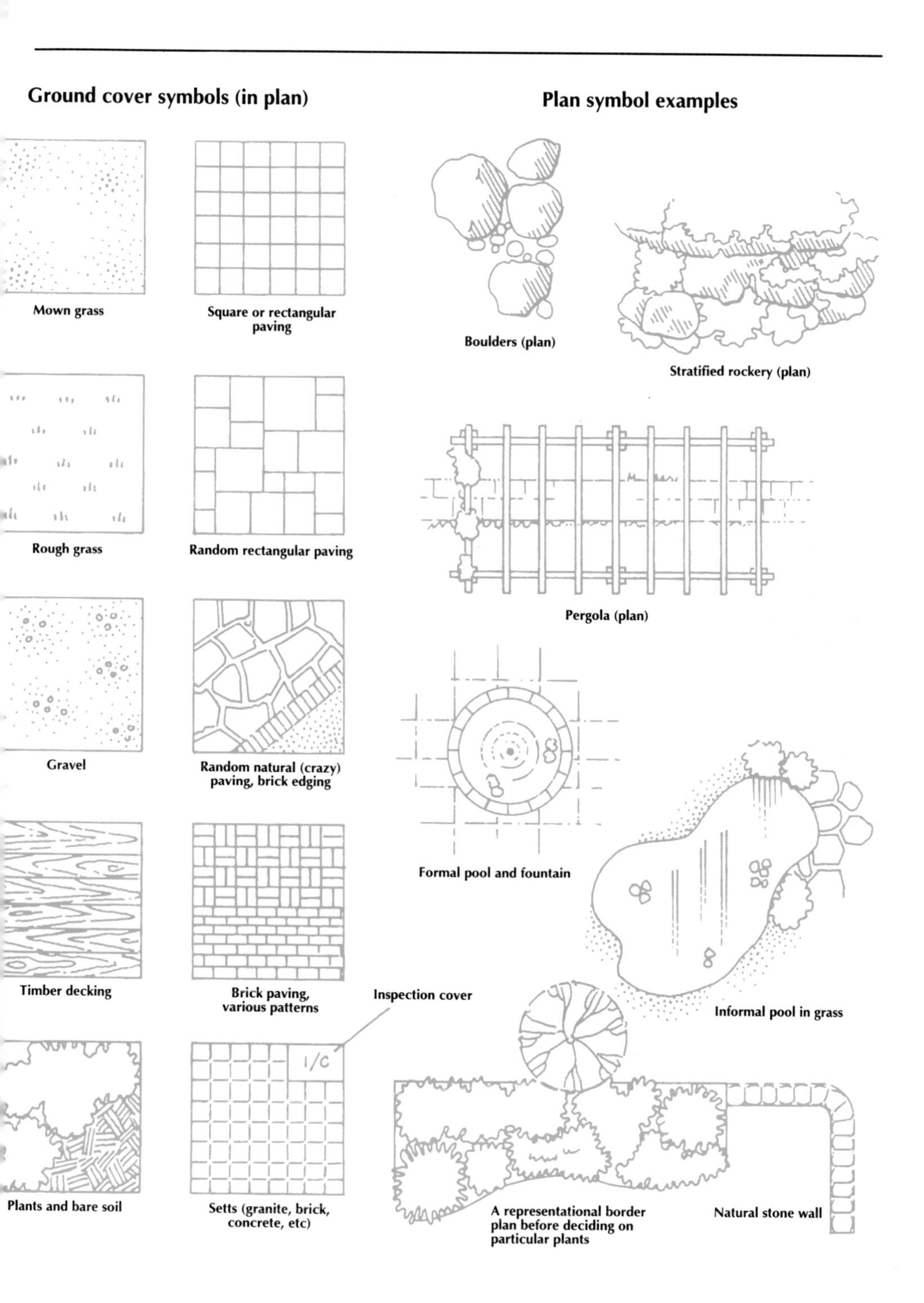
Ground cover symbols (in plan)
Plan symbol examples
Mown grass
Square or rectangular paving
Boulders (plan)
Stratified rockery (plan)
Rough grass
Random rectangular paving
Pergola (plan)
Gravel
Random natural (crazy) paving, brick edging
Formal pool and fountain
Informal pool in grass
Timber decking
Brick paving, various patterns
Inspection cover
I/C
Plants and bare soil
Setts (granite, brick, concrete, etc)
A representational border plan before deciding on particular plants
Natural stone wall

Drawing up the outline plan 3

The example opposite of an outline plan shows how a harmonious composition might be achieved taking into account the list of requirements featured on page 23.

Front garden

The existing driveway needed to be enlarged and resurfaced, preferably with material linking it visually with the house. On its left (seen from the road), an informally shaped lawn has been positioned in front of the garage from which access is gained to the area at its rear, at the same time leaving room for shrubs and a tree to distract the eye from the unattractive garage wall. To the right there is a formal rose garden and a weeping tree with other trees planned to the left, to achieve balance and to ensure that the house is attractively framed.

Paths and services

A path to the right of the house serves, via a new gate, both the kitchen door and the vegetable garden, with a surrounding hedge high enough to act as a screen but not so high as to exclude too much light.

Space has been found on the shady side for a greenhouse. It is usually better for a greenhouse not to be in full sun – on the south side of a wall, for example, as in summer it becomes too hot unless heavy exterior shading or some other means of cooling is provided. A greenhouse should not be positioned in permanent shade either (such as behind a high, north-facing wall), as it would then be too dark for normal greenhouse plants.

The greenhouse and small tool shed next to it are reached via a path and rose arch. Beyond this the path veers to the right, passing the shrub- and tree-screened cess-pit. Reasonable access is always needed to the cess-pit from the front drive. A minor cranked or angled path leads to it and this, in conjunction with planting, obscures a direct view of the unsightly cess-pit cover.

Recreational areas

Eventually the main path links with the shaded, secondary sitting area, which incorporates a small summer house backed by trees. These screen the house next door, but also ensure that the summer house sits well in the design, making it a subtle focal point. A short distance away the desire for a secret garden has been more than satisfied by the grassy "glade" which is completely hidden from view. This has a simple bench within it, where bird song or quiet reading can be enjoyed on hot summer days.

Beyond the glade the path divides. The main path continues, following more or less the far boundary, and eventually reaches a bench seat, positioned as another focal point and for rest and contemplation. The narrower path, meanwhile, veers to the right, passing through the centre of the "woodland" planting. Here a variety of plants and shrubs of different species, all appropriate to and thriving in the same moist, shady conditions, may be enjoyed at close quarters.

Taking care of wildlife

The proposed informally shaped wildlife pond echoes the general theme of the garden and will doubtless become the garden's focus in time. Because there is a natural mound on the far side of the area earmarked for the pool, some means of retention was thought necessary to allow a flat walking surface to be cut into it so that the path can circle the pool. To achieve this, and for its own contribution to the design, a dry-stone or rock retaining wall is constructed and planted with ferns and other shade-loving plants. A false spring cascades from its centre into the pool, creating movement and sound.

House and garden

The left side of the garden seems to be the ideal place for the gently curving pergola, which harmonizes perfectly with the general theme, being made of rustic poles and cross-beams. After emerging from the pergola, the path leads back to the front door via a gravelled area designated for shade-loving plants such as ferns, hellebores and hostas.

The terrace is formal in shape, but even though the rest of the garden is informal a degree of formality is normally acceptable this close to a house. Even so, sharp angular shapes have been avoided and planting visually softens the terrace outline.

Trees occupy the open areas but they have not been randomly planted. Viewed from different places, in particular the house windows, they have been positioned to frame various garden "pictures".

The outline plan

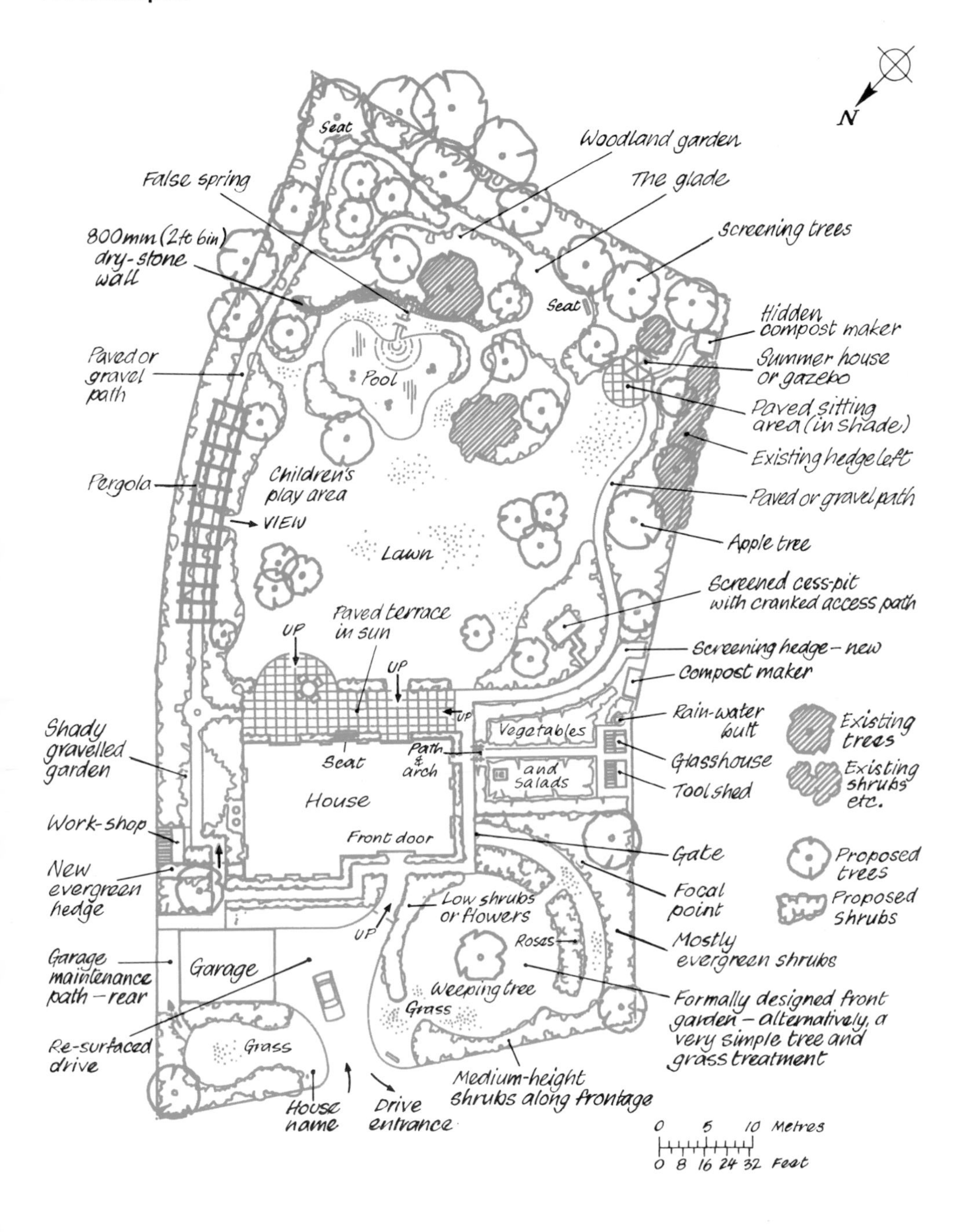

Cross-sections

Some gardens are on fundamentally awkward sites, and for these the designs have as much to do with overcoming environmental problems as with satisfying aesthetic or practical needs. This is certainly the case with sloping gardens.

Slopes tend to foreshorten the view of the garden: with steep downward slopes the garden simply drops out of view, while with upward slopes any horizontal planes above eye level are often unable to be seen. This foreshortening effect can be worsened if the site is terraced in an inappropriate way. It can be difficult to visualize changes in level. This is where cross-sectional drawings become an invaluable aid to the designer.

Measuring up for a cross-section

Cross-sections are based upon axes drawn through and across the garden plan at right angles to each other. If the garden slopes evenly or its design is simple then possibly only two cross-sections will be required, one drawn latitudinally and the other longitudinally. If, on the other hand, the slopes are uneven and run in several directions or the plan is complicated, then a series of cross-sections will be necessary. To ensure success in a sloping garden, full information on the extent of the problem is needed, so, before drawing a cross-section, establish precisely what the fall or rise in the ground is and over what distance it occurs. Always use the same scale, such as 1:100, for the cross-section as for the horizontal plan, to ensure compatibility between the two.

Using the cross-sectional drawings

First draw a cross-section (or a series of cross-sections) to show the way the garden slopes naturally, then another to show what is proposed. The proposed cross-section can be done in two ways, either in the form of an overlay or as a separate drawing. The overlay, especially if drawn on tracing paper, allows immediate comparison between what is there already and what is proposed and is therefore more useful.

Cross-sections showing proposals cannot usually be devised independently of the flat plan at the design stage. The two must be worked on together, testing ideas on the flat plan by observing their effects on the slopes, at the same time ensuring that the ideas are feasible.

Designing for slopes

If access to the garden is poor then cost alone might render the design impracticable. The movement of materials to and from the garden will be far more expensive if it has to be effected by hand in small amounts, using sacks or a wheelbarrow, for example. A cross-section will help to estimate volumes, quantities and costs in advance and may help to avoid some unpleasant shocks.

The existing garden plan before development

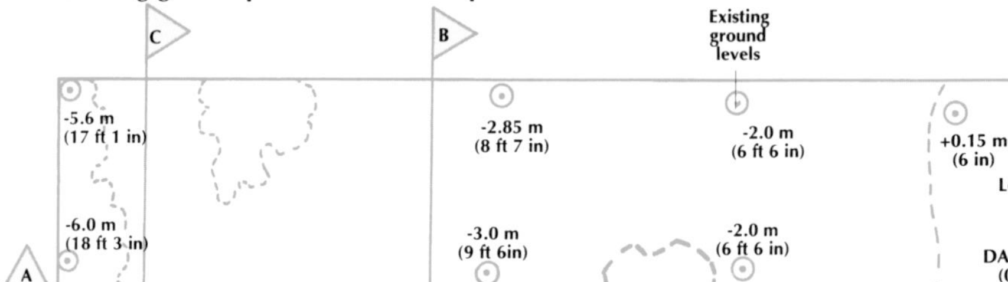

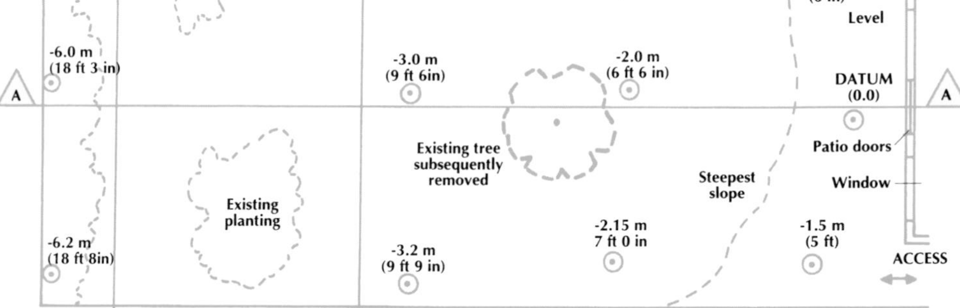

The diagram on page 42 shows a plan with the various axes of the cross-sections drawn in. The axes are positioned where information is needed about the existing ground falls. Circled dots indicate the points at which the original level measurements were taken. Datum has been fixed immediately outside the patio door and is expressed as 0.0.

Since the garden slopes downward relative to the house, the measurements are mainly expressed as minus quantities, for example -2.5 m (7 ft). There is only one measurement taken that is higher than datum at +150 mm (6 in). When a garden slopes up from the house level it is usual to express levels in plus quantities, for example +1.48 m (4 ft 6 in), keeping the datum at 0.0 close to the house. It is equally valid, however, to place the datum points at a distance from the house, particularly if the area to be designed is a more remote part of the garden.

Occasionally elements or objects not strictly on the cross-sectional axis are added in the form of an elevation to help with the comparison between the "before" and "after" plans, or to act as landmarks. For example, a sketched elevation of a fence or wall running parallel and close to a cross-sectional axis makes it much easier to visualize the slopes.

The diagrams below show cross-sections of the garden in its original state. In the first,

Existing garden contours (before development) in cross-section, A, B and C

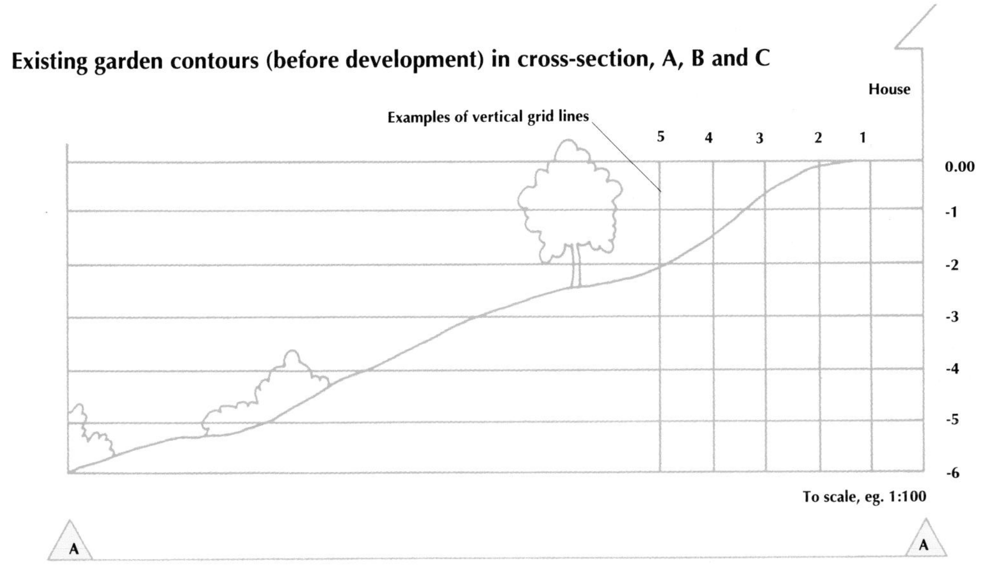

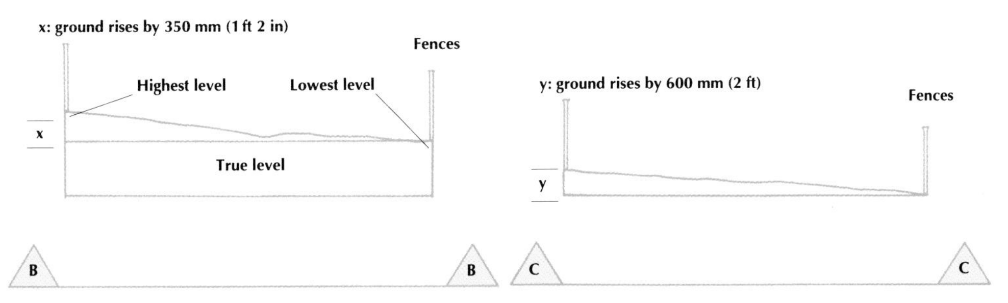

Cross-sections 2

longitudinal cross-section (A–A), the terrace (on the right, next to the house) has been chosen as the level for datum and is at almost the highest point. The far end of the garden is the lowest point. The distance over which the ground falls is known because it was measured and recorded during the original surveying process (see Information gathering: Site assessment, page 14).

Cross-sections, especially of very steep slopes, are best drawn in conjunction with a horizontal grid, evenly calibrated at appropriate spacings, for example 300 mm (1 ft), 450 mm (18 in) or 1 m (3 ft 3 in). The steepness of the slope and exactly where it occurs is then quite clear from the plan, but whether or not a grid is drawn a "true level" line is always necessary: without it, it is mentally difficult to compare the slope with a level and the cross-sectional drawing will be far less meaningful. To make the cross-section even clearer, vertical grid lines can also be introduced at the same spacing as the horizontals (see page 43). These help to indicate comparative distances.

The plan of the proposed design for this garden (below) has three cross-sectional axes corresponding with those drawn on the plan of the existing garden (see page 42). A–A is drawn longitudinally, running the length of the garden, while B–B and C–C run latitudinally, across the garden and at right angles to line A–A. Their precise routes are chosen at locations where it is necessary to know the effects the plan might have on the slope. Again, the arrows containing letters indicate the direction of view.

The cross-sectional diagrams on the right show the effects of the planned proposals on the slope and vice versa. The dotted lines indicate the original ground contours. The parts of the original slopes that will need to be reduced or built up are clearly visible when compared with the proposed levels in these cross-sections. Wall heights, numbers and proportions of steps and the size of the flat areas can now be accurately calculated or assessed and it might be necessary to amend the flat plan at this stage to accommodate any proposed changes. The

Examples of sections through B–B and C–C with corresponding directional arrows

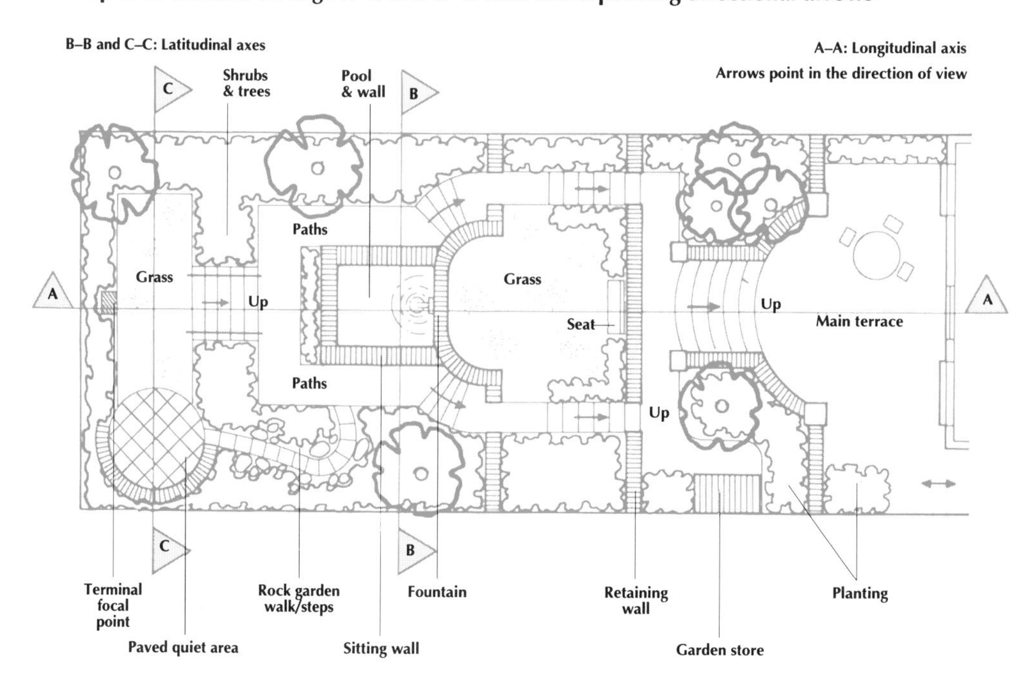

effects of making flat areas, such as the patio, on slopes can also be better appreciated on the cross-section. The angle of the slope might ultimately effect its proportions, but to help visualize the practical and aesthetic aspects of the plan as regards the rise and fall in ground levels and the height of the various features, add "stick people" to cross-section drawings.

Make sure they are drawn to the same scale as the cross-section and arrange them sitting and standing. An adult seated, stick person's eye-level will be approximately 1 m (3 ft 3 in) above the ground, and standing approximately 1.5 m (5 ft). These approximations are enormously helpful in calculating what is likely to be seen from different places within the sloping garden. A ruled pencil line drawn from eye-level to tops of walls, or slopes will indicate sight lines reasonably accurately. Bear in mind that even a low-growing plant, lavender for example, growing on top of a retaining wall, can remove a substantial part of the view beyond, particularly if the wall is already at eye height (see Designing the vertical, page 49).

The effects of the planned proposals on the slope in cross-section, A–A, B–B and C–C

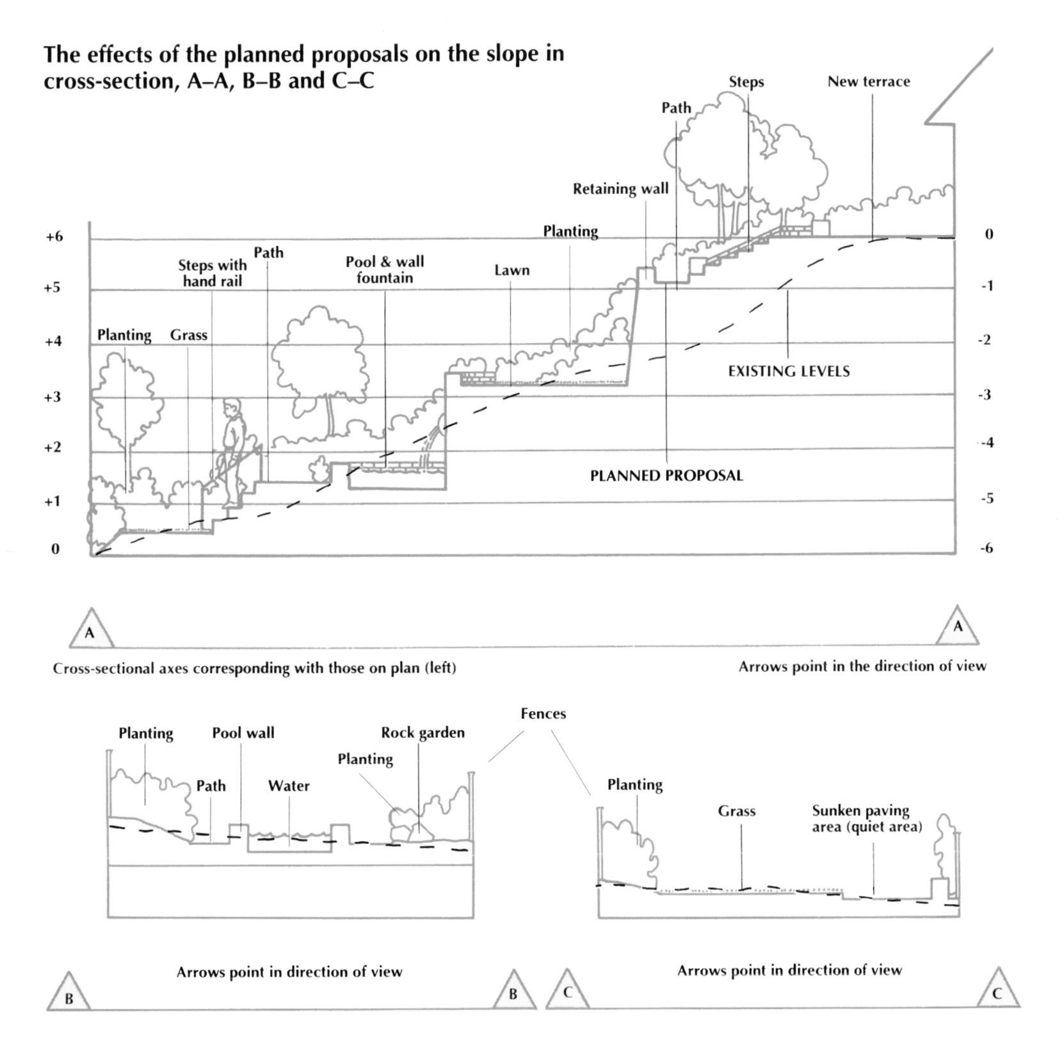

Cross-sectional axes corresponding with those on plan (left)

Arrows point in the direction of view

Designing the vertical

By this stage of the design process, the importance of composition and harmony can be more fully appreciated. But so far we have dealt only with the flat plan, in other words, designing on the horizontal plane. From this point onward, you need to start thinking about the garden's vertical planes too, so that each element fits into its proper place in the scheme of things and relates to everything else in the plan.

Vertical elements

The juxtaposition of vertical elements creates structure in a garden by interrupting the sight lines and by enclosing or compartmentalizing the garden. Vertical elements create spaces, interest and movement.

During the early planning stages all vertical elements must be imagined, yet they are as important as those on the horizontal plane and in some cases more so. Separate elevation drawings will be needed for some of the vertical features, but this will be dealt with later.

Selecting verticals

Some vertical elements, sheds for example, may be required for practical purposes only; others, like pergolas or gazebos, have practical and aesthetic roles to play, while others are chosen simply for the decorative contribution they make. Take care, as with ground shapes, that compositions of vertical elements are pleasing and harmonious as differing styles might easily conflict or compete for attention. Too many structures and features will confuse and make a garden look overpopulated (see illustration page 47, top): this risk is greater in a small garden. Individual vertical elements need space if they are to succeed on both practical and aesthetic levels and overcrowding will interfere with this.

Style and positioning

Continuity between existing architecture and proposed garden elements is essential in terms of style, materials, textures and colours. This is important for vertical features sited close to the house, which must be styled appropriately for the architecture of the building. A rustic pole rose arch seen against symmetrically formal architecture or a modern concrete screen set beside a thatched cottage, for example, would look out of place.

When positioning any vertical structures, including trees, take account of the views from all directions and not just those from the house windows. To form an idea of how their relative positions appear to change when seen from different viewpoints, move the plan around frequently during the design process and look at it from all angles. This also helps to prevent the plan from becoming one-directional.

As far as possible, arrange vertical elements as pleasing compositions or, where appropriate, as a series of goals to tempt the visitor through the garden. Pergolas or planted tunnels are excellent for this: viewed end-on or from the inside, they are strongly directional features, with the overhead and side "windows" giving tempting glimpses of the sky and garden; viewed from the side, they are delightful features in their own right and can screen one part of the garden from another.

Constructed and natural features

Of the vertical elements, those that have been constructed usually have the greater impact, since they tend to be more definite in shape and form than trees and shrubs. Trees and shrubs are, however, more versatile and especially useful for informal boundaries and partitions. They also make unrivalled foils for most constructed elements or works of art.

Some plants are trimmed formally, hedges or topiary for example, and so become architectural features, while some constructions such as rustic dry-stone walls appear almost as though they grew out of the ground.

A garden can be created entirely with trees, shrubs and plants but a garden made entirely of constructed elements is a contradiction in most people's terms.

The constructed elements in a conventional garden are usually adorned by or associated with plants, either to make the object look more attractive or more outstanding by comparison, or to soften its appearance in an attempt to integrate it with the natural elements.

Creating spaces

The open horizontal spaces of a garden are defined by the vertical elements and features which surround them. Without this definition, an area will lack identity and possibly even a sense of movement.

Using verticals for definition
The vertical elements creating garden spaces need to be chosen or designed at such a height that the area they surround functions as an independent space. Some areas can be planned to work as entities in their own right and also as part of the overall structure, but without obscuring nearby features which also contribute to the same design. Alternatively, the garden can be completely compartmentalized by creating a series of enclosed, individual outdoor rooms with little reference to any "grand plan".

Compartmentalized gardens can be exciting places with each individual "room" having its own function and proportion. Add character to an area by choosing the appropriate surround. A leafy unclipped hedge or shrubs will suggest informality; a clipped hedge, gentle formality; while walls or fences are far more formal. Some designs exploit this fact by creating a particular space as an extension of the associated architecture and patios are frequently designed in this context.

Height and scale
On a practical level, in compartmentalized gardens, vertical elements need to be tall enough

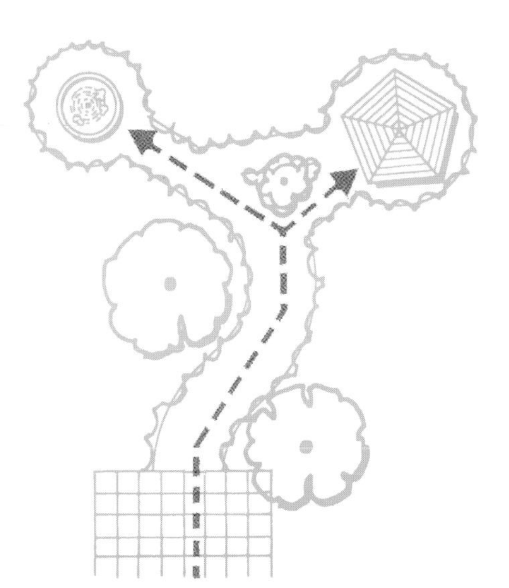

A zig-zag arrangement of vertical elements leads the eye (and feet) from one point to the next to provide interest and movement.

An example of an "overpopulated" garden with too many vertical features, each with its own unrelated style and form and each demanding individual attention.

A simplified version. The arch now forms a "gateway", the path is sufficiently interesting not to require a separate focal point. The summer house is glimpsed invitingly, its roof forming part of a composition of shapes with the nearby trees. The seat is partially hidden so as not to conflict visually with the arch. It is intended rather as a separate focal point to be viewed from another direction.

Designing the vertical 2

To be effective as a creator of space or as a partition, a vertical element needs to be high enough to do the job. Too low and the area within will simply appear as a ground pattern.

to define the space properly. Too low and the area within can be overlooked, losing its individuality relative to the rest of the garden. The divisions must reach at least eye level to ensure that the spaces within are not overlooked (see diagram left).

Problems with creating space

Spaces can be inadvertently "lost" as well as created. For example, conical or pyramidal trees, such as conifers, numerously planted make a small garden look even smaller, as the conical shapes act as distance gauges. Set against a formal boundary this visual phenomenon is exaggerated. The use of more rounded-shaped trees and shrubs has the opposite effect, particularly when formal boundaries are disguised.

Sloping sites

On sloping sites it is often necessary to create flat areas, for both practical and aesthetic reasons, but always avoid over-terracing. When any flat area is created upon a slope, it follows that the immediately adjacent slope to the front, the rear or both must be made steeper to accommodate it and there is an inherent risk

Since this is primarily a seating area, the surrounding hedge needs to be only as tall as a sitting figure to provide a sense of enclosure within.

In a small patio garden, the use of offset screens makes more of the available space.

that, from the newly formed flat areas, the rest of the garden may be partially lost from view (see Design principles: Cross-sections, page 42 and Structure, space and movement: Coping with sloping gardens, page 64). If distant areas of garden are removed from view in this way, they frequently remain unvisited.

In the smallest gardens there may be no practical choice other than to level the area closest to the house. This usually requires the creation of an embankment or some other method of soil-retention.

For structural and aesthetic reasons, it is usually better to have a stepped retaining system rather than a single vertical system such as a blank wall. The single system, usually taller, will appear closer and more uncompromising, while a stepped system will appear less so. Stepped systems can also provide an opportunity to grow plants, softening their visual impact, although planting at the top of an embankment can remove everything beyond from view. When an embankment approaches eye level, even comparatively small plants have this effect. The problem is exacerbated when the garden is viewed from a sitting rather than a standing position.

Identical paths, one (top) with an open, airy feel, the other (above) enclosed, more mysterious and atmospheric.

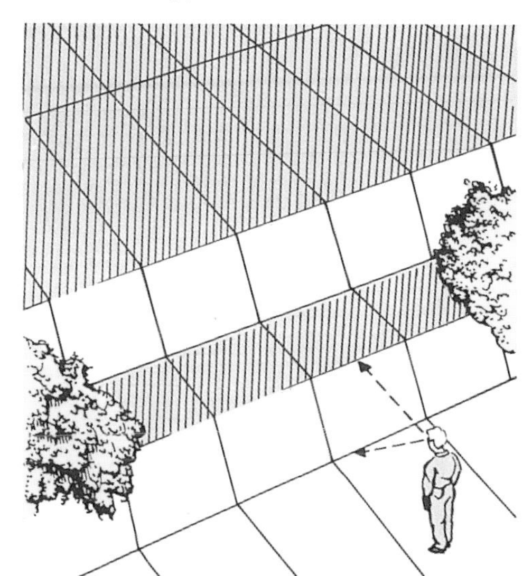

Terracing on a steeply sloping site must be planned with care if most of the example is not to be lost from sight. In this garden, only a partial view is afforded of the first level, none at all of the subsequent embankments.

Space is easy to lose when terracing ground that slopes downward. On the steepest slopes, terracing beyond the first level can remove almost an entire garden from view.

Movement

The way that spaces are shaped in a garden can suggest movement, but to what degree depends upon their proportions and perspective. The height of the surround relative to the size of the area within is critically important. The higher the surround, the smaller the area within it appears. A high surround will cast more shade within, to the extent that very small areas with high surrounds could be in permanent shade and feel claustrophobic.

Spaces can be used to determine the route or speed of progress through a garden. Try to encourage a sense and speed of movement appropriate to an area's function, whether it is a linking corridor or a place where it would be pleasant to meander.

Long, narrow areas evoke the greatest sense of movement and are often used to link "calmer" areas, although they can also be used to help to create atmosphere and structure.

Since vertical elements surrounding a space affect its sense of movement and the atmosphere within, height is the most influential factor – but form, texture and colour all play their part.

Horizontal spaces A and B are exactly the same proportion and size, but A appears open and airy while B is far more enclosed.

A

B

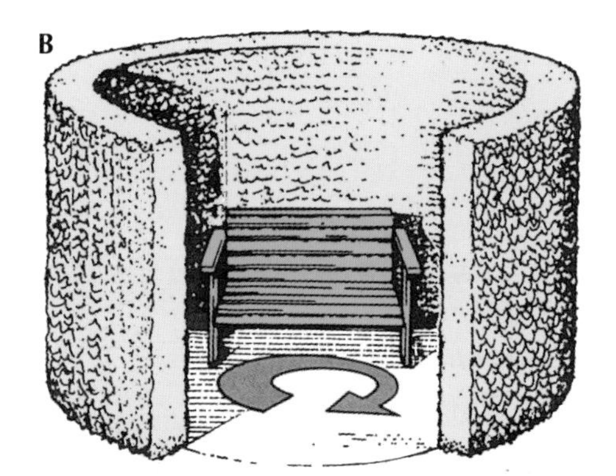

An equally proportioned area such as a square or circle (above) appears static. The height of the surround changes the quality of the space within.

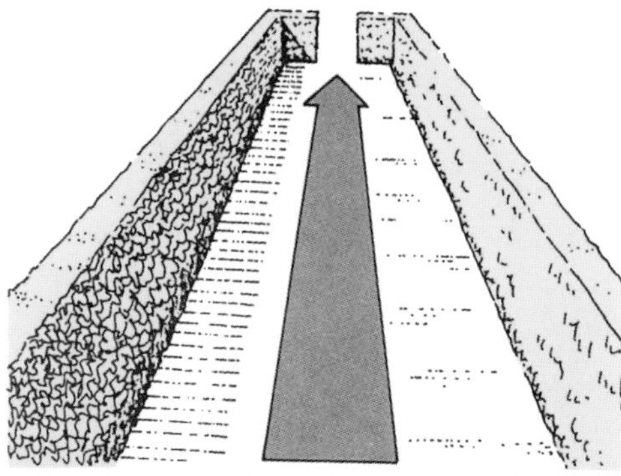

A broad rectangular area viewed "end on" encourages a slow, measured pace: the same shape entered or viewed from the side gives an impression of greater breadth but less depth and encourages radial movement.

The sense of movement is very strong indeed here because of the height of the surround. Even though the space is exactly the same proportion as that of the diagram on the left, this situation is almost oppressive.

Choosing ground coverings

Grass or gravel are neutral in texture and leave an area's inherent sense of movement (or lack of it) intact. Some paving materials or units are laid in patterns and the direction of the joint lines are significant in suggesting movement.

When choosing paving material, you must decide whether the space needs to be static or should have a dynamic effect. Parts of the garden such as sitting areas, for example, need to be static in feel: here a sense of movement could be unsettling. The choice of the ground surface and its associated patterning in these areas, has an important role to play, in addition to the height of the surround.

Consider the proportions of the paving in relation to the area to be covered: it can radically affect the area's apparent size. Drawing paving units to scale on the plan can help to indicate the most appropriate size.

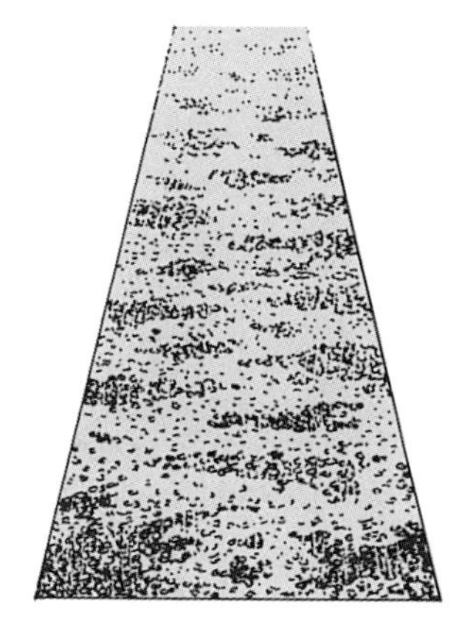

Gravel, like grass, is a neutral ground cover, having little effect on the perceived sense of movement.

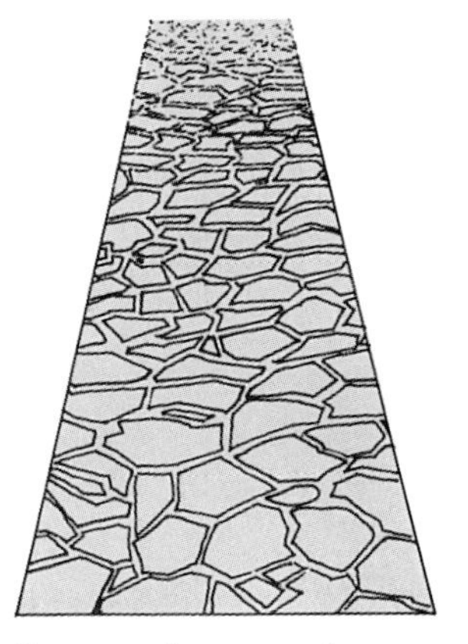

Crazy paving or random rectangular paving patterns tend to be neutral, with little sense of movement.

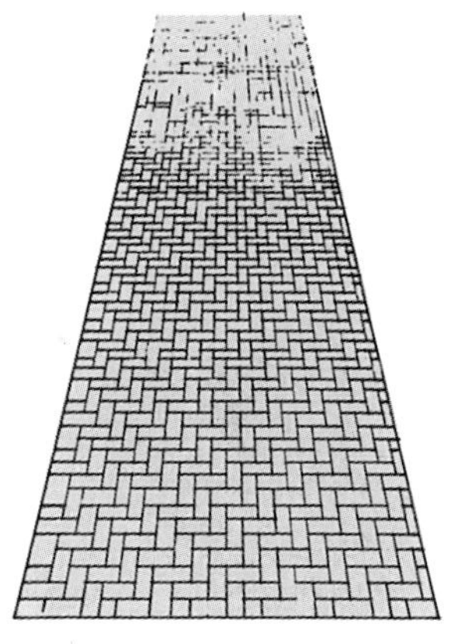

Diagonal "herring bone" pattern has a shifting effect.

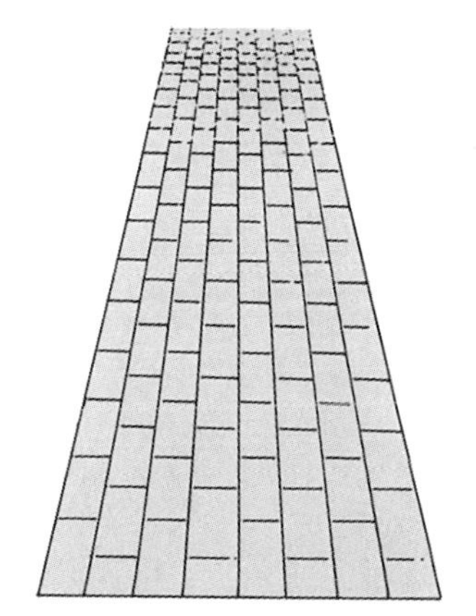

"Running bond", with its uninterrupted longitudinal joint lines, appears to lengthen the path or area.

"Stretcherbond" joints running uninterrupted across a path or area appear to widen it.

"Basketweave" brick paving pattern has a gentle sense of movement, or is static as an equally proportioned area.

Proportion and perspective

The principles of suggested movement and of the relationship between the proportions of constructed elements and their overall shapes apply as much to the vertical as they do to the horizontal plane.

The examples below illustrate the importance of the relative proportion of the covering material and the area being covered. The illustrations on page 53 show similar principles at work on a vertical plane: shadow lines introduced on the wall primarily by the joint lines, but also by associated planting, affect the perceived proportions of the wall. Achieving perfect relative proportions is more difficult when using manufactured products. These will probably conform to multiples of 100 mm (4 in) or 75 mm (3 in), eg a flat brick is approximately 225 x 100 mm (9 x 4 in).

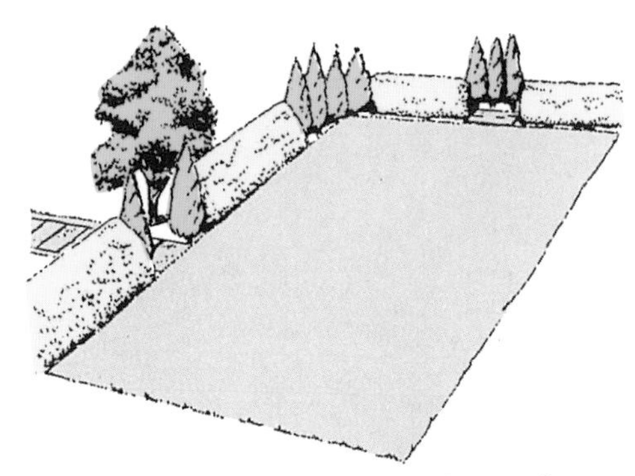

Gravel (or grass) is neutral and leaves the area's proportions intact, subject to the normal effects of perspective. Large areas of brick paving tend not to alter the perceived proportion of the spaces significantly.

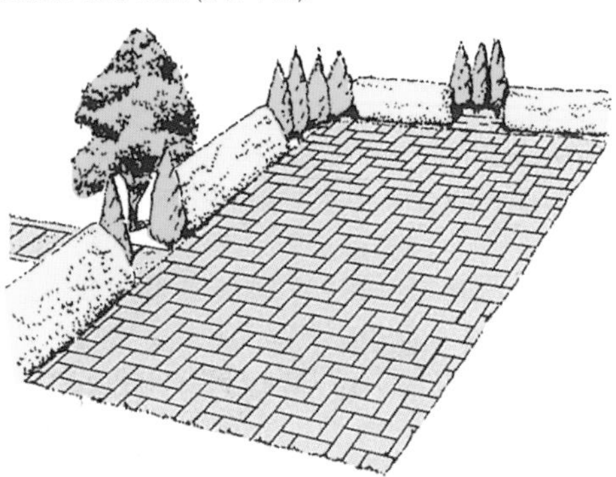

Small units relative to the overall size can make an area appear fussy and therefore it appears smaller.

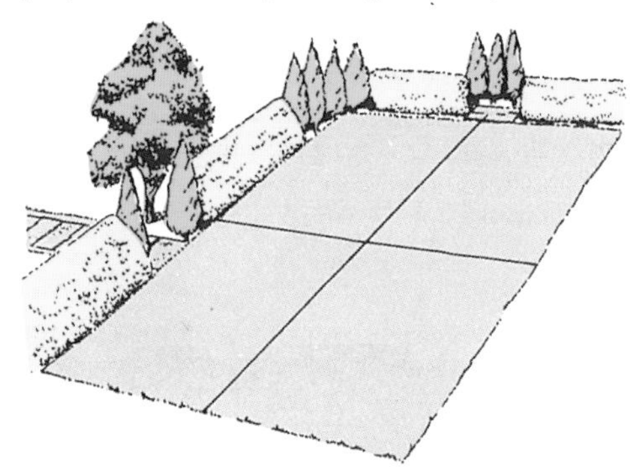

While the area still appears spacious, the units here are, perhaps, too large.

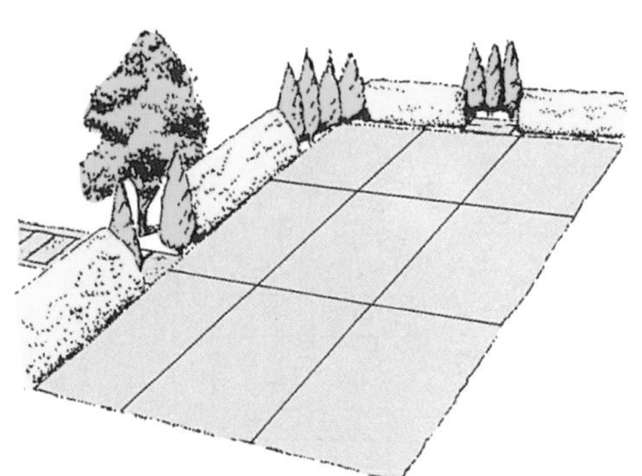

A satisfactory relationship between the units and the host area.

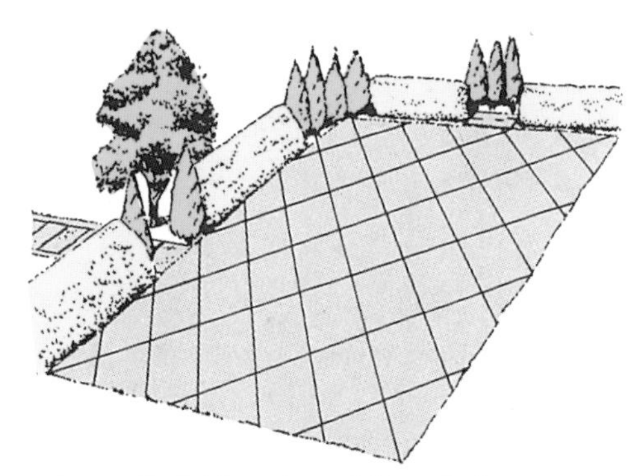

Diagonally laid paving of this relative proportion sits well in the area.

This wall appears longer than the same sized wall illustrated below because the mortar joints or predominant shadow lines are horizontal. The introduction of plants which have columnar or upright forms exaggerates this effect and is helpful in shorter gardens.

This wall is the same length and height as the illustration at thē top of the page, but it appears higher and not as long due to the verticality of the shadow lines. This effect is exaggerated by the associated rounded and horizontal plant forms.

Proportion and perspective 2

When designing the components and proportions of your garden, bear in mind that although the plan is drawn from a bird's-eye viewpoint, the realized garden will rarely be seen from directly overhead. A plan drawn to scale indicates the garden's size and proportion but suggests much more space than will actually be seen from a usual standing or sitting position. This is due to the effects of perspective, which can make a garden appear to be anything between two thirds and half its actual size.

To test the effects of perspective on the ground, mark out a shape with pegs and string, then view it from a distance. The shape will be foreshortened and the proportions different from those of the shape in plan (see Design principles: Shaping open spaces, page 34).

Designing with perspective in mind

To appreciate the foreshortening effects of perspective on your design, lay the plan flat on a table and look across it with your eyes 15 mm (½ in) above the surface. This represents, at a scale of 1:100 (⅛ in:1 ft), an eye-level view from about 1.5 m (5 ft) in a standing position. Positioning your eyes 10 mm (⅜ in) above the paper represents an eye-level view from about 1 m (3 ft 3 in) in a sitting position and further exaggerates the foreshortening effect. At a scale of 1:50 (¼ in : 1 ft) your eye will need to be 30 mm (12 in) off the paper, and so on.

False perspective

When the amount of available space is limited, introducing false perspective effects can increase the sense of distance. False perspective can be based either on the use of colour (see Design principles: Shaping open spaces, page 34), or on structural devices.

When a garden is viewed from one place, such as a window or patio, the eye tends to follow a specific axis. Ultimately the view terminates at the "vanishing point", where all uninterrupted visual lines, architectural or natural, appear to converge. It is rare for a perspective vanishing point to be visible, as in most cases boundary walls or other features intercept well beforehand.

Objects in the line of vision appear smaller the further away they are and this phenomenon can be used to create false perspective. Actively decreasing the size of features as they are seen

A perspective sketch gives an impression of the way a garden might look from a particular place. In this instance, the view (from standing position) at a patio window is taken as the picture plane (or frame).

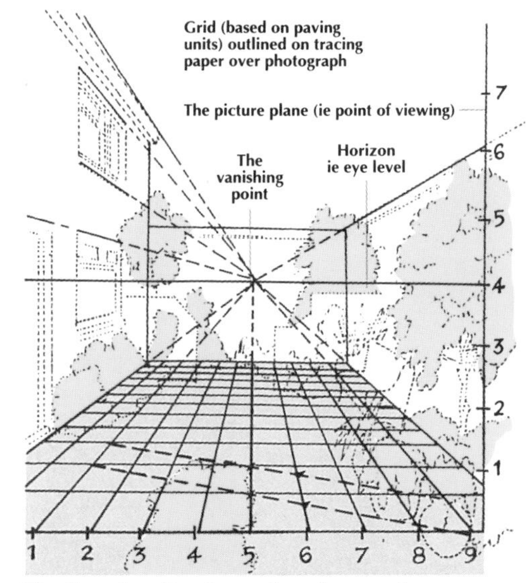

The lines leading from the picture plane toward the vanishing point cannot be drawn to scale beyond the picture plane. Scale calibrations can also be drawn along the vertical axis to achieve good proportion.

from a chosen viewpoint makes them appear to be more distant than they are, making the garden appear larger than its physical dimensions. In an enclosed, rectangular garden, for example, false perspective could be introduced in a number of ways which, in concert, would give the impression of a longer garden.

The central path might be designed so that it physically reduces in width as it recedes. This would be relatively simple to achieve with a gravel path, but if paving were used, the individual units would have to be cut progressively smaller as the width of the path reduced, in order to create the same effect. An arch, seat or other focal point at the end of the path could be made smaller than usual to add to the impression of distance. Trees, shrubs or bushes lining the path at "regular" intervals could play their part in the illusion by gradually reducing in height and being planted ever closer together as they reach the end of the garden.

Obviously, effects of this type work in only one direction. An appropriate site would have to be chosen with great care, or the effects may be counterproductive and make the garden seem smaller.

Planning for perspective

Sketching perspective diagrams allows you to test the effects of the planned vertical elements. Several different views are usually needed as it is difficult to draw an entire garden in perspective from one viewpoint. Start sketching at the front of the picture to avoid drawing over things which occur further back and are obscured by planting or by nearer objects.

Alternatively, photographs of the garden can be used. Enlargements are best at, say, 150 x 100 mm (6 x 4 in) or larger. Clip tracing paper of the same size over the enlarged photograph, then, taking the relevant information from the plan, sketch your ideas in pencil over the tracing paper. The photograph will be partially visible beneath the tracing paper to guide you.

Keep as much to the scale of the photograph as possible and, again, start by sketching in ideas at the front of the picture. Sketch your proposals accurately but not in minute detail: an impression is all that is required. Using separate sheets of tracing paper and a medium-soft pencil allow you to make as many attempts as are necessary to perfect the sketch, without damaging the photographs.

An enlarged photograph of a particular view taken from a central standing position.

The tracing paper overlaid and clipped to the photograph with pencil sketches of proposals.

Shaping horizontal planes

Although shaped and formed by surrounding features, the horizontal planes and spaces in a garden must exist in their own right. The contribution they make to the overall design is immeasurable, so never leave their shapes and proportions to chance.

Many garden spaces, apart from being planned for visual or horticultural appeal, will have a practical application, so make sure that they are suitable for their specific function, such as games, entertaining, sunbathing, reading, vegetable-growing and so on.

Style and contrast

What constitutes a pleasing shape is a matter of personal taste. Some gardeners prefer the formality of straight lines and geometric shapes: others do not. Well proportioned formal shapes have an inherent balance: informal shapes are often more difficult to perfect than formal ones, since informal shapes appear to be affected more on the ground by perspective.

A garden can, provided that it is sufficiently large, contain separate areas of many shapes and of differing styles, both formal and informal. The experience of walking through such a garden can be delightful and this can be further enhanced by the introduction of contrasting touches of formality to informal areas and vice versa.

Maintaining garden spaces

Spaces can be altered by a particular activity or by general wear and tear resulting from the whole family enjoying the garden. For example, a lawn can begin to lose its original shape following over-zealous or inaccurate edging and paths can spread or even be abandoned in favour of short cuts. This is where the garden plan comes into its own, since it helps to preserve or restore the carefully tailored shapes by becoming a point of future reference, thereby ensuring that the shapes' relevance and contribution to the plan is continuous.

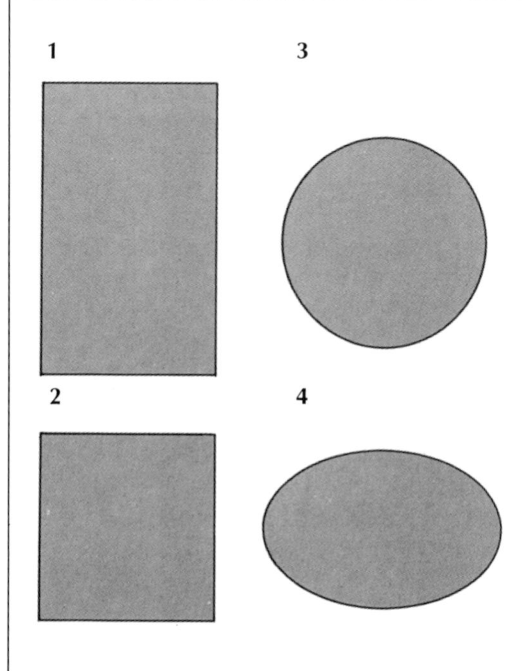

Formal geometric shapes are easier to incorporate into a design than informal shapes. The size of circles and squares can vary but, unlike other geometric shapes, their proportions cannot.

1 Rectangles are used in garden design more often than any other shape. The ancient Greek "perfect proportion" of eight units by five undeniably produces a good shape. Rectangles can be overlapped.

2 Squares are versatile and can be repeated in any direction or overlapped.

3 Circles are less versatile, particularly when set against, close to or overlapping other circles when they can create awkward "leftover" shapes.

4 Ellipses take on a very different shape when viewed in perspective and must therefore be incorporated with care as a garden shape.

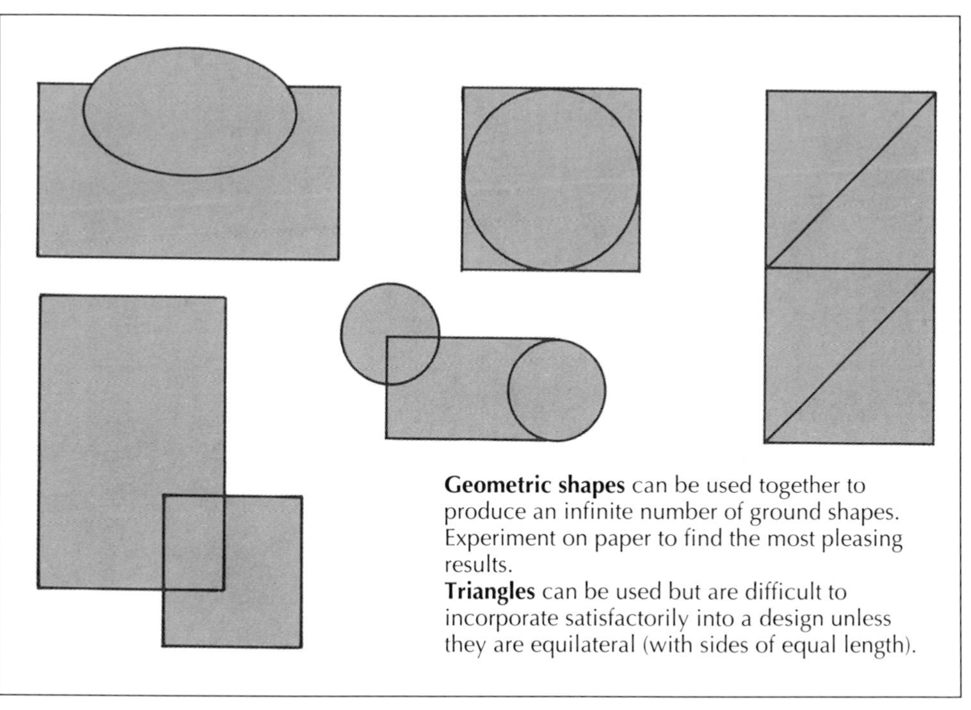

Geometric shapes can be used together to produce an infinite number of ground shapes. Experiment on paper to find the most pleasing results.

Triangles can be used but are difficult to incorporate satisfactorily into a design unless they are equilateral (with sides of equal length).

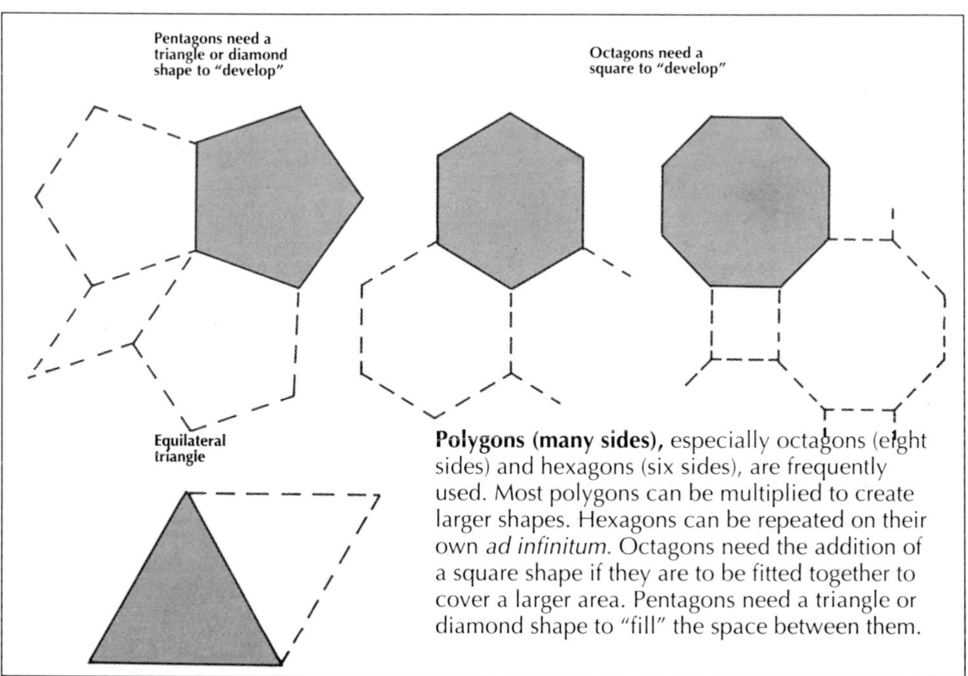

Polygons (many sides), especially octagons (eight sides) and hexagons (six sides), are frequently used. Most polygons can be multiplied to create larger shapes. Hexagons can be repeated on their own *ad infinitum.* Octagons need the addition of a square shape if they are to be fitted together to cover a larger area. Pentagons need a triangle or diamond shape to "fill" the space between them.

Partitions and focal points

Within the garden, structure can be created with a number of features, but partitions, focal points and more diffuse compositions create the sense of interest and excitement that makes even the smallest plot worth visiting.

Partitioning

Introducing partitions into a garden can make it appear larger rather than smaller. Imaginative partitioning can make a tremendous difference to small and medium-sized gardens and can be used to create spaces, each perhaps having a distinct function and atmosphere.

Garden compartments should be linked in a way that allows them to retain their individuality and sense of enclosure. Entrances and exits should be arranged adjacent to seats rather than opposite them, in which case they are in full view of the sitter.

Compartment size relative to the height of the surround profoundly affects the sense of enclosure. A large space with a relatively low enclosure feels far more open than a small space with higher partitions, which may also create more shade (see Structure, space and movement: Movement, page 50).

Focal points

Classical artifacts and statuary are usually linked with traditionally formal schemes.

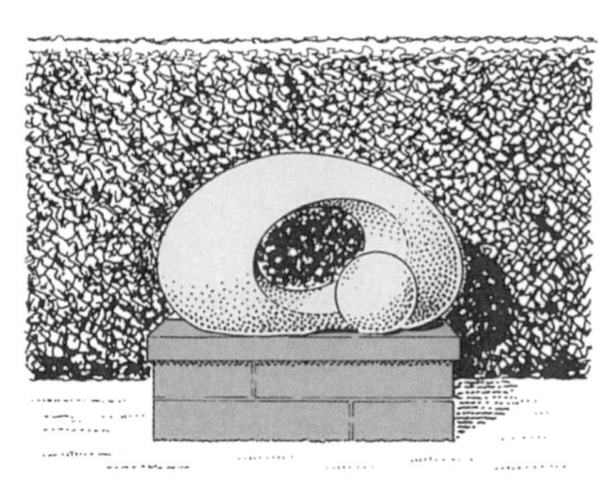

Modern sculptures in various materials look well in formal and informal "neutral" settings.

Sundials and bird baths, when used as focal points, combine function with ornament, as do seats.

Gazebos and summer houses are delightful focal points. Their style should not conflict with other forms of architecture nearby.

Focal points

Focal points are objects or plants lying inside or outside a garden that demand our special attention. More often associated with formal than with informal gardens, they are best sited individually as, when two or more focal points are seen together, a visual conflict is inevitable, especially if they are of different styles.

Focal points are used in large gardens as goals forming part of a planned route and arranged as a progressive series. After a particular focal point has been reached, the next comes into view and so on.

Individual specimen trees are perfect focal points, occasionally associated with circular or polygonal seats surrounding their trunks.

Practically any individual object or tree will serve as a focal point provided that it is significantly different from its background or immediate surroundings. For this reason, the background and surroundings should be carefully considered. Normally, a background of neutral colour and relatively uniform texture will ensure that the chosen focal point is displayed to the best effect.

Borrowed focal points

Focal points are useful for terminating a view within a garden in a satisfactory way, rather than it appearing as a dead end. But views lying outside a garden can also be incorporated into the design. These "borrowed" focal points can be as varied as a church spire or a coastline, but may be so dominant that the importance of other elements or lesser focal points within the garden is diminished.

Before designing a garden around a borrowed focal point, check what the implications might be. It might be necessary to reach an agreement with adjacent landowners, especially if stock-proof fences are to be reduced in height in order to create an unimpeded view of the borrowed focal point.

If there is a possibility of development in the surrounding area, the plan may have to be changed to conceal the view rather than to incorporate it.

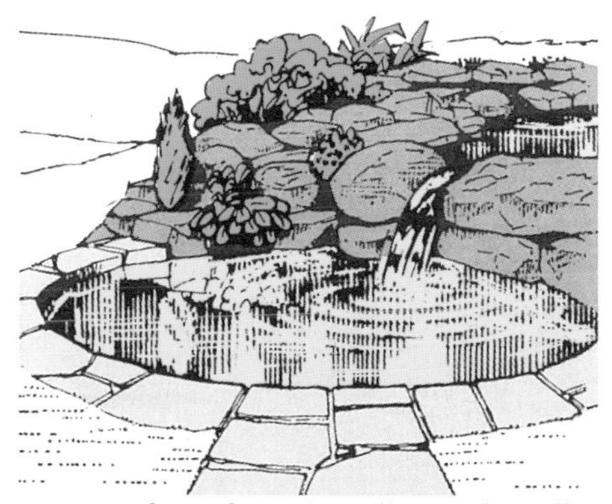

Water used as a focus formally or informally, whether still or moving, is irresistible.

Borrowed focal points, such as these distant hills, have been used for centuries to extend boundaries.

Compositions

Compositions
In informal gardens, individual focal points may be out of place and their role taken over by more diffuse compositions, for example, a grouping of several plants. These plant compositions are often subtle in effect but they must still be distinctive and distinguishable from the general planting. Some compositions can comprise trees and shrubs in combination with seats, garden buildings or other structures. In such cases the trees or plants are not there simply in subordinate roles, but form part of the overall picture where constructed and natural forms are brought into harmony. Compositions can be made with works of art or structures, provided that they are carefully presented as such and have an affinity with one another. The rule regarding two visible, individual focal points also applies to compositions: it is best to site different compositions individually, so that the one does not detract from the other and to avoid visual conflict.

All architecture, whether in the form of a house or garden buildings, makes a strong statement. Even so, most buildings, however large or small, can be improved by good foils

A pavilion reflected in a still pool, with trees and shrubs acting as foils. Their forms are indispensable, both individually and as components of the unified composition.

A single bench seat is at the heart of this composition, yet it would not work so well as a focal point without the contrasting shrubs and trees that surround it.

Compositions can be simple, as these three terracotta jars demonstrate.

Boulders, pebbles and a small gnarled tree combine to make a naturalistic focal point.

and framing. Trees and shrubs are excellent for this, bringing balance and harmony to the overall picture. Focal points need not be single objects; compositions are often more effective – especially so when the situation is informal.

Focal points and compositions can be used to disguise or draw attention away from unsightly features – raised gas or water tanks, for example – which, without suitable camouflage, could become focal points themselves. It may be tempting to hide large, unattractive features with a "wall" of fast-growing evergreens, but this usually only draws attention to the fact that something is being screened. Moreover, formalized groups of trees, particularly conifers, can grow into unsatisfactory focal points in their own right.

A better solution would be to use densely planted informal tree and shrub forms in combination with a small alternative focal point, such as a seat, which would tend to draw the eye downward. Informal tree forms break up unsightly architectural shapes. In winter, the bare branches of most deciduous trees can still soften hard outlines. Evergreens could also be used but most, except eucalyptus, take many years to become sufficiently mature to be effective. Eucalyptus, being so distinctive, may ultimately have the same effect as conical trees, drawing attention to the objects they are intended to disguise. In temperate climates, indigenous trees would blend in better since, as part of a screening arrangement, a degree of visual anonymity is an advantage.

Instead of being screened, this shed has become the centre of a composition. Its most visible side now has a light pergola with trellised sides fixed to it. Bold plants, including climbers, and a seat give the impression of an arbour. The shed, which was once a necessary but entirely functional item, is now making a positive contribution to the garden as an attractive focal point.

Screening

Sometimes it takes more than a focal point to counteract an unsightly feature. In many cases, screening can remove the offending object from view.

Tall unsightly objects or unattractive views just outside the garden can be concealed by screens placed near the main viewing position rather than closer to the offending object itself. The height of a screen close to the viewing position can be lower than one positioned further away. In principle, the further away the object relative to the screen and the closer the screen to the observer, the easier it is to disguise the object. But in many cases, even a relatively low screen may be inconvenient near the house. An alternative might be a constructed screen above a certain height, but cost and feasibility could rule this out.

Planning for screening
Deciding on the form and position of screens early in the design process ensures that the main part of the garden does not become obscured from view as the various planted elements mature. Sketches and annotated photographs should help the process.

In the example below, there is a commercial unit just beyond the garden boundary and the aim is to screen it from the house. The lines drawn from eye height to the chimney stack represent the angle of view and indicate the minimum height the screen needs to be. This changes as the viewer moves further into the garden, but not too dramatically. A planted bund (soil mound) or raised bed positioned at a distance can speed up the screening process by immediately giving the plants extra height.

Screening unsightly objects

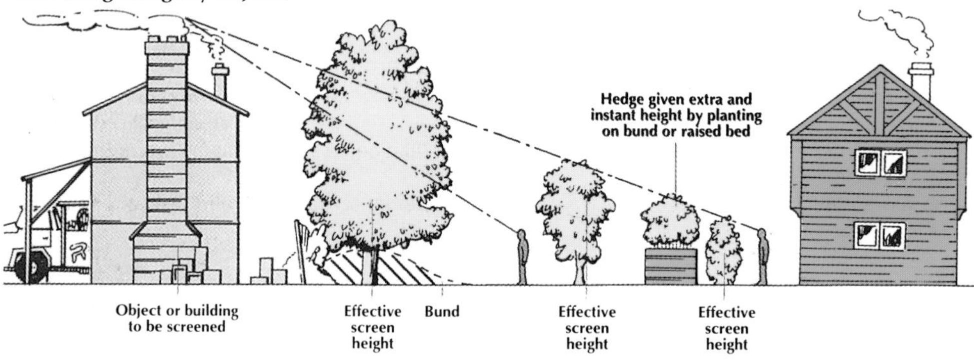

Trellis and plants The offending object is hidden behind trellis and planted beds.

Fences and walls can be used to conceal undesirable views.

Directing paths as screens
Curving paths can be used to screen unsightly objects provided that they are densely planted at the sides. In the example (page 62, bottom right) a path is combined with a decorative fence or wall and mostly evergreen plants. The screen is now an eye-catching feature in itself.

Overhead screening
In the smallest gardens screening may have to be achieved using tall planted trellis or with pergolas and arches. Vertical screening over 1.8 m (6 ft) or so, may need planning permission from the local authority.

The problem of being overlooked can be eased by using overhead screening: horizontal beams set on uprights to support planting. The direction in which the beams run and their spacing is determined by the position of the overlooking building. In the example below (left) the cross-beams run at right angles to each other, forming a grid pattern. This is because the patio is overlooked on at least two sides. In principle, when viewed obliquely from above, the beams obscure any view of the area beneath, but anyone underneath can look up and see the sky – if the planting is not too dense. This sort of screen can be installed anywhere.

Screening for mystery and concealment
Few gardens would not benefit from the addition of a little mystery. Gardeners who can see their entire plot at one glance run the risk of becoming bored with it sooner rather than later. The smaller the space, the greater the need for some hidden corner. Where all space is at a premium, a separate hidden area may not be feasible but it can still be suggested. Under these circumstances, screening makes a positive contribution to the design, whereas screening introduced to remove unwanted or distracting objects from sight is more a means of returning emphasis to the garden.

Unattractive features may lie inside as well as outside the garden. Compost bins fall into this category, as do dustbins and garden sheds. Whatever the unwelcome object, take care not to draw attention to it inadvertently by using the wrong type of screening. The screen should visually break up the lines or form of the offending object, making one wonder what lies behind rather than being a feature in its own right.

A patio screened from above

Focal points screened to avoid visual conflict

Coping with sloping gardens

Sloping gardens, usually more difficult to design and maintain than flat ones, have the advantage of being potentially more interesting. The design solutions for a garden which slopes upward from the front of a house, however, are quite different from those for a front garden sloping downward.

Slopes and visibility

Gentle upward slopes bring more of the garden into view than an equivalent flat area, but if a garden slopes so steeply that it has to be terraced, it effectively disappears from view once the slope reaches eye-level. The idea is to bring as much of the garden as possible into view.

Access and safety

Access is one potential problem, especially for garden machinery. If access is poor and the upper reaches of the garden are uninteresting, the chances are that no one will go there, resulting in a waste of both space and opportunity.

Steps and ramps (see Constructed vertical elements: Changes of level, page 134) must be as safe and convenient to use as possible. Ramps should preferably be no steeper than 1:20. Straight flights of steps and ramps are not always feasible in extremely steep gardens, in which case choose sideways, zig-zag or curving steps or ramps, as they allow a more gradual ascent or descent. In some cases maintenance

Reducing the negative effects of close retaining walls

A built-in wall fountain can be incorporated in the plan, or a ready-made unit added later.

A sitting wall with tiered planting

A rock garden can enliven a plain slope or a retaining wall in less formal circumstances.

Steps can be used to counter any impression of enclosure.

at the higher level might be possible only if a second set of tools and equipment is permanently stored there.

Focal points

Close retaining walls can look uncompromising, but there are various ways of softening their appearance by the introduction of planting or other focal points. Wall fountains are fascinating, especially when associated with bold plants such as bamboos, fatsias, grasses and irises, most of which could be evergreen to ensure year-round interest. A mysterious grotto built into a rustic stone retaining wall is always a talking point or, if this is not possible, enliven the wall with hanging baskets, pots and containers. If it is feasible, design the wall to be stepped with a series of flat planting areas in its face; this will both soften its appearance and provide planting opportunities. Night-time lighting, too, can create dramatic shadows to emphasize the wall's architecture.

Planting for slopes

Planted or grassed embankments are softer in appearance than walls and may be more appropriate in informal gardens. Choose grass mixes and plant varieties that thrive in a well drained situation, allowing for whether the embankment is in sun or shade. Grass is never easy to cut on a slope, so is usually a second choice to ground-cover plants.

Planting plans should allow for closer planting than would be usual in horizontal sites. The closer the plants are, the more rapidly they will spread and merge to inhibit weed growth. In drier conditions growth rates tend to be slower, so close planting also speeds up the ground-covering process.

Downward slopes

The illustration (above right) shows a house at a higher level than the garden. Under these circumstances the means of retention will be seen with the house as part of a composition. Ensure that materials used for steps, walls and paths are in harmony with the architecture of the house and bear in mind the colour of the hard landscaping when choosing the colour of flowers.

Gardens which slope down from the house appear more spacious than upward-sloping sites, especially if they overlook open country-

A house at a higher level than the garden

side. Similar gardens in the suburbs or in town, on the other hand, may overlook neighbouring houses and other buildings, in which case they might need to be screened (see Structure, space and movement: Screening, page 62).

The physical problems connected with steeply downward-sloping gardens are more or less the same as for those sloping upward, but the design solutions are different. Embankments, retaining walls and lawns, on looking back towards the house, are seen as a composition, unlike the view from the house of an embankment or a retaining wall.

Take extra care to ensure harmony and continuity in the design when a house, at a higher level, is seen in conjunction with any embankments, walls and slopes. This is usually the view seen from approach roads or driveways.

Upward slopes

Gardens which begin to slope upward close to the front or rear walls of the house present only a restricted view. Where retaining walls must be positioned close to the house, make them attractive enough to be a feature of the design (see Constructed vertical elements: Brick walls, stone walls, pages 126–33).

Drainage is an important aspect of design. When the ground slopes, surface rainwater drainage is generally very good, although this partly depends on the soil type or the surfacing.

Coping with sloping gardens 2

Consequently, if the house is at the bottom of a slope, an efficient drainage system is essential if flooding is to be avoided at times of high rainfall.

Always slope the paving down from the house to ensure that water does not collect close to its walls. The retaining wall should have drainage holes (weepholes) at its base which discharge water into a rainwater channel at its foot. The channel should be large enough to receive water from the sloping paving as well as from the drainage holes. From here the rainwater can be conducted to a ditch or drainage system.

If the slope is really steep, a series of intercepting lateral drains may be required. Under these circumstances, seek expert advice. The problem with providing drainage for sloping gardens is that, while efficient drainage is needed to protect property and construction, grass and plants often suffer as a result. Installing a controlled irrigation system incorporating water-retentive granules and mulching regularly usually solves the problem.

Creating flat surfaces in sloping gardens

Think very carefully before creating a flat area on a sloping site. A cross-sectional sketch will be of great help in illustrating exactly where the flat area might best be placed – minimizing, as far as possible, unnecessary and expensive earthworks. Access, too, will have a bearing on the costs and feasibility of major earth moving. Also, by using sketched human figures ("pin" people will do) drawn at the same scale as the cross-section but sitting and standing, you can see how the flat area will have an impact on the views in either direction.

The creation of the flat area can be done either by removing soil, building it up or "cutting and filling" – where soil is dug out on the high side, then heaped up and consolidated on the low side (to avoid latter settlement).

Creating flat areas on sloping sites may need, (depending upon the degree of slope) some means of physical retention on both the high and low sides. If the overall slope is gentle prior to levelling, then a planted or grassed embankment will be sufficient. New slopes created by the levelling operation intended for growing or planting should not exceed 40 degrees – to ensure stability. The question whether to grass, plant or pave the newly created level is up to you. Even if you choose paving, the area should not be truly flat to aid surface water drainage (see Horizontal surfaces: Paving, page 110). You are also likely to need an intercepting drainage channel on the high side, beneath the embankment, wall or other means of retention.

A sloping formal garden

The first plan (below) shows an asymmetrically formal solution to a garden which slopes upward from the front to the rear. Geometric shapes are used. The front garden is modest in size compared with the rear and it functions simply as a driveway. To the right a vegetable garden slopes gently upward, as does the service path at the left. The main terrace, which is lower than the rest of the garden, needs to be interesting at all times of year, hence the pool and the wall fountain in the retaining wall. Curving steps rise at its rear to the next level, which also slopes (apart from a circular level area at its centre). Achieving this flat area involved creating a curving embankment at the far side. Broad steps up another retaining wall finally arrive at a summer house, which is positioned at the highest point of the garden.

A sloping formal garden

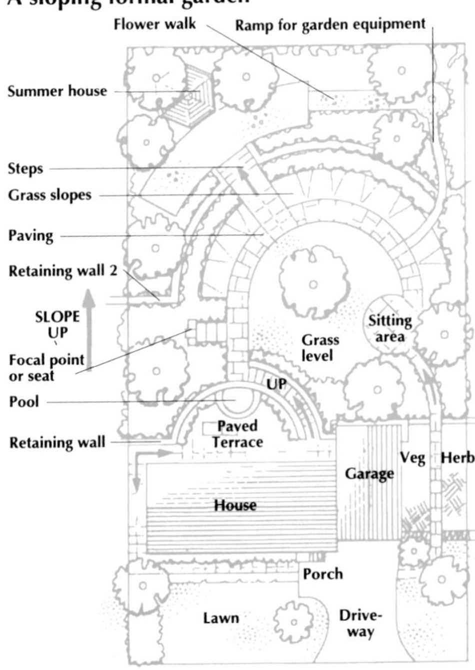

Design for a sloping informal garden

In the informal scheme for the same plot, the sloping service paths at each side of the house are for pedestrians and for wheeled garden equipment. The terrace is organic in shape and carpeting plants grow between random paving stones rather than in the more frequently used areas where they may become a nuisance. Rocks form the retaining walls and steps.

The second level with lawn is primarily for recreation, while the third and highest level is devoted to growing alpine and wild flowers. At the top right, the upper pool can be viewed from a concealed seat. Gravelled paths link the upper areas, making them accessible, particularly following inclement weather. Ground contouring has been avoided where possible and the garden conforms approximately to existing slopes.

Sloping garden with an asymmetrical theme

In the third illustration, which slopes downward from the front to the rear, all the shapes with the exception of the terrace and house service paths, are derived from polygons. Main steps are shaped to make an easy transition from the rectangular to the polygonal and are attractive features in their own right. Two levels of flat lawn are separated by the necessary retaining wall. Angled steps lead from the lowest to the middle lawn. At the opposite side, narrower service steps connect to upward-sloping paths. At the bottom left is a secondary sitting area complete with a small summer house. A small screened garden shed occupies the opposite corner.

Sloping garden with varying styles

When a sloping garden is large then different styled sub-gardens can exist together, providing that they are are not in visual conflict. Nevertheless, there might be a unifying factor – perhaps a paving material common to each. The idea of a varying style, sloping garden works well on steeper sloping sites when steps or paths lead from one area to another. However, as with most styles of garden, it is generally accepted that it is better to have the more formal areas near to the house, there being a logical affinity.

A sloping informal garden

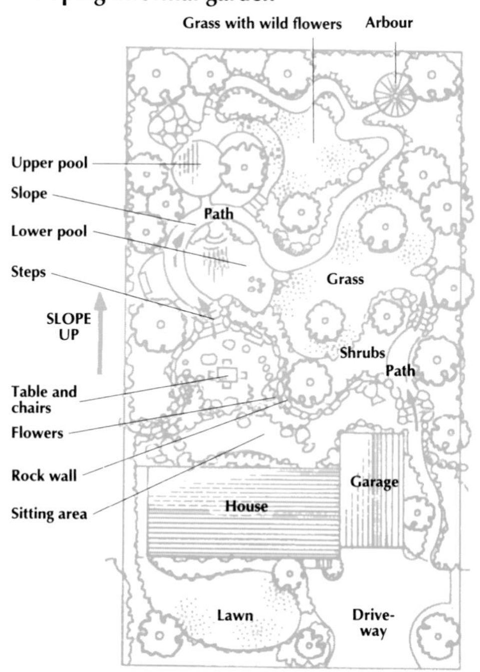

Sloping garden with an asymmetrical theme

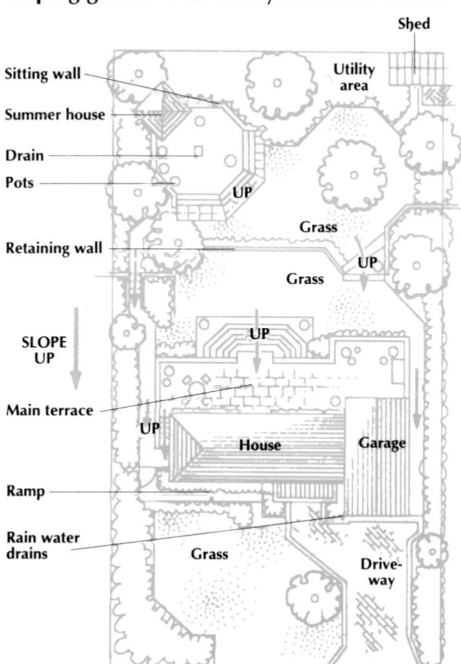

Style in the garden

The dictionary defines style as the "manner or expression of ideas". Most gardens conform to one style or another if they have been consciously designed. In some, the design follows the function, as is the case with most family or domestic gardens, while in others, such as ornamental gardens or bedding schemes, the design is intended purely for visual appeal. Some gardens are totally functional and are essentially without style, for instance a basic vegetable garden.

The style of a garden is often influenced by factors such as function, the environment, geographic location, shape, proportion, levels, associated architecture, the amount of maintenance required or the cost of realization. But there can be other influences, themes such as water features, roses, rock features or herbs.

If particular needs are to be fulfilled, this will also affect style. Gardens for the partially sighted, disabled or elderly will inevitably be different in style from a garden for a family with young children, say, or a conservationist. The style will be further influenced by the number of people for whom the garden is intended, whether an individual, a family or a community.

Formal gardens

1 A symmetrically formal garden with a single line of symmetry is illustrated below (left). One side appears as a mirror reflection of the other. The line of symmetry in this example passes through the centre of the garden lengthways. It could, under other circumstances, pass centrally from side to side yet the garden would remain symmetrically formal.

2 There are two central lines of symmetry in the second example, one running the length of the garden, the other at right angles to it. These quarter the garden. To be truly symmetrical, each of the four quarters must be an exact image of the others.

1 A symmetrically formal garden

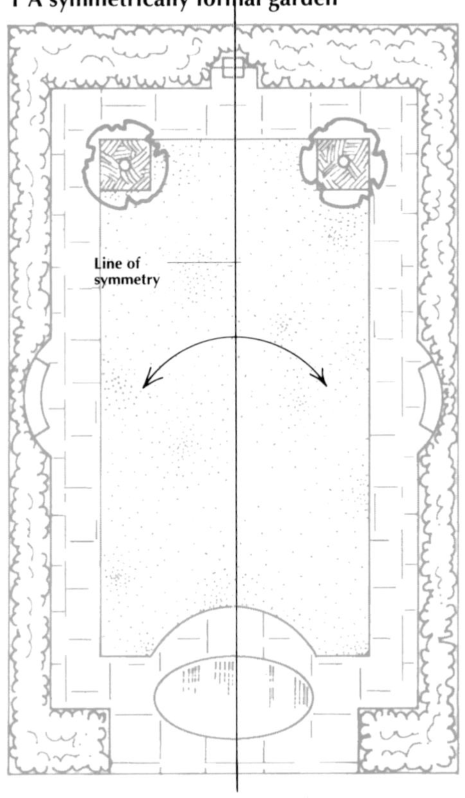

2 Two central lines of symmetry

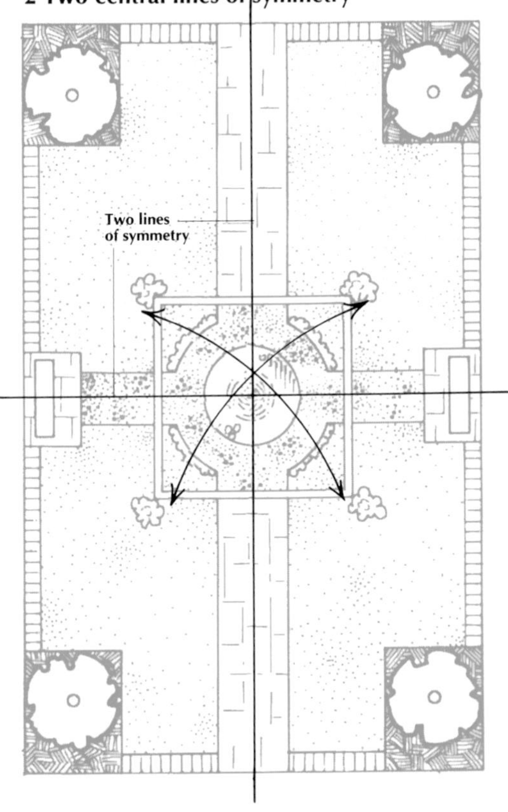

Many formal gardens of the past were designed to conform to the rules of symmetry. To achieve an area of true formality in an informal plot, a separate sub-boundary or boundaries must be created inside it and structured symmetrically within.

Informal gardens

3 Asymmetrical formality is a popular style in modern gardens. The formally or geometrically shaped planes do not conform to any lines of symmetry but are juxtaposed or overlapped to create interesting sub-shapes. Asymmetrical formality is the ideal style if a sense of order is preferred but without being too strict. To achieve this, try experimenting with different geometrical ground shapes.

4 Informal gardens can be very appealing, with free and natural forms and curving lines creating the vertical and horizontal planes. A degree of underlying order can be achieved, however, by linking curves based on part or whole circles and ellipses and allowing them to develop as flowing lines and free forms.

Achieving style in the garden

Having decided upon the style you wish to achieve, the next problem is how to interpret it. There are a great many possibilities: symmetrically formal, asymmetrically formal, informal, or as a series of smaller gardens, each with its own interpretation.

In some cases, the particular style may not result from free personal choice but may depend on what is appropriate to the situation. A formal "wild" garden, for example, would seem as incongruous as a "natural" rock garden in the corner of a town garden surrounded by high brick walls. Style must work on a practical and an aesthetic level. This is another aspect of garden "style" not based on the form or function, but rather on the garden as a setting.

3 An asymmetrically formal garden

4 An informal plan

Style in the garden 2

A garden combining symmetrically formal, asymmetrically formal and informal areas

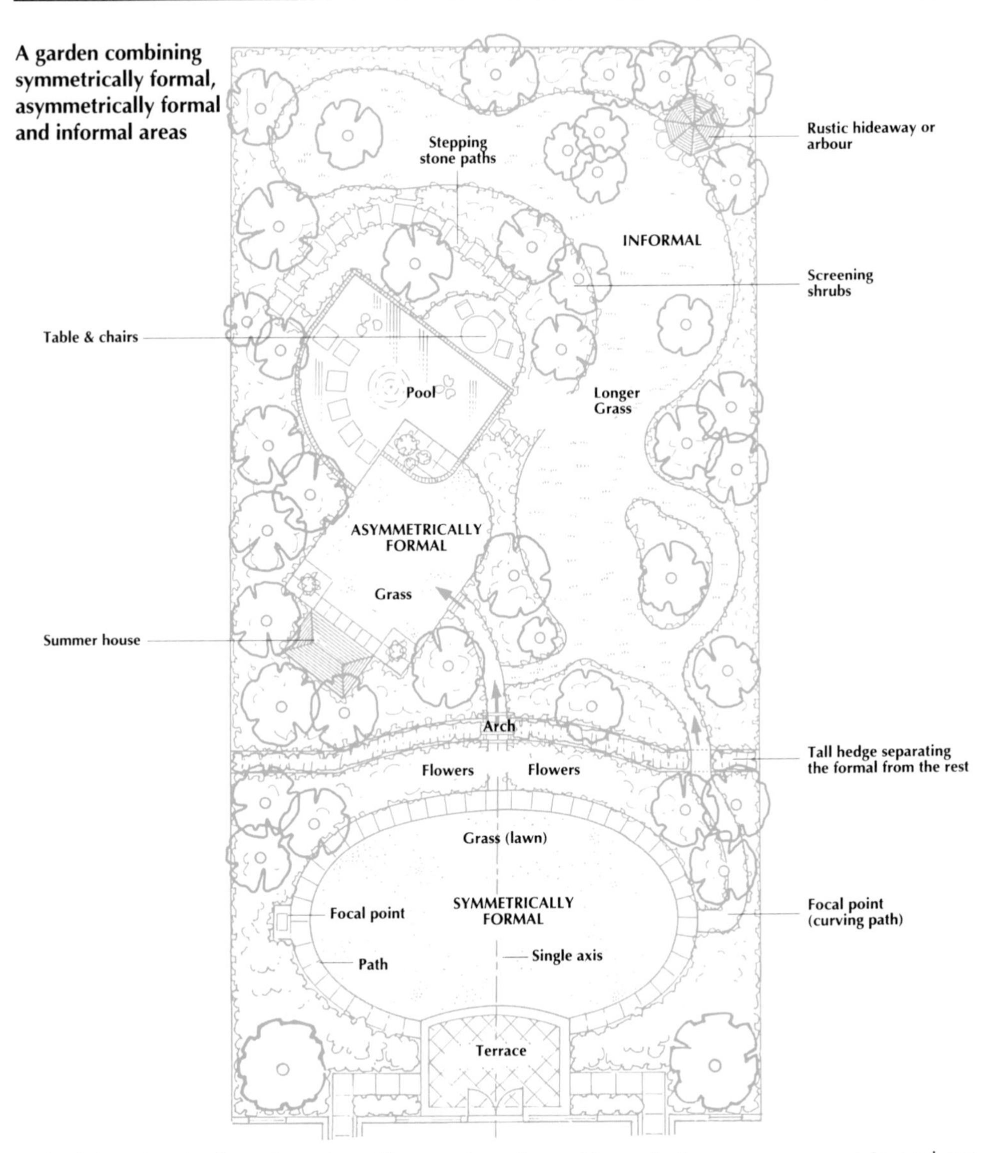

Linked formal and informal areas, as illustrated in the example above, create gardens of contrasting moods.

Traditionally, the area closest to the house is treated formally. A single line of axis terminates at the arch, from which point a path curves invitingly to the left, its destination tantalizingly invisible from the house. The path leads, via an arch in a tall evergreen hedge, to the next section, which is designed along asymmetrical lines. Ground shapes are geometric and are based on straight lines and true arcs. To the right is an informal garden where hidden areas create a sense of mystery and where wild plants, animals, birds and insects are encouraged. Although each section of this garden is different in character, style and shape, there is no visual or intellectual conflict. They are complete entities occupying their own spaces yet contributing to the garden as a whole.

Many small town gardens are designed to appear as if they grow out of the surrounding architecture. This inevitably brings continuity and a sense of aptness. Such gardens seem contained and intimate.

Out of town there is generally more space available but many gardens are still surrounded by neighbouring plots or are close to other houses. The best design solutions are often inward-looking, those which create an oasis of calm and at least partially screen the immediate surroundings.

Public gardens do not conform to the same rules as private gardens. They are often part of a broader design or townscape, relying on the interaction between the public and the structured elements for their success. Public gardens are mostly for the passive enjoyment of visitors and passersby.

Where gardens overlook beautiful views, a boundary can sometimes be disguised. This extends the garden by blurring the distinction between it and the landscape beyond. Views can be enhanced by being "framed" with trees. A dramatic view will dominate the scene: inappropriate objects placed in the middle-distance will be seen as interruptions.

Multipurpose gardens

An asymmetrically formal garden

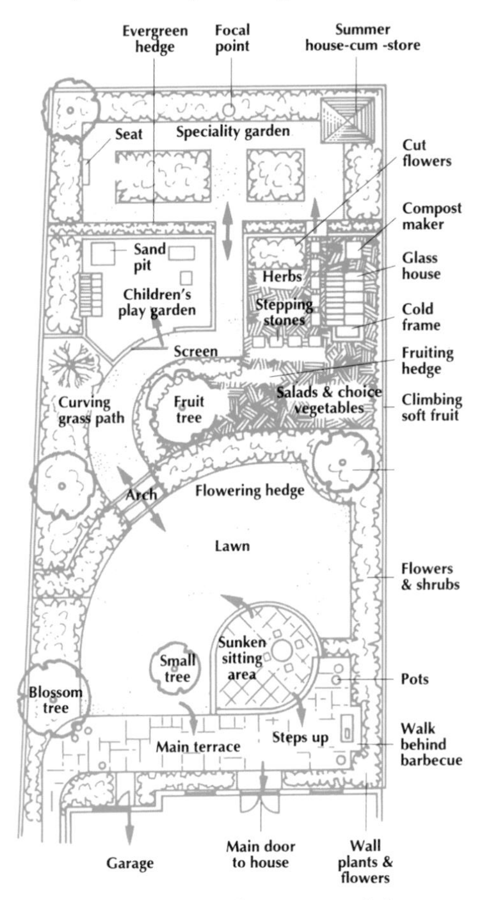

The creation of a garden is one of the most satisfying forms of expression. Possible permutations are endless: every garden is unique.

Early in the design process, the list of requirements suggests a style that fulfils the particular needs and expectations within the plot. In other words, the design based on the requirements is individually tailored.

The following pages contain a series of garden designs, tailor-made to suit particular tastes. These are intended as a source of ideas only, as it would be extremely unlikely that any of them would be completely suitable for use in any other context. Most plans can, within reason, be adapted or modified to fit a particular plot shape or proportion but there are elements that do not function below a certain size.

Gardens for families

One of the most common types of garden is for a family with children of different ages and with different needs and expectations. Although potentially more difficult to design than gardens with a simple theme or fulfilling a simple function, family gardens always make interesting projects. Following the guidelines set out in this book will not only make the process easier but more enjoyable too. The following "tailored" gardens illustrate the application of good design principles to the needs and expectations of the owner.

A large, asymmetrically formal garden for a young family

The main terrace is of a generous size in keeping with the proportions of the house. Paving is laid in a static, random rectangular pattern (see Horizontal surfaces: Paving, page 110) to increase the sense of tranquillity. On the right is a permanent barbecue area operated from the rear for convenience, while on the left the terrace is reduced to a service path turning the corner and eventually leading to the front of the house. A sunken sitting area, lower by some 300 mm (1 ft) makes an interesting adjunct and reflects the shape of the lawn, which is broad enough for recreational purposes and increases the sense of space. Its shape is defined by the flowers and borders at each side and by the flowering hedge. An archway with climbing plants frames an intriguingly curved path.

To the left is a play area created for young children, but the play house and equipment are made less conspicuous when viewed from the house because of the careful siting of this feature and because it is also lightly screened, perhaps with trellis, to give the sense of intimacy most children enjoy. When the children are older this area can be easily adapted for a different purpose.

On the right of the garden and screened by the flowering hedge (now with a dual purpose) is a herb, salad and vegetable garden. A small greenhouse and cold-frame are useful additions, as is a compost-maker. A view of the greenhouse roof from the main terrace could be distracting, but the evergreen tree planted in a forward position prevents this. The far end of the garden is separated from the rest by an evergreen hedge, but it is not so tall as to make this area appear small. Here, the owner's hobby may be indulged: a flower garden, roses, collections of a particular plant genus or even a water garden are all popular choices. If a water feature were chosen, a locked gate and fence hidden within the evergreen hedge would make the area secure. A summer house located in the top right-hand corner allows the parents to enjoy this area in privacy, but it could also be used as a store.

The whole plot is not truly rectangular, so the shapes of the areas within are designed to be complete in themselves and do not depend upon or follow the boundary lines. The irregularities are thereby absorbed by the shapes of the beds and borders and can, to some extent, be ignored.

An informal design for a family with older children and grandparents

Imposing an informal design on the plot illustrated (right) is the first challenge. A degree of informality has been introduced even in the shaping of the main terrace where house becomes garden. The terrace is gently curved at one end, giving it a more informal appearance than a rigid rectangular terrace, and surfaced with randomly sized and shaped paving stones.

The paved path allows the older members of the family, especially, to visit most parts of the garden at all times. For continuity, the path is laid with stone similar to that of the terrace, but is concealed for most of its length. This creates more interest and permits a close view of adjacent plants as it passes through various beds and borders.

Stepping stones take over from the path as it passes through an area of grass. These are more acceptable here as they do not form a positive line, as a path would, detracting from the more important shape of the lawn.

The circular hidden area is ideal for older children's play or activities, or would alternatively be a good place for a quiet read. Still concealed by planting, the path eventually leads to a rustic gazebo or arbour, chosen to be in keeping with the general theme of the garden. From here a beautiful view back up the garden is afforded, with a naturalistic pond forming part of the view. Its still, mirror-like surface reflects adjacent plants and sky and it provides a home for aquatic and amphibian life.

An informal or naturalistic garden

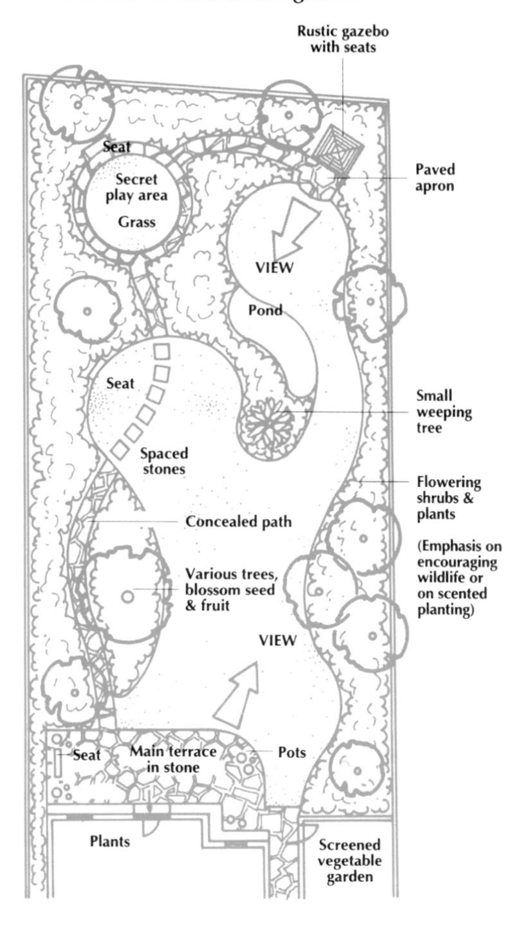

The informally shaped area of grass is the main feature of the garden. Intended for general use, it also makes an aesthetic contribution to the design. Depending upon the viewpoint, its shape will constantly appear to change and it will never be seen in its entirety, so interest will always be maintained. Wild flowers might be encouraged to grow if the grass is not intended to be a fine lawn and this would certainly be in keeping with the informal theme. If wildlife is to be actively encouraged, the plants, trees and shrubs should be selected accordingly; alternatively, a range of flowers and shrubs could be chosen purely for visual effect. Whichever choice is made, the design is mainly for passive rather than active enjoyment.

Multipurpose gardens 2

The multipurpose (or multi-interest) garden is styled to accomodate the various interests or recreational activities of one or more individuals. Such gardens tend to be busy places, when small, and the task for the designer is to ensure that the garden does not become too busy. Children's ball games on the lawn could spell disaster should potentially award-winning chrysanthemums be growing close by. A pergola to support overhead scented plants might, because of restrictions on space, be positioned too near the glasshouse, resulting in a visual conflict, and so on. Your early function plan should help you avoid most problems.

In smaller gardens, consider how some elements might take on a dual role, serving different interests at the same time. Examples could include a summer house fitted with blinds to accommodate garden furniture in winter; a brick barbeque fitted with removable fibreglass planters for flowers, decorative when the barbeque is out of use. Make low walls wide enough to double up as seats. Pergolas can support a grape vine, or other climbers. Cordon fruit trees can be grown as a screen.

The following plans illustrate a wide range of garden proportions and styles, showing how well, quite different purposes and interests can exist together in harmony.

Smaller multipurpose garden

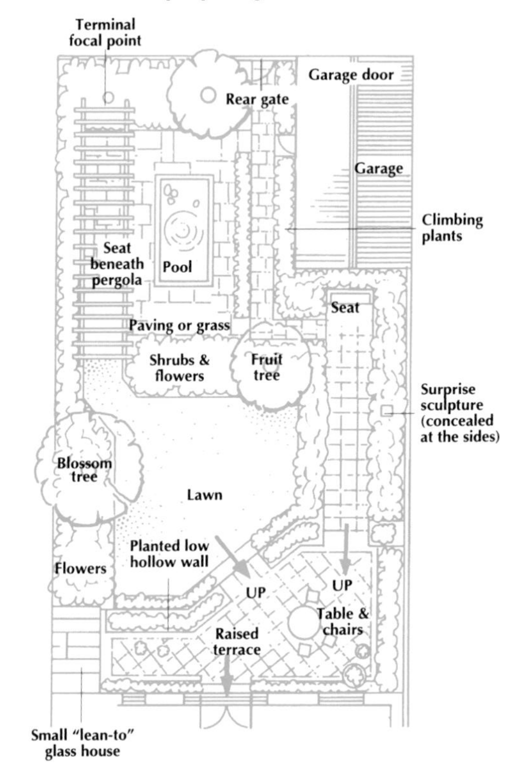

A smaller multipurpose garden

In the typical suburban garden of modest proportions illustrated (above, right), the garage takes up a considerable amount of space but has been incorporated into the design both to support climbing plants and as a foil for a seat. The seat, as well as being functional, is the terminal focal point for the main path leading from the terrace, which is raised to provide good views across the main lawn to the surrounding plants and flowers. Its angular shape creates a largish, open area next to the house, large enough to accommodate permanent garden furniture. Care has been taken not to place the furniture immediately in front of the patio doors, as this would obscure the view. On the left, a small "lean-to" greenhouse supplies the family with choice salad crops and is useful for raising plants, especially colourful annuals. Low, planted hollow walls front the patio and the stepped openings lead to other parts of the garden.

A long pergola leads to a concealed area on one side. The pergola supports scented climbing plants, while creating dramatic effects of light and shade. At its far end is a terminal focal point, such as a small statue, without which there could be a sense of anti-climax. A seat, partly concealed by the plants beneath the pergola, overlooks a paved or a grassed area. At its centre is a rectangular pool, set almost at ground level. This will ensure a maximum view of the water surface from the seat. The pool could be replaced, for the present, with a sandpit or a paddling pool if very young children are to use the garden. The surrounding planting has an aquatic theme, using bold architectural subjects such as brunneras, irises or fatsias, which, although not necessarily moisture-loving, give that impression to complete the illusion.

This area is linked to the service path, running parallel to the garage and now much narrower. On leaving the seat at the end of the main path, the path becomes simply a functional part of the design.

A long, narrow garden of mixed styles

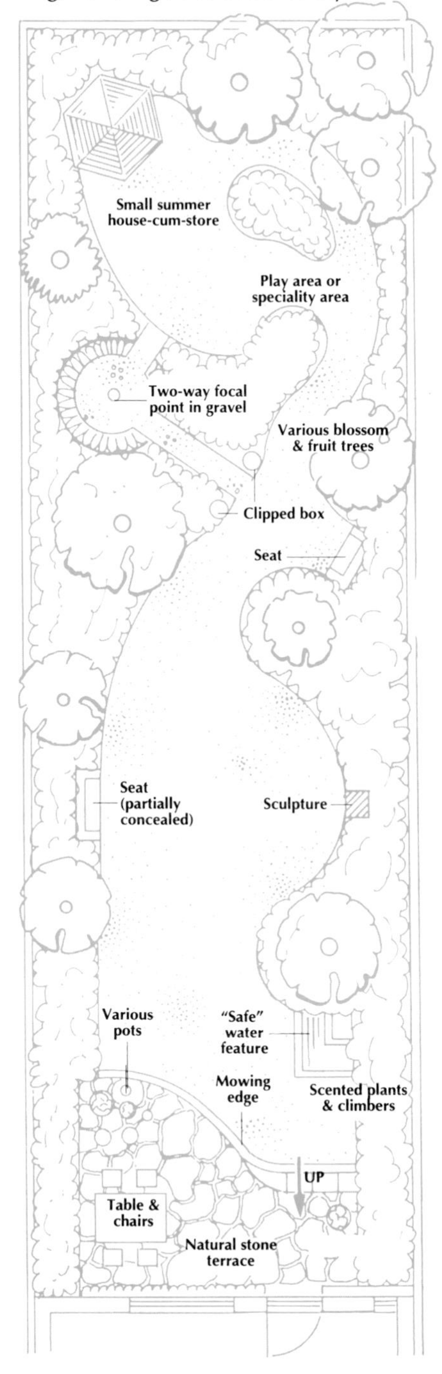

A long, narrow garden of mixed styles

For the most interesting effects, narrow gardens are best developed as a series of separate areas. This does not mean that each area has to be totally enclosed, just screened from view, one from the other.

The plan illustrated (left) is a mainly informal scheme of relatively low cost. The garden is created from grass, plants and trees, which are usually less costly per square metre than constructed features or paved surfaces.

A "safe" water feature is the main attraction, visible from the terrace, and the curved lawn provides ample opportunity for family recreation. About a third of the way into the garden, a partially screened seat is positioned opposite a sculpture or similar eye-catching feature. This is also partially concealed so that it can be enjoyed only from the seat opposite. Further on and at the opposite side of the garden is another seat, this time opposite a narrow gravel path, the entrance to which is marked by clipped box tree spheres. At the end of the path and circled by a low box tree hedge is a two-way focal point. A bird table or armillary sphere would be ideal for this position.

The area at the farthest end of the garden could be adapted as a play area, in which case the summer house would be doubly useful. A speciality area could replace the play area when appropriate.

Gardens for different age groups

A garden designed entirely for children needs to account for various age groups. Where children with a wide range of ages are expected to use the garden, it is advisable to separate one age group's activities from another. Very young children will generally not be able to join in with, or make use of, older children's games or play equipment because of their smaller size and restricted ability, and older children may scorn to take part in "childish" adventures.

Underlying any design for a children's garden is the unavoidable and obvious fact that children grow older and what they enjoy one year they may well have grown out of by the next. In a communal garden, successive generations of children will pass through and a wide range of equipment will be used to the full. This is not usually the situation in a private garden (unless an owner is willing to await the arrival

Multipurpose gardens 3

of grandchildren) and by definition all children's gardens are transient constructions. Bear this in mind when designing, as toys and play equipment will be used for a relatively short time and can never compare with games and activities born of the imagination.

Children's gardens

Above all, children's gardens should be challenging, intellectually stimulating and exciting places and, it goes without saying, they should also be safe places. For older children, however, the safety features should be in place but not be made too obvious, since a sense of adventure and imagined danger can be an enjoyable part of growing up.

A garden for older children

Older children will appreciate this garden because its design emphasizes adventure and exploration. The patio is generously proportioned for general use and for games like table tennis, chess and hoopla. The barbecue is a permanent feature and the focus of summer parties. A large open lawn can be used for more boisterous ball games and makes an aesthetic contribution to the entire scheme. In this area, the main focal point is a tree with a seat in its shade. A concealed path leading from the left of the patio immediately enters a vine-covered tunnel, providing dappled shade and occasional glimpses of the garden. On emerging from the tunnel, the path curves sharply past the end of the slide then dips beneath a timber bridge, continuing past a "safe" water feature to arrive at the rear entrance of a cavern constructed beneath an earth mound.

The alternative route across the lawn and over the bridge leads to a den enclosed by square section timbers set vertically into the ground to an approximate height of 1.5 m (5 ft). From here, the entrance to the safe, properly constructed subterranean cavern is reached by descending semi-circular steps. Opposite the cavern is the entrance to the sunken path, to the right via a ramp and to the left by steps. These also provide access to the top of the slide.

The entire garden is surrounded by hardy, child-resistant shrubs and trees. These unify the otherwise disparate elements and also provide year-round colour and interest for the adult members of the family.

A garden for older children

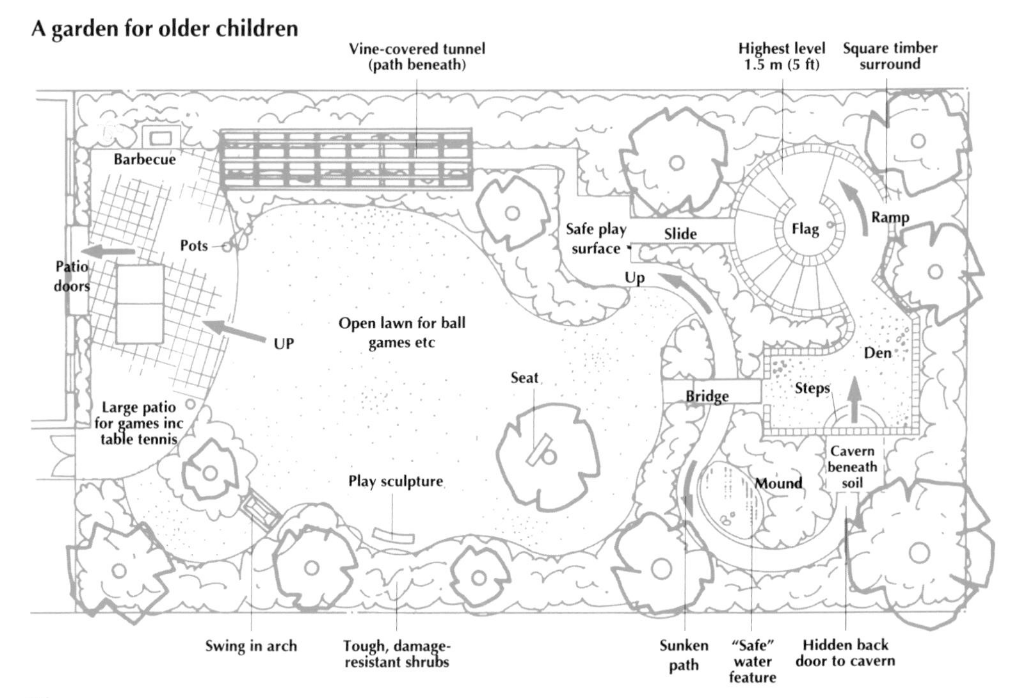

A garden for younger children

The design illustrated below for much younger children is contained within a smaller plot than the previous example. Most of its elements could be updated as the children grow older and, ultimately, the garden could be modified to fit solely with the parents' needs.

The area immediately adjacent to the house is paved in squares of two sizes: the smaller are pre-cast and the larger cast *in situ*, with numbers or letters marked on them by pressing pebbles into the unset, coloured concrete. A sand-pit, emptied and covered when not in use, lies adjacent to the shallow paddling pool, which is filled with fresh water each time it is used. Cleanliness is essential in both the paddling pool and the sand-pit in the interests of safety and hygiene.

A curving hedge divides the garden into three sections. Tucked away in the farthest section is a play house, either as a permanent or temporary feature, which provides the children with a degree of privacy. Close by is a robust, rounded "play" sculpture – perhaps a climb-on animal or fantasy figure – which not only brings pleasure to the children but acts as a focal point viewed from the house. This farthest area is reached via the arch in the hedge or the tricycle track which leads back in a strong curve to the corner of the terrace, where it also originates.

The middle section of the garden has a lawn at its centre with a play system incorporating a swing, slide and climbing net. The grass immediately beneath the equipment could be replaced with one of the many "play safe" impact-absorbing paviours.

The section closest to the terrace comprises a lawn or an alternative soft surface. At its centre is a weeping tree, such as *Prunus subhirtella* 'Pendula Rosea', which positively invites young children to hide from view beneath its umbrella of dense trailing branches.

On one side of the lawn a raised planting box meets the needs of budding horticulturists. Here, flower seeds can be sown and easy salad crops such as radishes or dwarf beans grown.

Trees have been chosen to encourage birds; a nesting box is fitted to the largest trunk. The flowering shrubs, as well as being attractive to the adults who will use the garden, have been selected to be robust, non-toxic and without spines or prickles.

A garden for younger children

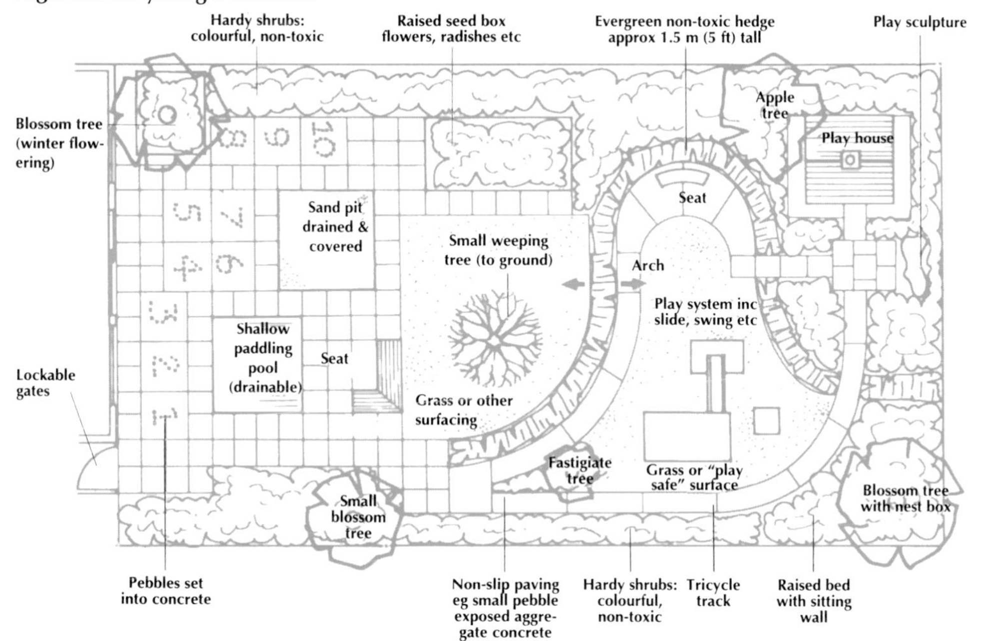

Small town/patio gardens

A wide, shallow garden

The wide, shallow patio garden poses particular design problems, especially when the boundary opposite the house is a wall or fence, which increases the sense of enclosure.

In the illustration below, this rather high wall is integrated in the design by fixing a mirror to it to create a *trompe l'oeil* effect or illusion (see Constructed vertical elements: *Trompe l'oeil*, page 142). Surrounded by slightly projecting bricks or timber, the mirror appears to be an opening to another part of the garden, an illusion enhanced by subtle adjacent planting and by the positioning of a sculpture or artifact, in this case a moulded terracotta figure, in front of it. To reinforce the illusion, the octagonal area in which the terracotta figure stands is paved with flint and pebbles and set at a lower level than the rest of the garden. Grass or paving covers the more open area and is surrounded either by a mowing edge or edging. On the right lies a secret sitting area, reached by an arch lightly clad with plants. On the ground, flints or pebbles are used again for continuity and to encourage moss to colonize the gaps. Bold evergreen plants, such as rhododendrons, enclose the seat.

A town garden

In the garden illustrated (page 79) the main view from the patio doors is of the table and chairs which, with a background of flowering shrubs, herbaceous plants and a small tree in the corner, form the focal point. The paving has been laid diagonally across the area to increase the sense of space and is pale in colour to reflect the available light. The overall shape of the paved area also increases the sense of space

A wide, shallow patio garden

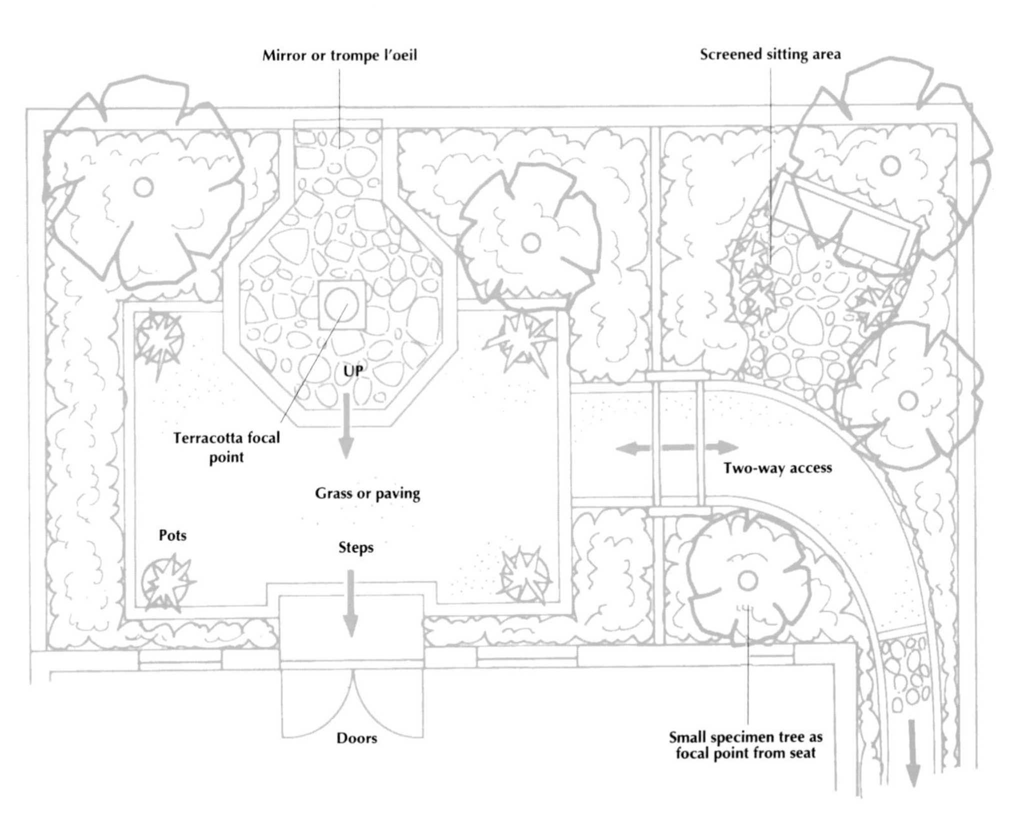

and, as part of it is screened from view, a sense of mystery is created. Only when visiting this hidden area or sitting at the table do the raised pool and wall fountain come into view.

The side of the screen facing the house has a sculpture or plaque attached to it, a focal point seen only from the kitchen window. This area between the screen and the kitchen window is a little lower than the rest of the garden and is intended as a more intimate sitting area. The paving is laid with uninterrupted joint lines leading away from the window to create an illusion of greater distance and to direct the eye toward the screen with its sculpture or plaque. Mellow bricks used as paving would bring a feeling of warmth to this small and separate area. Any sense of formality in this patio garden is offset by various potted plants, placed either in groups or individually on the paving.

A small, informal town garden

Provided that the formal boundary lines are concealed from view, this "jungle" garden is the perfect solution for even a very small plot. Despite its lack of size, a sense of mystery is created, with the farthest area concealed by the winding path and bold planting, which includes a high proportion of evergreens. Their year-round foliage screens the garden from neighbouring plots. An arbour positioned in the top left corner is the perfect place for solitude, while the patio, just large enough for chairs and a small table, is ideal for summer relaxation.

All paving is of roundish natural stone, which echoes in shape the many curves in the garden and acts as host to low carpeting plants in the less frequently used parts. If the garden is overlooked from above, the patio could have a pergola over it to provide privacy.

A town garden

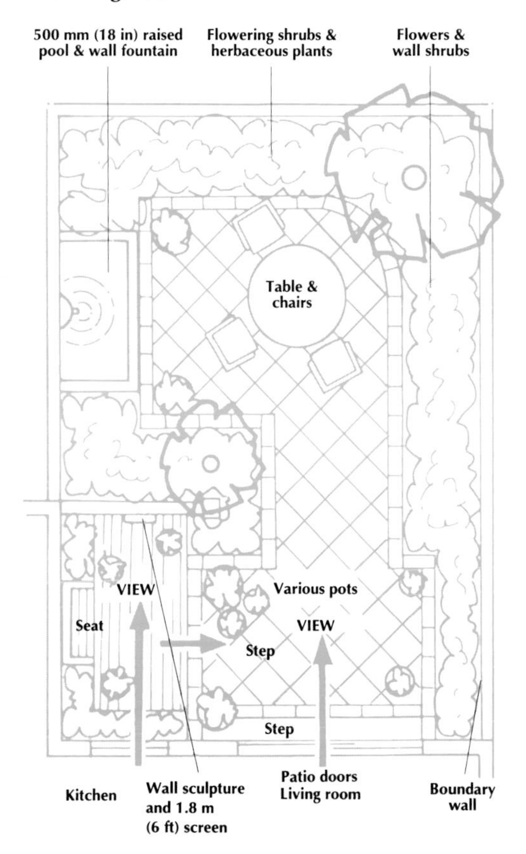

A small, informal town garden

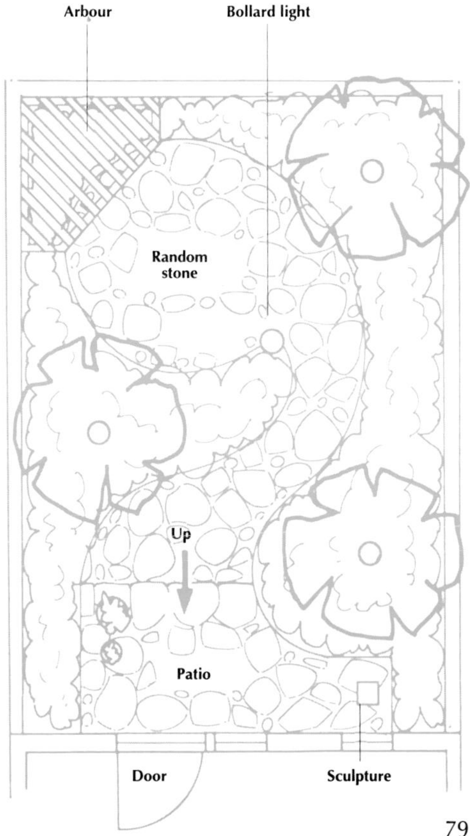

Front gardens

Regrettably, front gardens are often the poor relations in terms of garden design, yet their function, although different from that of gardens at the side or rear of a house, is equally important. Front gardens should bid visitors welcome and frame the house, complementing its architecture and acting as a setting for it. Another function of a front garden is to give importance and direction to the front door. On entering from the road or footpath, the front door should be the main focus of attention and never be hidden or its position obscured. When there is little or no side or rear garden, the front garden may have to take on a recreational role as well and this must be combined with the more functional requirements so that, as far as possible, these apparently conflicting uses are integrated in a coherent whole.

Parking and driveways

Most front gardens include a parking area and this calls for imaginative design solutions to avoid creating a totally utilitarian look. For safety there should always be an uninterrupted view of the road when driving out and, conversely, a good view from the road of cars emerging from the garden or driveway, although this often depends on the shape of the road. Where new houses are concerned, local authority planning permission to build is granted only when the driveway incorporates a suitable vision splay as part of the design.

A front garden based around a drive

The double gate of this typical front garden includes a pedestrian leaf for convenience. Where driveways slope upward, check that the gates will not snag the rising surface before they are fully open. To help avoid this, a double leaf rather than a single gate is better since the gate length is effectively halved. There are two reversing bays, positioned at either end of the drive, illuminated with a lamp. The drive is paved in a diagonal pattern that looks good

A front garden based around a drive

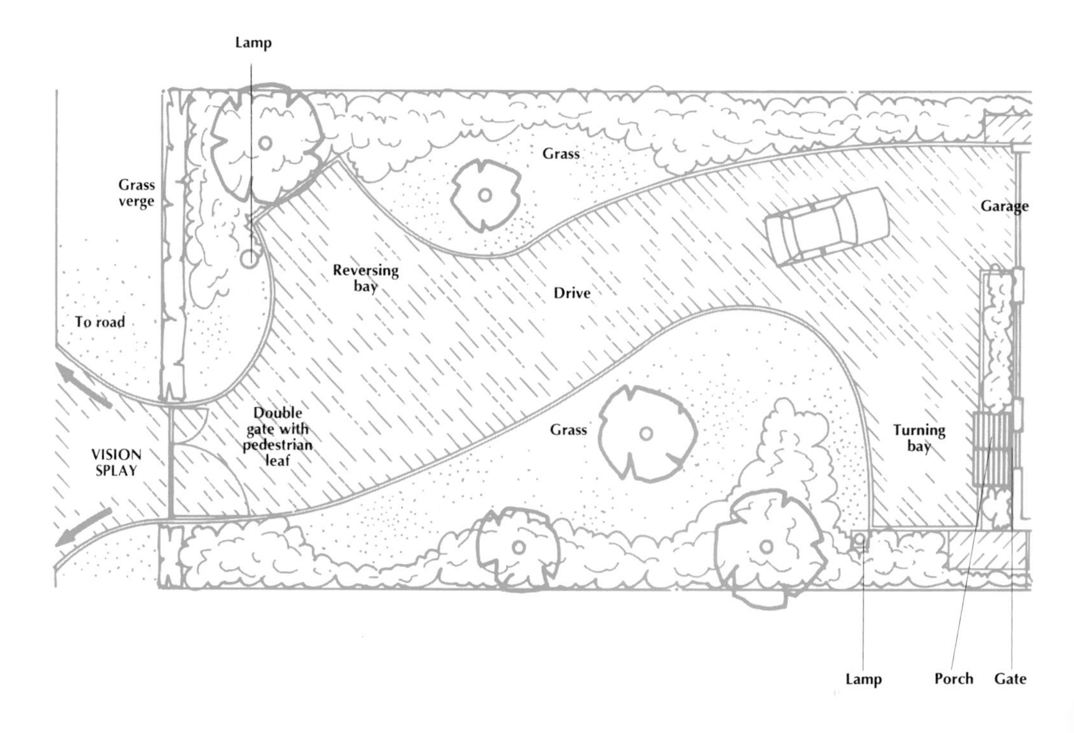

from any angle and is suitable for its strong and graceful curving shape. On a more practical level, dry-laid brick surfacing on a drive must have the joints running diagonally to the traffic flow (see Horizontal surfaces: Paving, page 114). The shape of the grass areas in the borders also balances the shape of the driveway. The garage is approached directly yet there is sufficient space in front of the porch for unloading or for quick access to the house in bad weather. Overall, the design is uncomplicated.

A shallow garden with two entrances

Turning bays are convenient but not necessarily attractive features of front garden drives. Where sufficient space is available it is far simpler to drive in at one side and out of the other. Many large front gardens which are shallow but wide can accommodate this system and under these circumstances the drive itself can provide the inspiration for the design, as in the example shown here. The entrances are splayed to make entering and leaving easier and safer, bearing in mind that other drivers could be approaching from either side. Gates could be fitted if security is essential. These could slide open if the drive slopes upward sharply from the road.

The brick paving pattern used is "neutral", eg diagonal herringbone (see Horizontal surfaces: Paving, page 110); the joint lines do not conform to the overall horseshoe shape of the drive, which is continued by the edging detail at the junction with the garage entrance. At the centre of the drive, steps lead up to the front door, identifying its position clearly. This is especially important in houses with modern doors which sometimes look similar to adjacent full-length windows. A planting of soft-leaved shrubs eases the line of the steps.

Opposite the front door is a raised pool and fountain, the shape of which complements that of the drive and surrounding border. A backdrop of bamboo or tall grasses would make an appropriate and attractive foil for the pool.

A shallow garden with two entrances

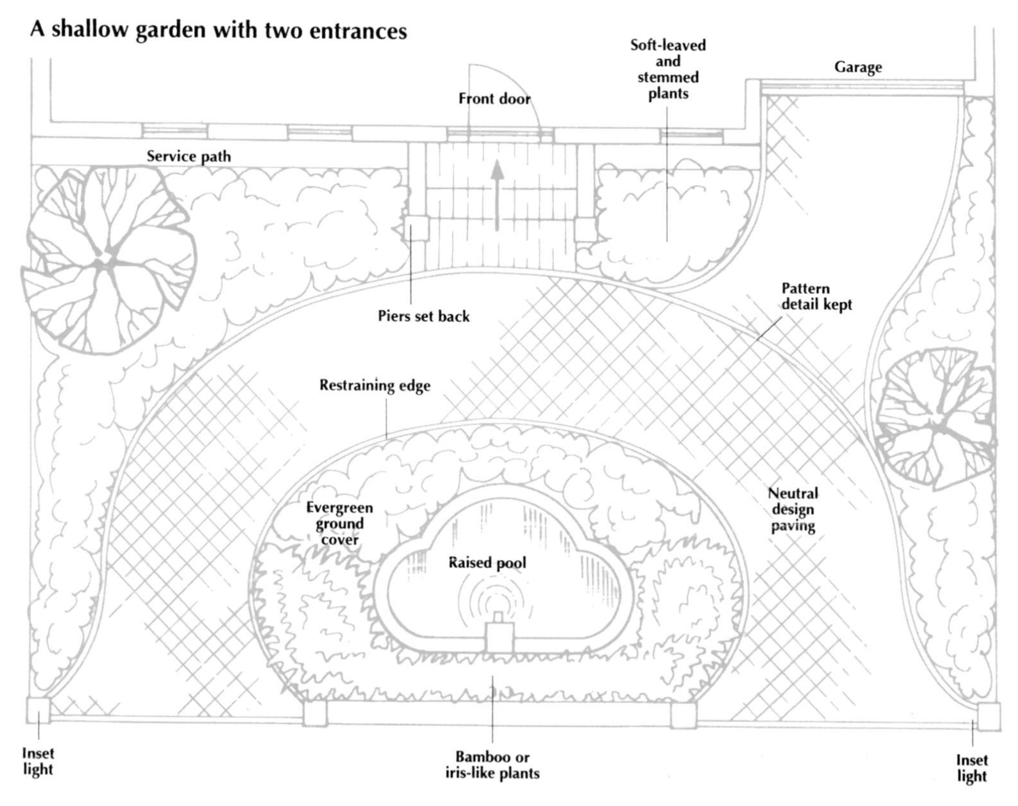

Front gardens 2

A small terraced-house garden

With enough room only for pedestrians and plants, parking is not even an issue in the tiny front garden illustrated (right).

The design is formal and intended to be compatible in style with an older house. The formal appearance of the surrounding walls sets the tone and their lines have been reflected within the garden. A path leads from the gate straight to the front door and could be surfaced with various materials such as brick, tile, gravel or stone, as preferred. In this instance, exposed aggregate concrete is used, edged with granite setts. On either side of the path, within the scalloped rectangle, low ground cover is used. Small-leaved ivy (*Hedera*), *Arenaria, Sedum* or *Vinca*, would all be suitable. Alternatively, grass or gravel could be used.

Because of the strength of the design, mixed herbaceous or annual, colourful planting is both appropriate and cheerful for the borders which flank the walls, in conjunction with the contrasting box tree spheres. Halfway along the path is a paved circle with a colourfully planted terracotta pot at the centre. This is large enough to be a focal point, but not so large as to impede the progress of visitors.

A small terraced-house garden

A sloping front garden

To avoid a direct view into the house from the road, or vice versa, the drive in the example (far right) curves sinuously. This also makes the ascent or descent easier in a steeply sloping garden, whether it leads up or down to the road.

This front garden has a naturalistic theme, so it is preferable not to define the drive too formally. Grass extends right up to the edges, but some means of restraint, perhaps unobtrusive timber strips, would still be necessary.

For continuity, the surface colour and texture of the drive is similar to that of the rock garden stones. Gravel from the same source would match perfectly, but loose gravel on slopes is not a practical proposition since it constantly migrates downward. As an alternative, tarmac or exposed aggregate concrete would be suitable, giving the appearance of gravel, but remaining fixed (see Horizontal surfaces: Paving, page 110). Whatever the medium, sloping drives, particularly those sloping downward to the house and garage, need an extra-efficient drainage system to avoid the risk of flooding. To make the drive easier and safer to use, it may have to be made wider where it curves and, to avoid collisions, boulders, rocks or any potential obstruction should be set back from the edge of the drive.

A series of pools provide a visual link between one side of the drive and the other, as does the grass at each side. This is an important feature of the design if the areas at either side are not to appear as separate entities. Similarly, tree and shrub plantings can be repeated at each side.

The pool and cascade arrangement would have to be designed according to the way the ground slopes, up or down, with the largest volume of water always being at the lowest level (see Water features: Water in the garden, page 148). There is no gate at the entrance to the drive as the more informal approach is in keeping with the concept of the garden as a series of open rock garden areas.

A sloping front garden

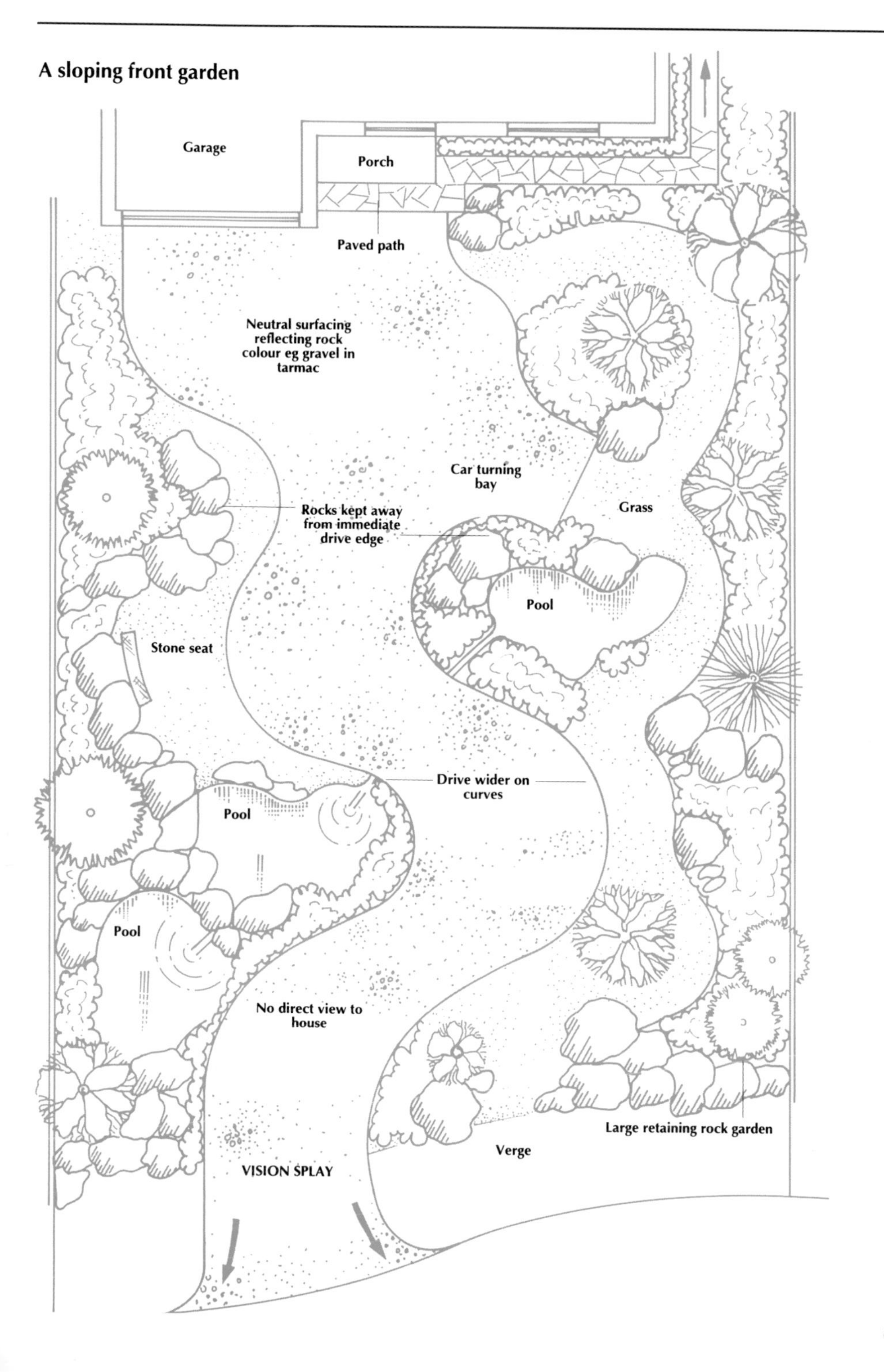

Cottage gardens

Cottage gardens are popular, but the style originated as a matter of economic necessity. Their original function was to supplement the diet of their owners with fruit and vegetables, while herbs for culinary or occasionally for medicinal uses were grown, too. Flowers tended to be planted only in odd corners to bring cheer to the otherwise strictly utilitarian productive areas. Victorian watercolourists produced a romanticized image from which the popular concept of the cottage garden was born.

Structure in the cottage garden

Undeniably they can be very beautiful, but the notion that a successful cottage garden can be created simply by gathering together a random selection of flowers and plants is a false one. As much thought must be put into the design of a cottage garden as into any other type.

The anarchic appearance of some cottage gardens belies the usually strong underlying structure, which must be able to cope with the seasonal nature of most flowering plants in terms of their colour, shapes and proportion relative to their neighbours' and the structure of the garden itself. The routes of paths and the positions of boundaries are important factors in this structure, which is usually formal but with any unwanted appearance of functionality being offset by carefully selected plants.

Framework and features

Always start by working out the horizontal framework of the garden, deciding the routes of paths according to their function. Then decide on the positions of seats, ornaments, sundials, bird baths and so on, all of which are popular ingredients of a traditional cottage garden. Finally, think about the plants.

Plant the taller subjects at the back and the smaller at the front, but leave room to experiment; the cottage garden is not the place for too much conformity in terms of colour and texture. Check flowering seasons or, if grown for foliage effect, when a plant looks its best. A balanced mixture of flowering and foliage plants will extend the garden's annual period of interest considerably.

Colour, as ever, is a matter of personal taste; some prefer controlled themes, others a riot. Of

A small cottage garden

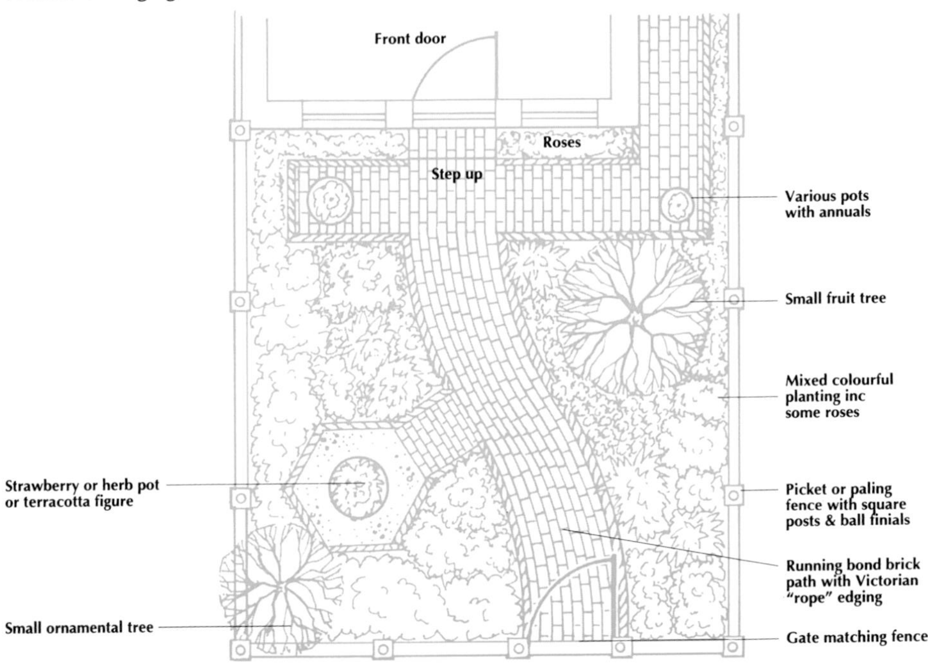

course, there will be a time, as with most gardens, when the cottage garden is at its best, probably during early to midsummer in temperate climates, because of the prevalence of biennials in the typical planting scheme.

Use traditional materials and surfacing, such as gravel, clay, brick, natural stone, terracotta and rustic timber for path edgings, as these are in keeping with the cottage garden style.

It is not necessary to live in a cottage to enjoy a cottage garden, as this style associates well with most types of informal architecture.

A small cottage garden

Many cottage gardens are very tiny. In the example illustrated on page 84 the gateway is not opposite the front door; a problem which is resolved satisfactorily by the construction of a graceful curving path. As the path is of uniform width, brick "running bond" is not only achievable but wholly appropriate, since it is strongly directional and has the effect of drawing the visitor towards the house.

To the left, waiting to be discovered among tall plants, is a hexagonal gravelled space edged with blue-grey (or red) Victorian "rope" edge tiles, as are all the paths. At the centre of the hexagon is a strawberry or herb pot, which fits in perfectly with the theme. Alternatives would be a small terracotta figure or sundial, depending on the aspect of the plot. A fruit tree screens the view of the less attractive side path and, in conjunction with the smaller ornamental tree situated nearer the front boundary, frames the cottage (or house). No soil is visible in the borders, since these are completely planted up with typical cottage garden favourites, including climbing roses.

A formal cottage garden

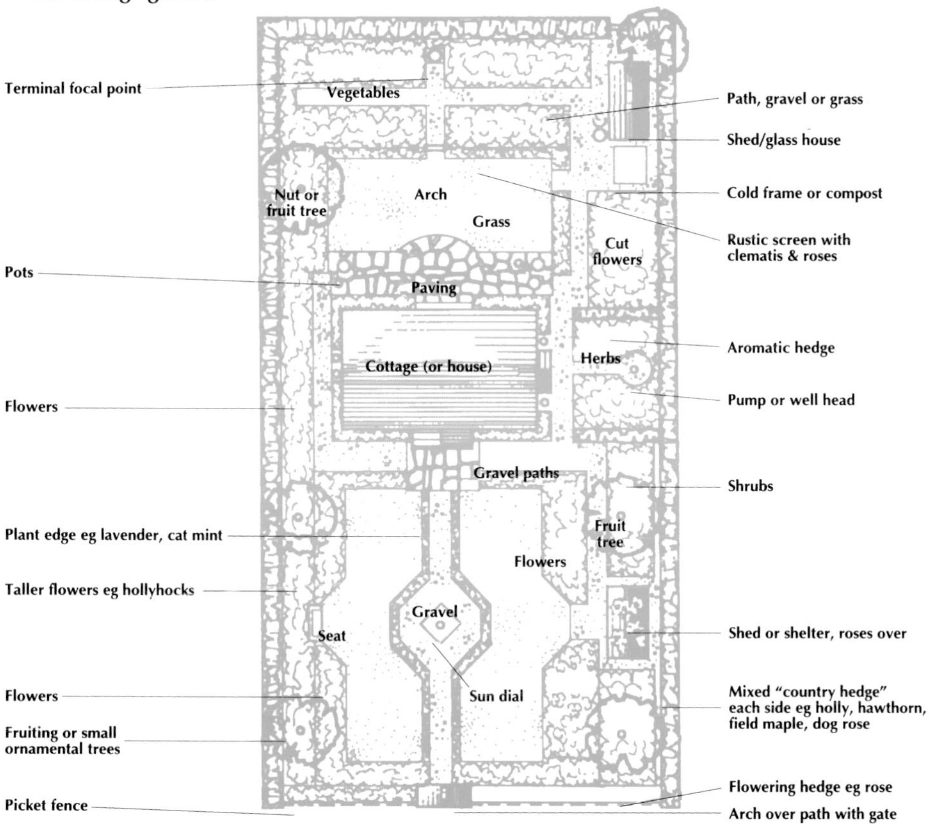

Productive gardens

The tendency with productive gardens is to hide them away. Neglected or out-of-season vegetable plots, it is true, contribute little to the visual attractions of a garden, especially if all other areas are well planned and maintained. This is a pity, since well grown, healthy crops can, given the right conditions, be as appealing as the other plants, with the added attraction of their being edible. Few will argue that fresh produce, taken from the garden and eaten straight away, can be bettered.

It is the tradition in some countries to ensure that productive areas make a positive contribution to the appearance of the garden as a whole, and they are given pride of place alongside the strictly ornamental areas. To ensure that productive gardens are both aesthetically pleasing and horticulturally successful they will need to be given the same consideration at the planning stage as all other parts. Detailed information regarding the siting, size, orientation, soils and climate of productive gardens is not within the range of this book. There are, however, several companion volumes in the RHS series (see back cover for details) which provide a thorough explanation of the best ways of establishing and maintaining productive gardens.

Designing productive gardens

From the point of view of their design, it is usual for productive gardens to follow formal lines, as this makes planning, crop rotation, cultivation and maintenance far easier than it would be in a plot laid out in an informal style. But there is no reason why a degree of informality should not be introduced. With imagination, the major part of a garden could be used to contribute to the family economy and be visually appealing at the same time, perhaps leaving some space for relaxation, too.

Herb plots are extremely popular in modern gardens. Although grown mainly for culinary purposes, some herbs have great visual, aromatic and even romantic appeal, and herbs from all over the world are now available. Even though this may mean growing the more tender types in protected pots, from seed, or as annuals in a border, the wider choice adds an extra dimension to herb garden design.

A formal productive garden

In this almost symmetrical, formal garden (right) the vegetables are grown in geometrically shaped areas arranged around an axis running longitudinally from the centre of the patio doors. The terrace and lawn are for family recreation and at each side, growing in large terracotta pots, are dwarf fruit trees, pruned either to form a pyramid or a spherical shape.

To the left of the terrace is a concealed serpentine path; to the right, a straight path. The latter is edged with lavender, cat mint, parsley or sage as preferred. Both the paths pass through arches, as does the path leading from the lawn. The three arches form part of a latitudinal trellis screen which supports various plants, some ornamental, others fruiting. If shade were a problem on the house side of the screen, gooseberries, Morello cherries and fennel could be grown, as these will usually cope well with less light.

A shed-cum-store is reached via the gravelled serpentine path, while the straight path leads to a cold-frame or alternatively a soft fruit cage, concealed from view from the house by

A formal productive garden

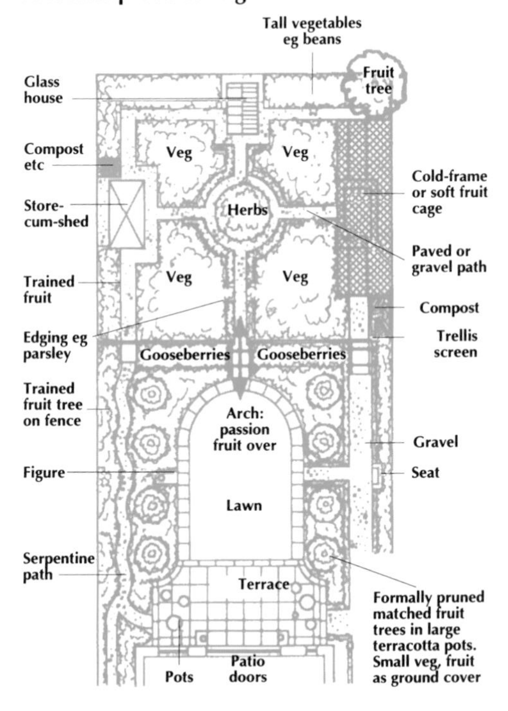

the trellis screen. Around a circular herb bed are areas designated to accommodate smaller vegetables, ensuring seasonal rotation. At the far end, taller vegetables and herbs, such as climbing beans and artichokes, grow at each side of an ornamental greenhouse, which is also the terminal focal point of the garden.

An informal productive garden

While formal areas are probably best suited for vegetable-growing, informality is the preferred style for most gardens. The example shown (below) features a terrace, lawn and pool as the only concessions to relaxation and play, while the remainder of the garden is productive. The design, nonetheless, encourages a visit to all parts on the basis of visual appeal quite apart from the need for maintenance. To enhance the theme of general informality, all paving is of natural or natural-looking stone. Near the circular pool, rocks have been introduced to provide a suitable place for growing many of the carpeting herbs such as thyme, perhaps with some associated alpine plants, too. All the trees have been selected to produce fruit or nuts, but are often as beautiful in flower as their strictly ornamental counterparts.

The area of garden further from the house is at a slightly higher level and is reached by steps or a ramp. The fruit trees partially screen the more utilitarian glasshouse and cold-frames on the left, while an evergreen performs the same function in the corner (far right) where a shed risks becoming an unacceptable focal point.

Across the end of the garden is a fruit cage made of black steel framing and netting. Black is the least obtrusive colour under these circumstances and the screening plants growing in front of it, climbing beans perhaps, render the fruit cage almost invisible

An informal productive garden

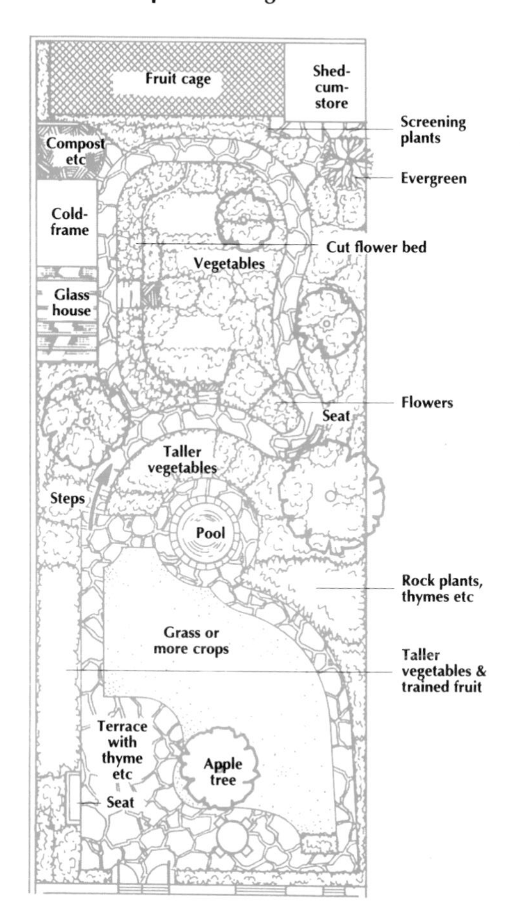

Small herb gardens

A garden, devoted entirely to herbs, could exist in its own right, or as part of a larger garden. Herbs are excellent container plants and these can be incorporated into the garden plan. Most herb gardens are informal simply because it can be difficult to assess the height and spread of different herbs and more difficult still to keep them within their limitations. However, you can give your herb garden a formal structure – by hedging it all around with rosemary, or another woody-stemmed herb such as lavender or hyssop. Keep the hedge neatly trimmed and it will serve as an excellent barrier to cold winter winds. Indicate the entrance to the herb garden with an ornamental feature such as an archway supporting a climbing, perfumed rose.

Access is very important when planning your herb garden. You do not want to tread across wet grass or rummage among other plants to get to the herbs. A gravel path dividing the garden into quadrants provides access as well as form. It could lead to a seat, or highlight a central focal point such as a sundial. In a simple, balanced arrangement such as this, the herbs growing in each quadrant can all be different without the risk of disharmony.

Informal gardens

Informal gardens are difficult to design because they lack the order inherent in the geometric shapes and straight lines of formal designs. The results, however, are by definition much closer to nature. Creating an informal garden within formal boundaries is difficult unless the boundaries can be effectively and permanently screened or camouflaged.

A large informal garden

This large, informal garden could be adapted to most tastes or interests. For example, a variety of plant species could be housed for the collector or, alternatively, species to attract wildlife for the conservationist. The drive and front garden are the only truly formal elements while the terrace, retaining a modicum of formality, is shaped to integrate with the general theme.

One feature, intended as a surprise, is the small cave or grotto at the bottom of the two flights of steps facing each other, set some 1.8 m (6 ft) down. The dry stone retaining walls at each side have shade-loving ferns and mosses growing in the cracks. In the corner of the garden is a sunken dell, which is home to shade-loving woodland plants, and this, too, is approached by winding paths and steps.

The fairly large, reflective pool is set within lushly planted borders and areas of less frequently mown grass. From the secluded shelter or gazebo (bottom right), there is a view back across the pool and grass. A mixed hedge surrounds the property, trees and tall shrubs forming the vertical structures. They could be indigenous shrubs, ornamental or fruiting trees, or a mixture of different types.

A large informal garden

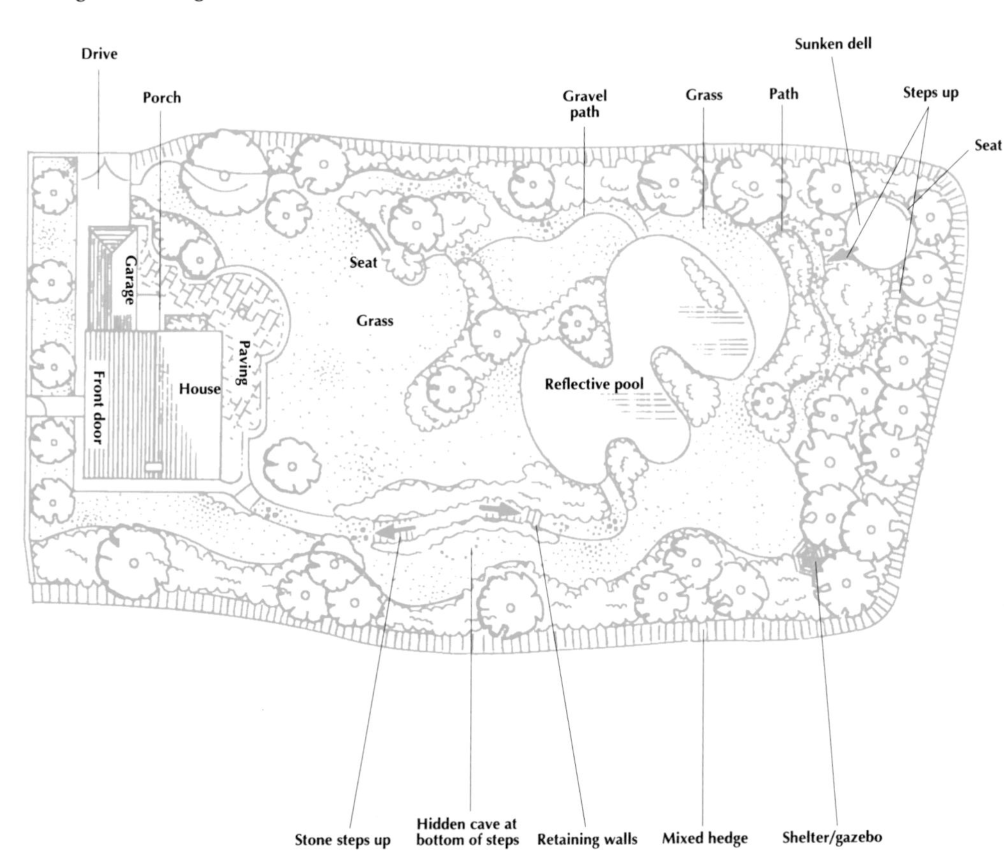

Seaside gardens

Seaside gardens must be designed within quite specific parameters. The plants have to cope with strong, salt-laden winds and, where holiday homes are concerned, periods of time out of season without regular maintenance. In season, when there may be other more interesting things to do, seaside gardens can still suffer from neglect. This should be borne in mind at the design stage if relaxation is the main purpose of the garden.

Coastal conditions

In temperate zones, proximity to the sea usually means moderated temperatures, enabling more tender plants to be grown, but the effects of strong, salt-laden winds may, in some circumstances, offset this advantage. It is common practice to include windbreaks in the designs for maritime gardens – indeed it is sometimes not possible to create a seaside garden without them. Plants and trees usually perform this function better than solid objects such as fences or walls. The former can, by filtering the wind, reduce its force while the latter creates turbulence in the garden, sometimes resulting in more damage than if there were no screen at all. Any screens, whether planted or constructed, should make a positive contribution to the design of a garden as well as being functional.

Maritime garden

The asymmetrical formal design solution below is for a seaside garden where the owners are in permanent residence. The main patio is set diagonally to face the boundary overlooking the sea, so from here the best views can be enjoyed. The terrace is raised to overlook the garden and includes a rear-operated barbecue for summer parties. Circular steps lead down to a lawn or gravelled area.

The retaining wall of the terrace doubles as a seat, as it is 300 mm (12 in) wide and 450 mm (18 in) above the terrace level. Near the boundary facing the sea, the planting has been reduced in height to permit a view toward the sea and to allow a telescope to be used, forming an interesting and appropriate focal point. Lowering the level of the grassed area provides more shelter and privacy, making it an ideal place for sunbathing. A sunken circular area,

Asymmetrical formal maritime garden

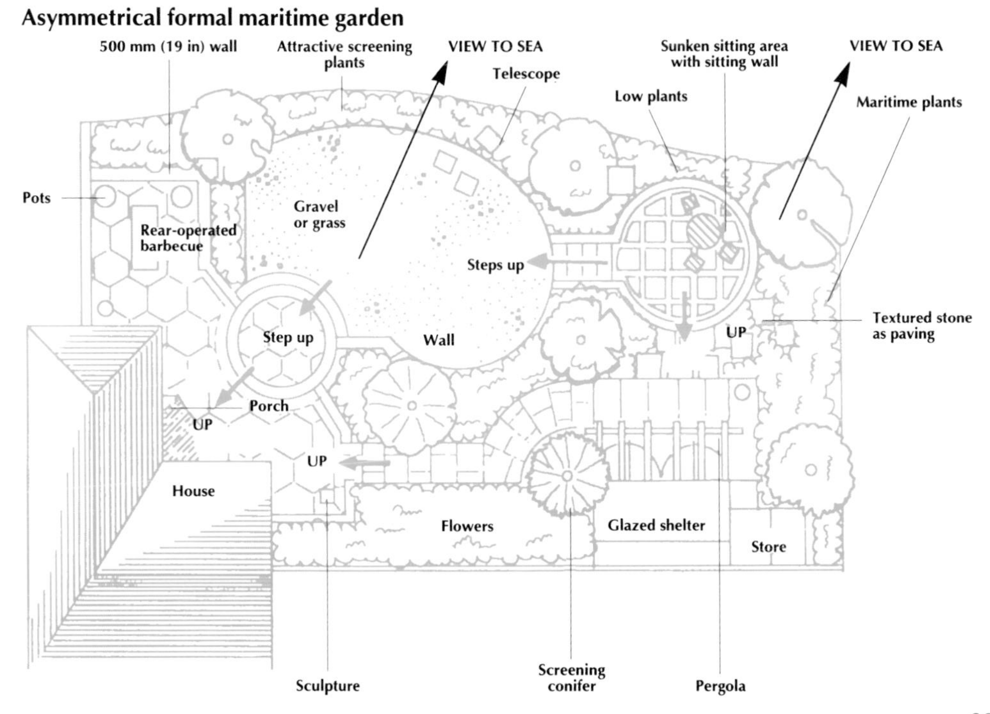

Seaside gardens 2

surrounded by a low retaining wall (ideal for sitting on), is reached by steps. At the centre is a permanently positioned table and chairs manufactured from timber, sunlight-resistant plastic, or aluminium. The table and chairs give the area a sense of purpose and are a feature in their own right. Randomly stepped paving units lead upward to a glazed shelter with a pergola attached at the front. This supports suitable climbing plants and provides a degree of shade. A gaily striped canvas awning would be an attractive summer-time alternative to a pergola.

A low-maintenance seaside or holiday home garden

In the garden illustrated below, the main paved area around the house is reached via a raised, paved rectangle with a low planted bowl at its centre. In the corners are short stone columns. The caps form the plinths supporting matched plants or pots. To one side of the house is a conservatory, glazed only at the front to prevent overheating in summer. One angled side looks toward an ornament or sculpture at the far end of a paved rectangle with planted pots.

A low-maintenance garden

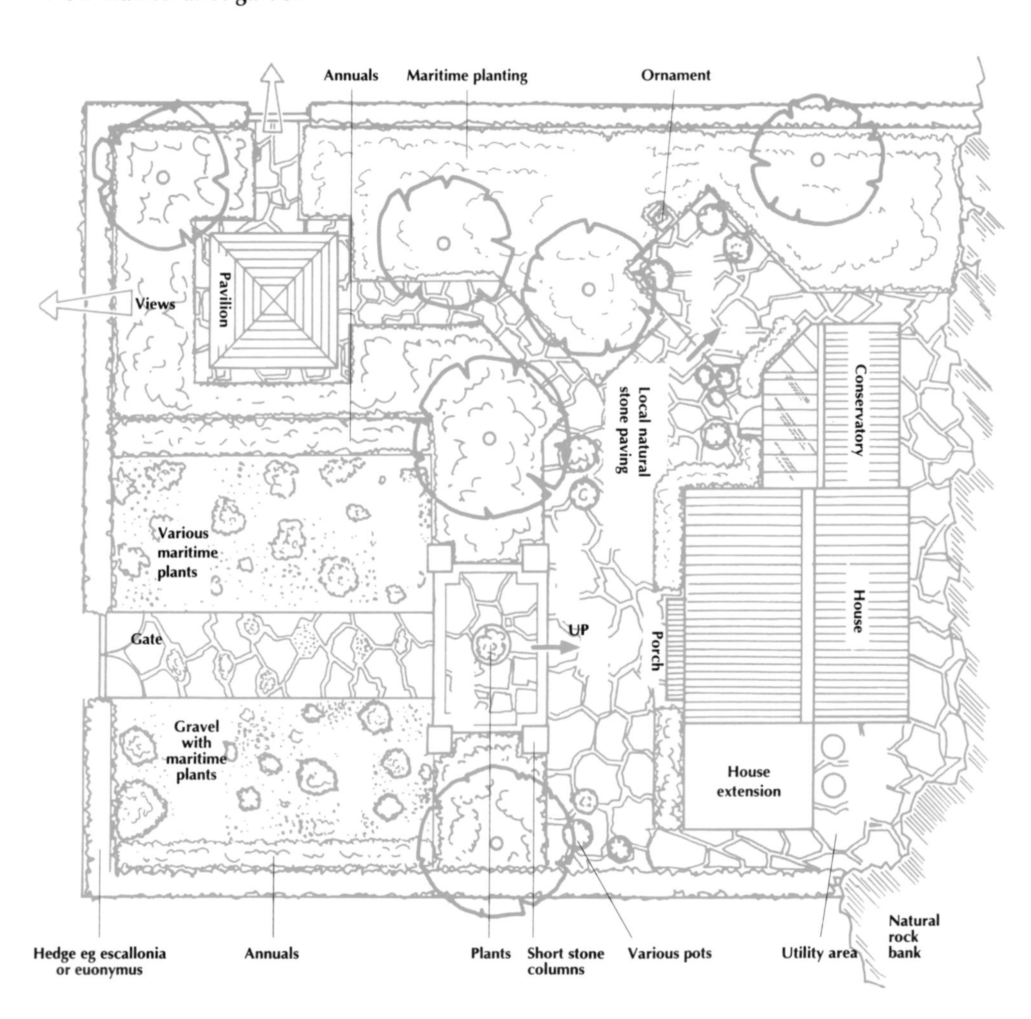

The area at the rear of the house, being close to an embankment, is utilitarian but, although it is not seen as much as other parts of the garden, indigenous plants growing in rock crevices are interesting, as are the sea birds nesting higher up. The planting has been chosen to cope with strong, salt-laden winds.

The best view of the sea is afforded from the pavilion which, set within trees and shrubs, is a feature in its own right. Every care has been taken to link its style architecturally with the house. Trees and shrubs will inevitably be sculpted by the prevailing winds to become an integral part of a seaside garden's character.

A small, decked seaside garden

The seaside garden of modest proportions illustrated below is completely decked on three levels. The surround is formed on one side by the house or apartment walls, two side walls 1.5 m (5 ft) high, one longer than the other, and tinted, ultraviolet-resistant glass panels supported by coated aluminium or timber frames. The major feature, second only to the sea views, is a raised circular plunge pool or jacuzzi. This is viewed not only from the windows but also from the seat set against the wall beneath the canvas awning. Between the decked surfaces and the surround grow a variety of colourful maritime plants, seasonally supplemented with others growing in pots.

An efficient irrigation system would be an advantage in a garden of this style, and raised decking can be designed in sections so that it can be lifted to allow irrigation lines to pots and planters to be introduced underneath.

A decked seaside garden

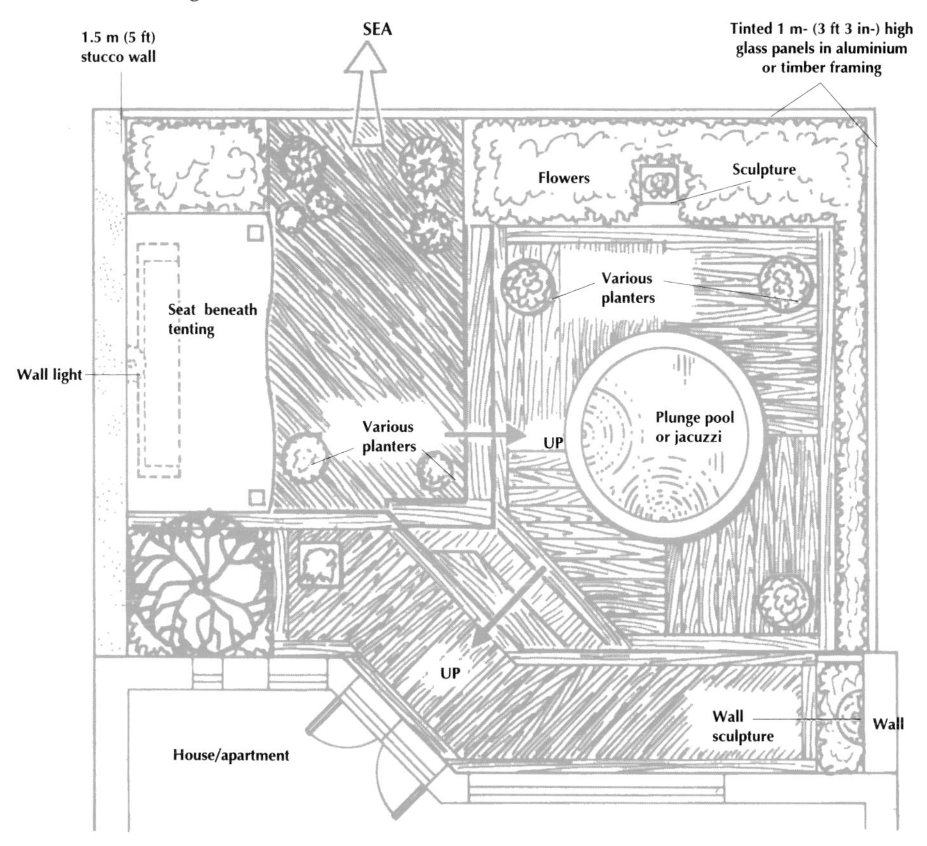

Cold, exposed sites

Apart from the personal discomfort involved, strong winds can cause structural and plant damage in a garden. When associated with high or low temperatures, dehydration becomes a possibility. Low temperatures introduce the wind-chill factor, which lowers the temperature even more. If the soil at ground level or in pots is wet, the problem is exacerbated further. For this reason, only the hardiest of plants should be used in cold, exposed gardens. Take your lead from what is growing naturally or successfully in the area. Native plants and trees, having evolved under such conditions, are an obvious choice but may lack the variety preferred by many gardeners, in which case some research will be necessary.

Creating shelter

A shelter belt can improve the situation but lack of space may leave room only for a constructed screen. There is often a dilemma when screening exposed gardens as many have dramatic views which are lost in the process. Under these circumstances, it would probably be better to decide which are the best views, then plant the shelter belts or erect the screens to leave a series of "windows". This not only enhances the views by framing them, but also creates sheltered areas within the garden.

Where a garden is cold because of its orientation (on the shaded side of a hill, for example, or because of local climatic conditions), the best solution may be to set about creating a series of micro-climate-creating hedges, shelters or buildings. At least the garden can then be enjoyed with a degree of comfort.

Choosing plants for exposed sites

The more exposed, cold and wet a garden is, the more limited the choice of plants and trees that can be grown successfully there. Under extreme conditions, indigenous species alone may have to be relied upon. This presents a challenge, but can still result in a garden that is interesting, attractive and functional. In such adverse conditions, a fundamental change of gardening philosophy may be necessary to avoid disappointment. For example, there is no reason whatsoever why a shelter belt should not be thought of as a contribution to the garden's visual appeal as well as acting as a foil to any formal elements within.

A large garden on a cold, exposed site

In this garden, "windows" have been strategically placed in the boundary using hardy, indigenous trees. Beneath the tree canopies, to form a screen at the lower level, hardy ornamental shrubs have been planted to supplement the mixed-species hedge which forms the first line of defence. By using mainly indigenous plants, success is more likely in hostile situations. Incorporating edible fruiting or berrying plants will make the hedge even more satisfying. Note that the deepest shelter belt is planted on the windward side. The open spaces are comparatively small to allow a greater depth of peripheral screen planting.

The terrace has been positioned immediately next to the house so as to gain maximum protection. To the left, a sunken circular area is protected by trees and a surrounding pierced screen. This could take the form of a brick wall or a timber fence, but the gaps in it allow the wind to filter through without there being any risk of wind turbulence on the lee-side. Opposite the sunken circular area is a productive garden for vegetable, salad and soft fruit crops, depending upon the available space. This has its own screen in the form of a flowering or productive fruiting hedge.

The main focus of the garden is the large circular pool, preferably still and reflective (wind strength permitting), but if a fountain is desired, use a spray head producing large droplets of water with not too strong a jet. Fine droplets in conjunction with high fountain jets are unsuitable in exposed gardens and result in the water being blown beyond the catchment area of the pool, which will then be rapidly depleted. Evaporation from the pool surface is inevitably more noticeable than in a sheltered garden and will make a built-in system for topping-up a necessity. Evaporation of water from the soil is also more noticeable in an exposed garden, making irrigation a more urgent requirement.

On the cross-axis lies a seat, the pool and a sculptured focal point. Hidden paths wind in and out of various borders and planting areas, both for effect and ease of border maintenance. Unseen from the terrace in the top left of the garden is a weeping tree with a circular or hexagonal seat beneath it, with views beyond the garden over lowered plantings and hedging. Care should be taken in the positioning of

A large garden on a cold, exposed site

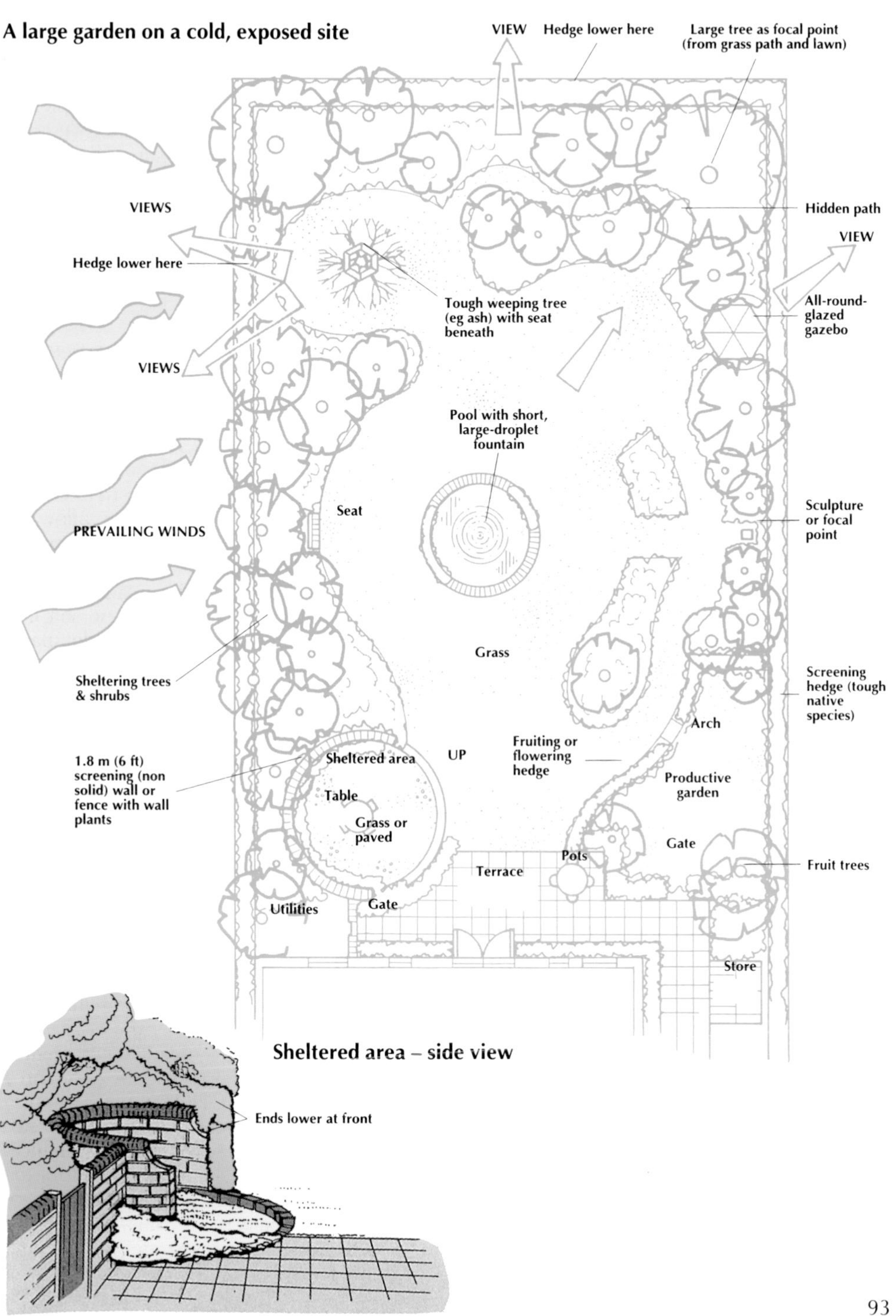

Cold, exposed sites 2

these "windows" of lower planting, since they could inadvertently become wind tunnels. Views both into and out of the garden can be enjoyed from the gazebo, which is double-glazed on all sides to allow year-round use.

A small patio garden for an exposed site

An architectural solution makes the best of this garden (illustrated below). Immediately outside the patio doors is the timber deck, furnished with various planters and with a broad step leading down to the main garden. This area has been lowered to provide greater protection from the prevailing winds. The excavated soil has been re-used to fill the raised beds which are supported by vertically positioned square-section timbers.

In the raised borders, screening trees and plants give instant height. These supplement the small-aperture trellis which screens and surrounds the entire garden. To the left of the deck is a small formal pool, backed with a continuation of the timber "wall", and over the pool is a vine-clad pergola.

A path on the left leads to an inward-looking seat which is also a focal point viewed from the house, and to the right there is a raised planter for flowers and herbs. Unseen behind the planter, a seat looks out over the open land or townscape.

Protecting cold, exposed sites (see right)

1 On the windward side, an arrangement of dense, hardy shrubs rising to a planting of trees makes the best shelter belt. Any shelter belt will be further improved if some permeable screen is added at its centre. To be effective, however, there must be a dense mass of planting and this is simply not possible in small gardens. Under these circumstances, a slatted screen or "pierced" wall probably provides the best solution, especially if hardy plants are established on one or both sides

2 A permeable barrier such as a hedge, slatted fence or row of trees allows the wind to filter through, dissipating its force.

3 A solid barrier is inappropriate in exposed situations. On impact, the wind increases in speed as it travels up and over the solid barrier; then, as it plunges down, it can cause extreme turbulence on the supposedly protected side, reducing air and ground temperatures there as well as battering any planting. Few plants can withstand strong winds from above.

A small patio garden for an exposed site

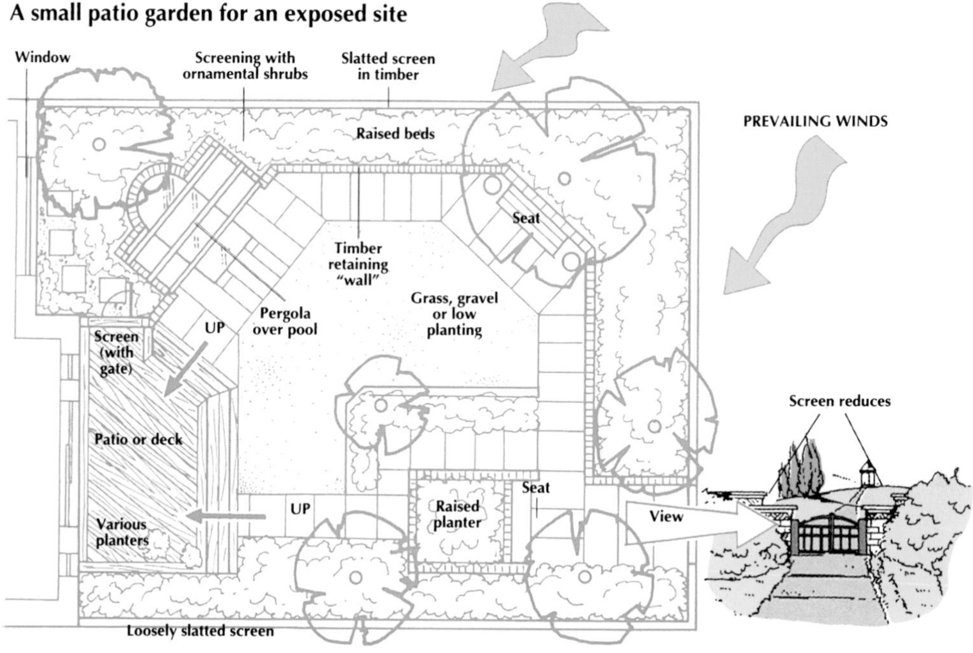

Cold, exposed sites

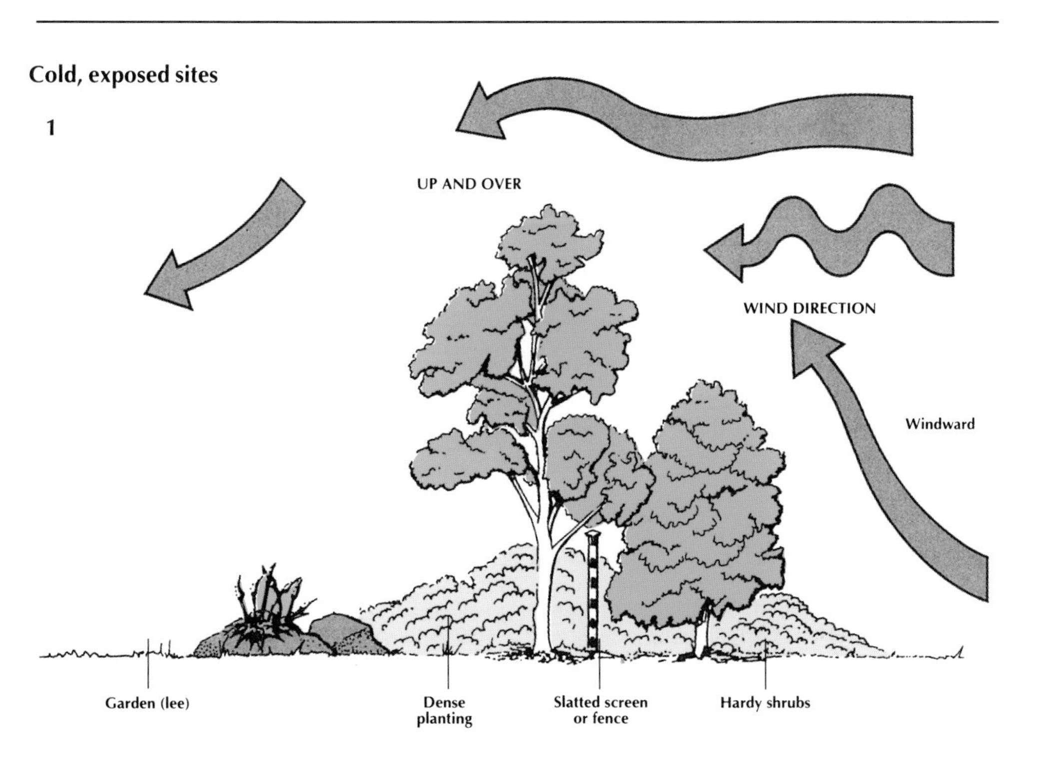

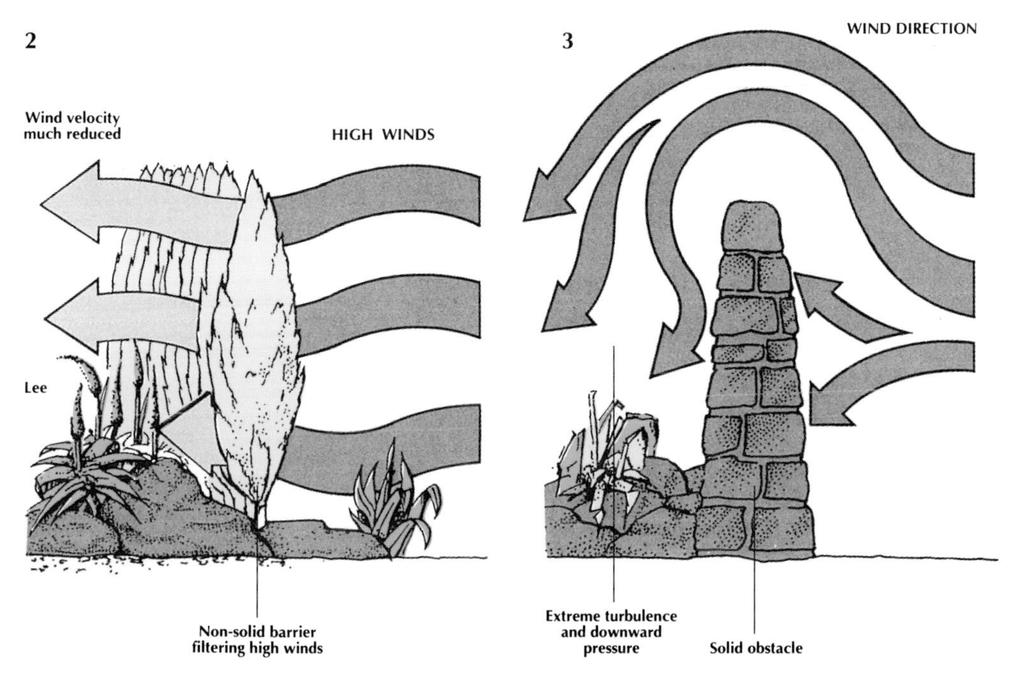

Hot, dry gardens

Shortage of water is always a problem in gardens in hot, dry climates and for those which have to be left unattended for considerable periods. To combat this, gardens can be specifically designed with drought-resistant plants.

This is known as xeroscaping, a modern word created from the Greek *xero*, meaning dry. Tough plants which are xerophytic, or naturally tolerant of dry conditions, are used in preference to delicate ornamental subjects from more temperate climates. These xerophytes, some of which have hitherto been considered weeds, include grasses, succulents and cacti and many narrow-leaved plants from dry, hot places. These are generally more efficient at conserving water than those with shiny or waxy leaves. Grey or silver-leaved plants are also a common sight in hot, dry places, having adapted to their environment by developing light-reflective leaves.

Hot, dry conditions are not confined to gardens close to the equator: temperate zones can be dry and hot in summer but damp and cold in winter. This poses problems for the designer, since there are comparatively few subjects that will tolerate such extreme weather conditions.

Creating shade

Shade must be created in a hot, dry garden if it is to be enjoyed in comfort. Parasols, pergolas, arbours and shade trees can all make a valuable contribution, but the selection of horizontal and vertical surfaces is also important. White house walls reflect sunlight, making the interior of a house cooler, but they can be dazzling to those sitting outside.

Similarly, paving that is too light in colour can be so reflective that people in the garden are uncomfortable without sunglasses. Conversely, dark or non-reflective paving absorbs heat from the sun and may be too hot to walk on, especially with bare feet. Pale "earth-coloured" pavings, including grey, are probably the best choices for surfaces in hot sunny situations, or gravel or chippings in a neutral colour.

Establishing a xeroscaped garden

An irrigation system might seem an obvious solution for the hot, dry garden but this would oppose the concept and function of xeroscaping. The idea is to work with the dry conditions rather than to try to change them, but there are steps that can be taken to help the xerophytic plants to thrive. A layer of gravel used as a mulch over soil has the advantage of storing any available water, which is then released as a vapour that will rise up through the plants. It also reduces evaporation from the soil beneath. Polymer granules, a fairly recent introduction, can be incorporated into the soil, where they store water to be used by the plants with minimal loss through evaporation. As there is a risk that birds may eat polymer granules left on the surface, make sure they are well dug in or covered by a mulch.

Asymmetrically formal hot, dry garden

One corner of this rectangular garden is defined by the house walls, and this is the site of the curved natural stone patio, where a parasol provides shade. Leading directly from the patio is a pergola, covered with climbing plants to create a cool walk to the far end of the garden. Approximately halfway along, a wall fountain cascades into a rectangular basin. The water is recycled by a small pump and the shady positioning of the pool ensures that evaporation is kept to a minimum. The sound of falling water is audible from most parts of the garden.

The path curves dramatically at the end of the pergola and this, in conjunction with the palm tree in the far corner, makes an excellent natural focal point. In the adjacent corner is a "dry pond", associated with boulders, grasses and xerophytic plants with leaves reminiscent of water or bog plants. Further on, an arbour with an open slatted roof offers a cool resting place. From here another palm (or hardier tree for cooler climates), together with more large round boulders, occupy the central area. This is gravelled and has carpeting and low sun-loving plants growing through the stones. A curved path runs from the apron of the arbour and sweeps around, eventually leading back to the patio. For much of its length, the edges of the path are hidden by plants growing at the sides.

Compartmentalized hot, dry garden

In the illustration on page 98, a longish narrow garden has been given a formal treatment and divided into four compartments. Each is distinct in terms of shape and style, but all four are designed around a central axis, ensuring that

Asymmetrically formal hot, dry garden

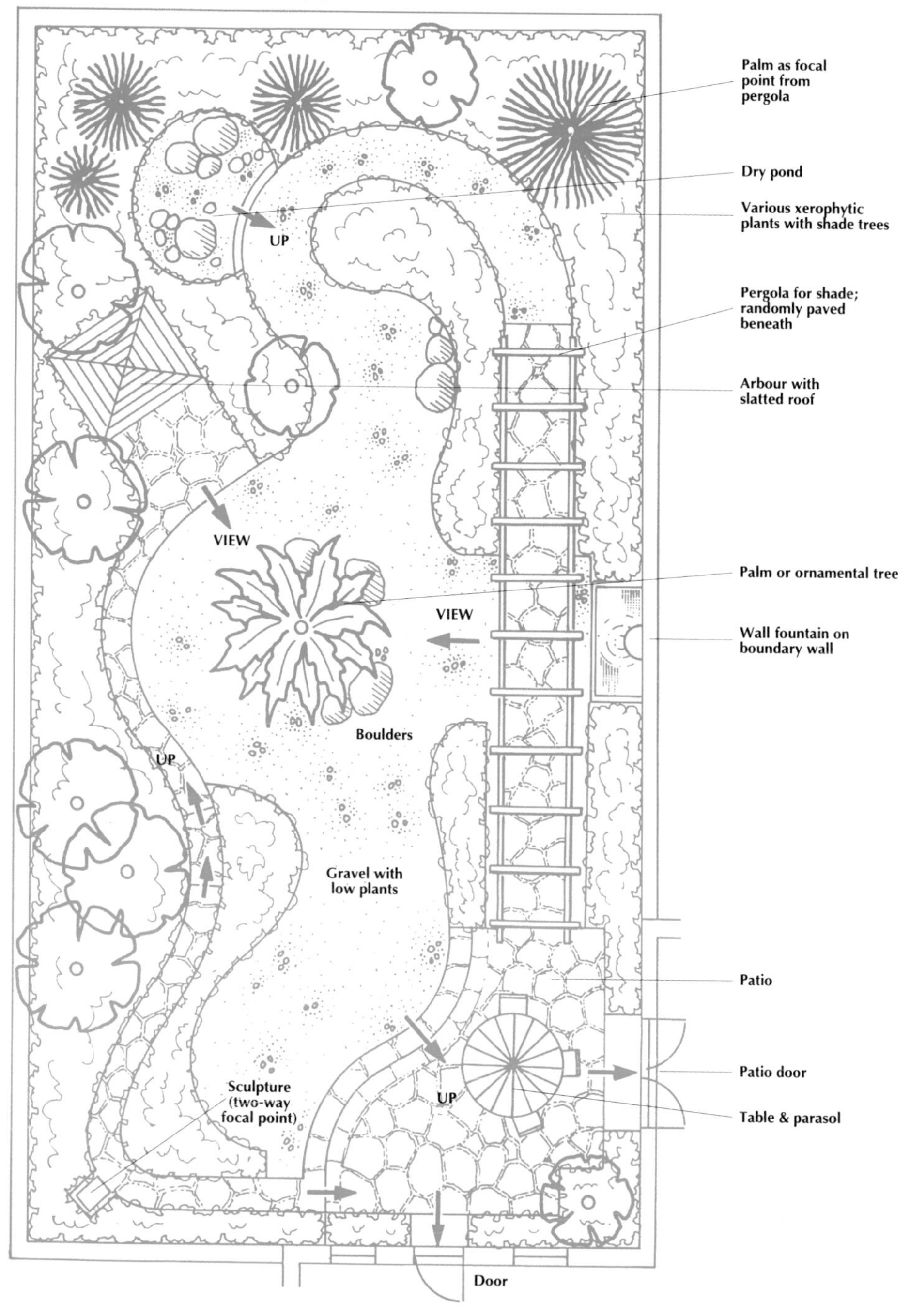

Hot, dry gardens 2

the sculpture, as a terminal focal point, can be seen from the patio. The compartments are surrounded by high planting, with the result that one cannot be seen from within the other.

The patio next to the house has a shady pergola above it, furnished with perfumed climbing plants. Extra colour is provided by potted plants. Just beyond the patio and flanked by colourful, perfumed plants and shrubs, is an open area of gravel. In each of the two far corners is an obelisk, which could be of the open trellis type, supporting climbing plants, or solid, in stone or metal. A step leads down to a short path flanked by tall, clipped blue conifer hedging, beyond which the curvilinear shape of the next compartment comes into view. In one corner is a stone seat, positioned opposite an armillary sphere which is encircled by low-growing plants. After a further step down, stepping stones lead to a rectangular space. Like all the other spaces, this is surrounded by shading high-growing shrubs and plants. Low evergreen plants cover the ground, and the stepping stones are positioned to lead to the various points of interest such as the small pool, the secret covered seat and the exit arch. To provide the desired visual effect, the pool need only be shallow and can be emptied when the house is unoccupied. The farthest area is for family recreation and includes a paved chess "board" with seats around it.

Informal hot, dry rock and decking garden

Although the diagonal timber deck and associated exposed aggregate concrete paths are angular, the general feel of the garden is informal. Shade is provided by a large parasol and a shade tree growing through the deck, with its roots in the cool soil beneath. The main area is gravelled and surrounded by large boulders and xerophytic, ornamental and indigenous trees and plants. The textured concrete zig-zag path at the left, hidden for most of its length, passes beneath a pergola constructed of sun-bleached driftwood. This supports climbing plants and vines, creating dappled shade beneath. In the far left corner is a concealed gazebo with open-slatted roof and sides to ensure that it remains comfortably cool within. Steps from the gravelled area disappear in a short tunnel below a large rock garden which is home to dwarf or prostrate sun-loving plants.

Compartmentalized hot, dry garden

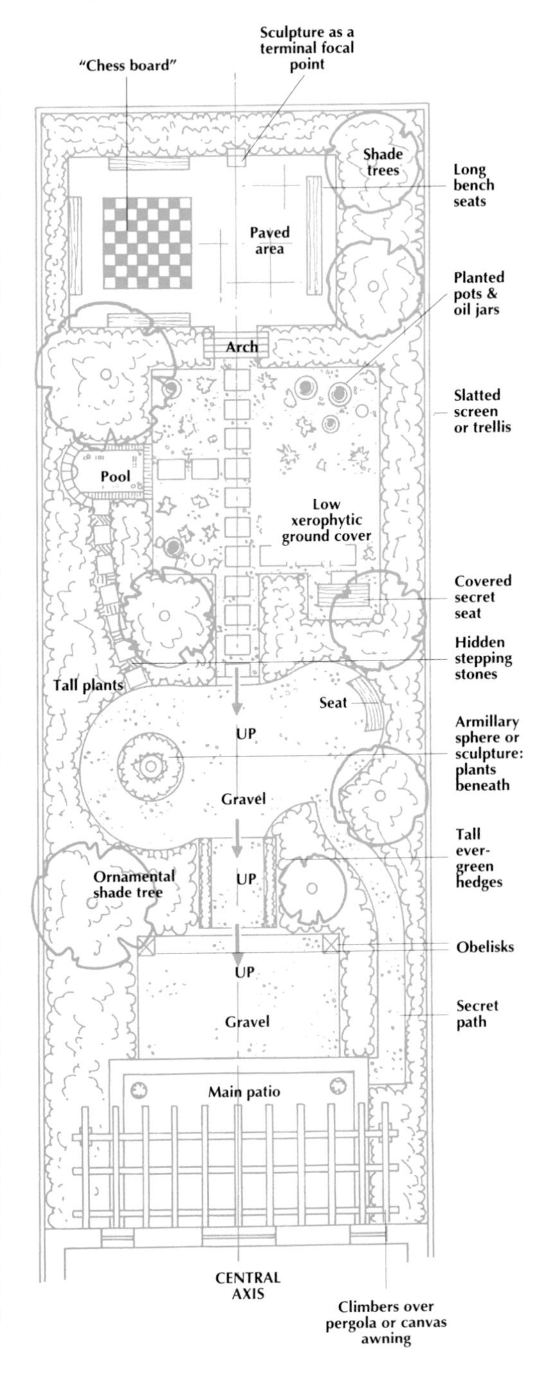

Informal hot, dry rock and decking garden

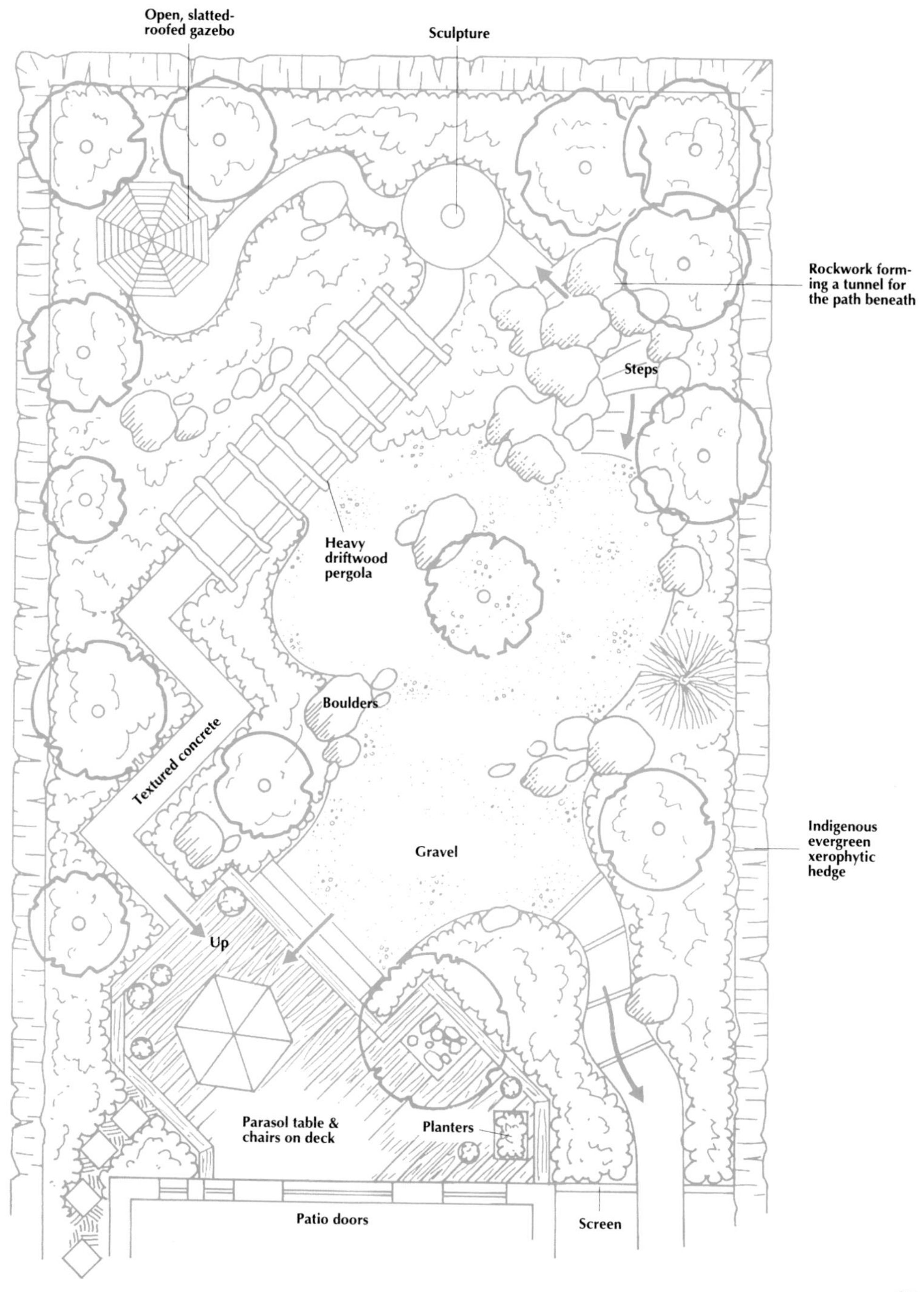

Specialized or themed gardens

Sometimes a garden is designed for a specific function or to have a particular theme: for physical recreation, for example, or growing a favourite plant group. In such cases, extra care is needed at the planning stage, especially when other members of the family, perhaps less enthusiastic about the main theme, have preferences of their own. With patient planning, however, seemingly contradictory requirements can usually be reconciled.

A formal rose garden

Possibly the most popular of all flowering plants is the rose. This is not surprising, considering the wonderful scents, varied forms and colours of the flowers and their fascinating and romantic history. Roses have set the theme for countless formal and informal gardens and the example shown here is of a symmetrical, formal rose garden.

The terrace is designed around a motif of overlapping circles formed by warm-coloured tiles and grey-mauve stone, which is the perfect foil for most rose colours. Carpeting plants grow at the periphery.

Two paths, one at each side of the garden, are flanked by pole and rope swags supporting climbing roses. These are underplanted with a low-growing rose or a traditional associated plant such as cat mint. The evergreen hedge acts as a foil to the lawn and to the white roses growing in front. At its centre is an arched opening, which permits a glimpse of the canal beyond, while the seat at the top of the garden, functions as a terminal focal point.

All these elements lie on the longitudinal central axis of the garden, while two minor openings in the hedge, situated at the sides, provide access to the path that follows the garden boundary on three sides, leading back to the outer edges of the patio.

In the two corners farthest from the patio are two standard trees which, for thematic continuity, belong to the rose family, for example cherry (*Prunus*), apple (*Malus*) or mountain ash (*Sorbus*). Between these are planted the taller shrub roses.

This design could easily be adapted to accommodate any plant group, such as irises or dahlias, but they would probably need to be supplemented with another genus in order to extend the period of interest.

An informal alpine and rock garden

Some alpines and dwarf conifers are so individualistic in form and cultural requirement that it can be difficult to incorporate them into a small, formal garden where well defined or straight boundaries are clear. Nevertheless, alpines, dwarf conifers and rock gardens are popular as garden themes (see Garden features: Rock and alpine gardens, page 166).

The small garden illustrated on page 101 has been designed with walls and rock garden forming the structure; the alpine plants and conifers simply furnish it. Since the garden is

A formal rose garden

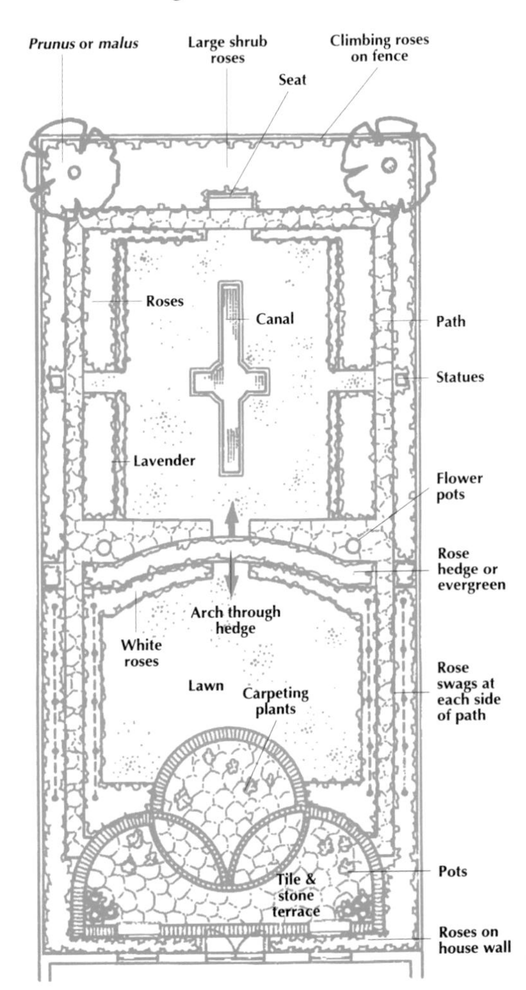

small, the plants can be placed individually, rather than in the large groups required for larger gardens. A paved path runs along the house wall, both for access and to limit the amount of gravel which might otherwise inadvertently be carried indoors. In the rest of the garden, gravel or crushed stone is the main horizontal surfacing because of its natural association with alpine plants.

The spiralling beds rise to approximately 750 mm (2 ft 6 in), supported by dry-stone walls which are similar in type and colour to the boundary walls. The spirals create vertical areas of light and shade, thus increasing the range of planting conditions in the soil joints. The areas at the top of the walls are suitable for growing a variety of subjects where well-drained conditions and soil types can be finely tuned to meet individual plant needs.

The dry-stone raised beds at the sides of the garden house the more robust alpines and conifers, while the surrounding walls host climbing plants which may be too invasive when grown horizontally and in varying conditions of light and shade. A small pavement rock garden (see Rock and alpine gardens, page 167) in the corner near to the house can be enjoyed from the nearby windows. Diagonally opposite, angled steps lead to the rock garden. Alongside the conifer bed, a circular window has been constructed in an extension of the boundary wall, providing a view of an interesting tree or shrub beyond.

The rock garden itself is constructed in a naturalistic, stratified way using stones similar to those used in the boundary wall but much larger. This makes for visual harmony and helps to integrate both the formal and informal aspects of the garden. The rock garden could be planted with undemanding alpine favourites or rare and more difficult species, according to the owner's personal enthusiasm. A small rock pool invites the visitor to pause and enjoy the sound of water gently cascading from the false spring above. The spring is activated by a concealed pump. A well-ventilated glasshouse provides winter protection for plants that are moisture- or climate-sensitive.

An informal alpine and rock garden

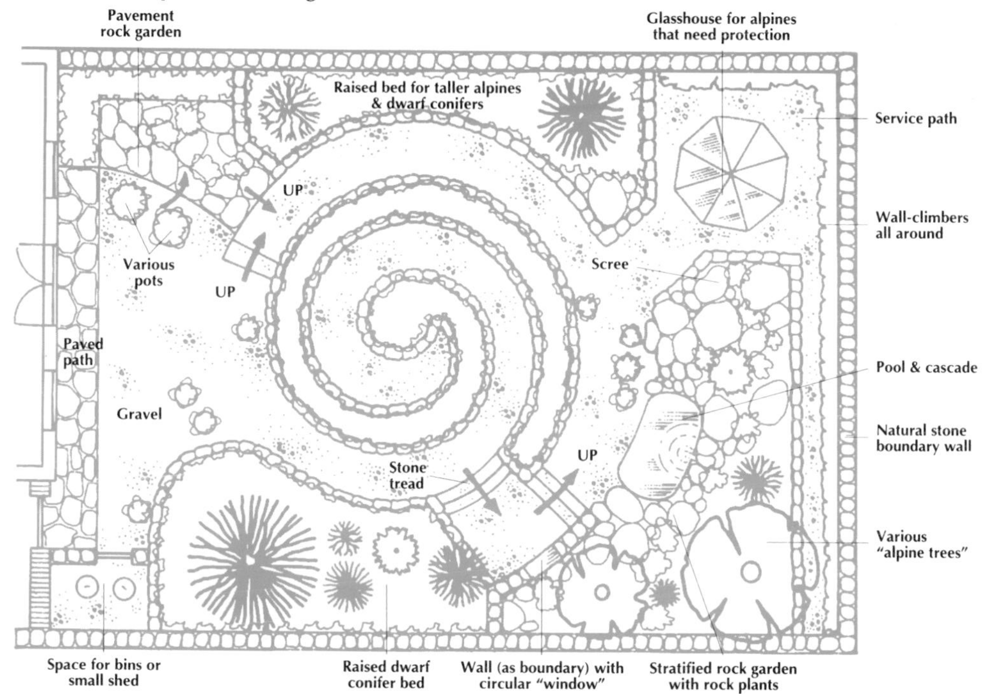

Roof gardens

For a variety of reasons, roof gardens need a different design approach and a different set of construction techniques from those used in ground-level gardens. Not least of these is the weight of the garden, which clearly has to be supported by the roof.

Even if there is a suitably sited flat roof available, it may not necessarily be constructed with enough strength to support anything more than the waterproofing system and the occasional visitor to carry out maintenance. Even then special timber walkways (known as duckboards) are normally required to spread the weight of anyone walking on the roof, and any further loading could invite serious structural damage to the building, even collapse. Never embark upon a roof-garden project without consulting a structural engineer. He or she should be qualified to decide whether or not the roof is suitably supportive, or what measures might need to be taken to make it so.

Placing roof garden features

Generally speaking, if a roof structure is not already strong enough, the necessary modifications are costly and disruptive. Where new houses are concerned, facilities for a roof garden can be part of the architect's brief at the outset, so avoiding extra expense later.

The strongest, most supportive areas of a flat roof are those close to the supporting walls. Usually these are at the periphery but, depending upon the size of the roof, supporting walls may cross under the roof as well. All the weighty elements of a roof garden should be designed to be as close as possible to the supporting walls with only the very lightest items at the centre. Unfortunately, there is always a risk of objects placed near the edge falling off the roof, so ensure that nothing top-heavy is included in the design and that anything that could be displaced by strong winds is secured to the decking. Do not secure heavy items to the structure of the building as this could cause structural damage in high winds or interfere with damp-proof courses (DPC).

Drainage

Never interfere with rooftop waterproofing, drainage systems or the DPC, including those in adjacent walls, either at roof level or beneath copings. To do so may result in the main house structure being penetrated by water. Unfortunately, this can happen when trellis, safety rails or deckwork are fixed.

A roof garden must be designed to ensure that rainwater is quickly discharged from all horizontal surfaces, as damage may be caused not only by water penetration but by its weight. Even a shallow depth of standing water can amount to an immense weight on larger roofs, especially if you bear in mind that just 1 litre of water weighs 1 kilo (1 gallon weighs 10 lbs, or 8 lbs for a US gallon).

Exposed situations

Wind funnelling and the wind-chill factor can present far worse problems at roof level than they do on the ground, damaging plants and causing discomfort to visitors.

In summer, a lack of shade combined with normal dark roof surfaces that absorb rather than reflect heat, can result in swiftly rising temperatures that will cause the compost in plant containers to dry out very quickly and also make the roof garden an uncomfortable place to sit. An irrigation system can help solve the former problem, while pergolas, awnings and planted trellis provide welcome shade and shelter for visitors.

Planting

Permanent plants for roof gardens must be tolerant of the cold stormy winds of winter. In very low temperatures the plants' roots and the compost in which they grow can be frozen. In summer when the compost heats up it can dry out completely. Either situation is detrimental to normal plant growth.

Since compost-filled pots and containers lack the mass of the soil at ground level, they are subject to greater temperature fluctuations. Only the toughest plants such as berberis, buddlejas and cotoneasters should be used on a roof unless year-round shelter, seasonally appropriate watering and a high level of maintenance can be provided. Annuals are popular choices for summer to supplement the tough structural plants that form the permanent roof-garden landscape, since they do not have to suffer the rigours of winter. Winter need not be cheerless, however, as winter-flowering pansies, bulbs and evergreens can all be used to great decorative effect.

Watchpoints for roof garden design

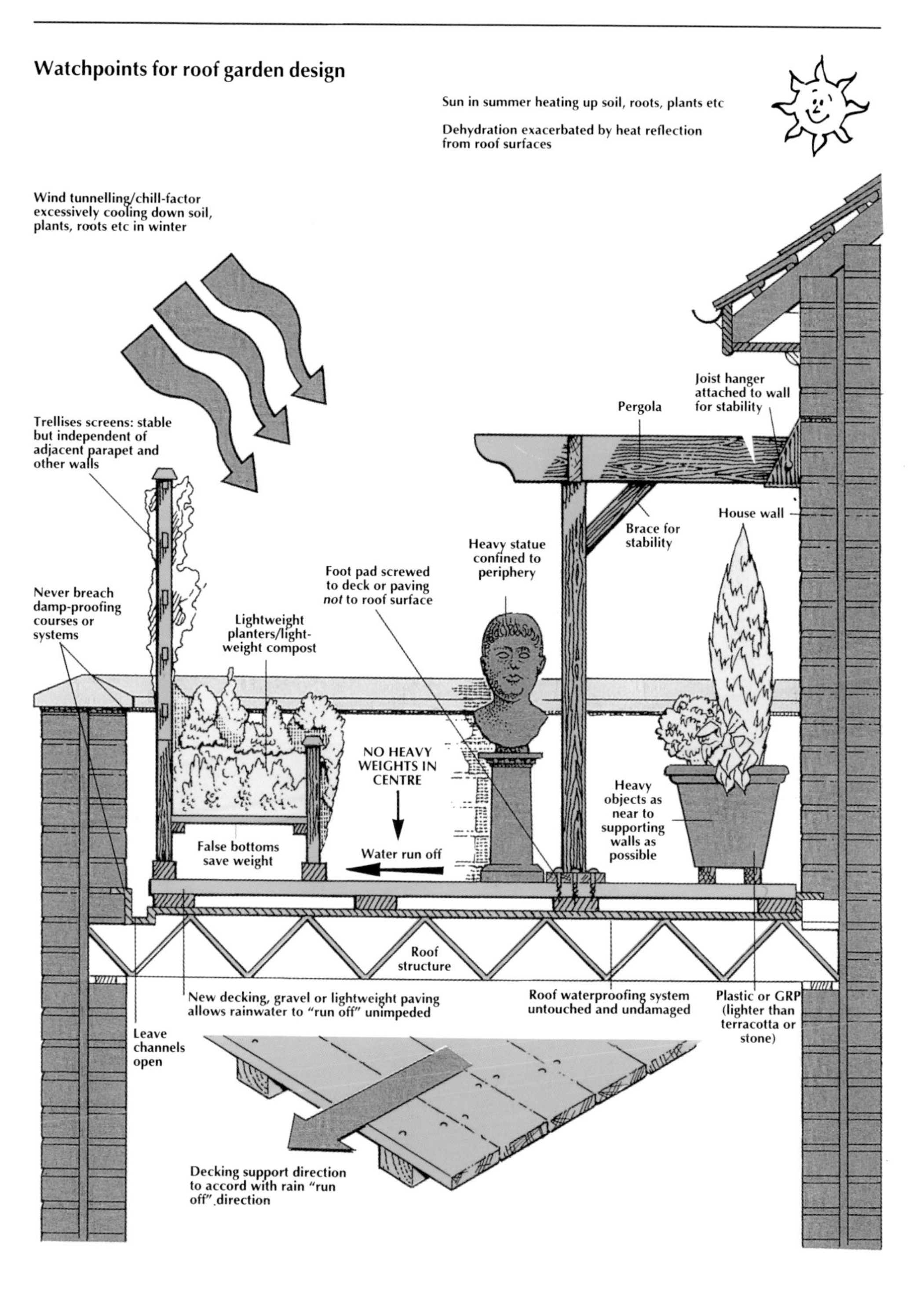

Roof gardens 2

When a roof garden is used only in summer and for the rest of the year is unvisited, then year-round plant displays are less important.

Automatic irrigation can be a boon on a hot roof garden where regular watering is essential. At ground level hand watering is problematic enough but on a roof, especially if water is not readily accessible at that level, it becomes even more of an onerous and time-consuming task.

A decked roof garden

VIEW
Parapet walls
Toughened glass panel
Heat-shielding wall at rear
Upper deck
Built-in barbecue with work top
Table
Built-in seat
Wall-mounted light
Lower deck
Planters
Patio doors
Planters with integral trellis screen
Various plants & shrubs
Plants & climbers in raised planter

A decked roof garden

In the roof garden illustrated (left), timber decking has been placed over the roof but it is made in sections so that it can be lifted should the need arise. Gravel makes a good alternative surfacing, ensuring good drainage, reasonable reflection of heat and an even weight-loading.

A built-in seat is positioned between free-standing planters which have trellis panels built in as part of their structure, thus overcoming the problem of instability and fixing. Ideally, trellis or similar structures should not be bolted to parapet walls as this increases the risk of structural damage to the wall in high winds.

The planters have gaps underneath to allow water drainage and are raised on feet. The more points of support there are, the more evenly their loads are spread over the surface of the roof. The permanent barbecue is a focus in summer but is screened from immediate view from the patio doors as it may appear less attractive in winter. A toughened glass screen allows an uninterrupted view beyond the garden and lighting extends the use of and the view of the garden at night.

Gardens for the disabled

The aspirations, needs and pleasures of gardeners with disabilities are no different from those of anyone else. Gardens can be enjoyed both passively and actively, to varying degrees, by everyone, but what is different for the disabled person is the degree of access possible, and this depends upon the form of disability.

The design of the garden must, as always, be tailored to meet an individual's preferences and needs but, unfortunately, communal gardens for the disabled can only ever be geared to the most common forms of disability.

Most people associate gardens for the disabled with raised flowerbeds or work benches. While these may be suitable for certain gardening activities and for particular forms of disability, they are by no means the universal solution. For example, where wheelchair users are concerned, a raised bed containing even low-growing plants blocks out the view of the rest of the garden which is visible to those who can stand.

Design criteria

Maintenance of raised beds can also be more difficult for wheelchair users, as tools have to be lifted and used at waist level. Even specially adapted tools can seem cumbersome and heavy under these circumstances. Downward movements, in which the ground supports the weight of the tools, are usually the easiest for everyone to handle.

Work benches, on the other hand, are generally more convenient raised to waist level, whether for disabled or able-bodied gardeners.

For the partially sighted or blind, different design criteria are applied but, again, the provision of easy, safe access to plants and other elements in the garden is most important, especially when the garden has been designed to have plenty of interest in terms of touch, smell and sound.

The cost of implementing a garden needs careful thought: the construction of a raised bed, for example, costs far more than the creation of a bed at ground level.

When constructing such a garden, safety is an even more important part of the design equation than is generally the case. Information and help for disabled gardeners is readily available from specialized organizations and the relevant charities.

A garden for a person with limited mobility (see overleaf)

Paving must have a non-slip surface, yet be as even as possible. In the garden illustrated overleaf, a flat natural stone has been selected, first for its pleasing and warm appearance and secondly to allow the curvilinear paths to be formed easily. A reconstituted stone would be an equally valid and lower-cost choice. Not all borders are raised since this would be both costly and unnecessary, but those that are have been designed to be broad and built to wheelchair height. This allows the gardener to move more readily from the wheelchair to the top of the wall, which can now be used as a seat. This is useful for maintenance and allows closer contact with the plants. There are no sharp corners and curves in the path are gentle enough to be easily negotiated.

Among the main features of this garden is a shed-cum-workshop, in which the enthusiast can prepare seed trays, prick out and pot on at any time of the year. There is also a hexagonal greenhouse with a sliding door for easy access and waist-high, space-saving benches. Any sitting areas should be designed to have room for wheelchairs and conventional seats. The shallow, ground-level pool and fountain fits into the curved shape formed by the raised bed and has a low barrier in front. A hooped arch supporting climbing plants makes a delightful entrance.

A ramp provides access to the rear house door. Ramps should, ideally, not be constructed with a gradient steeper than 1:20 in this or any other garden, for reasons of safety and comfort. Depending upon the time available or the ability of the owner to maintain the garden, the more open area can be gravelled for very low maintenance, turfed, or planted with some kind of ground cover such as camomile. Most beds can be maintained from a wheelchair by using special or adapted tools. The few areas of border out of immediate reach should be planted with more robust shrubs which have trouble-free characteristics.

A garden for a blind or partially sighted person (see overleaf)

Such a garden need not be bland or uninteresting. It is not necessary to sacrifice stimulation and interest in the pursuit of absolute safety. A well-designed garden will incorporate these

Gardens for the disabled 2

characteristics. In the example shown on the right, the main terrace is laid with a non-slip surface, making it suitable and safe for sitting, entertaining, alfresco meals and sunbathing.

At the point where the path leads away from the main terrace, there is a change in the texture of the paving intended to signal the change of direction or circumstance. This safety technique is repeated throughout the garden, for example, at path junctions, at the point where a ramp starts or finishes, at the bottom and top of steps and so on. Near the house and adjacent to the terrace, the open area could be laid with either grass or gravel.

The paths are interestingly arranged and, in some instances, confined by the retaining walls of beds and borders. These all have smooth sides and copings: brick and low relief, natural stones are ideal in this situation, as are bull-nosed stone coping or canted bricks (see Constructed vertical elements: Brick walls, page 126).

The raised beds make the plants more accessible to touch and smell. Taller plants do not, of course, need to be raised in this way.

Among the main features is a seat opposite a raised pool and fountain which produces delightful sounds of trickling water. There are also several sculptures chosen for their tactile appeal. The open-sided summer house is surrounded by perfumed plants and climbers, while a raised bed opposite contains plants chosen for their textural qualities and aromas. Trees have been selected to attract birds, bees and insects, the sounds of which will be particularly attractive in summer.

A garden for a person with limited mobility

Gravel access
Evergreen climber
Glasshouse
Bench
Floor at ground level
Flat coping for sitting and working
Sliding door
Reachable beds
Small pool with raised end
Flat coping for sitting & working
Hooped arch with thornless rose over
Easily maintained fence/ wall (rather than hedge)
Grass, gravel or low planting
Weeping tree
Compost
Potting bench
Flat "non-slip" paving
Fruit tree
Hand rails
Shed or shelter: climbing plants over
Door
Ramp

A garden for a blind person

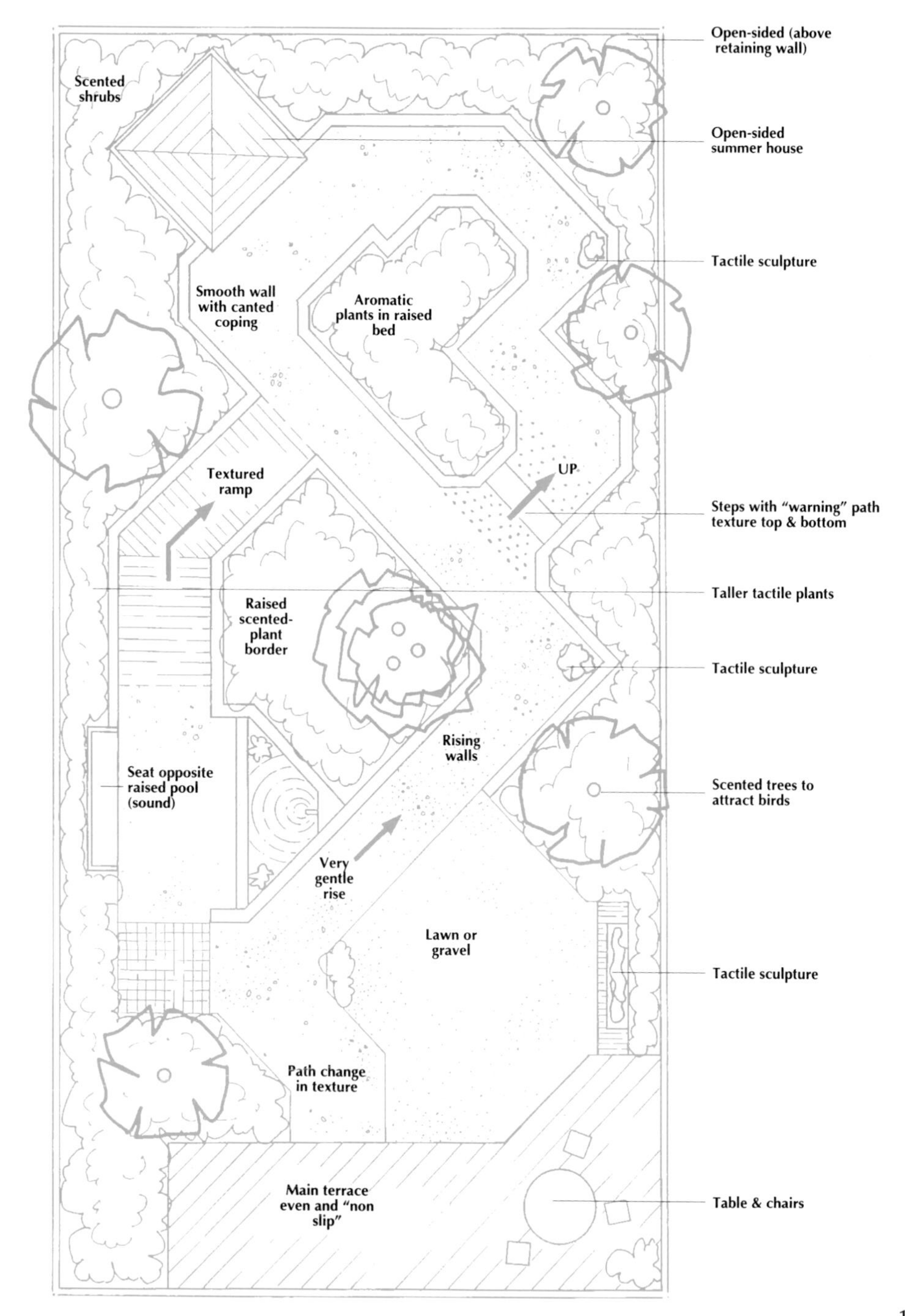

Low planting

The shape of a horizontal surface creates its own sense of movement, which is influenced further by the chosen covering: grass, plants, water or paving, for example, according to the area's proposed use and the desired effect.

As far as plants are concerned, once they reach a height where the shape of the planted horizontal surface is lost from view – the far side of a flower bed, for example – you must start to consider them vertical rather than horizontal elements. Under this circumstance, even the most carefully shaped bed, or border on plan will not appear as such in reality. This point is also worth bearing in mind when shaping truly horizontal areas which are formed by surrounding plantings, or any other vertical elements, for that matter. Harmony should always exist between horizontal and vertical elements.

Horizontal plantings

Planted horizontal surfaces take on functional roles too; grass is the most common ground cover and, as well as making lawns, is used in a similar way to create paving, between flower beds for example. The main reasons for its popularity are its unique attractiveness and usefulness as a foil to other garden features and plants. Choice of grasses depends on many things: proposed use, appearance, climate, siting, soil type and the quality of maintenance it is likely to receive. Some grass mixes are chosen for their appearance alone, others for their wearing qualities – where ball games or other active play is to take place, for example. In damp shade or on hot dry banks, different mixtures will be required.

Where grass is unsuitable, other low-growing plants can be used. As with any plant, its ability to grow well under given conditions will prevail over its appearance, and compromises have to be made according to circumstance. At the lowest level, plants having the general appearance of grass can be selected but many will not have the semi-evergreen properties

Dry shade *Lamium maculatum* 'Beacon Silver' can thrive in dry permanent shade: some other varieties of lamiums do equally well.

Hot dry areas Low plants for these areas often have bright flowers and silver leaves. Many of the heathers and heaths thrive here.

which grass has when growing in a temperate climate. However, it is worth considering subjects such as the low-growing thymes, sandworts (*Minuartia verna*), *Arenaria balearica*, mossy saxifrages and camomile (the flowerless varieties are best). Moss is used extensively in Japan as a close semi-evergreen cover but it enjoys being constantly shaded and moist – conditions not always available or even desirable in most gardens. In warmer or more sheltered places, taller subjects with more distinctive textures or colourful flowers can be used. These include the cheerful poached egg plant (*Limnanthes douglasii*) and, for frost-free climates, succulents such as hotentot fig (*Carpobrotus edulis*) or Livingstone daisies (*Mesembryanthemum*) grown in well-drained soils are colourful. The more permanent subjects include the prostrate cotoneasters, for example, and recently a range of very low-growing hybrid roses has been developed – perhaps the most well known being 'Nozomi'.

Taller ground-covering plants (just within the accepted definition) include heathers, geraniums, cytisus, genistas, vincas (usefully evergreen), a multitude of low conifers and ivies, ajugas and so on.

There are books devoted to the subject of ground-cover plants but, whatever is chosen, it should make both a useful and an attractive contribution to the garden. So often, subjects are chosen simply for their ability to facilitate garden maintenance or to fill awkward corners, but consider how they might make a good foil for other, perhaps more ornamental or sculptural plants – or trees – growing nearby. One only has to think of wild bluebells growing around beech or birch trees to be convinced.

Consider first the visual effect you are seeking to achieve from ground-cover plants, their function, the soil conditions and aspect, and then make the choice. Willing a particular favourite plant to perform the task to which it is unsuited is not the answer.

Low plants for foils or underplanting include lesser periwinkle (*Vinca minor*) and ivies. Bulbs such as crocuses are also useful in this context.

Low planting for permanent decorative effect Useful plants include ivies, evergreen euonymus (which can be pruned into shapes) and low hebes.

Paving

Paving is laid to fulfil many functions: as paths linking the various parts of a garden; as drives and for car parking; as patios for entertaining, alfresco meals, games and sunbathing. There are many forms of paving to choose from. Inorganic paving materials include gravel, natural stone (rectangular or randomly shaped), pebbles, setts, bricks, concrete, tarmacadam or asphalt and resin. Organic pavings include grass, sawn timber, bark, ground or chipped coconut shell and rubber compounds.

Flexible paving

Flexible paving systems are usually made up of loose stone aggregates and not bound within a rigid matrix, such as cement. When correctly laid, they absorb and dissipate the pressure of vehicular and pedestrian traffic, but to prevent them from spreading outward, flexible pavings normally require restraining edges.

Gravel

Gravel is the simplest form of flexible paving. There are three basic types:

Shingle Rounded stone pieces worn smooth by natural causes are available in sizes ranging from 5 mm (¼ in) to 20 mm (¾ in). Pea shingle is the best known type, similar in shape and size to a garden pea, hence its name. Besides being a good path or drive surfacing, shingle makes an excellent foil for plants or pots. It is not so suitable for sloping paths or drives as it tends to migrate downwards. The edging example shown below is of timber boards supported with stakes sawn off level with, or below the top of the board to facilitate mowing any adjacent grass areas. Shingle paths need a firm base with the surfacing itself approximately 50–75 mm (2–3 in) deep. If laid too deeply, it has a braking effect on any wheeled garden equipment, and also makes walking uncomfortable.

Crushed stone Crushed stone is derived from crushing larger rocks into flakes or shards. It is multi-faceted and does not have the same tendency as pea shingle to migrate on a slope. Pieces vary in size but tend to range from 25 mm (1 in) to 50 mm (2 in). Its colour depends upon the rock source. Victorian-style blue or red "rope" edging tiles are shown as the restraining edge in the example below (right).

Path gravel (self-binding) This consists of pebbles, shingle or stones held in a matrix of soil having a high clay content. It is best raked and rolled to produce a cambered surface, again over a stone base. Path gravel material is laid as a wearing surface to a depth of up to 75 mm (3 in), depending on the volume of traffic. Path gravel needs to be re-raked and re-rolled following heavy rain or frost. The camber, (the slightly arched form) allows rainwater to be shed to the sides of the path to drain harmlessly away. In the example below (page 111, left) the edging shown is brick with gaps left to allow rainwater to escape.

Shingle

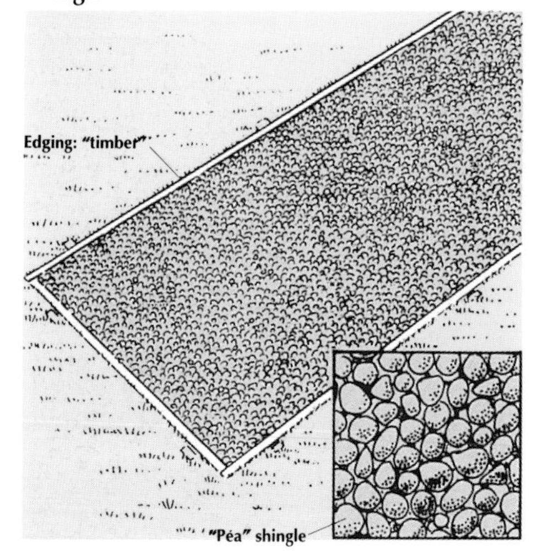

Crushed stone

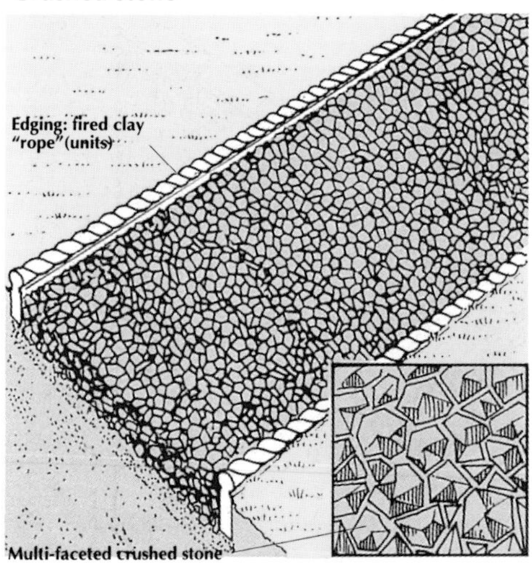

Tarmacadam
Shingle or crushed stone is the main ingredient of "tarmac", held in a matrix of tar. The numbers and depths of the courses or layers in a path or drive depend upon the expected traffic. Each course is made up of different sized stones and thicknesses: the largest at the bottom.

Tarmac surfaces can be "dressed" with rolled-in gravel or marble chippings. Coloured tarmacs are available but highly pigmented surfaces are vulnerable to damage from the tyres of power-steered vehicles, especially during warm weather, so consult an expert first.

Asphalt Asphalt is closely associated with tarmac. Usually black or grey, asphalt paths are more closely textured than tarmac, but less resistant to damage from oil and petrol spillage.

"Bull-nosed" units are an attractive and appropriate choice of edging, but as they are relatively thin they need to be backed up (haunched) with concrete.

Natural stone
Any stone used for paving should be frost-resistant and durable, so you should check both these properties with the supplier before ordering. The shapes of paving stones will depend upon the source and how the rock was created. Some paving stone is naturally flat and occurs in suitably thin strata; other types have to be sawn from larger blocks, and are more expensive. There are hundreds of stone types, among the more common of which are Portland, a limestone, York, a sandstone type, and granite, an igneous rock.

Natural stone paving patterns
Random rectangular This pattern uses slabs (or flags) that are basically rectangular in shape but of different sizes. The skill comes in laying the slabs so that uninterrupted joint lines do not extend too far in either direction, detracting from a random appearance. Random rectangular as a pattern tends to be static. A "riven" surface finish is the natural result of splitting stone rather than sawing it.

Regular sawn one size This regular pattern uses square or rectangular slabs of one size, although half sizes are sometimes used at the edges of a paved area. The pattern can have either a widening or lengthening effect depending on the direction from which the paved area is seen.

Regular coursed rectangular stone Blocks of stone set on edge form this positive and interesting pattern. It is made up of stones of differing lengths but similar widths in each row. Edging stones of the same type provide a stabilizing and attractive finish.

Random (crazy) paving This pattern comprises random-shaped pieces of stone set onto mortar, and is useful in informal schemes and where a path or terrace curves or is irregular in shape. For terraces, it is essential to choose

Path gravel (self-binding)

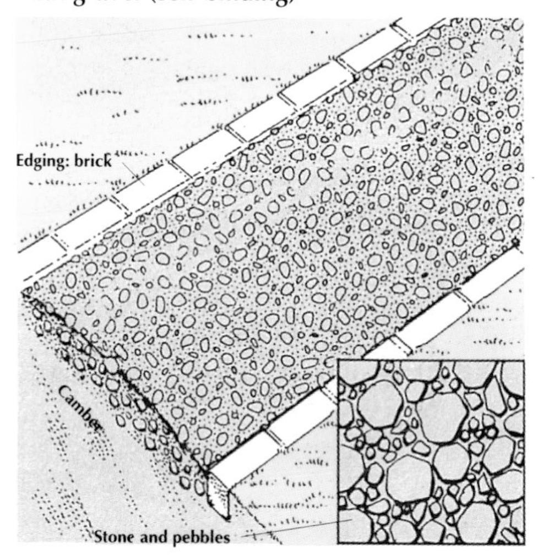

Tarmacadam

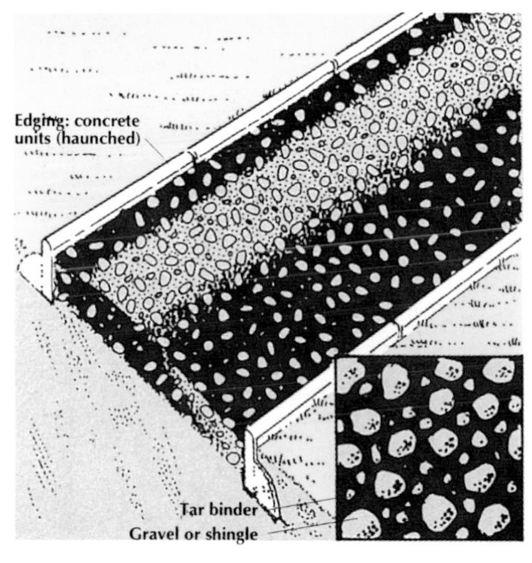

Paving 2

stone with a flat, even surface for safety and comfort, and to prevent furniture from rocking. Where random stones are flaky, as some are, and therefore liable to be damaged by frost, fill the mortar joints right to the top of the stone surface. This helps to keep the water out and reduce the risk of frost damage. Stepping stones cut from rounded pieces are excellent for lawn and border use.

Setts Setts are cubes or rectangular blocks cut from very hard stone, usually granite, varying in size from a cube of approximately 75 mm (3 in) to a rectangle of 150 x 150 x 250 mm (6 x 6 x 10 in). They can be laid in a wide variety of patterns. "Regularly coursed", using small units, creates a rather static appearance.

Pebbles Pebbles are smooth, water-worn stones. When imaginatively used and laid in mortar they can make beautiful and sometimes intricate patterns, especially when pebbles of different sizes and colours are used. Small pebbles need to be edged for stability, perhaps with brick, stone, setts or timber. In some circumstances, pebbles are simply placed loose upon the ground for textural appeal.

Reconstituted stone

Reconstituted stone paving is a mixture of natural stone aggregates and cement. Most units are moulded to resemble natural stone, and their final appearance depends on the texturing of the mould surface, the aggregate used and any pigment added. There are countless different textures to choose from: for example, smooth, brushed, stippled and exposed-surface aggregates. Most garden centres and builders' merchants stock a wide range.

Brightly coloured reconstituted slabs should be used with discretion as they may clash with the colours of adjacent architecture or plants.

Irregular rectangular paving The units shown below have been laid in a linear pattern which is made up of parallel rows of different widths, resulting in a strong directional feeling. The units themselves have a "rubbed" texture leading in the same direction as the uninterrupted joints.

Octagonal paving Octagons are a traditional paving shape for use in the garden. Made of reconstituted stone, terracotta or natural stone, octagonal pavers must be combined with small square units between them to be laid in a continuous pattern. These squares are often of a different colour or material.

Hexagonal paving Hexagonal paving units link well with modern garden schemes. A wide variety of colours and textures is available; the example shown below has a stippled finish.

Diagonalized square paving Diagonal patterns are used to minimize the sense of movement of paved areas. In the example on page 113 square units resembling terracotta tiles have been used. A stabilizing edge of brick or tiles would be appropriate, and would prevent the triangular pieces at the sides from being dislodged.

Mixed sizes Two sizes of paving are used in the example shown on page 113 to achieve a Flemish pattern. Brushing the surface of the paving units during the manufacturing process results in an attractive "non-slip" texture. This pattern tends to lack a sense of movement.

Equal-sized paving These can be square or rectangular, and laid with uninterrupted joints in either direction. If the slabs have the surface

Irregular rectangular paving

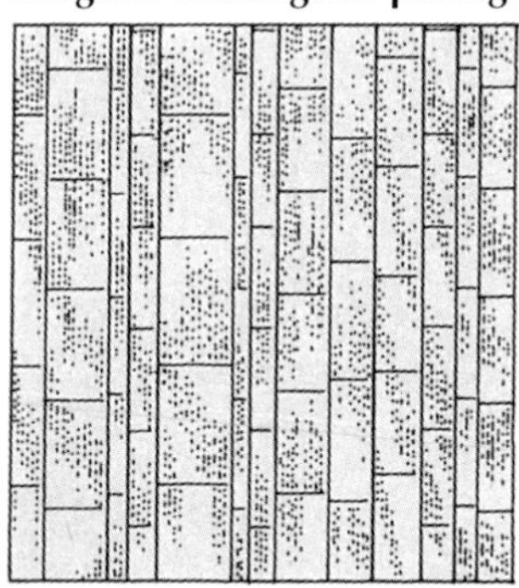

Octagonal paving

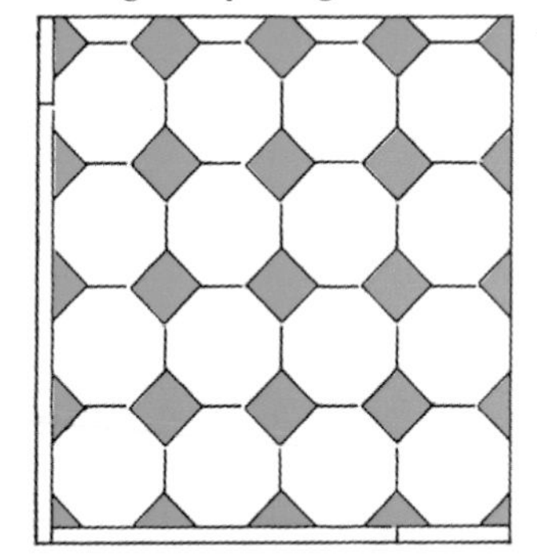

Hexagonal paving

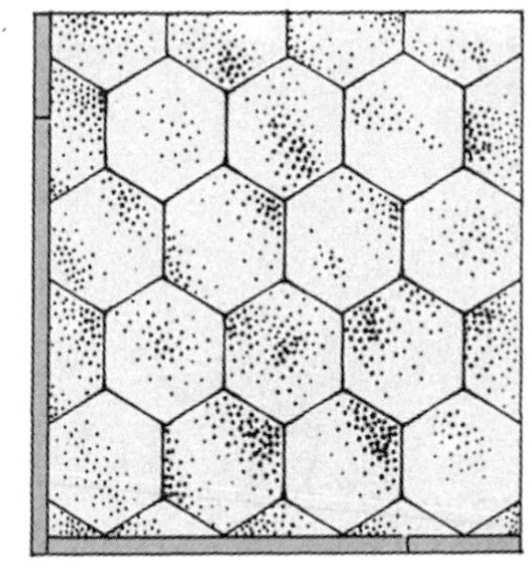

cement washed away during the manufacturing process to expose the aggregates within, the result is an attractive finish and a safe walking surface. The pattern is strongly directional.

Reconstituted stone paths
The range of unit shapes and sizes available is very wide indeed: when possible combinations of sizes, shapes – and colours – are added to the equation, reconstituted stone offers an almost infinite choice.

Where curves occur in paths laid with rectangular slabs, it looks better if the slabs are either cut to an angle to fit together, or if special shapes are made. Wide, tapering joints filled with mortar or pebbles suggest that the details were not worked out at the design stage.

Stepping stone paths
These are useful for crossing an area of lawn without interrupting its flow, and for borders and places in a garden where a conventional path would be obtrusive. Stepping stone surfaces in grass should be laid at or just below turf level so that the grass can be cut without damage to the mowing equipment or the stone.

Rectangular stepping stones These are better arranged in an orderly way. Haphazardly placed, they tend to look disorganized, not informal as may be intended. Spacing is a matter of convenience and function. To negotiate changes in direction the slabs should be shifted to one side or the other but remain parallel.

Circular stepping stones Circular reconstituted stones are popular in informal situations. They are available in a variety of sizes and are more convenient and longer lasting than log slices.

Concrete laid *in situ*
In the right context, well designed areas of concrete can enhance a garden's appearance. Being a "rigid" material, concrete must be properly supported with a solid stone base. Continuous concrete paths and paving must incorporate any thermal movement joints at intervals of not more than 5 m (16 ft). Without these it may crack. Concrete can be made to resemble other paving materials or simply left as it is. Texturing, marking or colouring will determine its final appearance, but expect colours to fade gradually. Earth colours tend to be more lasting than brighter hues.

Brushed and trowelled Smooth concrete could prove dangerous for pedestrians, but texturing before it sets will provide a non-slip surface. Path edges can be smoothed and rounded using a special trowel. This gives a neat finish and emphasizes the brush marks, the depth of which vary with the stiffness of the brush and the pressure exerted.

The thermal movement joints are made during the casting process by placing a timber strip horizontally between the shuttering to leave narrow open joints between sections. A 10 mm (3/8 in) width is adequate.

Brush texturing Soon after laying the concrete, effects ranging from swirling patterns to fan or shell shapes can be produced by using a soft brush on the trowelled surface. Raised, half-round, pre-cast concrete units could be used as edging to enhance definition.

Marked out By marking out unset, textured concrete with a rounded-end metal rod or pebble the effect of pre-cast paving slabs, random paving or even an abstract-patterned path can

Diagonalized square paving

Mixed sizes

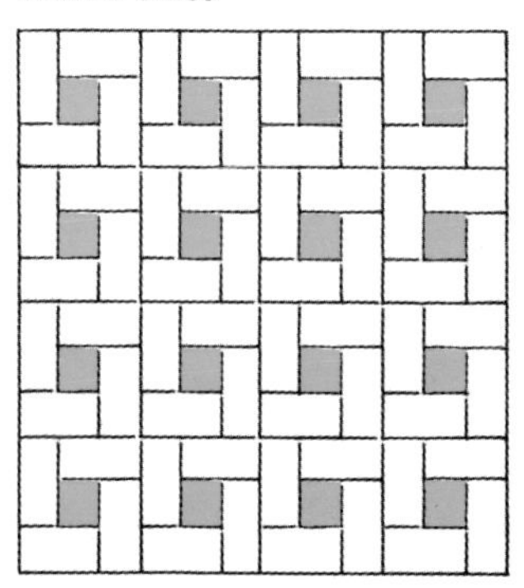

Equal sized paving

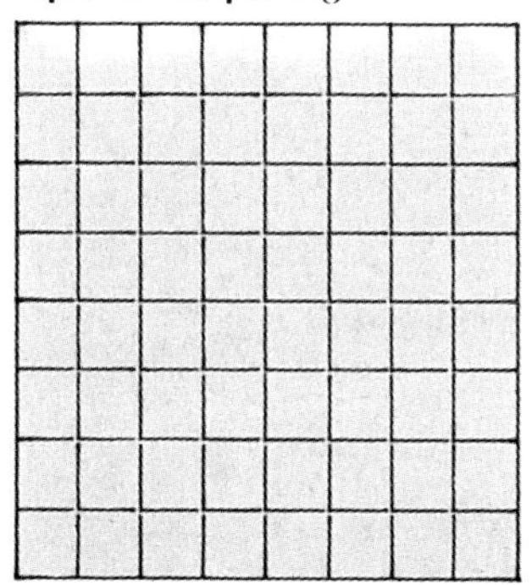

Paving 3

be achieved. Concrete brick laid diagonally at the sides in a traditional way suggests authentic stone paving.

Exposed aggregate concrete A basic or specially formulated concrete mixture can, prior to setting, have its surface carefully washed and brushed to remove some of the cement, so exposing the gravel and other stone particles that make up the aggregate. The sizes, textures and colours of the aggregate in the mixture and the cement itself will determine the appearance of the paving. Bricks laid flat would be suitable for finishing.

Mechanically impressed concrete This uses a fairly new technique in which unset, usually coloured concrete is impressed using a mobile hydraulic press. Most paving types can be imitated using this type of finish, ranging from natural stone to brick paving patterns, although mechanical impressing can be carried out only by specialists.

Brick paving

Brick, a traditional paving material, has been used all over the world for centuries. Choose bricks and patterns to match or harmonize with the colour and textural qualities of nearby architectural features.

Besides their appearance, the two most important properties for paving bricks are that they should be frost-proof and durable. In wet or icy conditions, very smooth bricks can become slippery, making them unsuitable.

Running or stretcher bond Depending upon the direction of the path relative to the direction of the uninterrupted joint lines in the paving pattern, this bond is described either as "stretcher bond", which makes the paved area appear wider, or "running bond", which has a lengthening effect and creates a strong sense of movement. Running bond is particularly suitable for paths with gentle curves.

Straight herringbone This has an interesting shifting pattern. It usually needs some kind of edging to ensure that the half-bricks used to form a straight edge do not fall away with use.

Diagonal herringbone This is the same as straight herringbone except that it is set at an angle, usually of 45 degrees to the main view or to the direction of the path. It needs an edging to secure the small triangular bricks at the sides. The pattern is useful for patios and for curving paths. The bricks can be laid flat or "on edge", producing a narrower pattern but they require a larger number of bricks and deeper excavation in order to achieve the same area and level of path.

Continuous or stack bond This has a modern appearance, and the brick direction can be varied to suggest widening, with the bricks laid with the long edges horizontally, or lengthening, with the long edges leading away from the viewpoint. Alternating panels of this pattern with bricks laid at 90 degrees to each other result in a chequered effect.

Basketweave Of all the brick paving bonds, this is probably the most "static", and is useful for sitting areas where a sense of movement is not appropriate. The bricks can be laid flat when each unit is made of two bricks (as in the example on page 115), or laid on edge where each unit made up of three.

Stable paviours Not a laying pattern, this is rather a description of a particular shape of

Running or stretcher bond

Straight herringbone

Diagonal herringbone

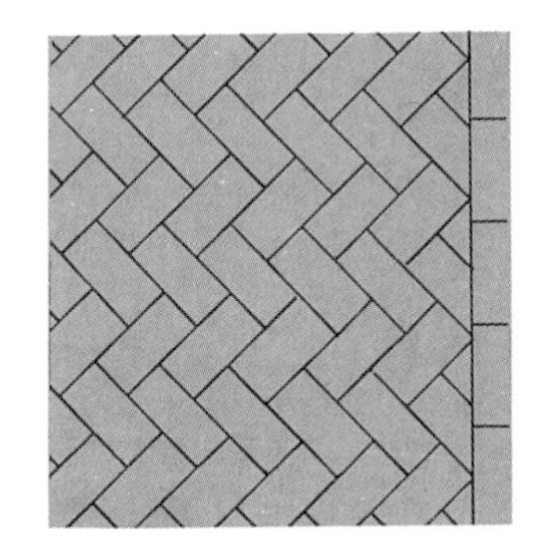

hard, impervious brick which was originally used in stables. Stable paviours are available either as "doubles", with chamfered edges and a centre valley, or "singles". They are butt-jointed (touching) rather than having mortar-filled joints. The chamfers (angled corners) give the appearance of conventional joints.

Diamond paviours Developed during the Georgian and Victorian periods, this type of brick is normally manufactured in blue, red or yellow fired clay. They are usually butt-jointed, and can be laid in practically any pattern. The name "diamond" refers to the pattern on the upper face which provides a non-slip surface.

Timber paving

Timber board paving is known as decking. For outdoor use, it should be treated with preservative, or a naturally weather-proof wood, such as oak or cedar should be selected. The longevity of decking is increased by raising it off the ground or laying it on a free-draining gravel base.

Board decking Imaginatively designed decking has appeal in most settings but especially where a modern look is desired. In many parts of the world, especially in the USA and Scandinavia, decking is a popular and traditional "paving" material, but it is less commonly seen in the UK.

Decking is usually left in a natural state when constructed of hardwood, but other types of timber can be stained and treated. Textured boards, such as those with a sawn finish, are safer to walk on than those planed smoothly, which can be slippery, especially when wet.

Timber setts Hardwood cubes or setts can be used in the same way as conventional stone setts. To add to their attraction, cubes can be laid with the end grain uppermost, preferably in a gritty sand bed. Sand should also be brushed in to any small surface gaps on completion. Setts laid in a diagonal pattern require a stabilizing edge.

Log rounds When sawn to 75 mm (3 in) or thicker, log rounds make excellent pathways or stepping "stones" in an informal situation. If softwoods are used, they will require regular treatment with preservative, but laying them over a free-draining layer of sharp sand will give them a longer life. Fill the gaps between with carpeting plants, granulated bark or gravel.

Coconut shell chips or granulated bark These are both good path materials for an informal situation, but must be laid on a proper base of stone or gravel if they are to last. The edging could be constructed from logs, laid longitudinally and fixed with pointed stakes driven in at their sides. This arrangement defines the path well and prevents the overspill of pedestrians or plants in either direction.

Other more unusual paving types include:

Clear resin-bonded aggregates Aggregates selected according to shape, colour and size are mixed with a clear, inorganic resin, then smoothly spread over a prepared base. The resulting appearance is of permanently wet gravel, but the surface is fixed. It is a popular finish for swimming pool surrounds.

"Safe play" composite material paving This impact-absorbing paving system is invaluable around play equipment of all types. It is based on recycled rubber products and available in a range of styles, sizes and dark colours.

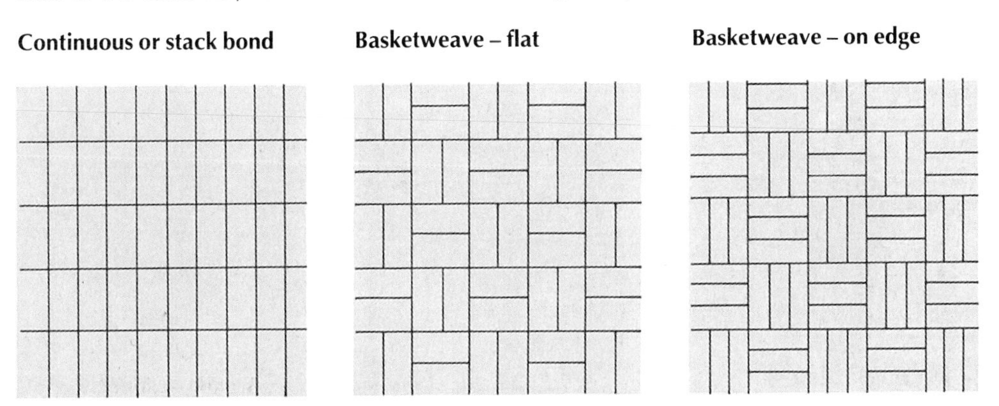

Trees and other plants

Vertical elements are, in general, more visible in a garden than horizontal ones. They are often deliberately positioned to conceal horizontal surfaces as part of a design strategy (see Structure, space and movement: Screening, page 62), and because they are so readily seen it is of the utmost importance that they should be well designed and maintained.

All too frequently, however, more attention is paid to the horizontal than to the vertical plan at the design stage, perhaps because the latter is more difficult to visualize. When creating a design, even though planning so often begins as a bird's eye plan, try to think of a garden in three dimensions rather than just as a series of flat features arranged on paper.

This is particularly important when including trees, shrubs, hedges and fences, which are all vertical elements, as are most constructions. Each of these must look attractive in its own right as well as working in the design as part of a composition.

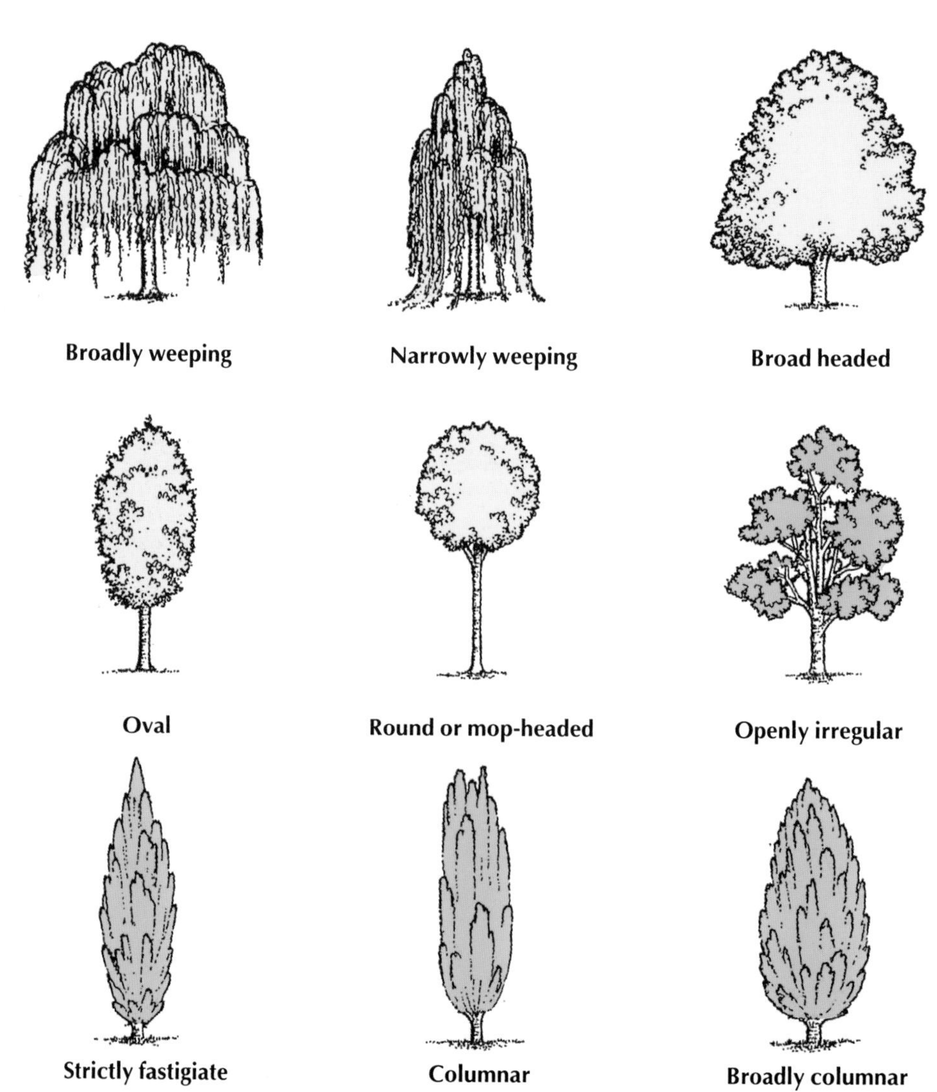

Trees in the design

Trees are probably the most important vertical elements in most garden designs, being naturally attractive. They can also contribute greatly to the structure of a garden either individually or in groups and represent a sound investment in the future development of your garden. Obviously, trees achieve their full potential only after a number of years. It is particularly important, therefore, to make the right choice of trees for the effect you want to create. Visit established local gardens to see successful tree plantings, and sketch ideas onto tracing paper placed over photographs of your garden to help you reach the right decision.

Tree shapes

Trees can be categorized according to their shape. There are recognized descriptions of these shapes: the more common are illustrated left and below. Choose the preferred or appropriate shapes and forms of the trees first, then consult a nursery catalogue to find which have these particular characteristics, which are the right size and which suit the site and soil where you plan to plant them.

The basic shapes and forms of evergreen trees are permanent throughout the year, but the mass of an evergreen is ever-present and most lack the sense of season of the deciduous types. There are qualities other than overall shape that might influence the choice of tree. Some, such as the corkscrew hazel (*Corylus avellana* 'Contorta') are grown specially for their winter appearance. Flower colour is mostly short-lived in a tree and should be only one of the reasons for choosing it; think, too, of the autumn, in terms of a tree's leaf-tints, bark colour, fruits and berries. Consider also the adjacent trees, how they will complement each other, and how they will look in a group at all times of the year.

Where trees are chosen to perform a particular function, check that they are suitable for the purpose. Here, as in other aspects of garden design, function may need to take priority over form. For example, trees planted primarily for wind screening should not only be tough, but it is better if they have close, supple branches and small leaves. These not only filter the wind efficiently, reducing its force, but they also yield a certain amount, so that the tree is not damaged.

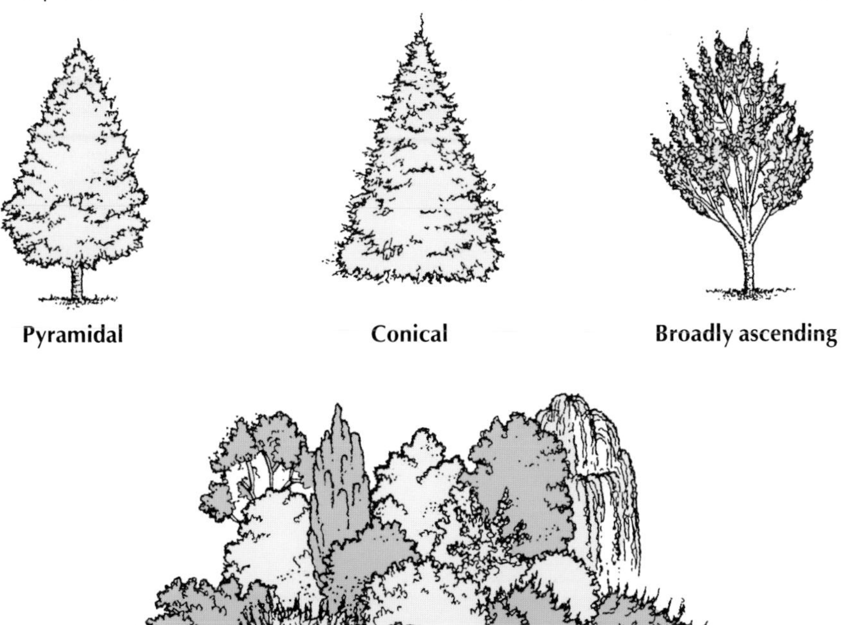

Pyramidal **Conical** **Broadly ascending**

A simple example of trees and shrub forms planted together in a harmonious group

Trees and other plants 2

Trees planted to create shade, are better chosen for their large leaves and wide canopies. If sitting is planned beneath, then the trunks should be clean up to 2 m (6 ft 6 in).

1 A familiar countryside view: a group of trees at the top of a hillock, which would make a distinctive focal point.

2 The structural planting of this weeping tree with a hexagonal seat beneath reinforces the calm appearance of the open area of lawn and is pivotal to the composition. The contrasting shapes of the surrounding tree forms emphasize the weeping tree still further. Strictly columnar trees have been avoided as being too strongly contrasting and lacking in subtlety. A spiky plant can be useful to emphasize a corner or bend in a path or border.

3 An avenue of fastigiate trees reinforces the formal appearance of the path as it leads to a gateway, contributing to the overall structure.

4 The rounder-shaped trees set further back from the path are structural too but less obviously so, suggesting a much gentler progress. In examples 3 and 4 (below), grass instead of the path would visually soften the effect.

Shrub shapes, habits and forms

These vary considerably, as illustrated in the examples (right) and make an important contribution to a garden's structure, whether used collectively or individually.

Shrubs can be grouped or massed to emphasize or exaggerate their forms and textures, with light and shade playing a large part in the effect. Others, such as grasses, bamboos and weeping willows, are planted for sound and movement produced when they are blown by the wind.

Direct contrasts in form and colour will work only occasionally; if overdone, they can appear unsettling and lacking in harmony. Again, since

Trees – structural qualities

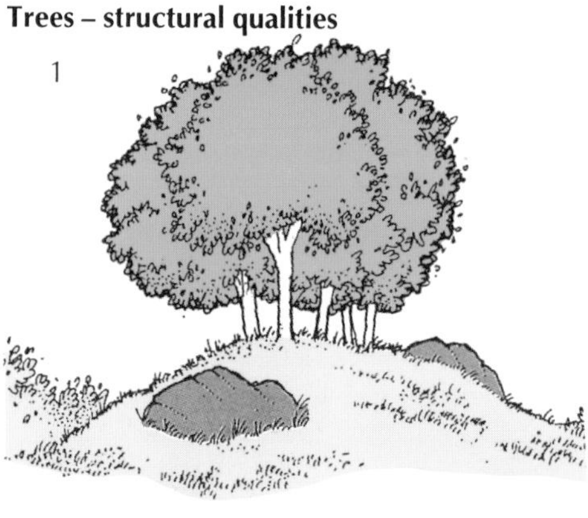
1

2

3

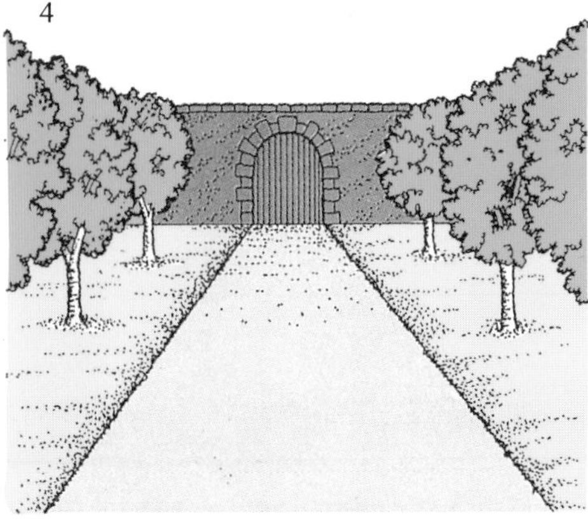
4

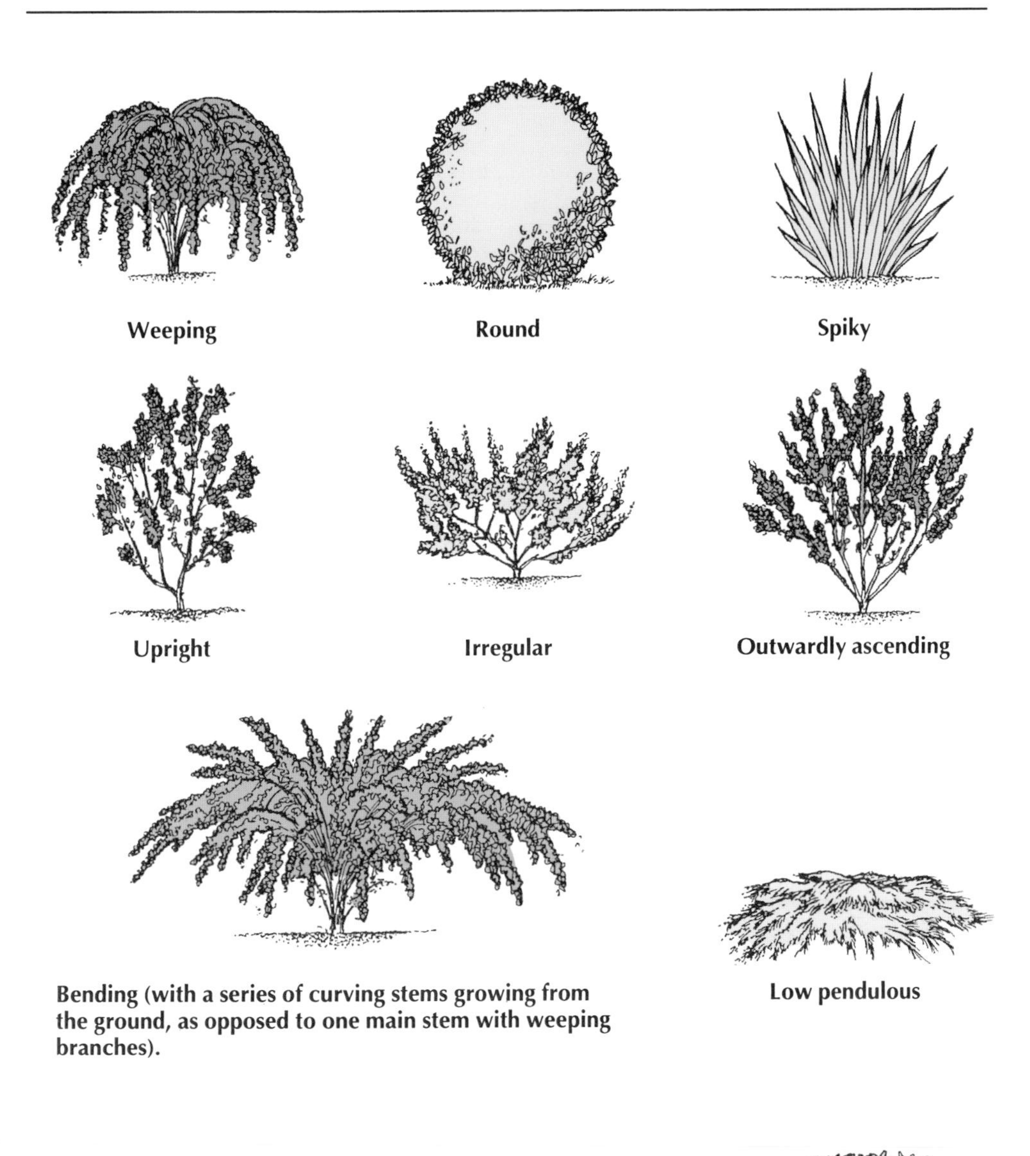

Weeping

Round

Spiky

Upright

Irregular

Outwardly ascending

Bending (with a series of curving stems growing from the ground, as opposed to one main stem with weeping branches).

Low pendulous

Prostrate

Low tufted

Broadly round or low oval

Trees and other plants 3

flower colour is transitory, shrubs should also be chosen for their other qualities to extend their season of interest. Most good nursery catalogues describe shrubs' year-round forms.

Herbaceous and other plants

Being mostly decorative, herbaceous plants, annuals and biennials make a far less significant contribution to the structure of the garden than trees and shrubs. As structural plants they work only during their growing and or their flowering season, which usually lasts from spring to autumn. Their decorative function is, however, important. Herbaceous perennials and annuals need a neutral foil to be seen at their best. A single-species hedge, such as green beech, yew or privet, is ideal for the purpose.

Designing herbaceous borders

When designing herbaceous perennial or annual borders, consider first the direction from which it will usually be seen. Mainly from the

Texture and form play important roles in any herbaceous composition

Tall flowering

Spiky

Curving, pendulous or grassy

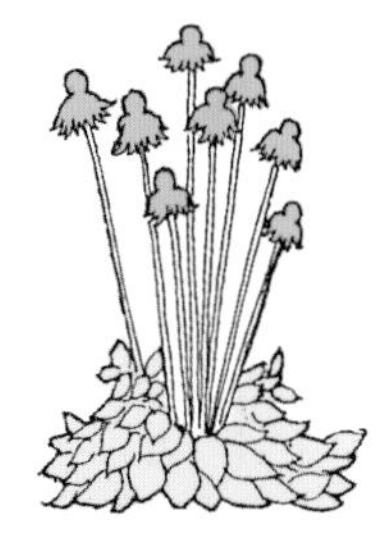

Top-flowering (bare stems)

Low hummock

Architectural, bending

front or end on? In the latter case, the border can consist of large blocks of just a few varieties to counter the foreshortening effect of perspective; a spotty effect might otherwise result.

When usually viewed from the front, the border can include a wider range of plants but there is an increased need to repeat plantings for continuity. Where taller herbaceous plants are grown, there can be a risk of their unattractive stems being exposed. Include smaller, bushier subjects at the front to disguise tall stems, but avoid planting in carefully arranged tiers. These always look unnatural and give the border a stiff, "stripey" look.

Plant textures and forms constantly change with the quality and direction of light and this has a direct effect on the decorative impression achieved. Experiment with forms and texture as well as colour as a way of extending the border's appeal. Remember that vibrant colours like red and yellow, for example, respond well to sunlight while colours such as blue or pale mauve look better in shade, sometimes even appearing to glow in the early morning or late evening.

Take risks to achieve interesting and unusual effects. If the overall result turns out to be unsatisfactory, herbaceous plants can always be moved at the appropriate time ready for the next experiment. Many of the great garden designers of the past and present have worked in this way to produce stunning results.

Selecting herbaceous plants

Apart from the specialist suppliers of a particular group of herbaceous plants, most mail-order catalogues include colour photographs which are an enormous help in putting a planting scheme together. Of course, there is nothing like seeing the real thing. So, visit as many nurseries, or gardens, famous for their herbaceous borders, as you can. Make a note of the orientation of the garden and the soil type to avoid later disappointment as herbaceous plants do have their preferences.

Forms and habits of herbaceous plants

Since there are many hundreds – if not thousands – of distinctly different forms, only the most common are illustrated below.

Broadly architectural

Delicate or fluffy

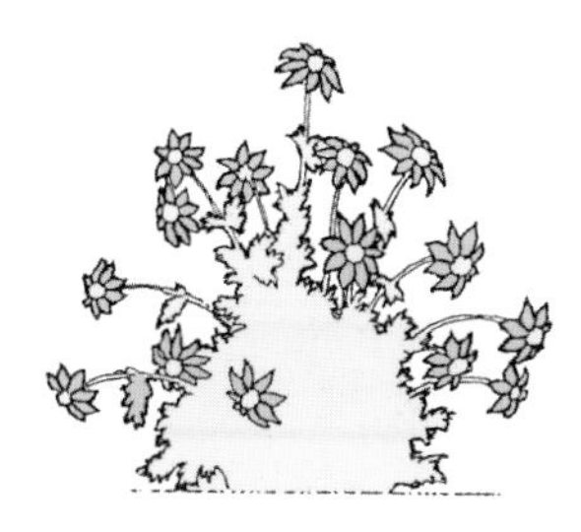

Outwardly flowering

Spiky

Bell-like or weeping

Thorny

Hedges

Garden hedges of all kinds are important in establishing the structure and outline of the design, but they may also play other roles. They screen for security and for privacy, they compartmentalize, they act as foils or backdrops for other plants and features, and can simply be attractive in their own right.

A hedging plant should be chosen for its natural growth habit, leaf size or texture relative to the way it will be sculptured or pruned. Different heights or widths fulfil different functions, ranging from a tall yew to diminutive edging box or lavender. Climatic and cultural requirements must be taken into account as hedge plants need as some, like yew, respond to formal treatments while others, like hawthorn, are better in informal situations. Larger hedge plants such as laurel and trees are planted as a single row and smaller types, such as hawthorn, blackthorn, beech or hornbeam, are planted in staggered rows to encourage greater density and impenetrability.

Clip or prune hedges to be narrower at the top than the bottom. This will allow light to fall on all surfaces, encouraging leaf growth to ground level. If hedges are allowed to bush out at the top, the lower branches will become bare and may die back.

Flowering hedges Flowering evergreen and deciduous shrubs and trees can be used for hedges, especially where ornamental effect is a priority, but where there is insufficient room for an additional flower border. Plants with a naturally bushy habit are best for this purpose, such as shrub roses, berberis, hebes and escallonias.

"Fedges" These are a cross between a hedge and a fence and are often used where space is too limited to accommodate the width of a hedge, or where an impassable boundary is needed immediately. The usual way of forming a fedge is to grow a climbing plant, such as ivy, over a chicken-wire or a chain-link fence. Uncovered timber posts give the fedge a more formal appearance.

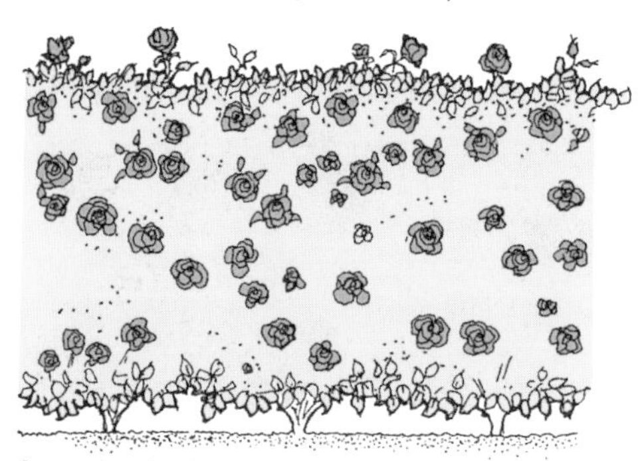

Flowering hedge

"Fedge"

Mixed hedge (summer)

The woven vertical stems of a "laid" hedge

Mixed hedges These are made up of a variety of indigenous species providing not only screening but a refuge for different wildlife eg birds and insects. Traditional mixed hedges might include hawthorn, sloe, hazel, elderberry, dog rose, snowberry, dogwood, holly, field maple or wild woodbine,depending on local conditions.

Mixed hedges need to be "laid" every few years to restrict their height and to maintain density and well being. This entails cutting part way through the vertical growths then bending them obliquely and weaving them together to form an impenetrable barrier. This is a skilled task best left to an experienced hedger.

Single species hedges These are made up of a single species of plant, such as privet, beech, hornbeam, quickthorn or yew. They can be used as neutral backdrops for other more ornamental plants or for providing positive garden structure and division. In the case of beech, alternating green and copper cultivars are sometimes planted to make what is known as a tapestry hedge with the varieties intermingling to produce blocks of contrasting colour. Tapestry hedges are less suitable as foils to other plants because of their own distinctive appearance.

Formal hedges These are indispensable in formal gardens, not only for providing structure but for contributing to the prevailing tone.

The degree of formality achieved in the hedge depends upon the plant type and the frequency and style of pruning: the most formal hedges are achieved by closely clipping yew or box and some of the smaller-leaved conifers. Since yew and box respond so well to very close clipping, they are popular as subjects for topiary work.

Stilt hedges In this variation on the formal hedge, dense growth is carried high on straight parent trunks or stems. Used frequently in formal gardens of the past, they were sometimes planted in a double parallel row.

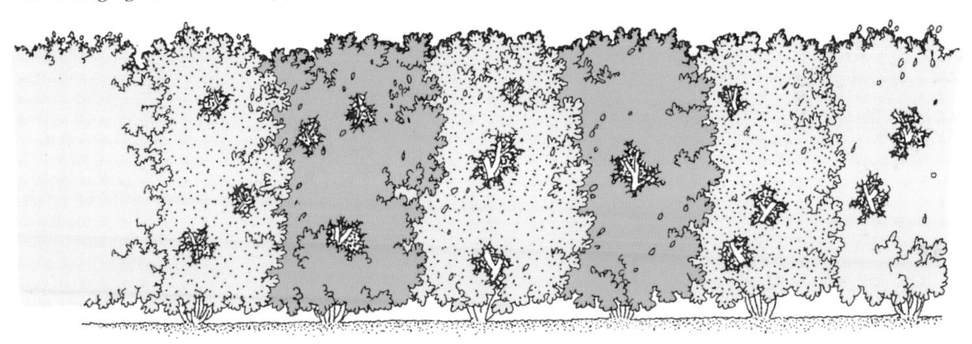

A tapestry hedge can involve two species, or different varieties of the same species.

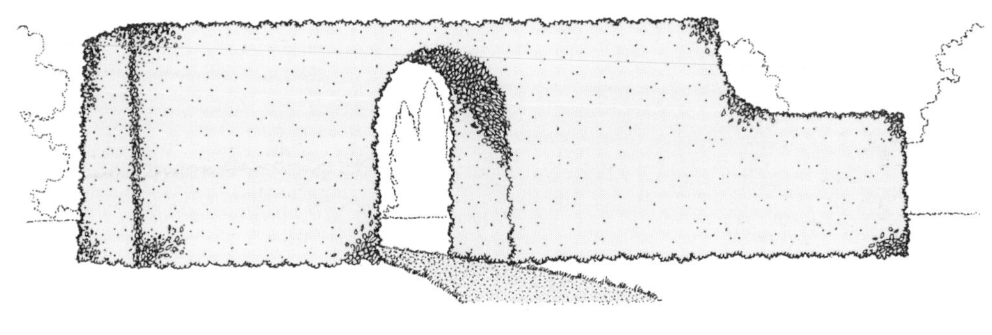

Formal hedge

Hedges 2

This style is useful where screening at a high level is called for but where an open view is required beneath. The example below shows a single-row stilt hedge.

Trained trees Fruit trees, trained horizontally or diagonally, make splendid screens. While not necessarily as dense as conventional hedges, they compensate for this by being productive and very attractive. Where divisions of fruit or vegetable gardens are necessary they are an obvious choice in the form of fans, cordons or espaliers.

Palisades A palisade comprises a row of spaced slender trees, the supple young branches of which are tied together to make overhead arches. To get them started, you will need a wire framework, but once the palisade has grown sufficiently to support itself, the framework can be removed if possible. Regular pruning is needed to maintain shape and size.

Pleached hedges Despite the maintenance required, pleaching is still popular. It comprises rows of clear-trunked trees, often limes or laburnums, with their supple, uppermost branches tied and interwoven together in the direction of the row. Sometimes they used to be grafted together. Formal double rows at either side of a grass or paved pathway are known as pleached walks.

Alley This form of divider or hedge is made by tying supple branches together overhead to form a tunnel. Flowering and scented plants can be used. Alleys need the support of stakes and wires during their formative years.

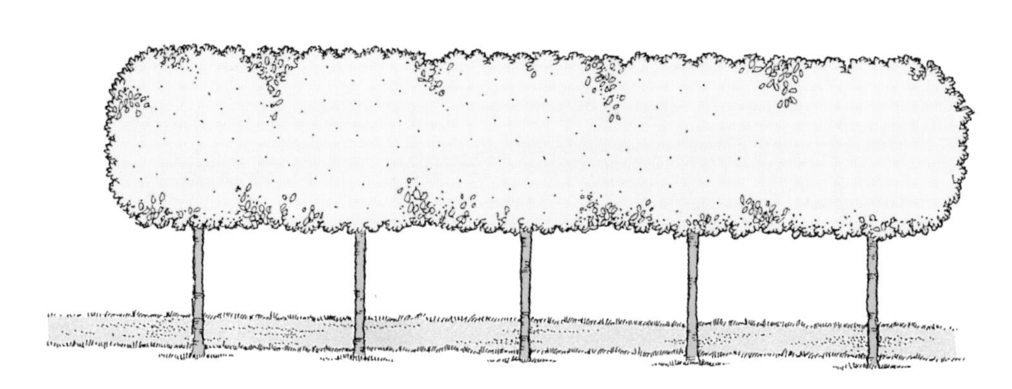

Single-row stilt hedge

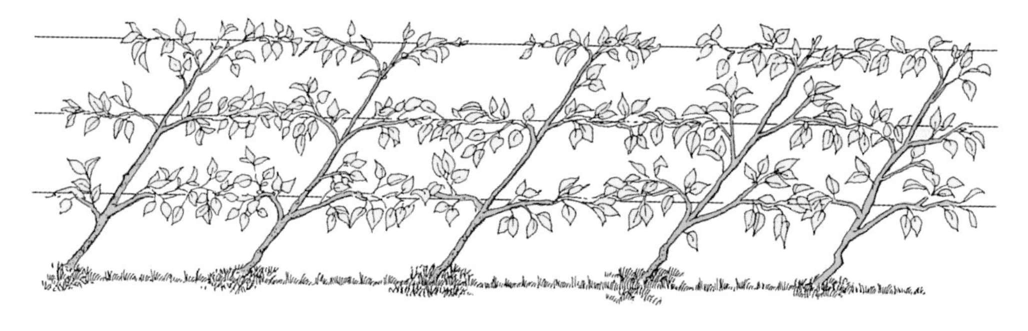

Cordon "hedge"

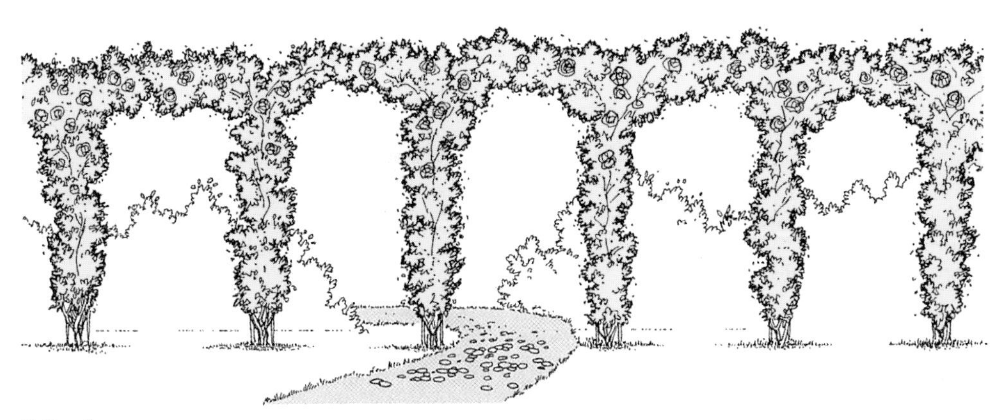

Palisade

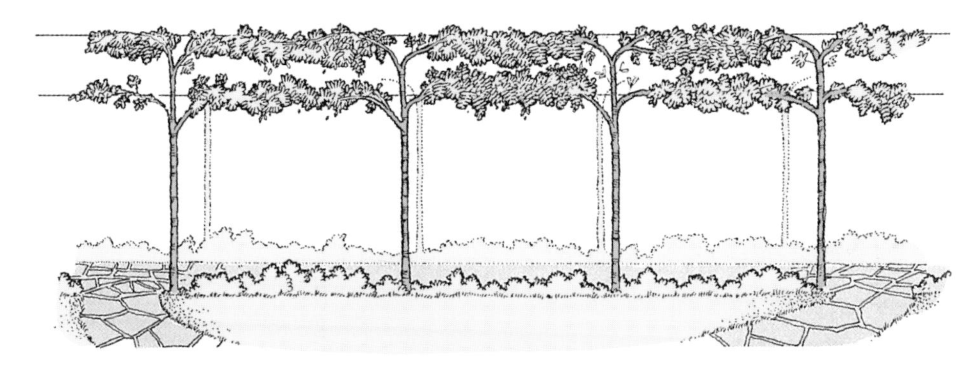

Pleached hedge

Alley

Brick walls

The shapes and forms of constructed vertical elements are a valuable part of a garden's design. Among the details to be considered are the style and overall appearance of the shadow patterns created by the construction materials or their arrangements. For example, old mellow bricks with recessed joints suggest characterful rusticity or great age, while precisely shaped concrete blocks, flush-jointed, look modern and sophisticated. The final choice of construction material should be determined by the function to be performed and the overall impression being sought.

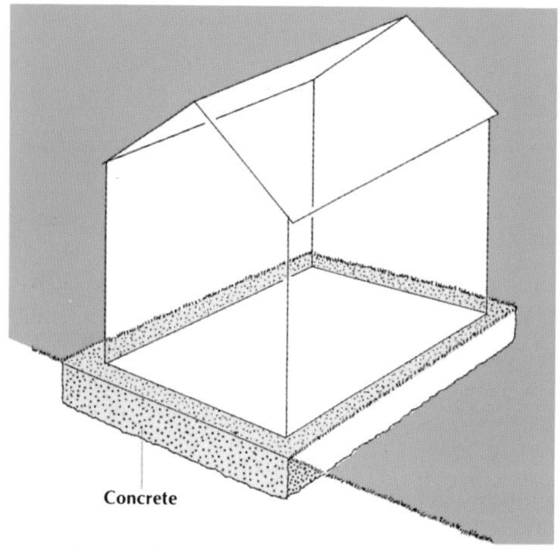

A typical raft foundation, suitable for a small garden building where a floor is needed as an integral part of the construction.

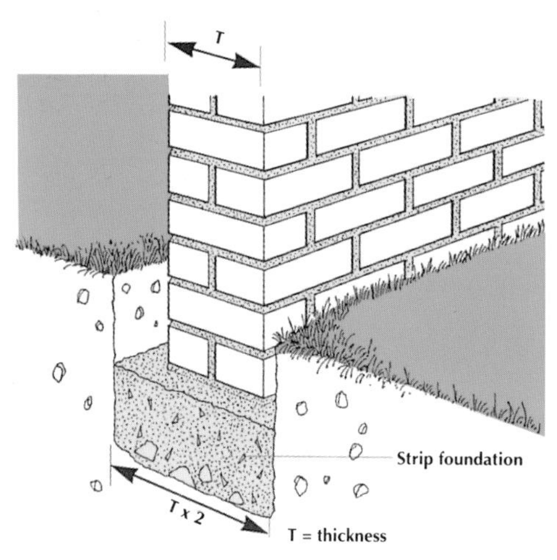

A strip foundation, set into the ground, is usually twice as wide as the wall it is to support. For example, it will be 450 mm (18 in) wide if the wall is 225 mm (9 in) wide.

Walls

Walls must be constructed safely and sufficiently strongly to fulfil their purpose. They must have adequate foundations, which means excavating and starting construction at a depth where the structure will be unaffected by any subterranean movement arising from natural causes or changes in foreseeable circumstances. Any movement in a foundation will inevitably be transferred to the wall above, usually causing damage. Foundation depths vary considerably according to the ground type and the wall being supported. Except for the very lowest wall, say 750 mm (2 ft 6 in) or less, expert advice should always be sought.

A foundation dug in clay soil, which shrinks in drought and heaves in wet conditions, for example, may have to be deeper than the height of the wall above ground, while foundations in a hard, gravelly soil, to carry the same wall, would be far more shallow. There are two basic foundation types used for garden walls: raft foundations, which carry an entire structure, and strip foundations, which carry only the walls of the structure. Foundations are normally made from concrete, but for a dry-stone wall they are formed by large blocks of stone and called footings.

Walls made to last

No matter what material they are constructed from, the walls that will last longest are those that resist moisture penetration from above and below, as damp walls are susceptible to frost damage. Copings on top and damp-proof courses (DPC) below help to prevent this.

In garden design, two basic wall types need to be considered: "free-standing" and "retaining" walls. A third type, "load bearing", unless for the very simplest structure, such as a low greenhouse supporting wall, must be designed by an architect, as indeed does any type of wall over 750 mm (2 ft 6 in) high. If abutting a public path, the permitted height is even lower. Local authority regulations should be consulted for constructions in this kind of site.

Free-standing walls

These are independent structures, typified by boundary walls, and must be of good stable proportion in terms of the ratio of height to thickness and length. Without additional support, free-standing walls should be constructed with an approximate thickness to height ratio of not less than 1:8, but with the support of piers equivalent to at least the wall thickness again, this ratio can be as low as 1:12. The spacing of piers depends on the wall's thickness and height as well as its aspect, but the rule of thumb is that the width between piers should be equivalent to three times the height of the wall. Vertical thermal movement joints are recommended at intervals not exceeding 12 m (39 ft) and not exceeding 6m (20 ft) from a corner.

Retaining walls

Retaining walls are designed differently as pressure will be exerted from one side. This means that the foundations must be deeper and wider than for other types of wall; there must also be free drainage at the rear of the wall and a low centre of gravity. Retaining walls work on a thickness to height ratio of 1:3. Never cultivate deeply at the front of an existing retaining wall, as this can remove ground support from its foundation, and the wall may start to move.

Brick walls

There are so many different types of brick that practically any effect can be achieved. Second-hand bricks are popular, especially where they produce an aged appearance, but new bricks have their place too. Check with the manufacturer or supplier that the bricks are frost-hardy before using them in a garden.

Bricks have an affinity with gardens that few other materials can match. Traditionally, bricks were used where stone did not occur locally but bricks can be just as characteristic of an area as indigenous stone can, so bear this in mind when selecting brick colour and texture. Constructed elements will look far more harmonious if the brick used is in keeping with nearby architecture.

Major brick bonds

The "bonds", or brick-laying patterns, used for walls make an important contribution to the look of the garden, just as they do when used for paths and paving (see Horizontal surfaces: Paving, page 114). The bonds are shown in the following examples with different coping or capping arrangements, but these are interchangeable. A common brick is shown (below left) with its parts named, as some brick bonds take their name from them. Some bricks have frogs, others do not.

Stretcher bond (below) This is the commonest bond, but in its simplest form it produces a wall of only 100 mm (4 in) thick, which is not stable over 900 mm (3 ft) high. Above this height, the wall would require additional support, from piers, for example. Each stretcher centrally bridges the joint above and below. This example has a "cock and hen" finish at the top.

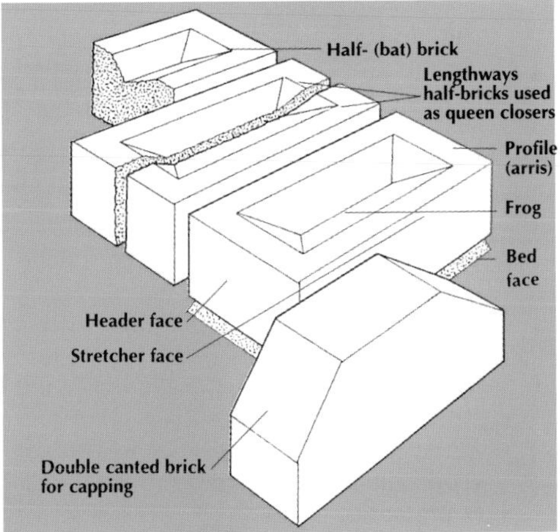

Anatomy of a brick

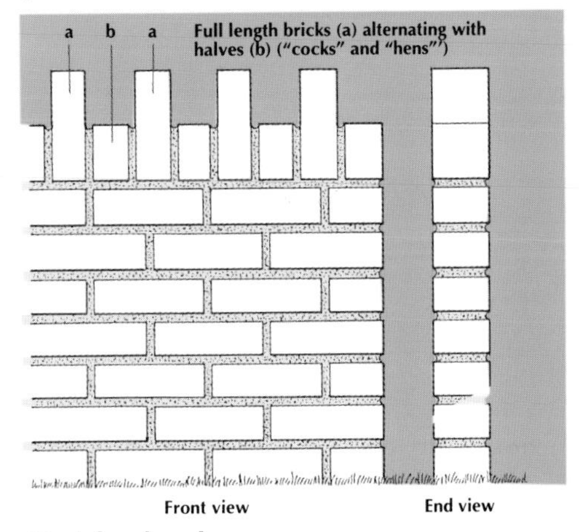

Stretcher bond

Brick walls 2

Flemish bond This is one of the most attractive bonds and comprises a stretcher alternating with a header in each course, or row. The header is positioned at the centre of the stretchers below and above. The "queen closer", a longitudinal half-brick (see page 127), pushes the alternating bricks along at every other course to make the bond work in respect of the staggered arrangement of vertical joints. A reconstituted stone coping with a waterproofing tile course beneath finishes the wall in the example below.

Header bond This is useful for negotiating curves as well as being an attractive bond. In the example below the wall is finished with "bull-nosed" capping bricks which are impervious to water and help to keep the wall dry while contributing to its appearance. A brick of a different colour from that in the wall can be used.

Flemish garden bond This has one header brick between three or sometimes five stretchers in each course. These arrangements are positioned centrally over those in the courses above and below. In the example below a decorative tile coping is provided at the top, and at the bottom, a double tile course also acts as a damp-proof course. Header bond is similar to stretcher bond except that the bricks are laid in the opposite direction and the brick headers rather than the stretcher faces are seen.

English bond This is the strongest bond and comprises courses of cross-headers alternating with stretchers placed side by side. It is used where strength is more important than appearance. Canted bricks (see page 127) laid on edge cap the wall in this example. As normal-sized bricks used at the end are easily damaged or dislodged, canted end blocks are used. These are similar to the other bricks but larger.

English garden bond Here the stretcher courses do not alternate with the header course. Instead there are three courses of staggered stretcher

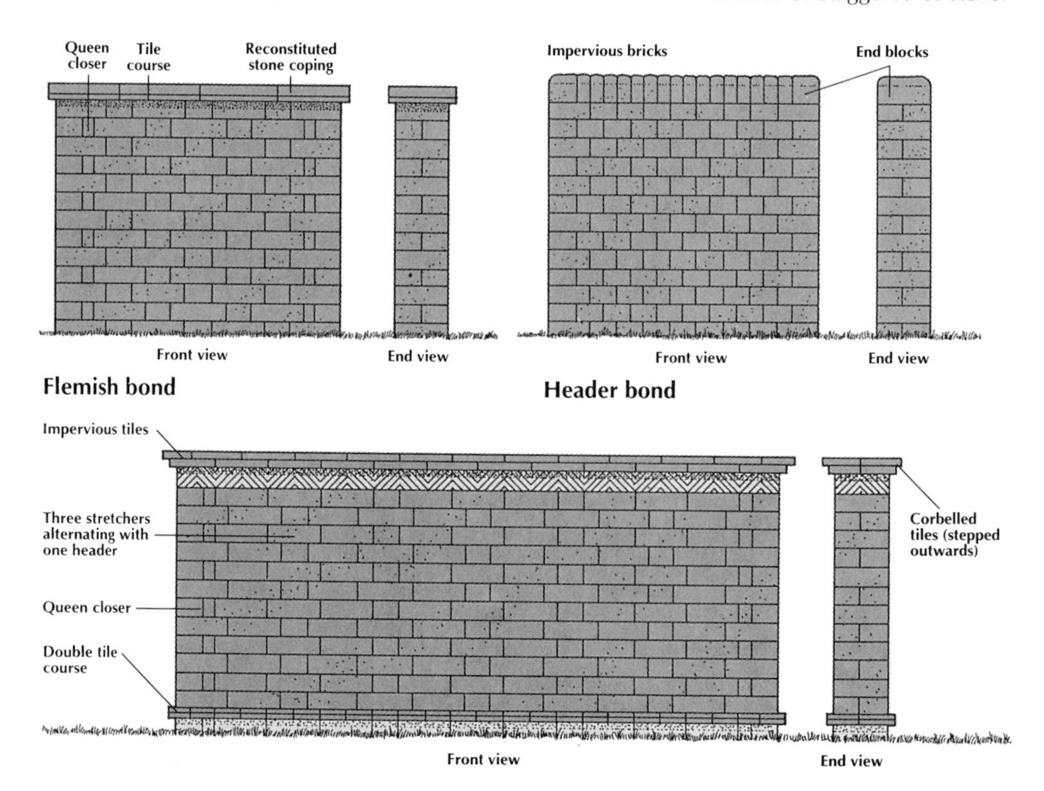

Flemish bond

Header bond

Flemish garden bond

courses to every one of headers. In effect, the header courses "tie" the stretcher courses together. Bricks laid on edge cap this wall but as the end bricks are easily dislodged, decorative metal "cramps" are mortared in, one at each end, to hold them in place.

Pointing and jointing

Mortar is used for both jointing and pointing. Jointing is a technique used to finish the mortar as the building work proceeds, while pointing is carried out as a separate job usually after the main construction is complete.

The mortar colour has a bearing on the appearance of a wall so, if a special colour or expensive mortar is required, for example, consult colour charts rather than leaving the shade to chance.

Flush This describes mortar cut to coincide with the face of the wall, resulting in a smooth-textured finish. It is useful if the wall occupies an exposed position as it keeps wind-blown rain from penetrating.

Once weathered In this style the joint mortar is pushed back at an angle with a small trowel, creating a series of strong horizontal shadow lines in a wall. "Once weathering" the horizontal joints and "flush jointing" the perpendicular joints exaggerates the horizontal shadow lines.

Bucket handle This name derives from the fact that a bent galvanized bucket handle used to be used to impress the mortar joint. This finish emphasizes each brick in the wall just sufficiently to create a series of gentle shadow lines.

Keyed This finish emphasizes each individual brick in the wall, or of the horizontal joints if the vertical joints are flush. Walls can be made to look longer by this means.

Square recessed This dramatic joint finish is not suitable for exposed sites. Rainwater can gather on the joint edges and is then driven by the wind into the wall's interior.

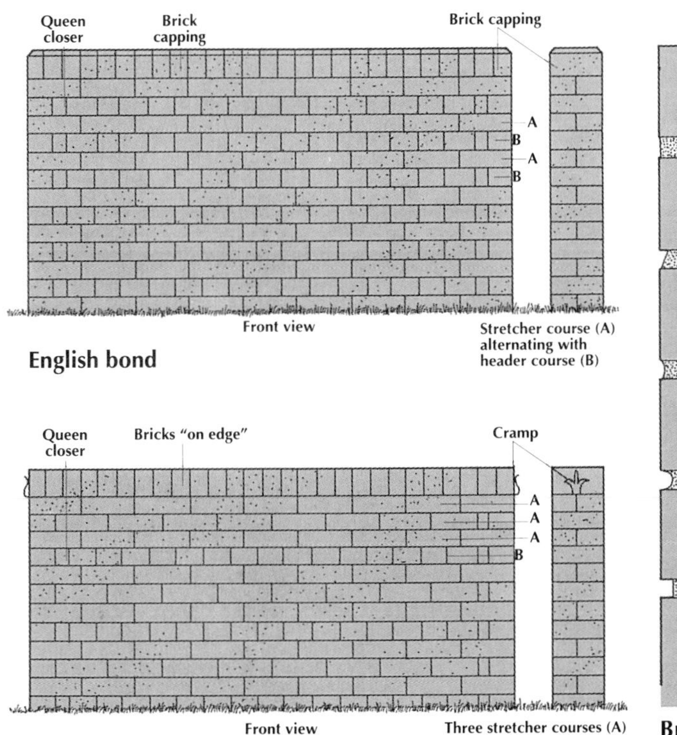

English bond

English garden bond

Flush

Once weathered

Bucket handle

Keyed

Square recessed

Brickwork mortar jointing (pointing) finishes (sectional views)

Stone walls

Random rubble (uncoursed)

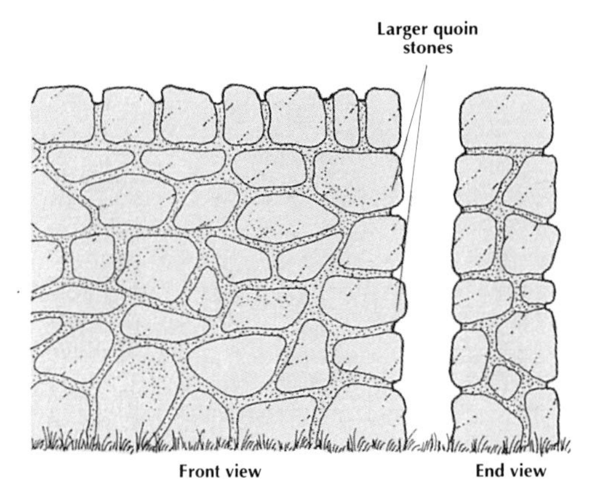

Random rubble (uncoursed) with thin stone

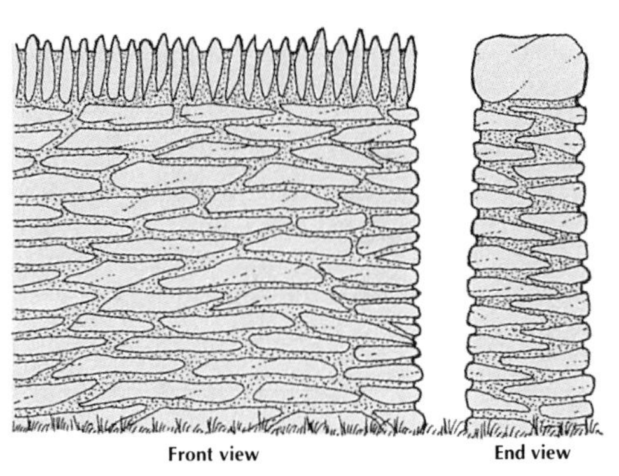

Random rubble brought to course

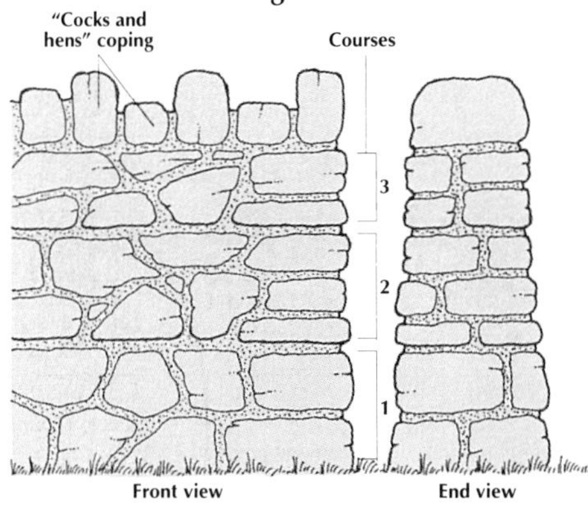

Random squared rubble uncoursed

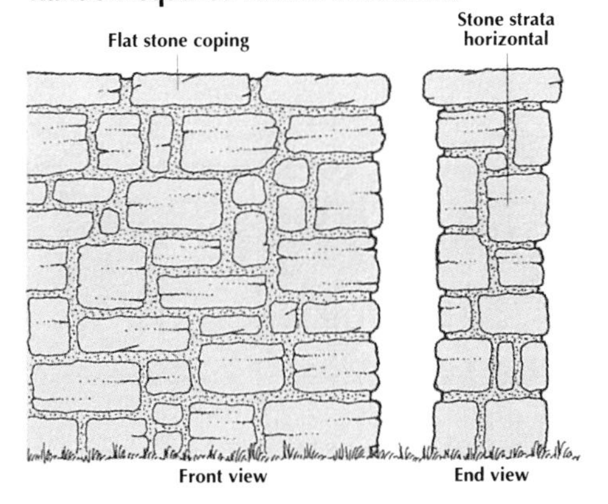

Stone (or rubble) walls also conform to traditional patterns or bonds which have developed for reasons of strength and appearance. Many traditional bonds have arisen from the use of a local stone, the way it was cut and shaped in combination with its inherent characteristics. For example, sedimentary rocks originate from compacted sand, clay and shells and should be placed in a wall "on bed", that is, in the same plane as that in which they were originally laid down. Laying them down on end, so exposing the compacted strata to the elements, can lead to weakness through the stone's delamination.

Stone bonds can be used to achieve many different effects, ranging from the rustic and naturalistic to the sophisticated, according to circumstances and the desired effect.

Stone bonds

Random rubble uncoursed The stone is of random shape and size, mortared together in a random way. The perpendicular joints are irregularly interrupted. Large quoin or corner stones are needed for stability if the stones used in the main body are small. A random stone coping is used to finish the wall in the example (top left). A variation of random rubble uncoursed is possible when thin stone is available.

Random rubble brought to course In this bond the stone is brought to a common level before the next band is built over it, and so on up through the wall. The bands are the courses. The choice of coping for this wall is known as "cocks and hens", which is a sequence of alternating tall and short stones.

Squared rubble brought to course

Courses
Sawn stone cope stone
Soil
3
2
1
Front view
Piped weep hole
End view
Reinforcement tied to foundation
Drainage material

Regular coursed square rubble

Differing course depths but each stone of equal depth within
Front view
End view

Cut and dressed regular stone blocks

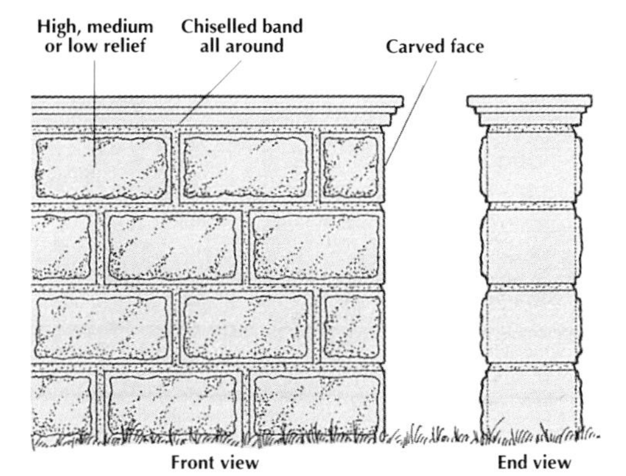

Random snapped flint

Soldier brick capping
Bonder
Tile (DPC) covers
Front view
Brick quoin
Tile course
End view

Random squared rubble uncoursed The stones are cut to blocks with a square or rectangular section. Stones can be precisely or approximately cut. Projecting flat stones are used for coping in this example. The strata of the stone is laid "on bed" as it was in the rock plane.

Squared rubble brought to course In this more sophisticated style the stones are sawn or cut to blocks with a square or rectangular section. The example (top) has a sawn, angled-topped coping. In a retaining wall, the backward slope at the front is known as a "batter". Drainage material at the rear is placed on top of drainpipes set in the wall's base, known as "weep holes". Waterproofing (tanking) is applied to prevent the wall from becoming damp and mossy. Reinforcement passes up through the centre of the wall from the foundations, usually by means of metal rods set in the foundation.

Regular coursed square rubble This bond is often recreated with reconstituted stone. Each stone is of a different length but a similar depth within each course, although the depth of the courses can be variable. The capping is of a regular coursed stone.

Cut and dressed regular stone blocks These blocks are of uniform size and laid in the same way as brick stretcher bond. Each block has a chiselled "frame" within which is a convex tooled finished area, usually worked to look like stone in high, medium or low relief, depending on the amount by which the tooled convex area projects beyond the "frame". A finely cut, moulded coping completes the wall.

Stone walls 2

Types of flint

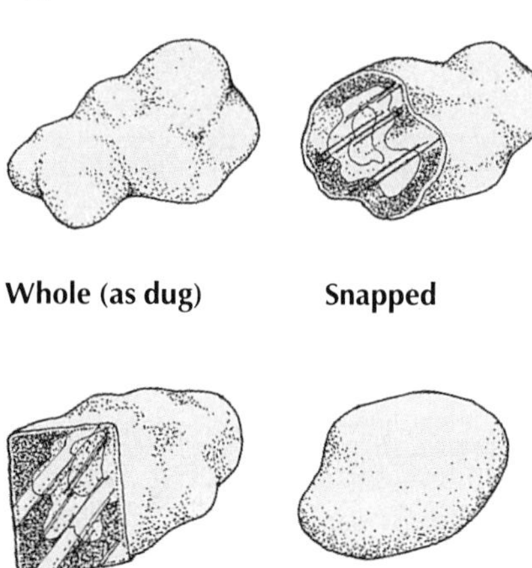

Common mortar joint finishes for stone wall

Flush

Over-pointed

Brushed or rubbed

Recessed

Snail trail

Bird beak

Detail of snail trail

Flint Flints are one of the most attractive of all the wall stones. Because of their usually small size they are associated with other materials, such as stone and brick quoins (corners), to make a stable and strong wall. Where only very small flints are available, "bonders" or "tie" stones are required to bond or tie the front of the flint wall to the back.

The illustration on page 131 shows a random snapped flint wall on a base wall with toothed quoins and a capping of brick. Tiles run beneath the brick caps and at the base of the wall is a damp-proof course (DPC). Brick bonders can be seen at the wall face.

Flints for wall building are used in different forms and bonds:

Whole flint These are as dug from the ground.

Snapped The dug flint has been snapped in half to reveal its glass-like interior.

Knapped Snapped flints cut to blocks with a square or rectangular section, now usually used for repair work only.

Water worn Whole flints worn smooth by river water or tides.

Stucco or render Stucco or colour-washed sand and cement render, often textured, is an attractive and economical method of finishing the sides of a wall. The supporting base and wall may be constructed of stone while the interior is of concrete block. The render usually oversails a base wall so that rainwater is discharged efficiently and coincides with a damp-proof course to reduce the risk of rising damp and subsequent frost damage to the render.

Mortar jointing and pointing

The stone wall types mentioned above are "mortar" bonded. As with brick walls, the mortar joints are finished off according to the wall's function and with regard to aesthetic considerations. Wall mortar joints are sometimes wider than brick joints but this depends upon the size of the stones used.

Flush In this style, the mortar joint finishes flat with the wall face.

Over-pointed With some stones it is difficult to achieve joints of an even thickness; over-pointing is then sometimes applied to cover the edges of the stones. This not only gives a rustic

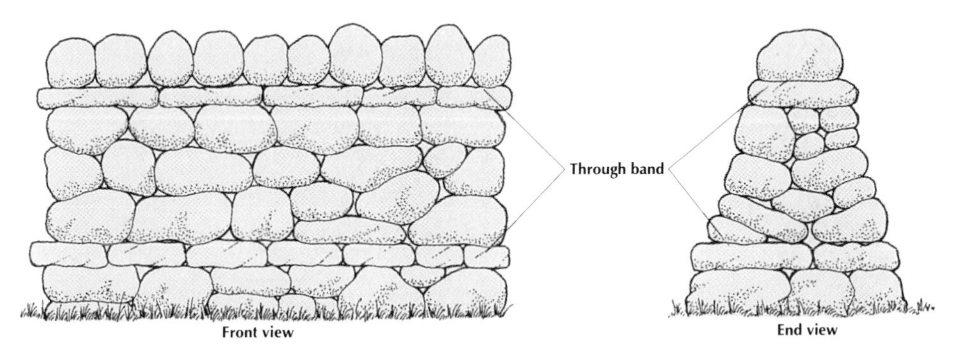

A traditional dry-stone wall, indigenous to the north of England, with projecting "through bands" and battered (sloping) sides. The sloping stones press inward and downward for greater stability and a low centre of gravity. Southern versions have "bonders", not through bands.

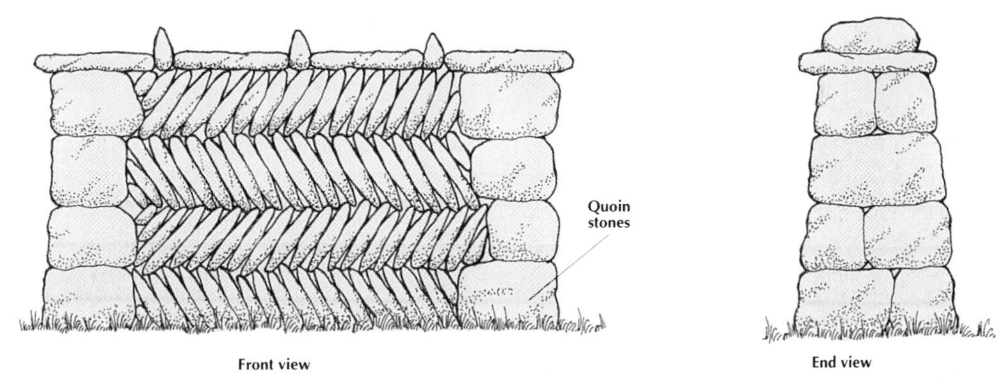

Dry thin stone walls use a vertical herringbone pattern. Large quoin stones at each end make the wall stable and flat coping stones help keep the rain out of the natural strata of the stones.

finish but is useful for making strongly stratified rocks more waterproof at the edges.

Brushed or rubbed This is possibly the most common finish. The mortar joint is, on completion, lightly brushed or rubbed back with sacking so that each stone is gently defined.

Recessed Using a pebble, a piece of hose or metal rod, the mortar joint is deeply impressed to emphasize each stone in the wall, creating a dramatic effect suitable for informal situations.

Snail trail Pointed mortar joints are smoothed over, then the mortar is scraped back from marked parallel joint lines. The smooth, precise shaping of the perceived joints resembles a snail's trail. This method is used to create an impression of carefully cut stone and accurate joints when ordinary rough random stone has been used. It is effective only when the mortar colour and texture resemble that of the stone.

Bird beak Also known as "twice weathered", this joint makes a feature of the mortar by working it with a trowel into a peak, following the routes of the joints.

Dry-stone walls

Dry-stone walls, originally a feature of farmland, are a favourite with garden makers. As the name implies, no mortar is used to bind the stones, merely the skill of the mason making each stone fit and hold together by the weight of the stones above.

Dry-stone walls differ in appearance and, to some degree, construction technique according to location and the local stone available. A trench is dug and larger stones are positioned at the base to act as a footing.

Changes of level

When level changes occur in the garden it is essential that the transition can be made from one level to another as easily and comfortably as possible.

The best way of achieving this is to construct steps or ramps.

Steps

Steps offer the most efficient way of changing levels. Besides being functional, they can make a significant contribution to the appearance of a garden, to the extent that they are frequently used as major focal points.

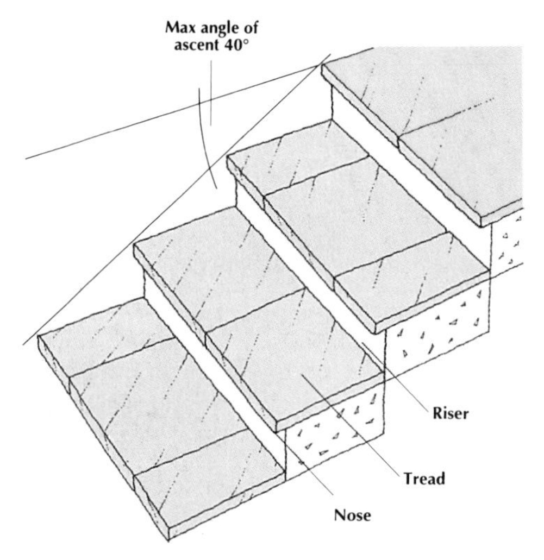

The angle of ascent should not exceed 40 degrees in a garden. The "nose" is the upper and outermost front edge corner of a tread.

Steps set within the lower area. Material used here matches the adjacent wall. Such steps need a handrail or wall at each side.

Curving steps are always intriguing. These are made of treated logs and consolidated gravel and are suitable for a woodland setting.

Multi-directional or zig-zag steps are useful for overcoming steep slopes in comparatively small spaces.

Steps should be in proportion with, and the same width as, any associated paths. They should be planned to be in proportion with the particular wall or slope with which they are associated and also with the garden itself. When too small they will appear mean or insignificant; when too large they can easily look pretentious.

Proportions for steps

A golden rule when designing steps is that every riser (the vertical plane) and every tread (the

These brick and reconstituted stone steps are half-in and half-out of the slope, making use of the space at both top and bottom.

Stone steps are the ideal choice for a rock garden or informal setting. These are entirely contained within the slope.

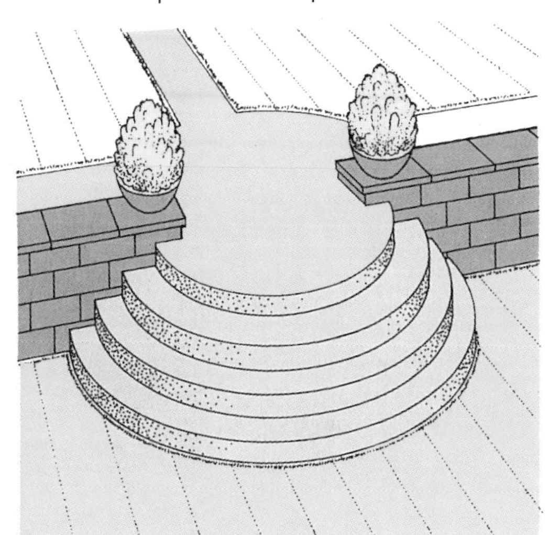

Semi-circular steps are one of the most popular styles. They are excellent for announcing a view from the top.

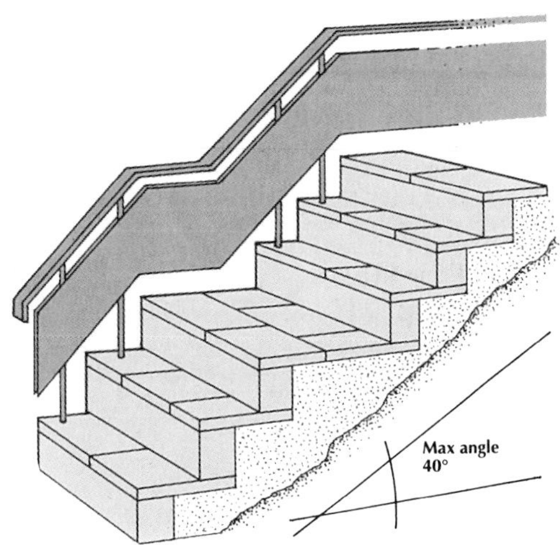

Offsetting the joints of paving used to form the treads of steps helps to avoid unsatisfactory continuous joint lines.

Changes of level 2

horizontal plane) should be consistently proportioned in the same flight. Where steps are created from natural materials such as rock or logs it can take some effort to achieve this, but an uncomfortable, even dangerous, ascent or descent will result if the steps are not as regular as possible.

About every 10 or 12 steps, there should be a landing to allow a short respite and the size of the landing should be a multiple of the size of the tread, front to back, again to allow smooth and safe progress.

There is a recognized relationship between the size of the riser and that of the tread: the deeper the tread, the shallower the riser should be. Garden steps tend to have deeper treads and shallower risers than their domestic counterparts, so they are less steep.

For reasons of safety, the risers of garden steps should not be less than 100 mm (4 in) or more than 200 mm (8 in). The table below gives a range of dimensions for well proportioned steps. Their precise size and style, however, ultimately depends upon the height to be achieved and the space available.

Riser (top–bottom)		**Tread** (back–front)	
180 mm	(7 in)	280 mm	(11 in)
165 mm	(6½ in)	330 mm	(13 in)
150 mm	(6 in)	380 mm	(15 in)
140 mm	(5 in)	410 mm	(16 in)
130 mm	(5½ in)	430 mm	(17 in)
115 mm	(4½ in)	450 mm	(18 in)
100 mm	(4 in)	475 mm	(19 in)

Calculating step sizes

Low risers and deep treads generally appear more elegant, especially when the steps are broad from side to side. On the other hand-high risers and shallow treads look more purposeful.

Calculate step dimensions by comparing the horizontal space requirement and availability with a simple cross-section showing the height to be overcome. This will help to determine the correct riser-to-tread ratio. The amount of space available at the top or bottom of a proposed flight of steps helps to determine their position and form.

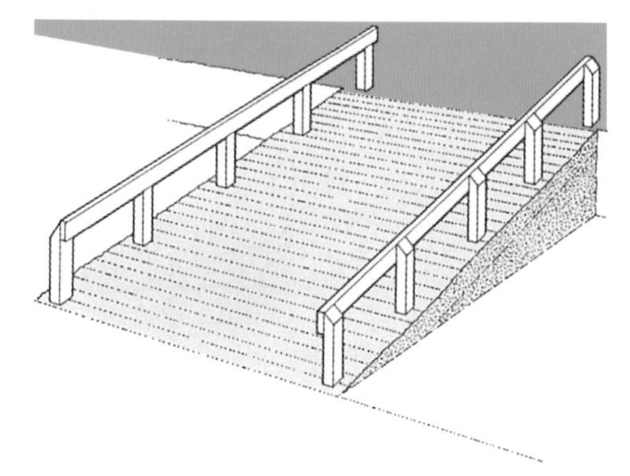

An example of a 1:15 gradient ramp, useful for general purposes, such as moving wheelbarrows or lawn-mowers and where space is limited. A handrail makes the ramp safer to use. The textured surface provides a good grip for shoes and wheels.

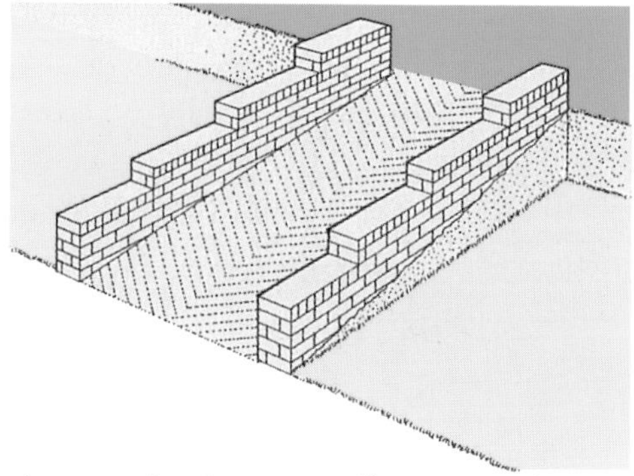

An example of a 1:20 gradient ramp. The shallower slope makes it more suitable for moving "ride on" machinery. The surface is best made with tamped concrete or bricks laid in a chevron pattern, which also assists in shedding rainwater quickly.

A curving ramp with safety walls showing how the gradient increases at the inside edge of the curves. Deeply jointed diagonal paving provides a non-slip surface, as would bricks laid in a herringbone pattern.

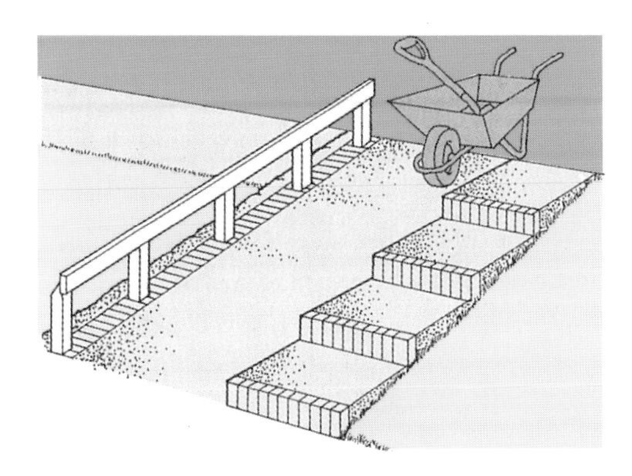

Where a garden ramp is needed, perhaps to and from the vegetable garden, this might be combined with steps as illustrated. For pedestrians only, steps are usually more comfortable to negotiate than a ramp. Ramps should always have some protective device at the sides. In this example a low rail has been positioned on one side and steps on the other.

Ramps

Ramps are preferable to steps in sloping gardens where wheeled equipment is used. There is a limit to the gradient of a ramp beyond which it may become difficult to negotiate.

For general gardening purposes 1:15 is regarded as the maximum gradient. Where wheelchairs, pushchairs and certain "ride on" equipment is concerned, a gradient of no less than 1:20 is recommended for safety and ease of use.

The space required to achieve comfortable gradients should be worked out at the planning stage, when the available area and the height involved can be considered together. When space is limited, curved ramps might provide a solution but be aware that a gradient varies across the curve and is steepest at the inside edge, so make sure that the maximum gradient limit is imposed at this point rather than at the outside edge.

Ramp construction

Ramps are normally laid *in situ* with concrete, paving stone, or bricks. Where paving stones and, especially, bricks are concerned, it is better to mortar them in over a concrete base. Many bricks are now manufactured to be "dry laid" (butt-jointed on a bed of sand), but on ramps some slippage can occur due to the downward pressures of wheels and pedestrian traffic. This problem can be exacerbated by heavy rainfall penetrating the butted joints and washing the bedding sand away.

Ramps and safety

Ramps can be surfaced with the same material as adjacent paths and other surfaces but it is more important that they provide a secure grip both for wheels and footwear. For this reason, avoid smooth surfaces as they are potentially dangerous in wet or icy conditions. Loose gravels are not suitable as gravel tends to migrate downward with use and the steeper the slope, the more quickly this happens. Permanent surfacing, such as brick, stone or concrete, is therefore best.

When making a ramp with concrete or brick surfacing, tamp the concrete down or lay the bricks to form downward-pointing chevrons. This provides a grip for shoes and wheels and encourages rainwater to drain off.

Trellis

Trellis is used to provide structure, decoration and support for plants – often all three. It has played an important role in gardens for hundreds of years. Trellis patterns and styles vary enormously. Standard panels are widely available, but the more ornate trellises call for specialized manufacturing techniques. Trellis panels can be used individually or as part of a series to form larger garden structures.

Wood, often pine, is the main material used for trellis work but occasionally metal and hard plastics are used. Softwoods must be treated or painted with a non-toxic preservative to make the trellis weatherproof, but hardwoods do not have to be treated in this way.

Standard square trellis This is often fixed to a wall as a plant support; if free-standing, it is supported at each end by posts. It is versatile and can blend in well, but look out for architectural clashes. The sizes of the slats and apertures vary according to quality and design.

Diamond trellis Diamond trellis is a favourite with garden designers. The diamonds can be achieved either by rotating square trellis units through 45 degrees or by altering the angle of the battens to make true diamonds. If it is to be stable and long-lived, diamond trellis must be framed and capped.

Decorative trellis arches These can be purchased from specialist manufacturers and painted or stained to link them with the colour of other timber features in the garden. They make excellent supports for climbing plants and add a romantic touch to a garden.

Heavy trellis When privacy is required without a sense of total enclosure, heavy trellis could be the answer. In the example shown, the trellis is set at the top of a wall. A wall used for this purpose would need to be thicker than usual to accommodate the supporting posts; or, preferably, the posts can be set into the ground immediately against the wall on the inside of the garden.

Trellis with different sized slats The slats or battens making up the trellis need not all be the same width. Attractive effects can be achieved by using different size slats, perhaps set horizontally, diagonally or in combination. The simple example shown here has slats running vertically and horizontally but it includes a larger diamond within the gable top.

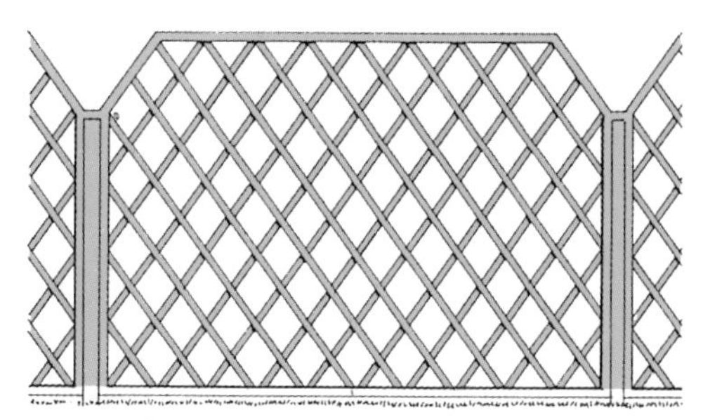

Diamond trellis

Arched trellis

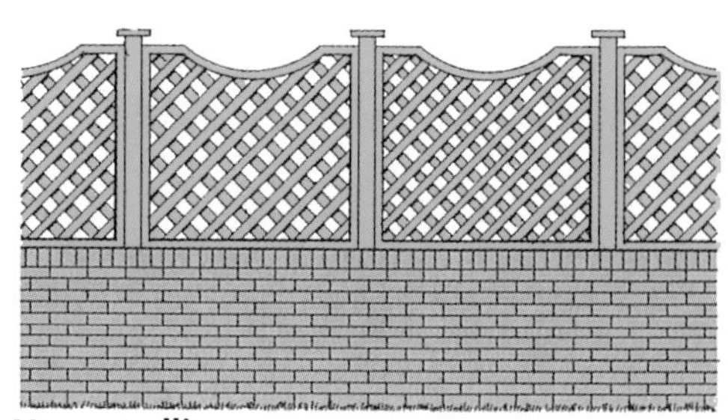

Heavy trellis

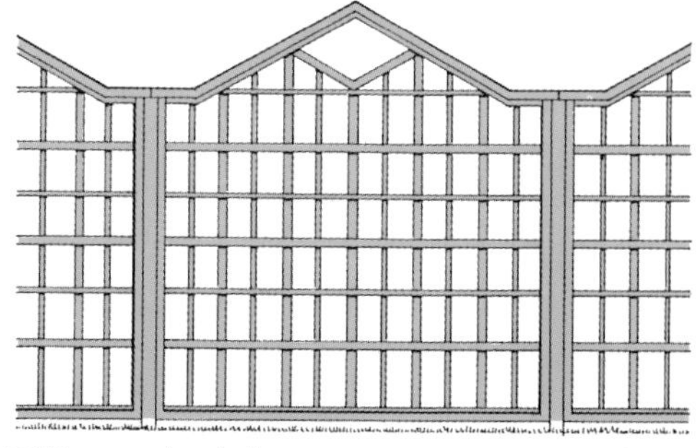

Different sized slats

Fences

Fences can be used for various purposes: as a means of enclosure or demarcation, to protect the plot against trespassers or livestock, as a shelter from wind and rain; or as a screen to increase privacy. These practical applications do not, however, mean that fences have to be utilitarian in appearance: there are ways of making them an integral part of the design.

Post and rail fence (split timber)

Materials

Fences are usually made of timber but concrete, metal, wire and plastic are among the many alternatives. Styles vary considerably according to the materials used and the function the fence has to perform.

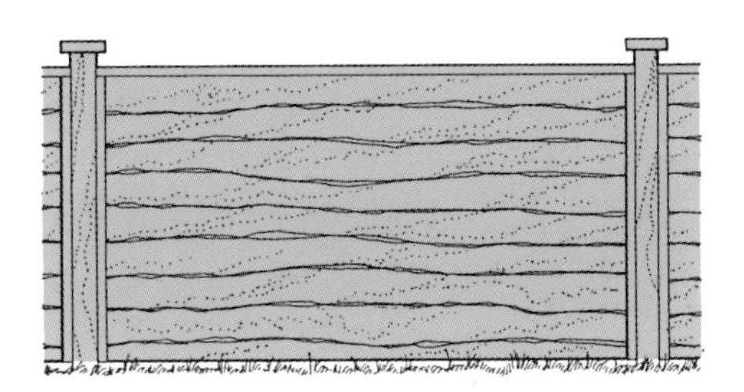

Overlap panel fence with "waney edge"

Wood fencing

Post and rail fence In rural areas where fences need to be stock-proof rather than decorative or screening, post and rail fences provide a popular solution. There are two basic types: sawn timber and split timber. Treated softwoods make up most of the sawn types, while untreated oak and chestnut are used for splitting and look attractively rustic.

Panel fences Most fences used in town and suburban gardens are the panelled types comprising wooden slats fixed together horizontally and framed. Available in many sizes, they need to be supported with posts which are either cut from wood or manufactured from concrete. While concrete posts are the less attractive they are more durable, although pressure-treated wooden posts set in spiked metal sockets driven into the ground are a good alternative.

The two basic panel fence types are interwoven and overlap. When the lower edges of the overlapping slats are naturally undulating, the style is known as "waney edge".

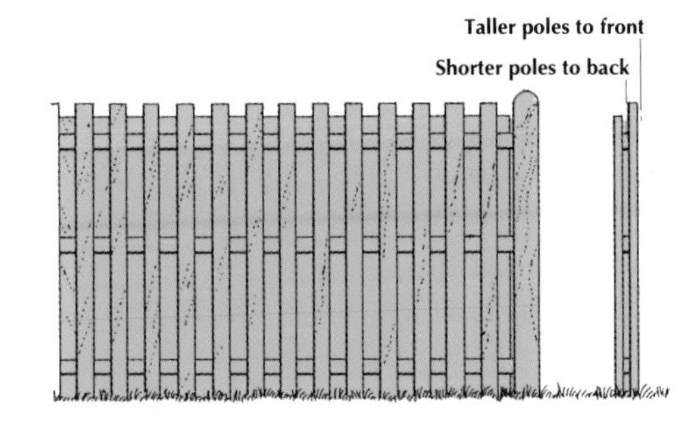

Hit and miss "palisade" fence

Hit and miss "palisade" fence This is made up of poles split in half lengthways and nailed to horizontal rails in a staggered pattern, providing complete privacy yet allowing the wind to filter through: important if wind-damage is to be avoided on the lee side (see page 92).

Close-board fencing This is one of the most expensive types of fence but it is also the most effective in terms of screening and strength. The best close-board fences are made entirely from hardwoods such as oak, which weathers gracefully to a soft grey colour. The capping and the gravel board at the bottom resist water

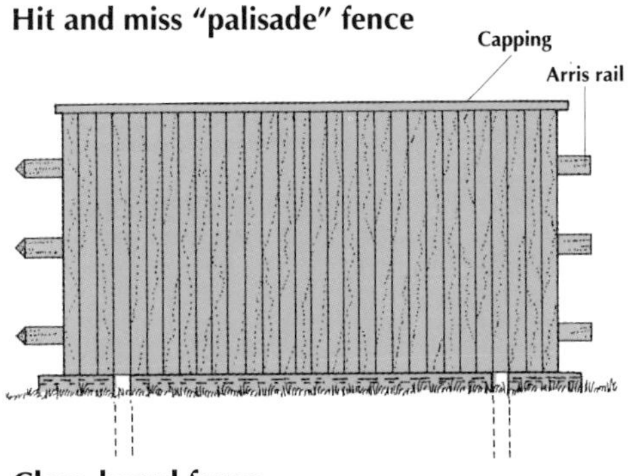

Close-board fence

Fences 2

penetration but can be detached and replaced if necessary without affecting the main fence. An attractive series of vertical shadow lines characterize this style.

In the overlap type, the boards are "feathered", which means that they are narrower at one side than the other.

Chestnut paling This fence type belongs in an informal setting. Made from split chestnut branches and bound vertically by two or three horizontal twisted wire strands, it makes a perfect temporary fence as it can be rolled up and stored when not in use. It can also be erected as a permanent feature and makes an excellent host for climbing plants.

Split hazel (wattle) or willow (osier) fences These are panels of basket work, available in a range of sizes and unsurpassed in the garden for an instant rustic look or for supporting plants. They are also used in open situations where a more solid fence could blow down in high winds. Wattle hurdle in particular weathers very quickly, becoming unobtrusive in a matter of weeks.

Picket fence What could be more delightful than a rose- or clematis-clad picket fence? It can become an attractive feature in its own right, evocative of the cottage garden idyll. A picket fence can either be painted or left untreated in its natural state. There are many forms, ranging from the simple flat-topped version to the highly decorated. The examples shown here (middle right) have half-round and pointed finishes.

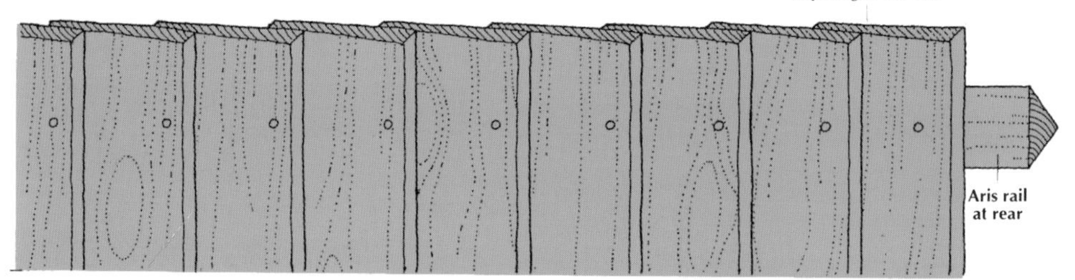

Close boards "feathered" and overlapped

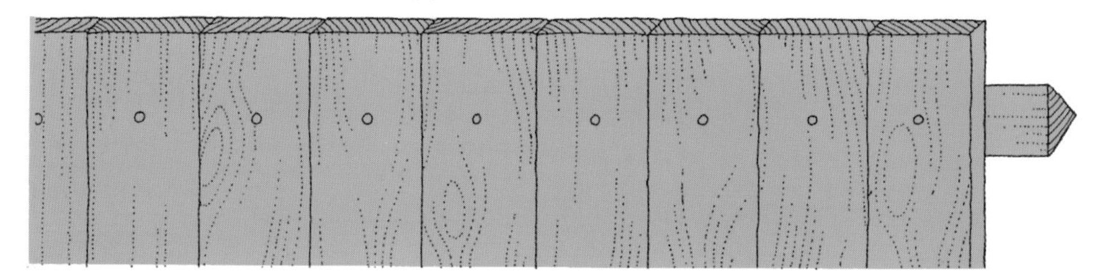

Close boards straight and butted

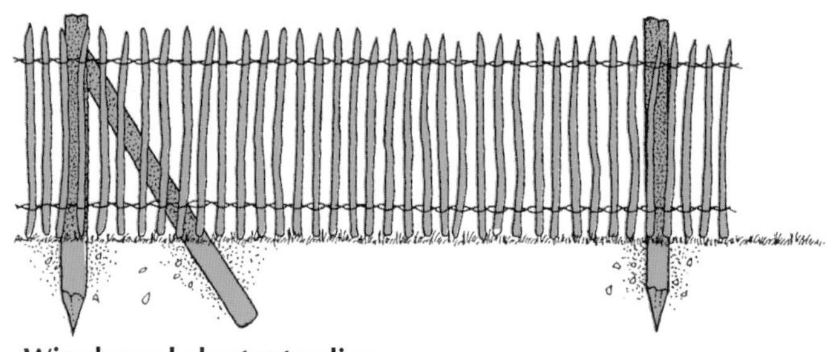

Wire-bound chestnut paling

Detail

Metal fencing

Vertical bar fencing: "unclimbable" fence This is made of vertical round iron bars, looped at the top and held together with rails in rectangular sections. Usually associated with country gardens, this is a long-lasting alternative and it is usually painted.

Railings These are normally associated with town front gardens and were traditionally made of vertical iron bars with cast-iron finials or arrowheads. Railings are now manufactured in less expensive aluminium alloys and are available in a wide range of patterns. They are often painted in traditional colours such as black, white or dark green.

Continuous bar fencing (estate fencing) This is a traditional means of enclosing fields or estates. The fence is made of horizontal wrought-iron straps and round vertical bars. It is still available, but it is expensive.

Chain-link fence This is generally accepted as the least attractive type of metal fencing but it is functional. Black or dark plastic-coated types blend into the background shadows of plants and shrubs, making them less obtrusive. Chain-link fencing makes a good impenetrable core for hedges with staggered planting at each side. Eventually the fence itself is lost from sight as the hedging plants grow up to conceal it. Sinking the chain link into the ground 450 mm (18 in) or so makes it rabbit-proof, too. Chain-link fencing is available in sizes ranging from 1m (3 ft 3 in) to 4.5 m (14 ft 6 in) in height; the latter is often used for tennis court surrounds.

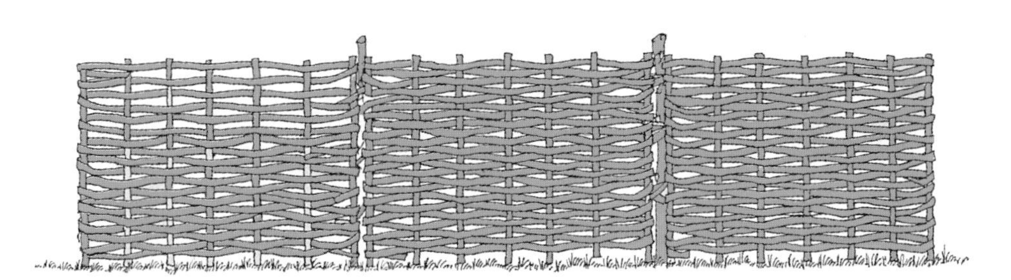

Split hazel (wattle) or willow (osier) fence

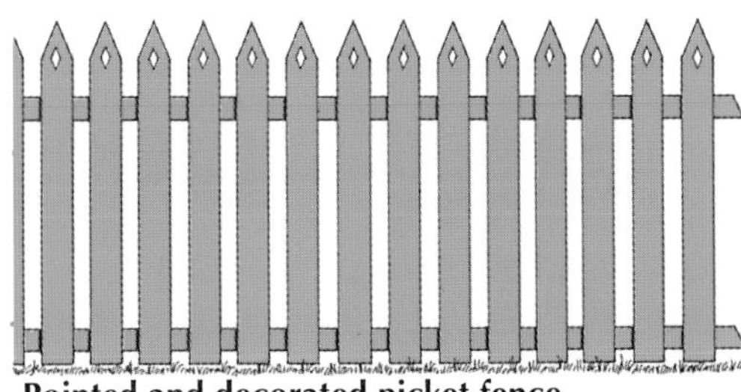

Pointed and decorated picket fence

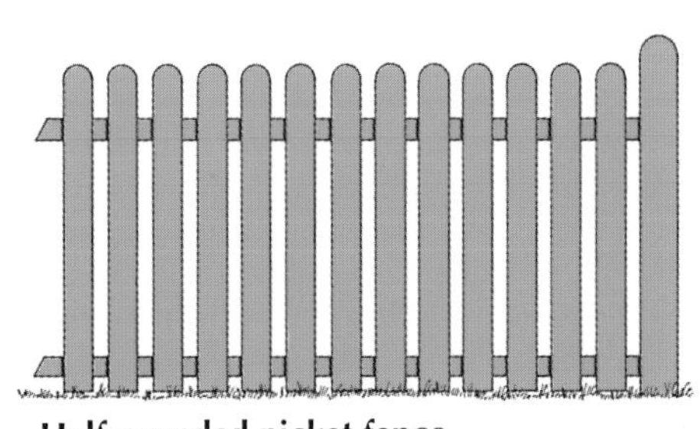

Half-rounded picket fence

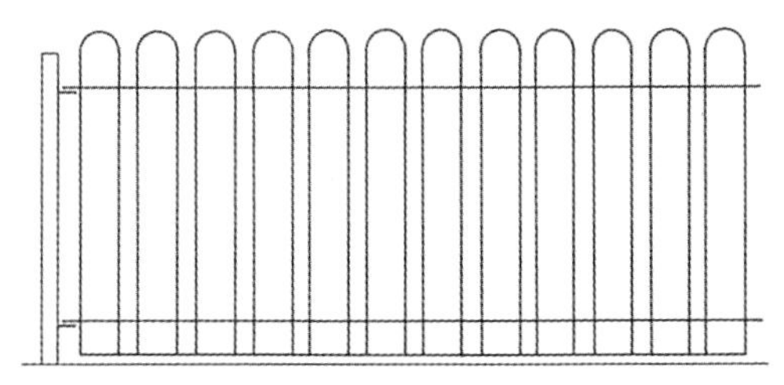

Vertical bar fence

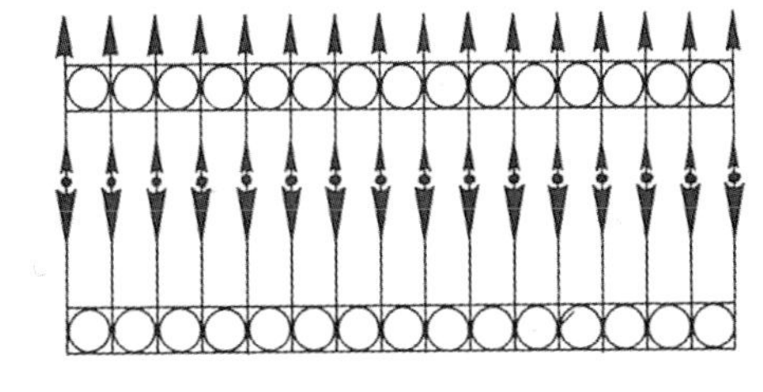

Railings

Trompe l'oeil

The practice of deceiving the eye using *trompe l'oeil* techniques has been elevated to an art form. In garden design it is almost always used to make a garden appear larger.

There are four devices commonly used for this: optical illusion (often involving trellis), mirrors, murals and false perspective.

In this trellis *trompe l'oeil*, the view beyond is partly obscured – in reality, there is very little space. A dark-coloured wall with green ivy climbing up it, for example, gives the impression of distance. Should more space be available behind the trellis, plant grass or lay a light-coloured path with blue-flowering plants to suggest greater distance. Trellis *trompe l'oeil* can be free-standing, as this one is, or it can be fastened to a wall, but a free-standing trellis is best set within a neutral foil, such as a yew hedge.

Mirrors are used to create a sense of space in confined spaces. Provided that they are made of weatherproof toughened glass and are strongly supported, mirror *trompe l'oeil* features can be used in a variety of situations.

In the example shown here, the mirror has been recessed into a moon gate, but it could just as well have been positioned a metre or so beyond the moon gate – on a far wall, perhaps, – thereby allowing hidden access to a path running behind the wall. This ploy makes the garden appear twice its real length, once the reflected image is added to the true distance between the front of the garden and the wall.

False doors or gates are useful for *trompe l'oeil* and give the impression that there is more to the garden than there really is. In the example shown here, four small diamond-shaped mirrors are set into the door, making it appear that there is another garden beyond.

Half-thickness metal gates, which appear to be of normal thickness when reflected, can be used in conjunction with mirrors. The gates, which can be made to look authentic with hinges and latches, should be removable to allow them and the mirror to be cleaned.

Murals can be effective both indoors and out. A previously dismal basement has been transformed in this example by a simple, brightly coloured mural, using exterior quality paint. In conjunction with real potted plants, the illusion, while never entirely convincing, is fun and cheering.

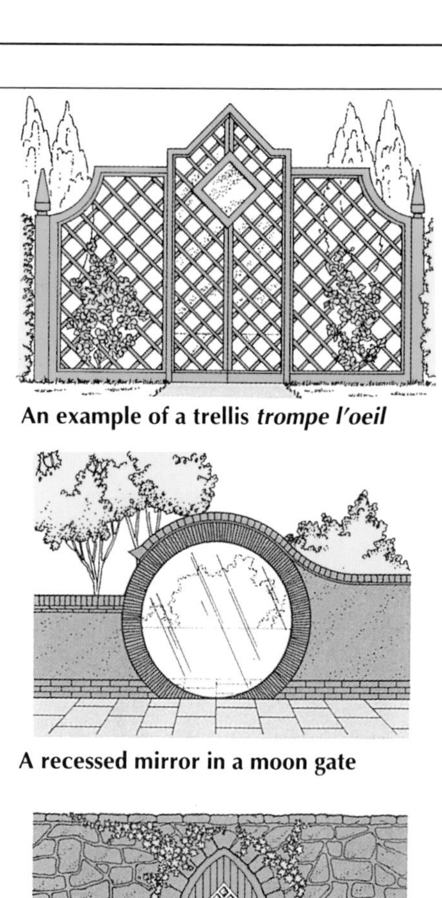

An example of a trellis *trompe l'oeil*

A recessed mirror in a moon gate

A false door

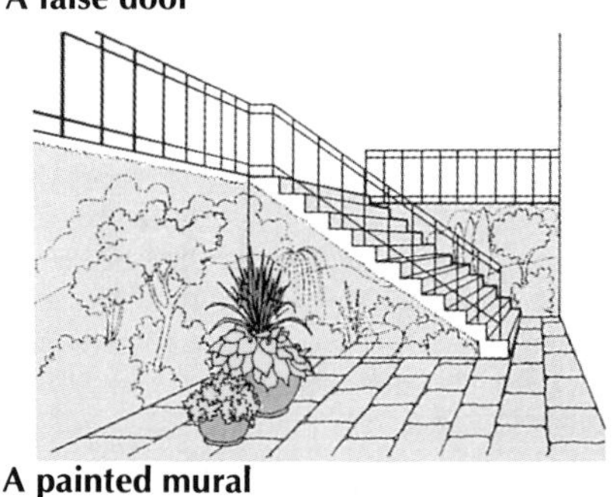

A painted mural

Arches and pergolas

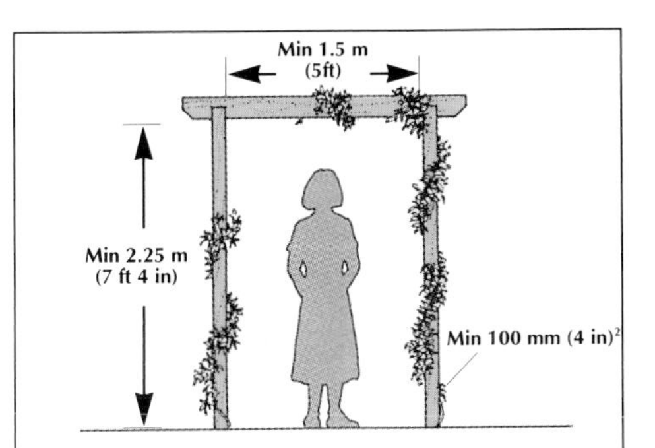

1 A small pergola

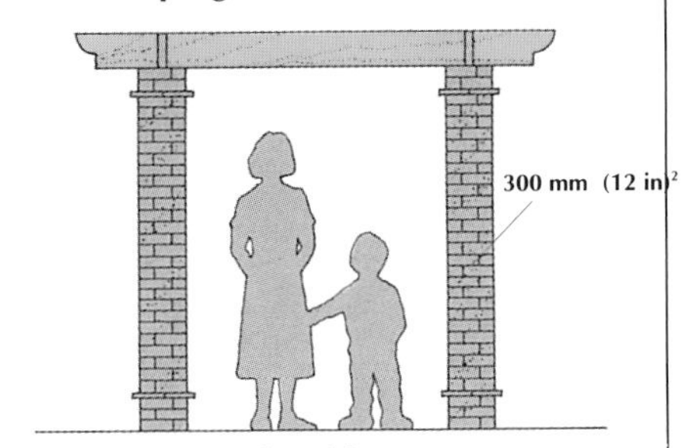

2 A larger pergola with stronger supports

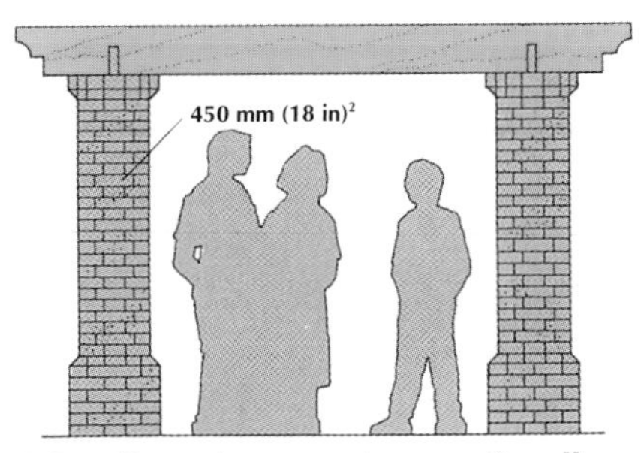

3 Sturdier columns and proportionally sized cross-beams

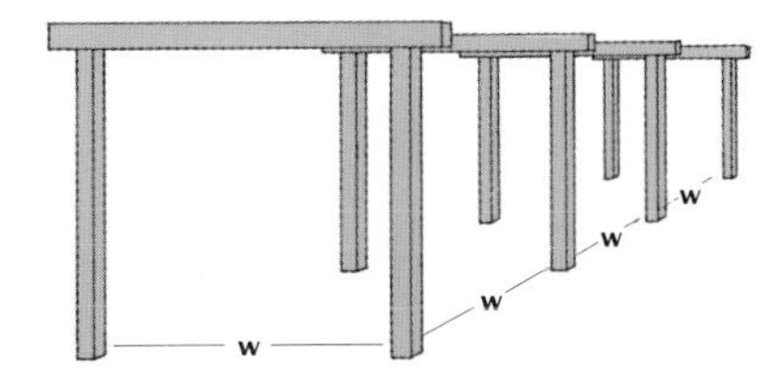

4 Length as a multiple of entrance width

Arches and pergolas are two of the most romantic elements that can be introduced into any garden. They have no real practical application beyond acting as a support for climbing plants, but for those who wish to experience the sheer pleasure of cool dappled shade and summer scents, what could be better?

Pergolas and arches are strongly directional from within and can, sideways on, act as a screen within the garden as a whole.

Structure of pergolas and arches

The vertical supports of pergolas and other similar structures, should always be well founded or set deeply in the ground. It is easy to undercalculate, or simply overlook, the considerable weight that the cross-beams and the plants they support, impose. Add to this the weight of rainwater, or snow and the risks of wind and it is easy to see why the supports must be strong. A pergola without corner braces is a potentially unstable structure.

The columns should also be strong in themselves as, under sufficient sideways pressure, brick or stone can crack, and timber may break. In the case of stone or brick columns, this risk can be greatly reduced by steel reinforcements running from the foundations to the very top of the column. Indeed, it is sometimes allowed to project above, as a means of fixing the bearers, and hidden under the climbing plants.

Proportions for pergolas and arches

The proportions of a pergola or arch are determined by several things. The height should always be adequate for adults to walk without stooping, with sufficient space above to accommodate hanging branches or long flower racemes. The width will be determined partly by the number of people expected to walk through at the same time and the garden space available. The wider the span of the pergola or arch, the stronger and larger the supports should be. The length of arches and pergolas is determined by the amount of available garden space not only in absolute terms but also in relation to the other features you have planned for the garden.

1 A small pergola of a minimum height of 2.25 m (7 ft 4 in) from the ground to the underpart of the cross-beam. The width of the entrance is 1.5 m (5 ft), which is sufficient only

Arches and pergolas 2

for a single individual to pass through, allowing for the outgrowth of plants. The supporting posts are in proportion to the size of the cross-beams and should be about 100 mm (4 in) square or more.

2 This larger structure can accommodate two people walking side by side but requires stronger supports. The main support columns are 300 mm (12 in) square, slightly thicker at the base.

3 In this large pergola, intended for more than two people to walk through at a time, the supporting columns are increased to a width of 450 mm (18 in) square and are thicker at the top and base for reasons of appearance. In each case, the columns are in proportion to the cross-beams.

4 The length of a pergola is often designed to be a multiple of the entrance width. This may not always be possible if there is a finite space in which the pergola is to be fitted lengthways. Under this circumstance, the supports should be spaced evenly over the length of the structure. The sense of enclosure can be increased by spacing the supports more closely than the equivalent of the entrance width.

Vertical supports

You should bear in mind that the vertical supports for arches, swags and pergolas are visually more prominent than the cross-beams, since the latter are frequently obscured by plants and are positioned above eye level. Supports deserve your special attention in the design and there is a large range of styles and materials available:

Sawn square timber post, with or without planed-off, or "chamfered" corners.

Composite post, made up of perhaps three or five minor posts fixed together in a variety of different ways.

Cast iron or aluminium columns

Reinforced brick columns which could also use special coping and plinth capping bricks.

Reinforced natural or reconstituted stone columns

Concrete filled and reinforced fibreglass which is mainly designed to resemble turned stone or marble.

Round smooth posts which can be topped with various finials in order to achieve a smart and sophisticated look.

Overheads

The overhead timbers of a pergola comprise the bearers, or joists, which carry the cross-beams and the cross-beams themselves. Both elements can have plain or decorated ends. The bearers are placed and fixed immediately over the supporting posts or columns so the spacing of the bearers coincides with that of the supports, while the cross-beam spacings can vary. The closer together they are, the greater the sense of overhead enclosure.

Dimensions of joints and cross-beams vary with the overall proportions. The greater the distance between supports, the more substantial the timbers need to be. For the narrowest span this could be 20 x 150 mm (¾ x 6 in) and for the widest, 75 x 300 mm (3 x 12 in) or more.

Styles of post and overhead

1 The bearers here have been laid flat and are decorated with carving at the ends. Since they are laid flat, the beams need to be extra thick to carry not only their own weight without bending, but also that of the climbing plants.

2 The safest means of fixing is probably the "crossed half-joint" in which the timbers, bearers and cross-beams finish at the same level and lock into position together. They are then screwed or nailed together. Another style, know as "partial cross-jointing", follows a similar principle except that in this case the bearers or joists are not notched: the cross-beams only have rectangular notches which fit over the bearers. This produces an elegant finish.

3 This sturdy rustic pole arch is strong enough to carry dense climbing plants. Peeled, treated poles will outlast the more attractive untreated, bark-covered poles.

4 These rope swags are supported by round posts, using unpainted hardwood or painted softwood. The diameters of the posts depend on the overall scale, from 75 mm (3 in) to 125 mm (5 in), with height and frequency as required. Ropes can be single, double or treble to carry the weight of the plants. They are usually of 25 mm (1 in) diameter. Synthetic fibre ropes outlast those made from natural fibres. Wisterias, roses and clematis are perfect plants for training along swags.

5a and b Many metal arches are available as kits in a variety of styles. The ones shown here are semi-circular- and ogee-shaped overheads.

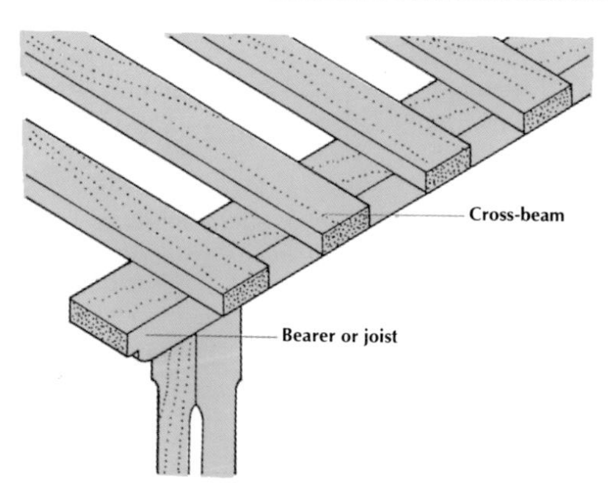

1 Bearers laid flat

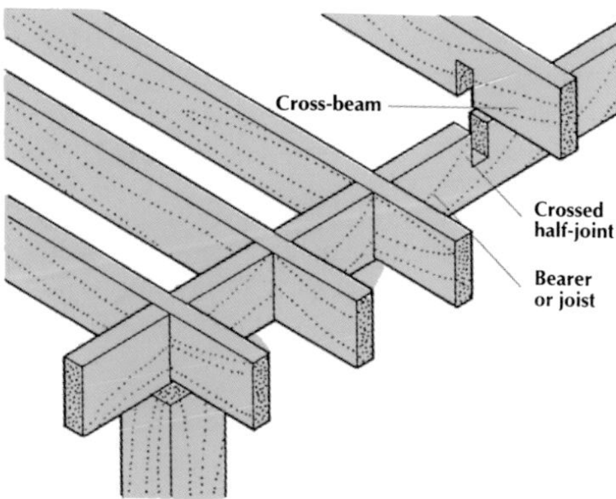

2 Partial cross-jointing

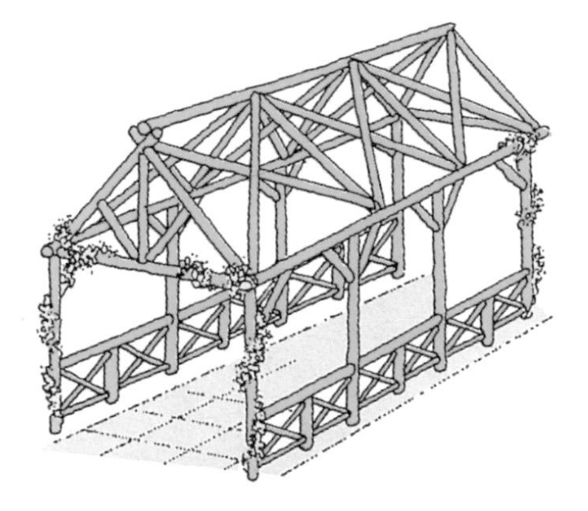

3 Rustic pole arch

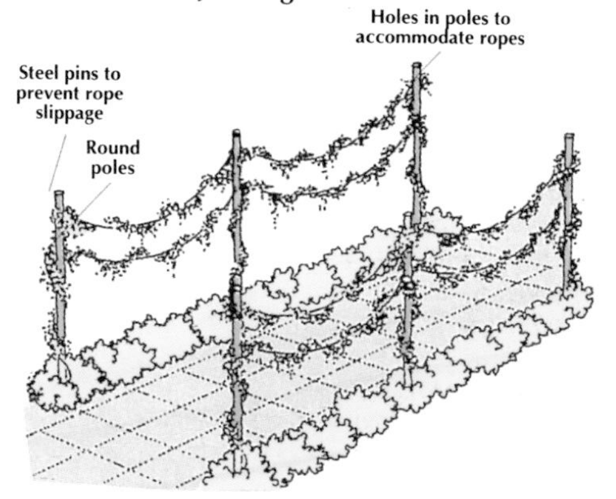

4 Round posts supporting rope swags

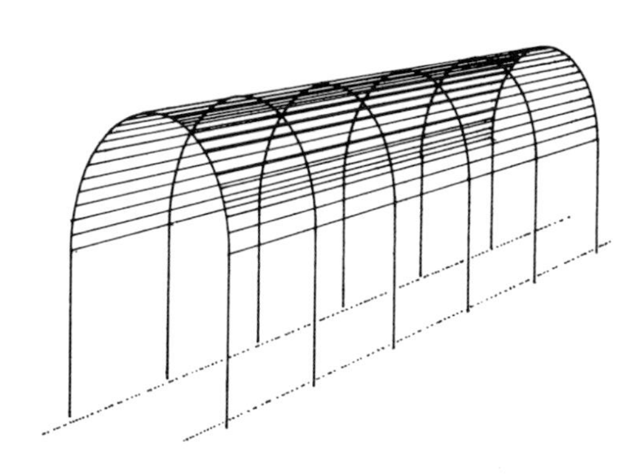

5a Metal arch with semi-circular overhead

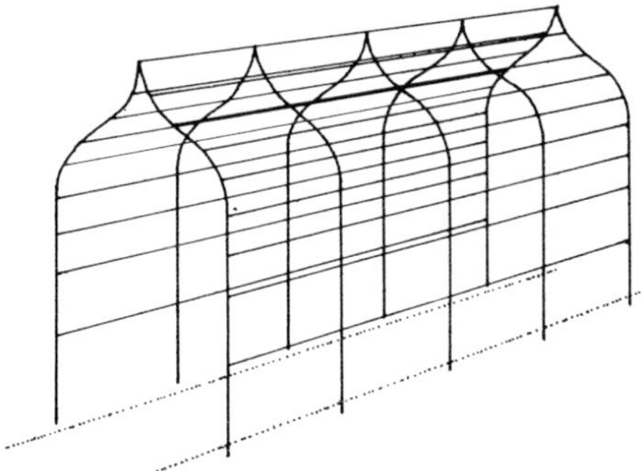

5b Metal arch with ogee overhead

Gates

The primary function of a gate is to permit vehicular or pedestrian access while maintaining security and privacy but, as with many things connected with gardens, they have taken on an independently decorative role, frequently as focal points.

A gate can be a solid or an open structure, the former reinforcing the sense of enclosure, the latter allowing tantalizing glimpses of the garden that lies beyond. Gates are made almost exclusively from timber or metal, so their design has been influenced by the way these materials can be worked or fashioned.

Due to their weight, most gates must be hung on strong supports or posts, otherwise they will fail to close or open. It is not unusual for wider gates to be split into two, which has the effect of dividing the weight between two supports, although this is occasionally done for decorative purposes alone.

Types of gate

The ever-popular five-barred gate has migrated from the farm to the garden and is both elegant and practical.

In the example shown below, a pedestrian leaf has been fitted using common stop posts. In gardens, five-barred gates are often painted rather than left in a natural timber state. Some have a wire or plastic brush or skirt at the base to deter rabbits.

A pretty picket gate is shown below opening onto a cottage garden. In the same spirit, a Victorian-style arch has been constructed over the gate and is adorned with climbing roses.

This solid, arched gate has been decorated with diamond moulding and could be painted a glossy rich colour; dark green or blue is popular. Custom-made ornate hinges decorate it further. The wall on either side has been specially designed with piers to incorporate the gate, and the closely clipped evergreen hedge links the two together.

Steel bar gate This attractive style, available in a range of patterns from many outlets, is excellent where good security is required but not a sense of complete enclosure. Gates of this type are welded together and treated with special coatings to prevent corrosion.

Wrought-iron gate These are available in many different forms, some simple and others highly decorative. This fantastical design is set into a wall which acts as its support as well as a suitable "backdrop".

Five-barred gate with pedestrian gate

Picket gate with arch

Door with moulded pattern

Steel bar gate

Decorative wrought-iron gate

Gazebos and summer houses

Gazebos, summer houses and arbours are all popular elements in the garden. While summer houses and arbours are meant for sheltered sitting, gazebos are vantage points from which beautiful views may be enjoyed. Since they often do not have solid roofs, save perhaps a canopy of climbing plants, only fine weather sitting is possible, but gazebos are for looking at as much as for looking from. Summer houses and arbours also make good focal points but have a more practical application. Summer houses are best placed at a distance from the house. Too close and their purpose as an alternative sitting and viewing area is defeated. Arbours, originally made of entwined branches and twigs, are more appropriate in a natural or woodland setting, again providing shelter and the opportunity to commune with nature.

Gazebos, summer houses and arbours
There are countless types of summer house, ranging from simple self-assembly kits to large buildings, which are literally summer houses containing all modern conveniences. Out of sight of the house, there is an opportunity to experiment with style.

A traditional timber summer house, roofed with shingles or wooden tiles.

The classic simplicity of this stone summer house would suit a formal or informal setting.

This pseudo-classical gazebo supports climbing roses. Gazebos can succeed as visually isolated structures.

This arbour resulted from tying or weaving supple, slender trees to form an enclosure, as in the original definition of the term.

Water in the garden

There is little doubt that, whatever form it takes, water becomes the main focus when it is included in a garden. Because of this, its form and placement must be chosen with the utmost care. Water has such an irresistible appeal that where other eye-catching features exist its introduction will be a potential distraction. To prevent this, think about how the existing features might be brought together in a mutually complementary way, perhaps using the water's reflective properties or water plants as the catalyst.

Where a design does not have other features to consider, or is starting from new, this almost magical element can be exploited imaginatively to the full.

The effect of water in the garden

There are many reasons why the introduction of a water feature can improve the design of a garden. One is the way in which water reflects adjacent elements, planting and the sky, which makes the pool and consequently the garden appear to be more spacious. Sound is another delight of water and in warmer climates it is valued for the impression of coolness it produces.

Water in some form or another, as a habitat for fish, amphibians, insects and visiting animals and birds, is an almost essential element for the wildlife garden. Planting is an integral part of water gardening, as almost any water feature provides an opportunity for growing a wider and more varied array of plants.

Where a garden has sufficient space to accommodate larger bodies of water, swimming pools are popular. Boating or fishing enthusiasts would need even greater areas of water to indulge their hobbies, but these are outside the scope of this book.

Choosing water features

Some form of water feature is suitable for practically any garden style, as ponds and pools can conform to both formal and informal treatments. Lakes suggest informality while canals are formalized rivers, their slow movement suggesting tranquillity. Rills, for the most part, are narrow, fast-moving canals, waterfalls and cascades. Either formal or informal, they are lively and dynamic, depending upon height, movement and sound for their success.

Fountains

There is little to compare with the effervescing vivacity of fountains, although they are inherently formal features and can, therefore, look a little out of place in informal pools unless sensitively designed and positioned. Wall fountains are extremely useful in confined spaces where an eye-catching feature is required in combination with the pleasant sound of running water.

Height, water pressure, jet arrangement and droplet size determine the final form and effect. There are numerous fountain heads available from specialist outlets and catalogues which show exactly the type of jet produced. Apart from being beautiful, fountains also help to aerate the water and are worth including for this reason alone.

When choosing a fountain be sure that the pool in which it is placed is large enough to catch all the water droplets, even on a breezy day. This will ensure that the surround stays dry and that water is conserved, obviating the need

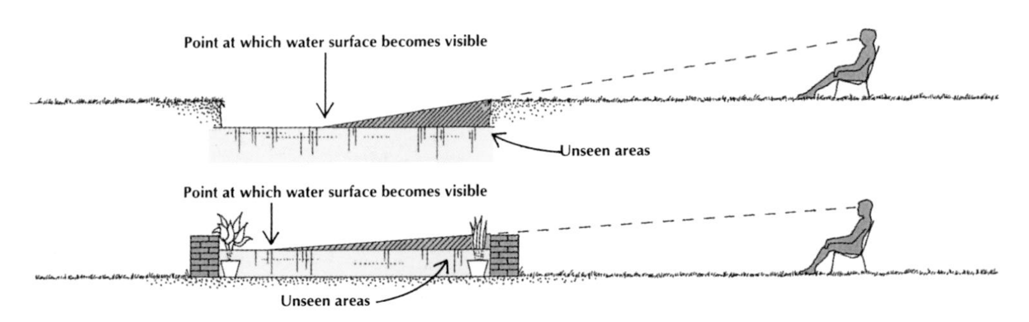

In this raised pool, little of the water surface is seen as it is at almost the same level as the sitter's eyes

for frequent topping-up. Water loss through evaporation is greatest in fine droplet fountains.

Maintaining water features

When designing and positioning a water feature, ensure it is neither in full sun all day nor in constant shade. Too much sun promotes excessive algae growth, while shade, in combination with falling leaves and litter from nearby or overhanging trees, results in unhealthily low oxygen levels. Frequent cleaning will then be necessary. The condition of water is always improved with aeration by artificial means, with fountains and spouts, or by natural means using plants. Help the process along by keeping approximately 30 percent of a pond surface covered with plants such as water lilies. This reduces water loss by evaporation and oxygen depletion in summer.

Water in perspective

The principles of space and movement in the open areas and horizontal surfaces in the garden are equally important when expanses of water are being designed. When horizontal land forms are viewed in perspective they appear to close up and look smaller than when seen on plan (see Design principles: Shaping open spaces, page 54). The phenomenon tends to be exaggerated where bodies of water are concerned. This is because the surface of the water is often below that of its immediate surround, so from a distance less water is seen. This is true also when water is raised closer to eye level, as in a raised pool.

Try to take this effect into account during the design stage by laying the plan on a flat surface close to eye level, then viewing it end on (see diagram opposite). Another technique is to mark out the pool on the ground, go back to the house or patio, then sit down and look at the proposed pool shape from this level. This gives a realistic impression of the finished shape as it will appear from a frequently used vantage point.

Diagram 1 (right) shows an informal pool in plan form with surrounding planting and an island. Diagrams 1a and b illustrate how the same pool will appear from a standing, then a sitting position. Plants at the front of the pool conceal much of the water surface, as does the island. For this reason, avoid creating islands in small ponds. The fact that the water surface is lower than the ground exacerbates the problem. Achieving the planned effect would involve making the pond larger from front to back by as much as two or three times.

Viewed from further back even less of the water surface would be seen. In informal situations even a fairly short grass surround, combined with the lower level of water, can greatly reduce the view of the pool surface. Water plants in the foreground could conceal it completely.

The effects of perspective

1

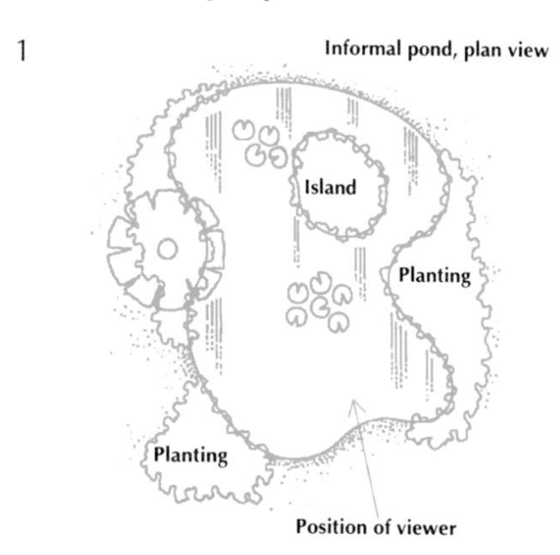

1a

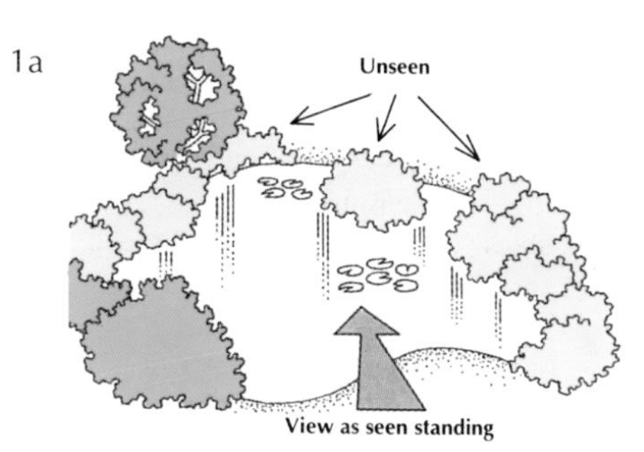

1b

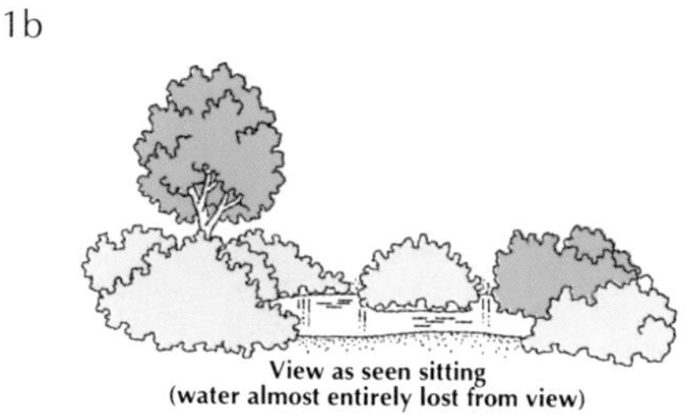

Water in the garden 2

Creating water features on slopes

Water, as is well known, always flows to the lowest level, apart from in very special natural circumstances sometimes found on mountains or moorlands where impervious soils create suspended water hollows.

Artificial pools on slopes rarely look convincing when the ground slope can be seen to continue beyond. To reduce the artificial impression, use the excavated soil from the pool area to create a bund (mound) on the low side of the pool. The bund should be a natural-looking shape if possible. Too uniform and the bund itself might suggest that the pool is not natural. When it is complete, plant up the bund with trees and shrubs, including evergreens. These will inhibit a through view and suggest that the slope has terminated. The pool or lake will then appear to be occupying the lowest area where water would naturally collect.

When creating a water feature on a steep slope, remember to include a flat area for access rather than allowing the slope to extend right down into the water, as this can be dangerous. On very steep slopes, when it may be impractical to create a single body of water, a series of minor stepped pools will look more natural and be easier to construct. Large areas of water on slopes will inevitably create logistical problems and be expensive to contrive.

Make sure that there is sufficient space for the chosen water feature to work well aesthetically, practically and in terms of proportion. Allow plenty of room, too, for marginal planting. If uncontrolled, rampant plant growth can greatly reduce the open water surface.

Water features

The examples (right and overleaf) show a selection of formal and informal features.

1 Small patio pool with a "bell" fountain Low fountains are best for small catchment areas, as tall fountain heads and fine droplets can result in a pool being depleted through evaporation on breezy days.

2 Undulating fountains These were originally operated mechanically by altering the water pressure. Modern undulating fountains are operated by computer and they are still as beautiful and popular as ever.

3 Informal cascades In the example shown here, projecting rocks interrupt the water flow. Sunlight striking the fast-moving droplets creates a fresh, sparkling effect. The sound of rushing water is also attractive.

4 Floating tap fun fountains No garden should be without a touch of humour. This type of fountain consists of a "floating" water tap, not apparently attached to anything, continuously running into a bucket. In fact the tap is supported and supplied with water by a rigid, clear plastic tube which is attached to a pump hidden at the bottom of the bucket. The water is pumped upward inside the tube, and then it overflows inside the mouth of the tap to run down the clear pipe on the outside.

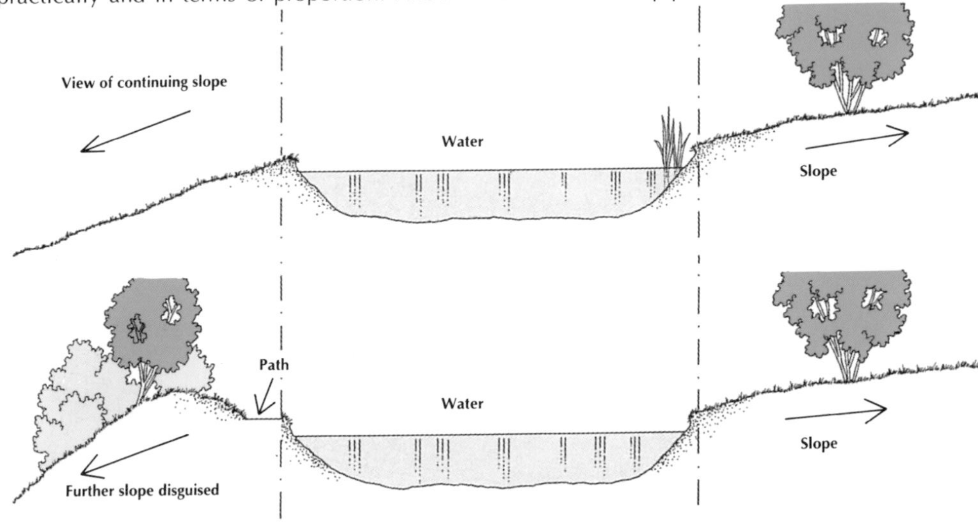

5 Wall fountains Where water at ground level is inappropriate for reasons of safety, this could be considered a "safe" water feature.

Wall fountains are available in many styles made from stone, metal, terracotta and fibreglass. Tiny submersible pumps are housed in a water-filled bowl and pumped via a small bore-pipe to an outlet: in the example illustrated, a lion's mouth.

Wall fountains can be used equally well as planters, especially in winter when they should be drained of water as a precaution against frost damage. A small-leaved decorative ivy would make a charming substitute for the trickling water of summer.

Other attractive water features for the garden might include:

Tiered fountains Ranging from simple sprays to highly complicated patterns, tiered fountains create focal points that overwhelm most others.

Sculptured fountain Sculpture has long been associated with water because of the attractive symmetry of the reflection. Sculpture can be incorporated as a fountain head, which is useful where space is limited.

Revolving sphere fountain In this novel feature a polished granite, marble or metal sphere rotates freely in a socket, raised slightly by the pressure of water from beneath.

Bowl fountain For a small patio this feature,

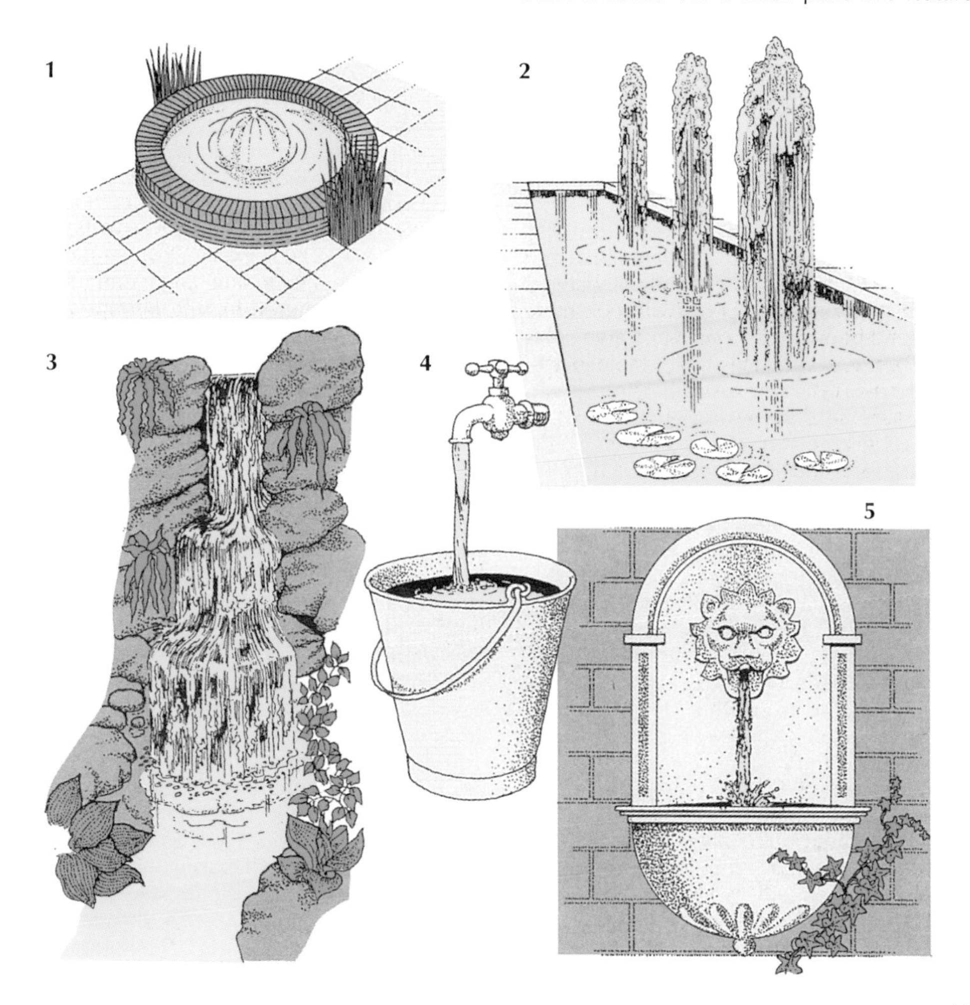

Water in the garden 3

which can be made safe for even young children if it is filled almost to the brim with black pebbles, is an ideal focal point. A small jet appropriate in height to the bowl's diameter brings the fountain to life, powered by a concealed pump. Line the inside of the bowl with a black pond sealant to make it waterproof and to make the water surface more reflective.

Rock pool Rock pools are a delightful addition to the garden either as individual features or as part of a series, but you should aim to make them look entirely natural. There should be no liner visible anywhere. If a series of pools is to be constructed, the bottom pool must be significantly larger than those above to ensure that it is not noticeably depleted when the pump activates the waterfalls.

Capped spring head This could be a natural spring or an entirely artificial construction, using a submersible pump. The spring head could be fitted with an ornamental mask (as in the illustration page on 153, bottom right) and gush into a "dipping pool".

Rill Originally a narrow stream running through a meadow, similar features can be formalized for garden use. The great landscape gardeners of the past included rills for their movement, sound and as a gentle surprise.

Stream Make an artificial stream look as natural as possible and conceal evidence of liners at the bottom and sides by disguising them with turf, plants, gravel or rocks.

If rocks do not naturally occur in the garden or are not used elsewhere, avoid lining the stream sides with them, at least above ground level, as they will give an immediate look of artificiality. If rocks do occur or are planned as part of a water or rock theme, place them as naturally as possible and place more in other areas adjacent to the stream. For continuity, use broken stones of a similar type to rest at the bottom of the stream. If a flexible liner is in place use only smooth stones to prevent the liner from being damaged.

Formal cascades Formal cascades have no real practical function. Nevertheless, they are eye-catching and stimulating, with endless design possibilities. They should be considered only for naturally sloping gardens, as the earth-moving that would otherwise be necessary to create the required contours and terracing, could be prohibitively expensive.

Millstone fountains Worn millstones were traditionally used for these features as they have a hole in the centre but the "stones" are now mainly manufactured from fibreglass.

The concept is simple: a shallow dip in the upper surface is fed from a reservoir below the "stone" up through the hole in the middle via a submersible pump. The water overflows evenly down the sides and disappears through pebbles or stones, to be collected and returned to the reservoir for recirculation. This is fast becoming one of the most popular "safe" water features.

Safety factors

Because water is so attractive, especially to children, safety must take priority over appearance in water features (see Safety in the garden page 186). It is well known that even the shallowest water can prove fatal to the very young. Rather than take any risks, a pool or pond should be omitted from your garden plan altogether, or its inclusion postponed until a more appropriate time.

If a water feature is already present in a garden that is to be used by children, then it should be securely fenced off with lockable gates at the access points. Alternatively, cleanly puncture the bottom in one or two places to ensure adequate drainage (these punctures can be repaired later) and fill the pool with soil. It can then serve as a moist shrub or flower bed in the interim period.

Raised shallow pools with walls 600 mm (2 ft) or so high are not quite as dangerous but, even so, these are not suitable in an area where young children will be playing unless constant supervision can be guaranteed. Alternatively, it is possible to fit a lockable steel mesh cover over small pools.

Designing water features for safety Conventional sunken pools or ponds should not have plain sloping sides, especially if they are constructed using smooth liners. These can be very slippery and once a child or even an adult has fallen in, it is not easy to climb out. The deeper the pool, the more difficult this is. Instead, arrange the sides as a series of inward-sloping steps, which will make it much safer.

Where concrete is used to line the pool, texture the steps by very rough brushing or tamping before the concrete dries, to make it even easier to climb out.

Choice of feature

Open areas of water contribute enormously to the appearance and atmosphere of a garden, but there are situations in which they constitute a real hazard. A small garden, in which space for children's play is concentrated, is an obvious example. On sites like this, "safe" water features like wall, bowl or millstone fountains come into their own. In each case there is no depth or open space of water to secure, and each feature can be quickly emptied and refilled as and when the need arises.

When including an area of water or a water feature in your designs, there is no reason why you should not control exactly how you would like it to appear and in what form. Its realization, however, is quite a different matter and it is a good idea to consult a specialist. Wrongly installed, your water feature may fail aesthetically as well as practically. A water specialist may even guarantee the feature. Advice can also be sought on what sort of plants to use from the range of marginals, floating or bottom-rooting types.

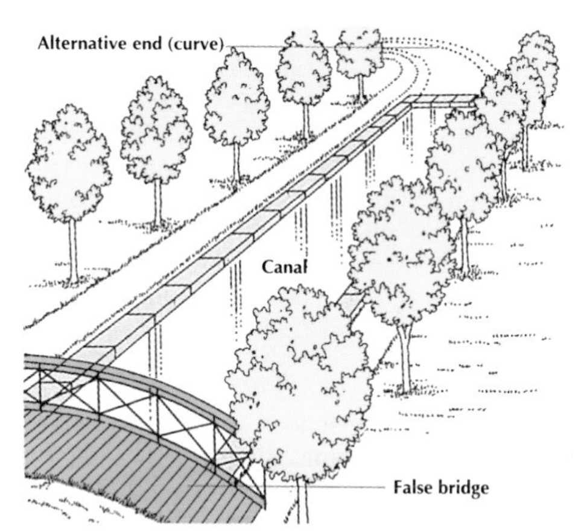

This rectangular "canal" reflects the sky and the tree avenue. The far end could curve out of sight, to suggest even greater length.

Tranquil, still and mysterious, this lake reflects both sky and surround, thus increasing the sense of space.

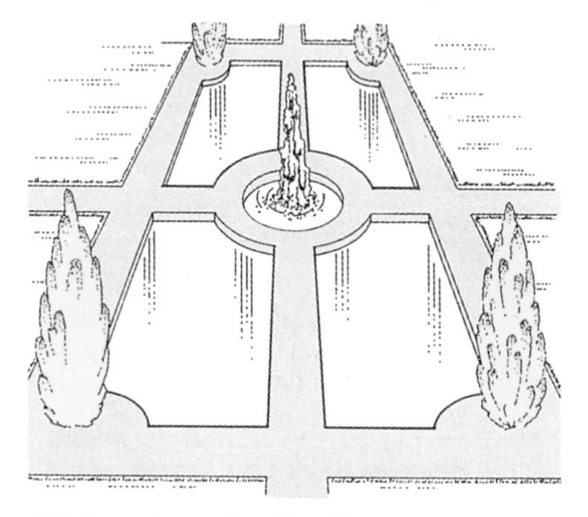

This formal pond's still, reflective surfaces are designed to contrast with the central pond, emphasising its frothy central fountain.

A formal water feature on a small scale is appropriate in a small garden, especially as the pool surround doubles as a seat.

Pumps

Pumps

If a stream or waterfall is required on a flat site where water would not normally be expected to flow, then considerable site alterations need to take place. Changes in level are usually needed for this and, especially in an informal setting, the stream or waterfall must appear as an entirely natural phenomenon. In any event, an electric pump will be required to move the water around.

There are two basic types: those which are placed outside the water in a special waterproof chamber and those which are placed in the water and known as submersible pumps. Submersible pumps are popular in smaller water gardens, as they are convenient to use and simple to install, but any type of pump needs to be kept cool when in operation.

Deciding on the power

The advice of the supplier should be sought when determining the power of pump required. It is all too easy to choose a pump that is not powerful enough.

Good catalogues will list a range of pumps and their performance ratings, expressed in gallons per hour, relative to the height and distance of the outfall or fountain head away from the pump. The higher and greater the distance over which the water is to be moved (known technically as the "head" of water) the more powerful a pump needs to be.

Water is a heavy element weighing 1 kg per litre (10 lbs per gallon or 8 lbs per US gallon) and with a natural propensity to run downward. In a waterfall system there can be a huge weight of water being pumped continuously. Furthermore, it is pumped through pipes which have a restrictive effect on the flow, so the right pump is essential, as is the appropriate pipe size.

Pumps for waterfalls

The bottom pool in a waterfall or cascade system is the place for the submersible pump, because it is from here that most of the water is abstracted. The design of the bottom pool must take account of this: the pool should not empty by half when the pump is turned on.

In this respect, formal pools are more difficult to design than informal pools because the vertical sides of the former act as a visual level gauge, emphasizing any depletion. Informal pools with gently sloping sides are easier to design as it is not so obvious when the waterfall system is operating, especially if the pool has a gravelled bottom and sides.

The route taken by the water as it is pumped up to the top of a waterfall, then flows back down to the pool.

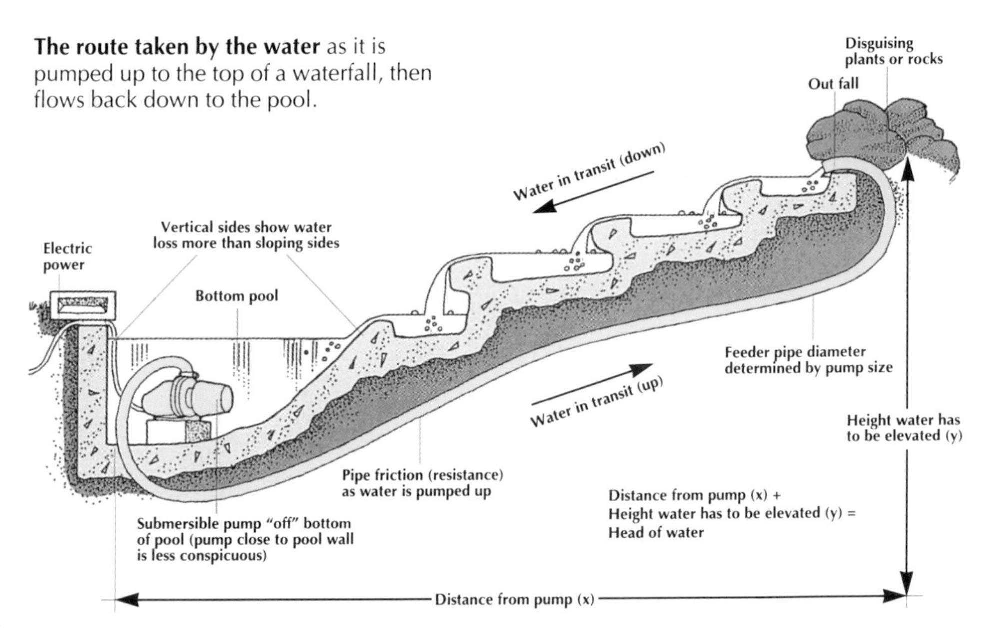

Methods of water retention

Pool liners

Various materials can be used to create pools: choice depends on their availability and the feasibility of construction or installation. Ease of access to the garden influences costs, applying not only to construction materials coming in but also to any excavated materials going out, so the volume of the pool is important.

Puddled clay

In areas with a clay soil, this technique has been used to create ponds for many hundreds of years. The clay must be flexible, impervious and have a low silt content. A layer of lime used to be placed beneath the clay to discourage root penetration or animal activity which could cause the pond to leak. Today, low-grade plastic sheet provides a more economical and effective alternative. The sides of a clay pond should not have more than a 20-degree slope: any steeper and the clay particles could slip downward, leading to water loss. Shrubs and trees should be planted well away from the edges of a clay pool and invasive aquatic plants such as willows, poplars, large bamboos and some sedges should also be avoided, as they could penetrate the clay, causing it to leak.

Liner pools

Flexible liners are less costly per unit area than concrete and are convenient. Butyl or PVC, for example, can have long lives, though polythene is suitable only for short-term use. Flat sheet liners are not so easy to use in formal pools, which often call for awkward folding at any corners, but specialist firms can make liners to match specific pool shapes. If correctly fitted, flexible liners should not be visible above the water line and this is essential if the pool is to appear natural.

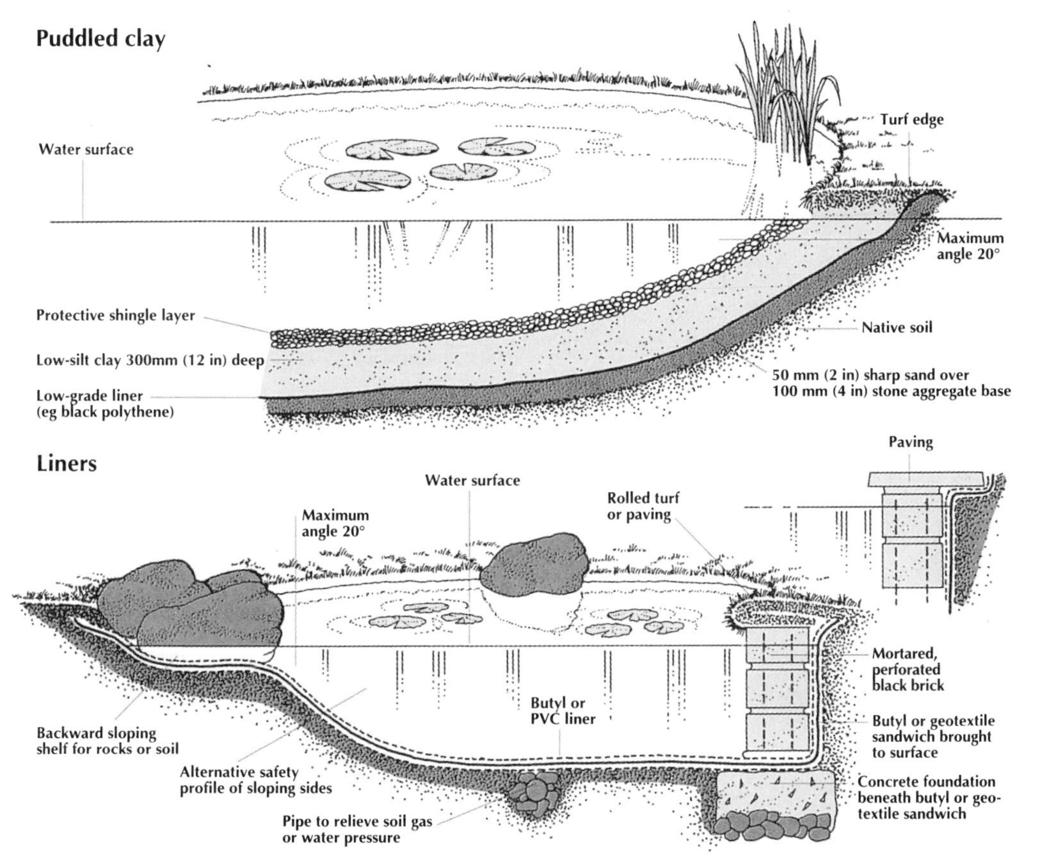

Water retention methods 2

Rigid liners
Rigid liners, manufactured mostly from fibreglass, are pre-formed in geometric or informal shapes to make instant patio or rock garden pools. Their artificial-looking edges can be disguised with rocks, plants or grass. Old leaking pools can also be repaired using fibreglass sheets and resin.

Above-ground pools
If they are built with walls about 300 mm (12 in) thick and 450–600 mm (18–24 in) high, these features can also provide supplementary seating. Most materials can be used in their construction: real or reconstituted stone, brick or timber are all suitable, although the interior needs to be waterproofed either with waterproof mortar or a proprietary pond sealant.

In rigid pools the internal walls should slope upward and outward so that, in winter, expanding ice can move harmlessly upward, rather than outward as it will if trapped against vertical sides. An overflow at the proposed water level will also reduce the risk of ice lifting or otherwise damaging the pool coping.

Informal concrete pools
These should ideally be dish-shaped in section and deepest at the centre, whatever the plan form. This reduces the risk of cracking due to differential loadings, which is common where there are several separate deep areas. To be truly waterproof, concrete must be consistent in mix, well compacted and be of uniform thickness not less than about 150 mm (6 in). If it is thinner than this, it will probably have to be waterproofed using a pond liner.

Rock or planting shelves should slope downwards and backwards to ensure stability. The edges of a concrete pool can be disguised with plants and rocks. A natural internal appearance develops more quickly if the concrete sides are textured rather than smooth.

Formal concrete pools
Formal concrete pools can be cast using shuttering, or they can be constructed as retaining walls over a base. In larger pools, steel reinforcement is needed to counter internal and external pressures.

To prevent dissolved cement chemicals from harming aquatic life, fill the pool but wait at least six months before introducing any creatures into an untreated concrete pond. Then, change the water but do not scrub the pool sides. The spontaneous appearance of water beetles and daphnia (water fleas, for example) is a sign that the water is uncontaminated.

Waterfalls
Although more ambitious in scope, the construction of a waterfall is not very different from that of a pond. Both concrete and flexible liners can be used to channel the water.

Above-ground pool

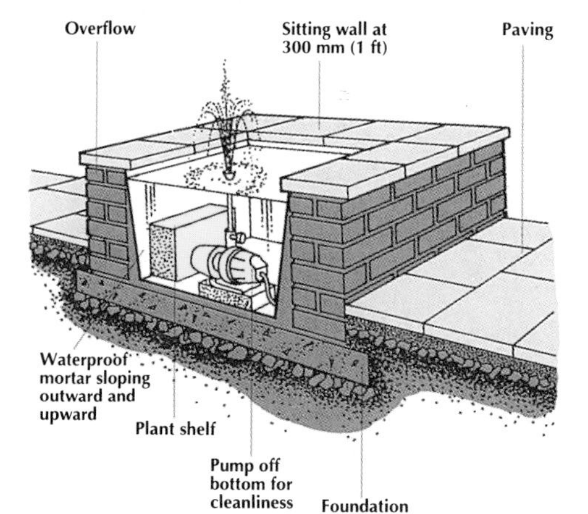

Rigid plastic or fibreglass

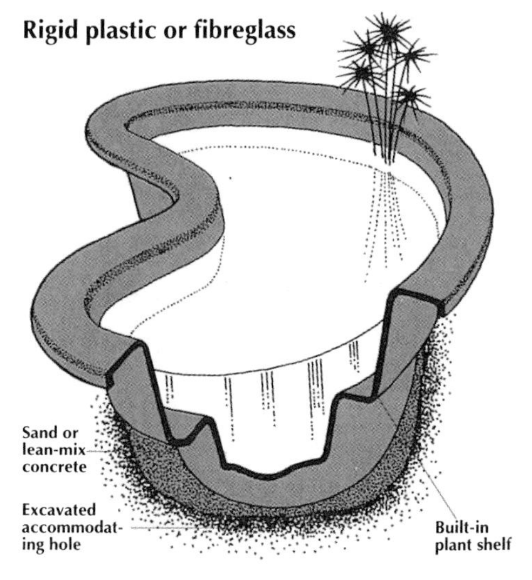

Concrete

Since concrete shrinks and expands in response to changing temperatures, often resulting in cracking, it cannot be used for the construction of long water courses.

To overcome this problem, concrete streams and water courses are constructed as short overlapping units, as in the examples below (and on page 154), with the rear wall of each section and the corresponding sides always higher than the anticipated water level. There is the added advantage, when a waterfall is constructed in this way, that a series of stepped, independent minor pools is formed. When the circulatory pump is switched off, water is retained in these minor pools and the "stream" does not run completely dry. The sides and bottom of a concrete stream or waterfall can be made attractive and natural-looking by placing stones or gravel against or on them.

Flexible liners

While flexible liners do not have the same thermal movement problems as concrete, it may be difficult to obtain very long and narrow strips suitable for forming stream beds.

To achieve the desired effect, shorter lengths can be used but overlapped, as illustrated. Smooth loose stones or rocks can be placed on the bottom and sides for a natural effect, but sharp stones may penetrate the liner and should therefore be avoided.

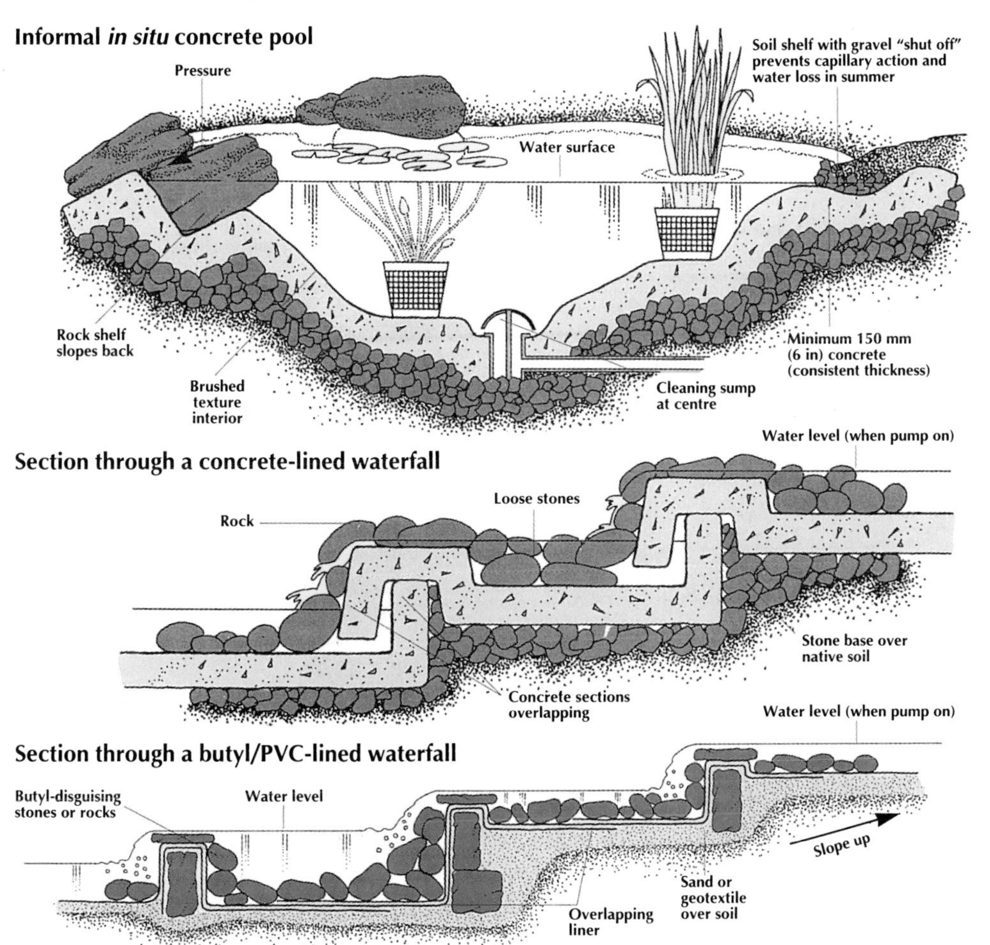

Swimming pools

Swimming pool brochures contain a vast array of shapes, proportions and depths that can be tailored to a family's individual requirements and budget. Siting can be problematic in itself if the garden is small or awkwardly proportioned.

The first requirement is to position the pool where it will receive the maximum sunlight, for the comfort of the bathers. In temperate zones, bear in mind the time of day and the time of year the pool is most likely to be used. In some cases over the period of a year the pool might be looked at far more than it is used and it will certainly dominate the garden if in full view.

The next requirement is that the pool and its surround or decking is large enough to meet the family's needs. Size should not, however, be the overall deciding factor at the expense of the rest of the garden which is, after all, the setting for the pool. The shape of the pool, both the outline and the internal profile, is also important and should be determined by the use to which it is to be put, whether simply for fun or for serious exercise. For example, adults diving will require a much greater depth of water than children playing.

Pools in context

Swimming pool surrounds or decks should always have a non-slip surface for reasons of safety. Stone, concrete, brick and timber are all extensively used. Choose the colours of the surround to associate with the broad area of water colour and adjacent architecture.

Interiors are usually blue or turquoise, making the water look particularly inviting in warm or hot climates. In cool climates, however, extra care must be taken with colour association if the pool is not to look out of place.

In temperate zones, turquoise is not a natural reflected colour and can jar with the softer colours and light qualities that prevail. As an alternative, consider a black or dark blue interior. Viewed obliquely, this transforms the water surface into a mirror reflecting sky and surroundings. As for the water itself, this remains clear and inviting while, out of season and left uncovered, it takes on the role of an ornamental pool and in frosty weather the mirror-like surface looks far more natural than turquoise.

Disguising a pool

Swimming pools with covers do not usually contribute positively to a garden's visual appeal and, for this reason, covered pools are best placed away from major views or axes. By surrounding them with screening plants, the view is improved and, simultaneously, a sheltered micro-climate is created.

Construction materials include concrete, fibreglass, plastic or metal. Most pools are built directly into the ground, some only partially in the ground while others, mainly the framed, plastic or metal varieties, are entirely above ground, posing the greatest challenge in terms of garden design. When the sides are visible, they have a strong visual impact and, unless the

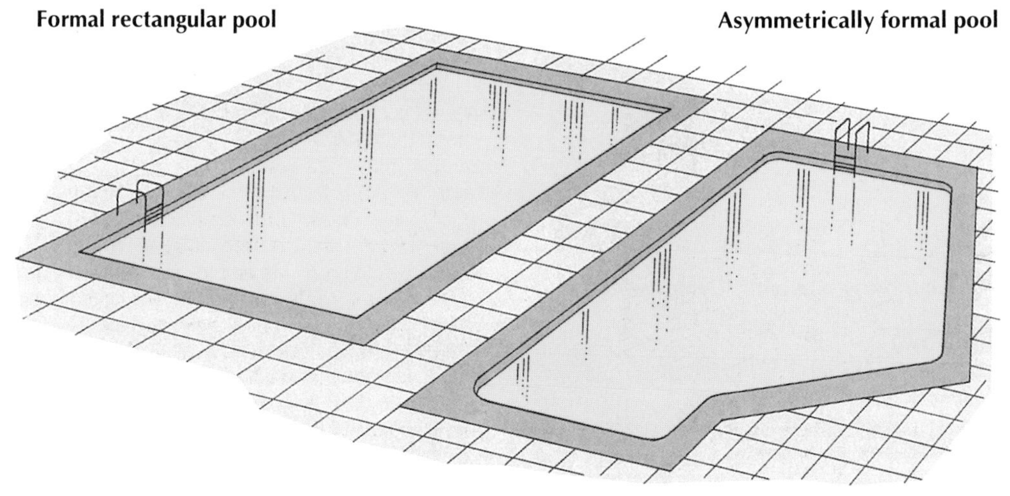

Formal rectangular pool

Asymmetrically formal pool

pool itself is of an attractive design, dense planting, at least on the side from which the pool is usually seen, is the best design solution.

Swimming pool water needs to be filtered, purified and perhaps heated, too. The equipment for this may require separate buildings, as may facilities for changing and showering. Such buildings can dominate the pool they serve, so careful planning is required to ensure these structures blend into the rest of the design.

Artificial swimming pools in natural settings are possibly the most difficult to integrate. In temperate climates, the favoured turquoise or pale blue interior may be even more conspicuous but popular informal shapes can be made more acceptable surrounded by bold, leafy plantings.

Pool types or styles

Formal rectangular pool A rectangular pool (see illustration, page 158) is generally acknowledged to provide the maximum space for swimming, but the shape is rather stark. The addition of semi-circular extensions known as Roman ends can make it appear more graceful. Roman ends can be functional too and frequently incorporate access steps at the shallow end or a spring board at the deep end.

Asymmetrically formal pool Most domestic pools fall into this category. Although attractive, they often call for ingenious design solutions to fit the associated paving or decking around the pool, as well as link it with the surroundings.

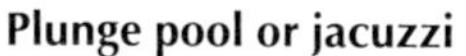

Plunge pool or jacuzzi

Counter-flow swimming jet or jacuzzi Both these features have only recently become widely available for domestic use. With a counter-flow swimming jet, swimming takes place against strong directional water currents produced by powerful pumps, so that little or no forward movement is achieved. Jacuzzis also have water currents but these are multi-directional and work in combination with warm to hot water. Plunge pool and jacuzzis can be accommodated in a much smaller area than a conventional swimming pool, but they must be installed by a specialist.

SWIMMING POOL SAFETY

Swimming pools pose a particular threat to children and, for that matter, any non-swimmers. After all, they are intended to be attractive and inviting so, in case the attraction should prove irresistible, access must be limited and controlled, perhaps using a strong chain-link or picket fence with a dense flowering or evergreen hedge. When safety overrides any other considerations, position a swimming pool near to the house so that there will be more chance of hearing cries for help if someone is in difficulty. Leave several life belts permanently floating in the water, just in case, and provide plenty of space around the side of the pool for climbing out. Safety fences around any open pool should not, for this reason, be positioned hard against the water's edge.

Pool covers should be maintained in good order and the devices used to attach them to the sides must be kept taut. Roller covers must always be fully extended with no gaps around the edges when the pool is not in use and completely rolled back and secured before anyone enters the water. In some ways, it is better not to have a cover at all rather than one under which someone can become trapped.

All paving and decking should be finished with a non-slip texture, as smooth paving and planed wood can become dangerously slippery when wet.

Jetties and beaches

The true function of a jetty is to provide access to a boat or raft, without the user getting wet feet. Jetties are usually associated with larger areas of water where a boat might be useful or necessary for a variety of reasons, although they also provide a useful vantage point from which fish can be fed or simply admired, allowing a clear rather than an oblique overview. Some designs include jetties and boats in the smallest gardens, simply presented as a tableau.

Beaches provide access to and from the water for humans, animals, amphibians and birds, while protecting the pool liner beneath, especially when flexible types such as butyl or PVC are used.

A beach should comprise round pebbles or pea shingle rather than stones, which have sharp edges and are likely to puncture a liner. To be convincing, the surface beach material should be of an adequate depth – at least 150 mm (6 in) is a good rule of thumb.

Some designers include beaches simply because they like the look of them, rather than for any practical reason. To help a constructed beach look as natural as possible, try to match any locally occurring stone or pebbles, even if only in colour.

Beaches placed at the windward end of a pool need to be regularly cleaned because it is here that wind-blown scum and litter collects.

Jetty and beach combination

Bridges

Bridges are required where a large pond, river or stream prevents access from one part of the garden to another, but they can be made extremely decorative, too. If placed so that they are seen chiefly from the side or obliquely, as they are in many famous gardens, they make the most attractive composition subjects.

Scale and proportion

Scale is an important factor when deciding on the style and proportions of a bridge. The bridge should always be of an appropriate style and in scale with the body of water over which it passes. A large ornate bridge spanning a narrow pool or stream will look pretentious, while a narrow plank bridge over a wide expanse of water will look and feel dangerous. Similarly, a bridge designed along classical lines will look out of place in a modern garden.

Positioning

A bridge can effectively terminate the view of a pool or stream if inappropriately placed, so position it with care, or it may make the water feature look smaller than it is. To ensure that the pool or stream appears to continue beyond the bridge, make sure that the bridge is raised high enough above the surface of the water for light to be visible at the other side. It does not matter that there is little or no stream beyond the bridge: if the intention is to make a garden look larger, this trick of perspective will help.

As with most other decorative garden features, bridges benefit from having a good but uncompetitive backdrop, such as a laurel hedge. Alternatively, use a bridge as the centrepiece of a design composition.

Materials

Bridges can be home-made, assembled from kits or designed and constructed by professionals. For bridges intended to be functional rather than purely decorative, except perhaps for the simplest plank structure, it is essential to consult an expert. The materials commonly used for bridges include timber, stone, concrete and metal, used separately or in combination.

Rustic pole A rustic pole bridge (see below) is an excellent choice for an informal setting.

The poles will be longer lasting if they are treated with a preservative, but this usually means stripping them of bark, the very feature that lends them their great charm. Hardwood poles can be used as an alternative; it is not essential that these be treated and the bark can then remain, although all the bark will drop off eventually.

All bridge-supporting poles need to have been treated or to be made of hardwood if they are to stand permanently in water. Oak and elm are particularly suitable hardwoods for this purpose. The bridge foot-boards can be made of poles or rough-sawn timber, as shown; both are safe to walk on.

Rustic pole bridge

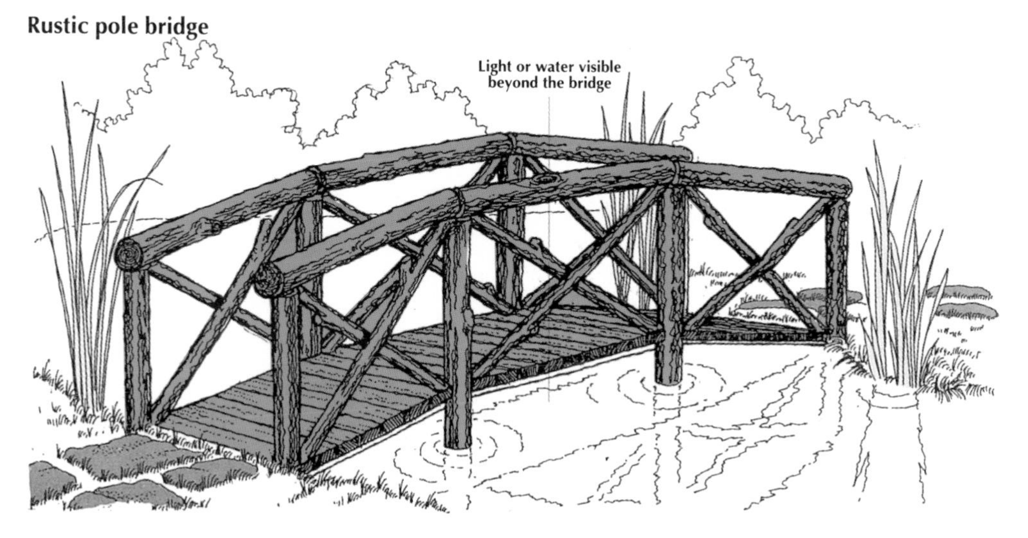

Bridges 2

Stone bridge The robust stone construction illustrated below could alternatively be designed to look formally elegant, depending on the style of the garden, perhaps using balustrades rather than a solid wall to give a less massive appearance.

Stone bridges need to be based on strong foundations and are usually constructed over a concealed reinforced concrete span or steel joists. The attraction of the stone bridge illustrated below owes as much to the setting as to the bridge itself.

Metal bridge Most modern metal bridges intended for gardens are prefabricated as a single unit or in sections for on-site assembly. Designs vary widely, from gothic to modern, from utilitarian to abstract, and they are available in a variety of finishes. Metal garden bridges commonly range in size from 2 m (6 ft 6 in) to 6 m (20 ft) or more. The greater the span, the heavier the construction, since a bridge has to carry not only the loads imposed upon it but also its own weight.

Timber walkway (causeway) The walkway in the example below changes direction to make the walk more interesting.

Used in conjunction with bog gardens, with which they are frequently associated, walkways provide an excellent means of access. There is a sense of intrigue as the walkway winds in and out of the taller aquatic plants. In

Stone bridge

Metal prefabricated bridge

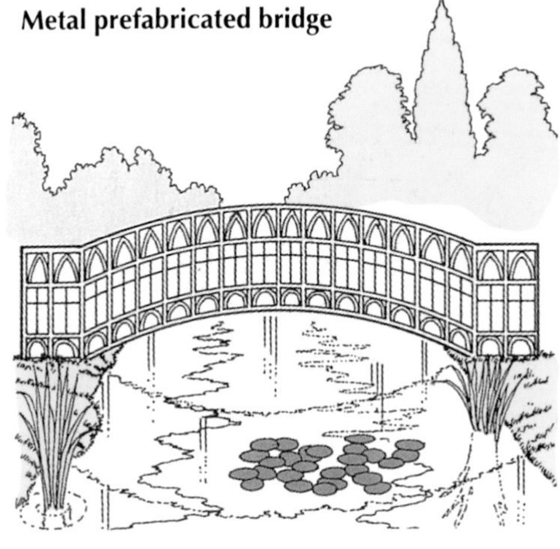

Timber walkway (causeway)

some examples, narrow spaces are left between the planks, allowing a tantalizing glimpse of the water below.

The introduction of lighting illuminates the walkway and extends its use into the evening. Ideally, walkways should be made of hardwood, particularly the supporting posts which stand in water.

Stepping stones

Stepping stones in water achieve the same effect as those in grass, allowing safe and easy access without creating unwanted divisions in the space. This characteristic is particularly advantageous where an uninterrupted flow is crucial to the design. Stepping stones look best if they appear to float just above the surface of the water, with a dark, narrow shadow.

Stepping stones can be of equal or of different sizes and their routes can be straight or curved, but for safety they must be spaced with care. The distances between the stones should take account of the differences in stride between adults and children. Normally, the gaps left between stones range from 150 mm (6 in) to 300 mm (12 in) but whatever is decided, it should be consistent.

The stepping stones should be large enough to allow plenty of room for the whole foot to be accommodated easily. Having to aim at a small stepping stone is not only inconvenient but potentially dangerous, so a minimum size of 500 mm (20 in) square is recommended.

Artificial stepping stones

In pools with flexible liners, it can be difficult to add stepping stones. The concrete foundation for each stepping stone needs to be in place first (see cross-section below). Over this a protective layer is laid to prevent damage to the liner, perhaps of geotextile (a tough woven polymer protective "cloth"), then the liner itself of PVC or butyl, followed by another protective layer. On this is placed a constructed support, such as a mortared concrete block painted black, so as to be unobtrusive, then the stepping stone itself.

The stepping stone should be carefully mortared into place with a little oversail: 20 mm (¾ in), for example, all around the concrete block. Too great an oversail can result in the stone being dislodged should weight fall on the edge rather than the centre. In concrete pools, stepping stone supports can be built directly onto the flat pool floor.

Natural stepping stones

Natural stepping stones lend themselves more readily to fast-flowing brooks and streams than to still, formal bodies of water where their water-worn appearance is unconvincing. They are often smaller and are placed closer together than those set in larger, deeper water features.

Artificial stepping stones

Cross-section of stepping stones

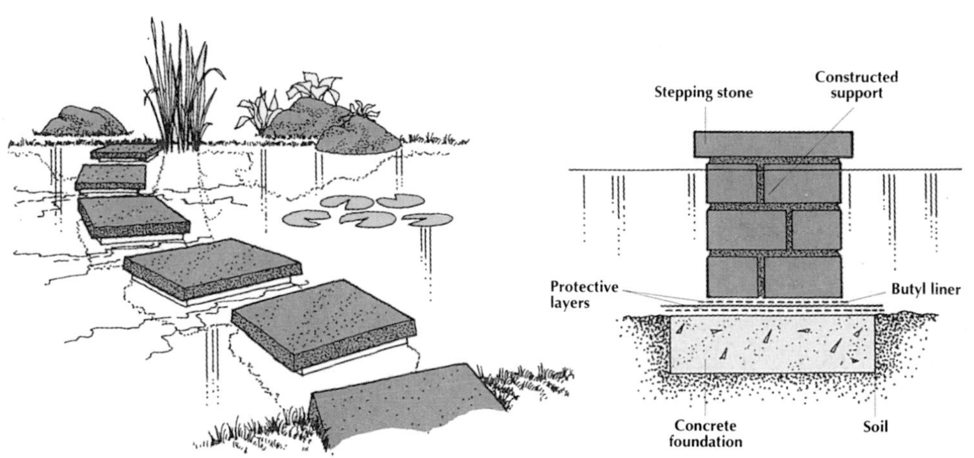

Grottos and caves

Grottos and caves associate most naturally with water or woodland gardens. They can be dry, contain small pools and dripping water or be an integral part of a larger water feature. They are ideal places for growing ferns, mosses and other plants which revel in shady conditions. It is essential that their construction is strong and stable, particularly if the intention is that visitors should go inside. Seek professional advice in this matter.

Rock garden cave A cave can be designed as part of a rock garden. The example shown below has a shallow reflective pool as its floor and the sound of water dripping down the rear wall can be heard from outside, adding to its attraction. A cave entrance does not need to be very high or wide, simply in scale with the rock garden, perhaps no more than 1 m (3 ft 3 in) or so.

A grotto as part of a pool The size of the grotto depends on the size of the pool of which it is a part. It could be large enough to accommodate a small boat, which could be the only means of reaching it, but grottos do not necessarily have to be accessible. Lined with flints, pebbles or shells and in combination with unseen running water, a small grotto could be the focal point of the water garden.

A rock garden cave with small "mirror pool"

Grotto as part of a pool

Grotto with circular window and stone steps

Cave beneath rock garden with waterfall

Grotto with circular window and stone steps This grotto (page 164, bottom left) could be part of a rock garden or an independent feature placed within a mound. Its roof and walls are of reinforced concrete which has been well disguised with flints or stone, both inside and out. To add to its charm, the grotto is set well down into the ground and is reached by stone steps, with ferns and mosses growing in damp shady corners. A shaft of light shines through a circular window set into the rear wall, illuminating a stone seat. The floor is patterned with pebbles and shells in the traditional manner.

Tunnel Concealed beneath a rock garden, this tunnel has a cascade on the outside, which leads into a pond or swimming pool. If the latter, the tunnel could also be used for access to an underground pump or filtration room. Ivies, ferns and other shade-loving plants have colonized the internal walls.

Cave or grotto This large rock garden incorporates a grotto-cum-cave with a waterfall within. The pool is large enough for irises and other marginal plants to grow in it and in spring it becomes a nursery for frogs and toads.

Formal grottos Grottos need not be informal or naturalistic, as this example demonstrates. Close to a house of similar architectural style, this structure comprises a series of arches supported by pillars and a long chamber at the rear. The internal walls of the grotto are studded with pebbles. Positioned centrally at the rear, a wall fountain gushes water into a rectangular pool. The pool is set below ground level and has shade-loving aquatic and marginal plants growing within it.

Rock embankment and grotto

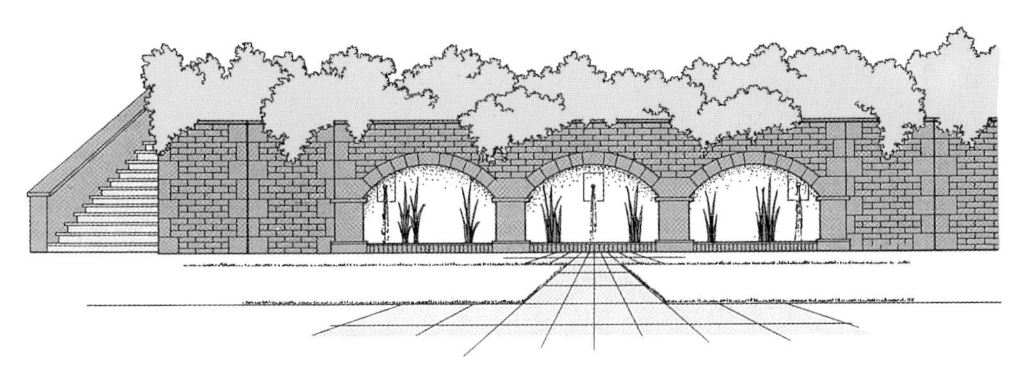

Formal grotto

Rock and alpine gardens

Used imaginatively, rock gardens can enhance the structure of the garden as a whole or simply exist as a feature within a garden.There is a fascinating range of alpine plants, the cultural requirements of which can readily be met with a rock garden. A range of different microclimates and soil conditions can easily be created within the same garden.

Rock gardens created to accommodate collections of specialized plants, intended to be viewed and enjoyed at close quarters, are quite different in design from those in which the sculptural qualities of the rocks are the main attraction, in association with larger shrubs or trees. The latter type usually comprises larger rocks with fewer individual planting pockets and plateaux.

Blending a rock garden into the garden

Rock gardens made up of equal-sized stones heaped up in the corner of a brick wall, perhaps even with a stream issuing from the top rather like a "wet volcano", never look convincing. Even in the smallest garden a rock garden should be designed to have the most natural appearance possible, using local stone where available. A couple of rocks can be introduced nearby but independent of the main rock garden to help blend the feature into the garden as a whole. There are various forms a rock garden can take.

Stratified rock garden This type is designed to resemble eroded bed-rock with the strata of the rock clearly visible, or an escarpment with soil pockets or plateaux which are ideal for planting up. Use the largest rocks that can feasibly be imported, ensuring that they are well founded and laid so that they slope inward toward the centre of the rock garden. This makes the structure more stable and safer to maintain and encourages rainwater to run back into the soil pockets where it is needed, rather than draining off. By adding different compost mixes and grits, plants with different cultural requirements can be grown.

Boulder rock garden Boulder stones, shaped by glacial activity or water erosion, are not generally found naturally in a stratified state. Because of this they look out of place in a conventional stratified rock garden, but they can be arranged in a way that allows their sculptural qualities to be enjoyed. The tone of a boulder rock garden is determined by the surrounding and associated planting. For example, the same

Stone laid to suggest natural stratification

Stratified rock garden (cross- section)

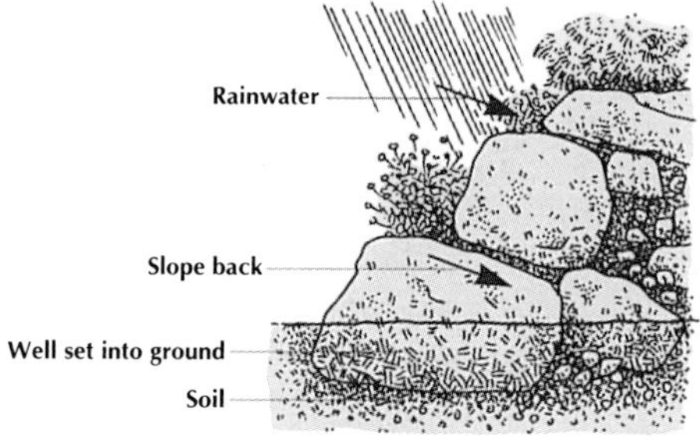

Boulder stone arrangement

Boulder rock garden (cross- section)

group of boulders planted about with different grasses, yuccas and succulents in a gravelled setting creates the impression of an arid zone, while a planting of hostas, ferns and rodgersias in a mossy, shaded setting will suggest moist conditions.

Pavement rock garden This is an excellent way of growing favourite alpines, especially when a conventional rock garden cannot be accommodated. Large flattish stones are the most suitable and must be of sufficient size to step on safely and to allow for the sideways spread of the plants. The joints between the stones should be approximately 25–50 mm (1–2 in) wide and a lime mortar (one part cement to two parts lime and ten parts sand or stone dust) can ease the bedding of the stones and make them stable.

Compost pockets can be created, wider than the finished joints if necessary, before the stones are laid, then planted up once the pavement is in place. Given adequate drainage, individual cultural conditions can be created between the pavement stone joints in the same way as the soil pockets of a stratified rock garden. Invasive alpines should be confined by clay pots sunk into the soil, again before the stone is laid. Pavement rock gardens can also be established at the periphery of a patio: a useful device when space is limited.

Scree A natural scree is a mixture of soil and eroded stone debris which has fallen from rock outcrops above. These conditions can be recreated in a garden either as an independent feature or in association with a stratified rock garden, providing the perfect opportunity for growing a range of xerophytic and other specially adapted plants (see Hot, dry gardens (xeroscaping) page 96). The cross-sectional diagram shows how an artificial scree is constructed. Most types of stone can be used but crushed limestone supports probably the widest variety of plant subjects.

Dwarf conifer gardens Dwarf conifers vary so considerably in shape, habit and colour that it can be difficult to make them part of the structure of a garden. This is the reason why they are more appropriate as an individual collection where they can be enjoyed at close quarters, or as features in an alpine garden since there is a natural affinity between them. Always check the ultimate height and spread of conifers sold as "dwarf" varieties: some can still reach 2 m (6 ft 6 in) in height.

Pavement rock garden

Pavement garden (cross-section)

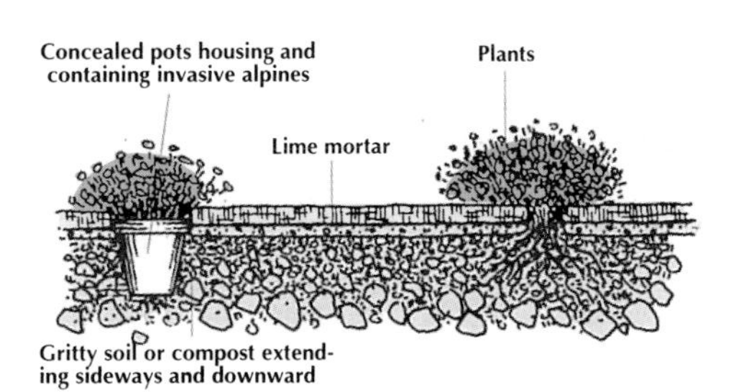

Scree

Cross section

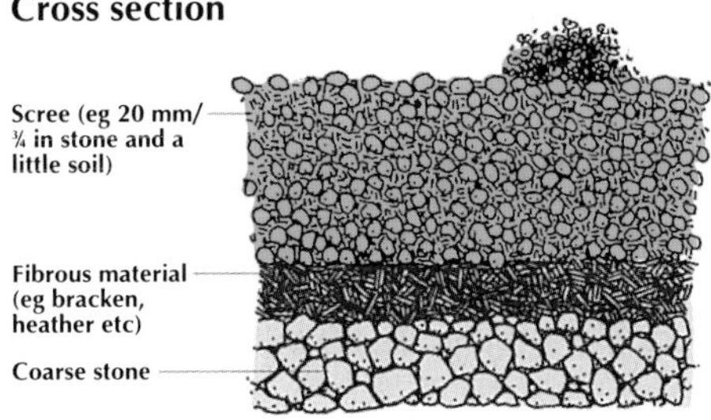

Wildlife gardens

Wildlife conservation as a theme for a private garden is a fairly recent and exciting concept. All conscientious gardeners recognize the serious effects of the continuing loss of wildlife habitats. Social pressures on the environment and modern farming techniques are alleged to be the main causes, but gardens can provide opportunities to create alternative habitats for some species.

It is true that the wildlife garden is not the place for the tidy-minded, or for those who wish to use the garden only for passive relaxation. It requires dedication and commitment, but the rewards are great.

In a tiny plot, planting a single shrub chosen to attract insects and birds can help, while at the other end of the scale some owners of large gardens are developing them as miniature eco-systems.

Planning for wildlife

The creation of a wild garden is a fascinating challenge. Some people think of it as a way of avoiding regular maintenance, but this is not so. Wildlife gardens need to be as well maintained, or rather managed, as any other type but in different ways and with different priorities. A well planned wildlife garden accommodates a wide variety of animals and native plants, plus a few trusted strangers.

To be practical, the needs of the owner's family and those of a wildlife habitat must go hand in hand, with the area designated for the family probably located nearest the house.

Wildlife ponds

Space will determine the size and complexity of the wildlife garden beyond, but where an area of water can be included this will

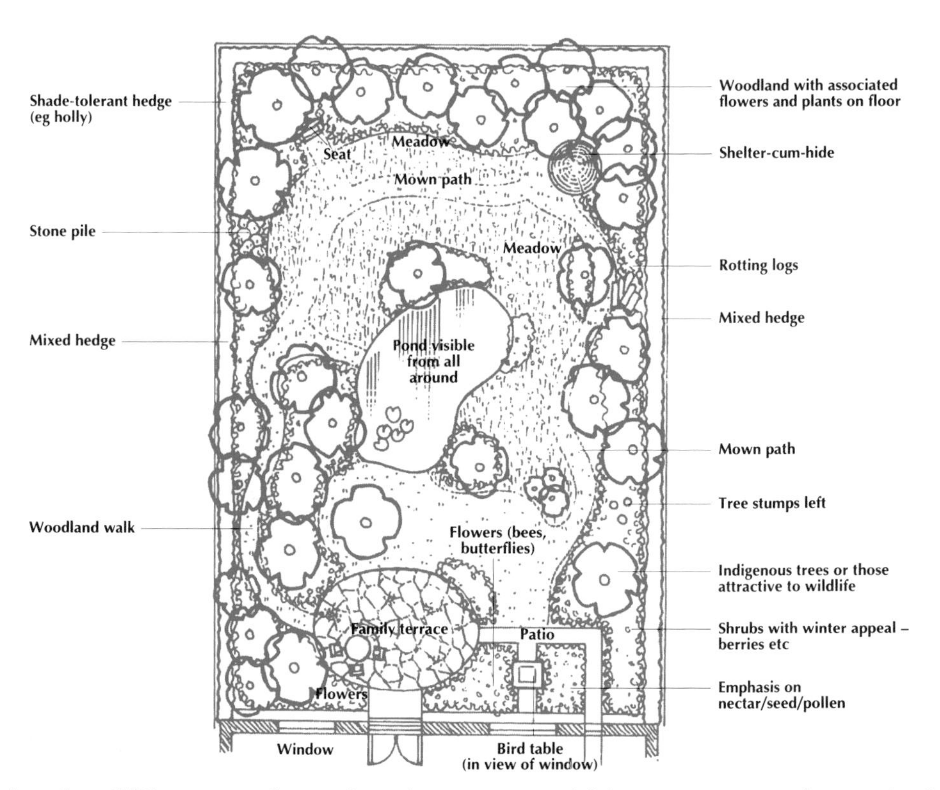

A plan of a wildlife conservation garden The family's domestic needs take second place to the main theme. Many features intended to tempt wildlife are incorporated to make it attractive to visitors, yet it is visually satisfying and practical for the human users.

inevitably become the natural focus. A wildlife pond can be created with a flexible liner sandwiched between protective geotextile layers resting on the native soil. The lining should be well concealed all around. The sides of the pond must be sloped very gently (at a maximum of 20°), since shallow sides are more accommodating to emergent plants, provide easy access for animals and amphibians and help to prevent the soil particles from sliding down to the bottom of the pond.

Having gently sloping sides means that the pond will have to be quite large to achieve the minimum ice-free water depth of 600–750 mm (2–2 ft 6 in) at the centre. An allowance also has to be made for a 150 mm (6 in) soil layer at the sides and bottom for growing plants. The soil layer should be of low-nutrient clay or sub-soil and free of sharp stones which might penetrate the lining.

Wildflower meadows

Wildflower meadows are not simple to achieve. Herbicides or fertilizers must not have been used in the immediate area for at least 18 months, but existing lawn grasses are unlikely to be a good basis for the meadow, so will need to be removed. This might be achieved by lifting the turf and stacking it for use elsewhere after composting or, alternatively, by covering the proposed meadow area with black polythene sheets for a year or so, to kill off all plant growth underneath.

When the area is ready the wild flower and seed mix to be sown should be tailored precisely to the garden soil type, pH and aspect. Consult a specialist in advance for advice about this and about sowing rates and times, which are also critical.

Never expect a wildflower meadow to become established quickly. It can take two years before the meadow begins to match expectations. Even then some flowers will need to be resown annually; the field poppy (*Papaver rhoeas*), which self-sows only on newly-disturbed soil, is an example.

Cutting the wildflower meadow is also important and the appropriate frequency and season will vary according to the kinds of plants grown. Make sure the clippings are always removed to prevent too much plant food returning to the soil and to inhibit fungal growth.

Bird table

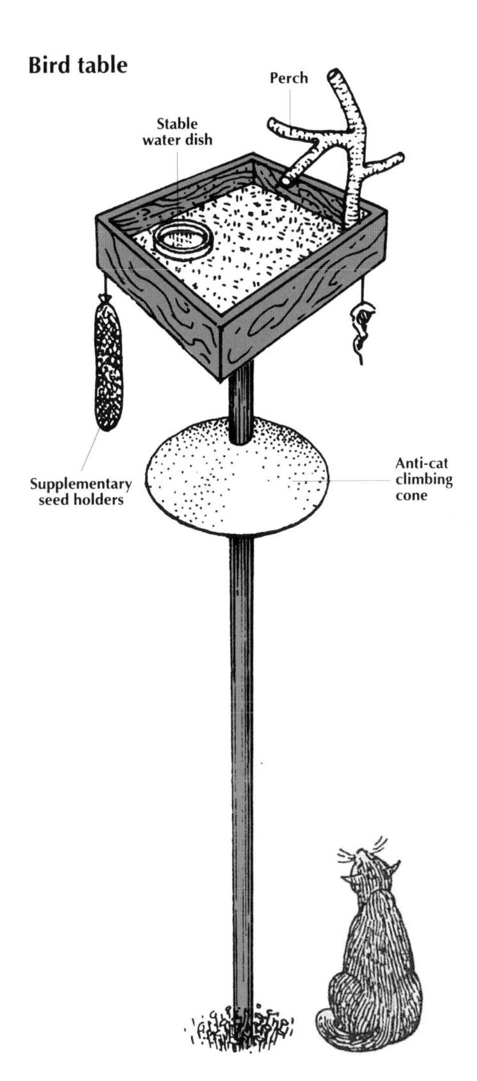

A basic bird table: the tall stand and cone help to keep predators at bay

Where suitable indigenous grasses are already growing and herbicides or fertilizers have not been used, wildflower "plugs" (of small plants) available from some nurseries, can be used. These succeed in established grass sward when seed may not, but if seeding is preferred, the existing grass must be thoroughly and deeply scarified beforehand and all debris removed before sowing takes place.

Wildlife gardens 2

Providing habitats
Trees and plants for a wildlife garden should be selected not only to attract birds, insects and animals as visitors but whenever possible (migrating species excepted) as permanent residents. This is probably the most important function of a wildlife garden.

To help establish young trees on embankments, sink a black plastic plant pot up the slope from the stem at the time of planting. Water poured into the pot will then go straight to the tree's roots rather than running down the embankment. Fill the pot first with crumpled, small-mesh chicken wire to prevent insects, frogs and toads from being trapped inside.

There are many ways in which a garden can be made attractive to wildlife.

Bird tables (See page 169) These range from the basic DIY types to the sophisticated. What is important is that the table is accessible to birds yet safe from predators.

Decomposing logs attract various forms of wildlife including insects, small rodents and fungi. Small ferns and various algae can also take hold, adding further interest.

Bumble bees are usually welcome in a garden. Create a home for them by fixing a flower pot into an embankment, angled so as not to collect rainwater. A layer of fine wood shavings at the bottom will be appreciated by the bees.

Rock or boulder heaps with small spaces left between them will soon be home to various insects, toads and slow-worms.

Various nest boxes encourage bird species

Decomposing logs

Sunken pot for bumble bees

Rock or boulder heaps

Bird nesting boxes

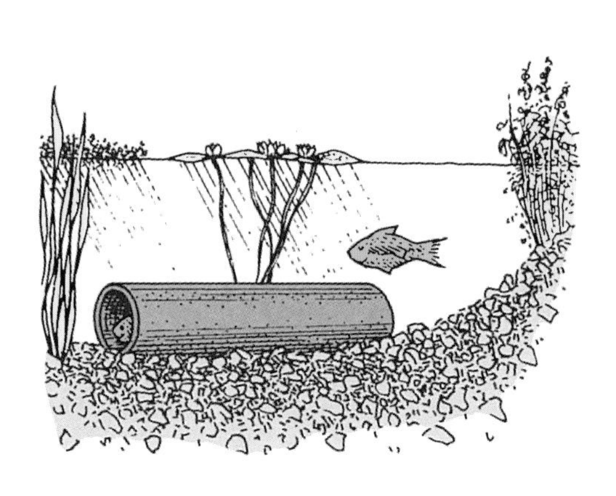

Open-ended pitch/fibre pipes

whose precise nesting requirements may not be met by the trees. The RSPB provides information on the dimensions of the boxes, hole sizes and perches to suit particular species. Boxes, like bird tables, should be positioned well beyond the reach of any predators. Pergolas, arches and redundant swings all qualify as supports from which to hang bird-seed containers. A thorny climbing rose might be used to discourage cats.

Some wildlife pond owners may have mixed feelings when they receive a visit from a heron. To minimize fish losses, provide a refuge for them by placing a number of pitch fibre pipes (pipes used in road drainage works) open both ends and 100 mm (4 in) or more in diameter, at the bottom of the pond. As they are black they soon merge into the soil at the bottom. Alternatively, make the pond extra deep (see Safety in the garden, page 186), remembering that a heron is a wader, not a diver.

To encourage moths and other insects to come to feed, paint a slurry patch onto the side of a tree or two. The slurry is made from a mixture of treacle and ripe bananas with a dash of beer or stout to give added incentive. To attract nocturnal moths and insects, hang a translucent light in a tree or on a pergola. A clear outer cover is essential to prevent moths or insects from injury through direct contact with the hot bulb.

Dried moss, hay and short pieces of string are good nesting materials for birds. Loosely bundle a mixture in some wide mesh sacking, then tie it to a tree branch from late winter onward.

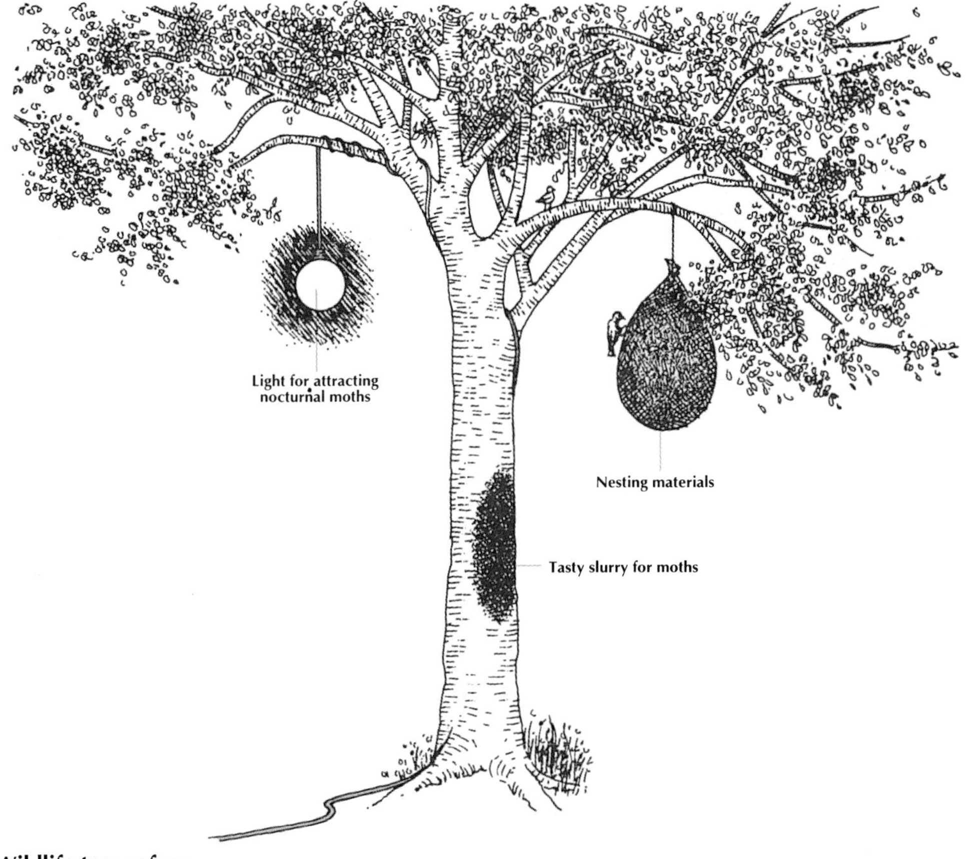

Wildlife tree refuge

Relaxation and play

To many families, facilities for play will take precedence over other garden features. Since features specifically for children are needed for only a relatively short time, they can usually be accommodated without too much trouble, then adapted as the children grow up.

Other facilities for sporting activities may be more permanent. Tennis courts and swimming pools are obvious examples and they must be designed to fit in with the garden's structural elements. Tennis courts need high fences to surround them and, although using black or dark green wire helps to minimize their impact, this is effective only when set against a background of foliage shadow.

Swimming pools become focal points for better or worse. They can be screened with trees but this takes time. Some facilities can be included unobtrusively and fairly easily: putting or croquet lawns may go almost unnoticed when not in use.

Problems usually arise with this sort of feature if they are added when a garden is already in place or on its way to maturity. The closer the new features are to the house, the greater their impact. But it is a question of priorities: some gardeners are proud of their sporting or games facilities and are pleased to show them off, while others camouflage them, preferring to see trees, grass and flowers.

Making space for relaxation

Relaxation can range from doing nothing but lying on the patio or lawn, through weeding the border and growing vegetables, to playing a vigorous game of tennis. Some research will be necessary to ensure that there is enough room for the various recreational activities – not only for their own sake but also so that they can be placed in a pleasing setting in the garden.

Games and recreational facilities

Even passive recreation takes up more space than may be imagined. For example, a lounger needs an approximate length of 4 m (12 ft) and, allowing for access at the sides, a normal dining table and four chairs need a patio width of 4 m (12 ft) at least.

A child's swing requires a minimum distance, back to front, of 4 m (12 ft) to allow room for the swinging movement, or more, depending on the height of the structure.

The space needed for patio chess or draughts varies depending on the size of the squares and pieces used, ranging from multiples of 150 mm (6 in) square upward if standard concrete or clay tiles are used. Alternatively, ready-made rolled or rigid chess "boards" can be purchased, complete with lightweight pieces. The example (bottom) is based on a multiple of 300 mm (12 in) plastic black and white square tiles.

A child's swing

Patio chess or draughts

Table tennis A full-sized table, fixed or moveable, is 2.74 x 1.5 m (9 x 5 ft), but allowing extra room for "run back" – approximately 2 m (6 ft 6 in) – the total playing length is 6.74 m (22 ft).
Swimming pools are limited in size by the available space and the budget, but below 8 x 4 m (22 x 12 ft), adult swimming becomes difficult.
A child's see-saw takes up about 2.5 m (7 ft 6 in) by at least 250 mm (10 in) and, when in use, the width required is far greater.

Slides are typically about 3 m (9 ft 9 in) long. Space should be allowed for a safe landing, which could increase the length required by 1.5m (5 ft), making a total of 4.5m (14 ft 9 in). Slide widths range from a minimum of 500 mm (20 in) upward, but plenty of room must be left for running round the sides for another go. Climbing frames and action equipment vary so much in size and proportion that only careful study of the many catalogues available can

Table tennis

Swimming pool

See-saw

Children's slide

Relaxation and play 2

indicate how much space is needed. As a guide, for a multi-activity frame allow between 2.5 x 3.5 m (8 ft 3 in x 11 ft 6 in).

Tennis must be the ultimate garden game but a full-sized court including "run back" at each end measures 36.57 x 10.97 m (120 x 36 ft). Added to this there is usually a path all around for access and maintenance. A version known as "short tennis" can be played in a smaller space, with a court of 13.4 x 6.1 m (44 x 20 ft). Tennis courts are best sited east to west to avoid having the sun shine directly in the faces of the players.

Croquet is virtually synonymous with warm summer days and lush green lawns. A full-size croquet lawn, which must be flat, takes up a great deal of space: 32.0 x 25.6 m (105 x 84 ft). It may be difficult to achieve this on a sloping site without major cut-and-fill terracing work.

A vegetable plot, an area for retreat and recreation for many gardeners, can be almost any size or shape, although rectangular is perhaps the easiest to manage.

The size of the plot will be determined by the number of people for whom the plot is to provide vegetables and the type of crops it is intended to grow, ranging from main crop potatoes to the choicest vegetables and salads. At the RHS Wisley Garden, there is a series of model vegetable gardens each measuring 27 x 9 m (90 x 30 ft) and each planned to keep a family of three supplied with basic vegetables for a year, if properly managed.

The choice of site for a vegetable plot is important and depends on soil, aspect and shelter. Vegetable gardens are best on gently sloping, well-drained loam, with a sunny, sheltered aspect.

Tennis court

Croquet lawn

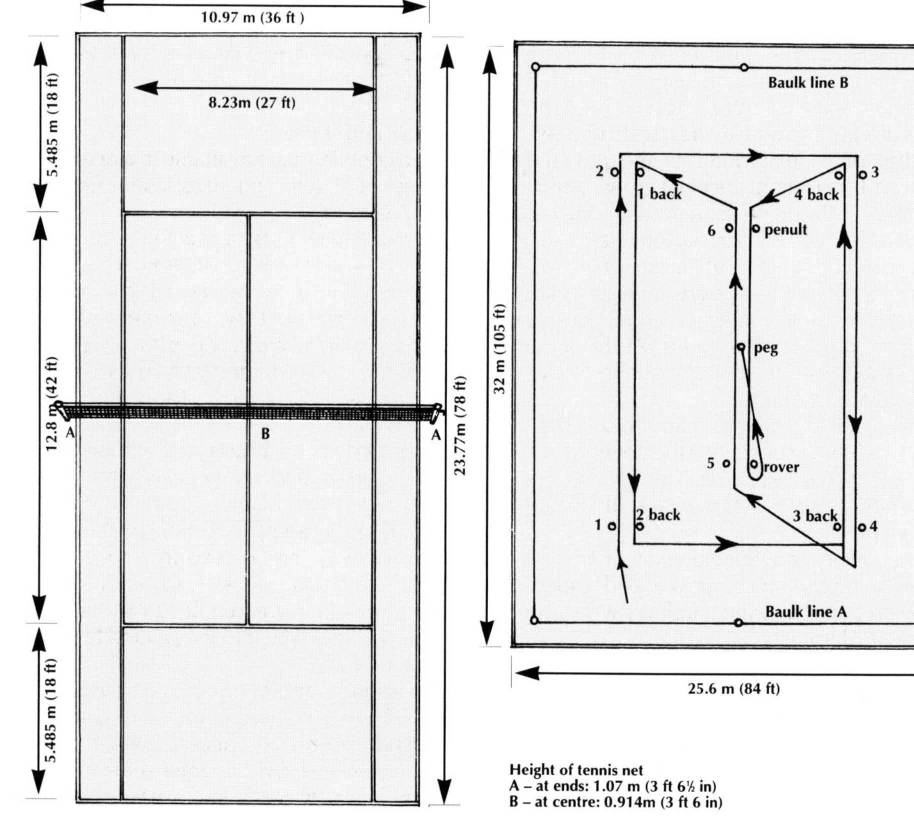

Pots and containers

Planted pots and containers can be used in conjunction with other planting in beds and borders, or to grow plants within areas of hard surfacing. Specific conditions can be created in containers to suit plants that might not otherwise thrive in a particular site or soil.

Pots and containers are available in a variety of materials including terracotta, concrete, stone (real or reconstituted), various metals, glazed earthenware and plastic. Some gardeners like their containers to follow a theme; others are happy with a random selection.

Adverse weather conditions

Containers used outside in a temperate climate should not only be frost-proof but also shaped to allow frozen soil or compost to expand harmlessly inside, otherwise the container may crack open. Containers with straight sides widening outwards toward the top are best. Narrow-necked pots or containers should be completely emptied of soil and plants at the onset of cold weather if they are to stay outside. With few exceptions, pots need to be well drained. They also need to be placed carefully: in permanent sunshine during hot summers the contents of a pot can quickly heat up to temperatures that may be harmful to the pot, the compost and the roots of the plant growing in it.

To cope with these extreme conditions, choose sun-loving plants, water regularly and use a porous pot made of unglazed terracotta, for example. Pots of this type absorb water, then release it slowly, through evaporation, cooling not only the pot but its contents. At the same time, the water vapour creates a humid microclimate around the plant.

Pots and their contents can freeze right through in winter, especially if the pot is poorly drained and the compost wet. This in conjunction with cold winds is detrimental to all but the hardiest of plants.

A good nursery should help you to make the right choice. If you want to grow a tender specimen, be prepared to bring it indoors when the temperature plummets.

Pots in groups

When arranging pots in groups, try using odd numbers and different sizes, with the tallest at the rear if they are to be viewed mainly from one side. If the composition is more of an "island" within the patio and intended to be enjoyed from all sides, experiment by placing the largest or tallest pot at, or near, the centre.

Form and shape

The relationship of form and shape between plants and containers is as important as that between colours: one must complement or harmonize with the other. Try to seek out the natural harmony of shapes when choosing plants for specific containers: shape and "weight" should combine as a pleasing whole. A large or dense plant in a small or delicate-looking container can easily look off-balance.

Creating an harmonious composition based on the position and shape of the plants is also important. A tall conical dwarf conifer placed at the centre of a flattish bowl, for example, could look out of proportion, but when the same tree is positioned off-centre and other, less rigid plants added to soften the conifer's geometric shape, it can make a pleasing and balanced composition. The illustrations on pages 176–177 are examples of balanced plants-to-container relationships.

Materials and styles

Pots and containers are available in a bewildering range of shapes and sizes, made from all kinds of materials.

Terracotta (clay) pots, since they "breathe" and absorb water, are considered superior to other types by keen gardeners, but always check whether or not they are frost-proof. Clay pots have many imitators, with plastic probably second favourite, but nothing can quite replace the natural affinity of terracotta with gardens the world over.

Stone or terracotta bowls make good focal points or centre-pieces, especially when filled with lower-growing plants.

Clay land drain pipes, if frost-proofed by dipping, or glazed, can be used to grow a wide range of alpines or herbs. A variety of sizes, arranged upright in a group, look very striking. Sink them a little way into the ground to make them more stable.

Prefabricated planters or containers made *in situ* may have to be used in roof and patio gardens with restricted access when large containers are needed, or larger prefabricated containers can be assembled on site.

Pots and containers 2

Planters made of planks or railway sleepers (ties) can be used in informal garden situations to give a robust appearance, with the planks or sleepers sawn to size and bolted together. Sleepers or ties are pre-treated with preservative, so they are long lived, but you should treat any timber obtained direct from a supplier, with non-toxic preservative.

Many stone (real or reconstituted) container styles are available. Choose a style that suits the garden or patio. Real stone pots or containers are, however, much more expensive than reconstituted stone since each is individually cut or hand carved – a time-consuming process, but the results are usually beautiful. The choice of stone for use in a temperate climate must be carefully made, as non-durable types can deteriorate in frost, suffering the same forces of expansion and contraction as the frozen soil within. There is always an increased risk when importing natural stone and terracotta pots from warm environments into cold climates, so always check before you make your purchase that your pot is frost proof. As a rule, pots and containers carved from stone have a small, and close granular structure (Portland stone, for example). Some of the more obviously stratified stones are not suitable because of their inbuilt lines of weakness, along which cracks can easily form.

The "stone" pots and containers available form most garden centres are, more often than not, reconstituted stone. In other words, the original stone has been ground down and mixed with cement, then moulded into shape by mechanical means. The cheaper pots are

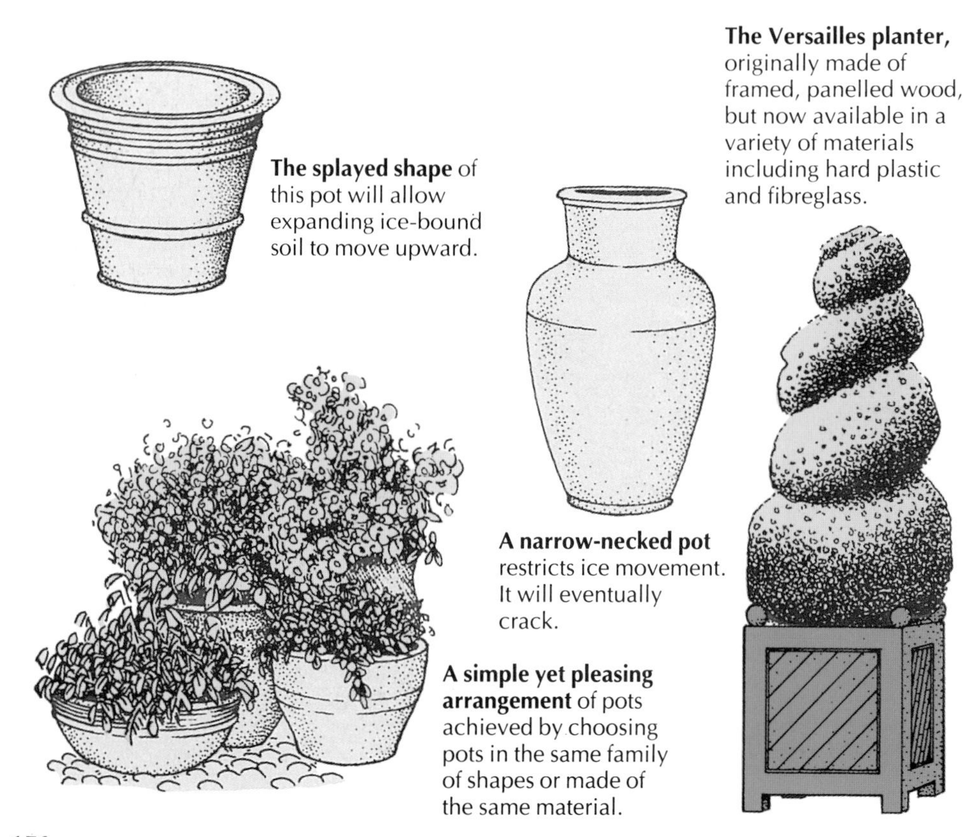

The splayed shape of this pot will allow expanding ice-bound soil to move upward.

The Versailles planter, originally made of framed, panelled wood, but now available in a variety of materials including hard plastic and fibreglass.

A narrow-necked pot restricts ice movement. It will eventually crack.

A simple yet pleasing arrangement of pots achieved by choosing pots in the same family of shapes or made of the same material.

made from basic concrete, sometimes coloured. To achieve a suitable strength, reconstituted stone containers are usually much thicker than their terracotta counterparts, and size for size, are much heavier. They do not allow the plants to "breathe" as terracotta does, and most are impervious to water so efficient drainage holes are essential.

Metal pots are very hard-wearing and those made from bronze or lead improve with age. Copper pots should be lined (including the upper rim) with plastic, as rainwater and air combine to cause copper salts to form and these are poisonous to plants when they come into contact with the stems, leaves or roots.

Hanging half-pots could provide the answer where space is limited or where a bare wall needs to be brightened up. These are available in reproduction stone, metal and terracotta.

Old chimney pots, particularly the decorative Victorian variety, make unusual plant containers or, individually, distinctive focal points.

Strawberry pots are often used to grow other trailing plants. Originally made of terracotta, they are now available in other materials, including plastic.

Modern fibreglass or rigid plastic containers are mostly of a geometric shape and may have a textured or smooth exterior. Some also have self-watering systems within, making them ideal for roof and patio gardens.

Before buying them, make sure that plastic or rigid plastic pots are proof against ultraviolet light damage or discolouration.

Old stone sinks and horse troughs are eminently suitable for miniature gardens. Their popularity means they are in short supply – if you must have one, be prepared for some expense.

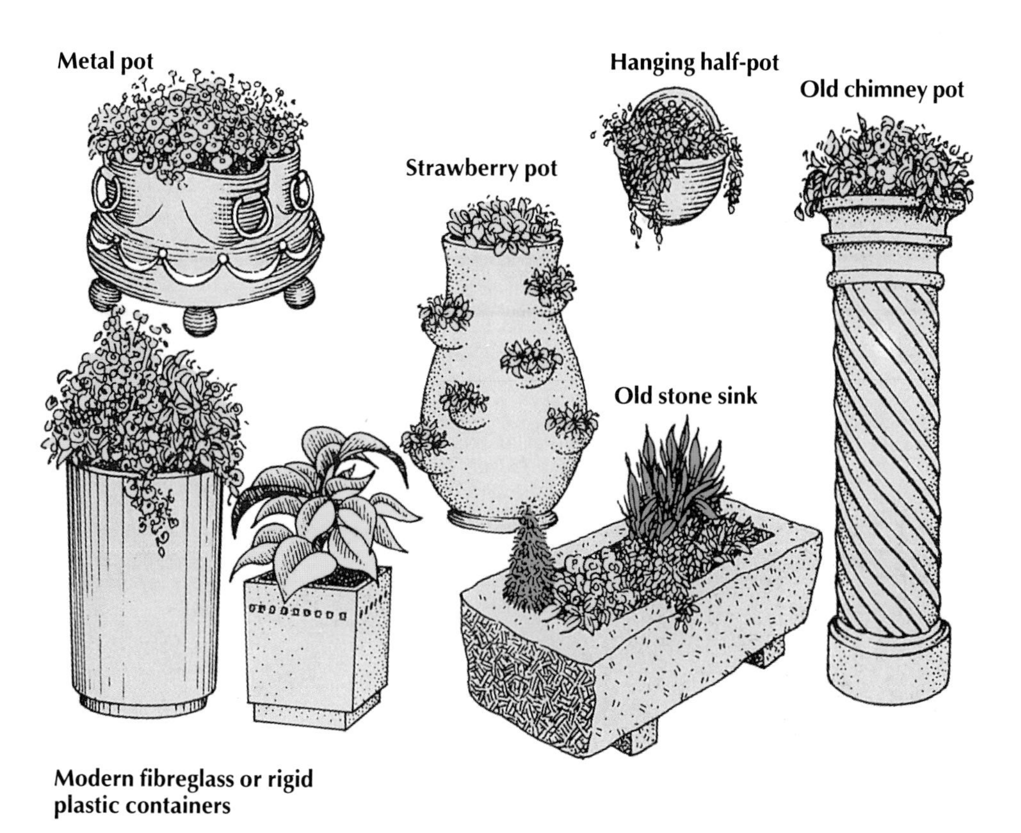

Lighting the garden

A still largely unexploited aspect of garden design, lighting can dramatically transform a garden so that it appears quite different at night. It can make a garden more accessible at night and also increase security by deterring burglars.

Practically any effect can be created, from the most subtle glow to the highly theatrical illumination and, with imaginative circuitry, the lighting can be altered to suit the mood of the moment.

Successful lighting must be planned carefully, and basic ideas for the whole garden are best incorporated at the initial design stages. The effects of artificial light and shade are, however, sometimes difficult to anticipate, unlike the shape of a tree or shrub. For this reason, be prepared to modify initial ideas when the circuitry is in place. The intensity and direction of lights can be altered and clear or diffused lights tried out until a satisfactory result is achieved. This can be done only at night, of course, on a trial-and-error basis.

The alternative is to employ a garden lighting specialist who will have knowledge of a range of fittings and their potential effects. Ask to see a portfolio of work before coming to a decision; it may provide inspiration as well as demonstrating the specialist's skill.

Light fittings

Some light fittings are meant to be seen and will be on show both day and night. The ornamental standard lamps on page 179, for example, at night light a large area because of their height but during the day can act as focal points in their own right. Other fittings, usually of an unobtrusive colour and shape, are intended to be hidden from general view and only their lighting effects seen.

There are fittings that emit a general light, such as the translucent globe (below left) which provides a diffused glow. These are useful for all-round illumination of path corners, shrub beds, trees and so on. Others are directional, emitting well defined shafts of light. These are called "spotlights" and can be used to pick out an individual feature from its surroundings as a night-time focal point. The spiked spot (below left) and other general-purpose mobile units are intended to be moved around the garden and

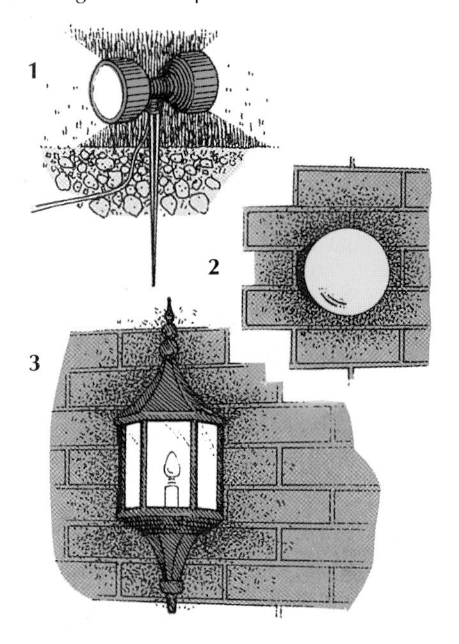

1 Twin-headed spiked spotlight
2 Translucent wall globe for general use
3 "Period" coach lamp on wall

A sunken spotlight housed below ground under a toughened glass cover has a theatrical effect up-lighting a tree.

are powered with a trailing cable. Depending on the lens type, these can give either a general glow or a narrow beam. Some versions are intended to be permanently mounted on a fixed base and typically provide low-level illumination at a path curve. Such units are inconspicuous within the adjacent planting during the daytime.

Positioning lights

It is disconcerting to visitors when, in darkness, the house name or number cannot be read, or a path or drive route is obscure. Well lit driveways and front doors are welcoming and safe for visitors and well designed illumination to a house front can place a different accent upon its architecture with usually pleasing results.

As a general rule, path lights are best when placed at or just above ground level. Plants and trees look better "up-lit", with the light positioned below and pointing upward, than "down-lit", as their forms and textures can then be better appreciated from a normal standing or sitting position. The dramatic effect of a sunken spotlight up-lighting a tree is illustrated on page 178. Down-lighting, by contrast, is particularly effective for statuary of human form, which can look rather sinister when up-lighting is used.

The effects achieved by well positioned lights can be dramatic, but over-use will result in the same confusing effect as when too many daytime focal points are visible at the same time. Take care also to direct bright lights away from main viewing positions, such as the patio or house windows. Lights shining directly into eyes or just visible to one side can be uncomfortable and will also obscure the view of the garden.

Levels of lighting

Never over-light the garden. In addition to having a disturbing effect on any wildlife, it tends to make the garden look so similar to the way it appears during daytime that the exercise seems rather pointless. However, insufficient lighting, with just the odd light at a distance, may make some of the farther areas appear remote or unfriendly. Feelings of vulnerability may also result if a sitting area is well lit while the area all around is in darkness. It is better to create a

A high-level spotlight, in this case attached to a sturdy branch of an adjacent tree, provides dramatic down-lighting.

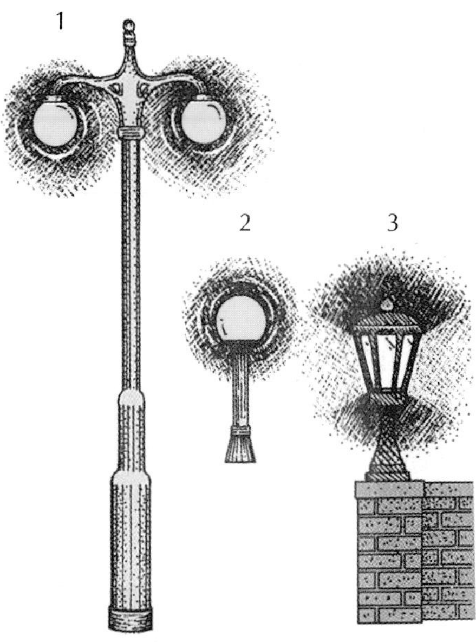

1 Full standard lamp (globe form)
2 Half standard lamp (globe form)
3 Quarter standard lamp set on a wall pier

Lighting the garden 2

balanced scheme, with areas of comparative light and shade in conjunction with occasional brighter accents.

Functional lighting

One of the first areas to be considered for illumination, apart from the area immediately surrounding the house and patio, is probably a swimming pool.

Underwater lights are available for both ornamental and swimming pools in many styles. In the swimming pool, special waterproof fittings are fitted to be flush to the pool sides and bottom for safety's sake. These can make swimming at night as appealing as in the day – sometimes even more so. Alternatively, floating lights can look very effective. Specially made for the purpose, they are normally battery-operated.

Good lighting, preferably on separate circuits, will make other recreational areas of the garden not only useable but also inviting in the evening: the tennis court, putting green and croquet lawn can all be used during twilight hours if sufficiently well lit.

Coloured lights

Coloured lights add a further dimension to garden illumination. Of the range of coloured bulbs available, red and green are the most commonly used. Green light is mysterious but, when shining on human skin, it is distinctly unflattering; yellow has a similar effect. Red imparts a warm glow which might not be welcome on a hot evening, when the cooler effect of white or blue light is preferable. Blue light, because of its longer wave length, usually looks diminished and fainter than yellow and red lamps of equal wattage.

Installing garden lighting

It is important when installing any garden lighting or power circuits that a qualified electrician or lighting engineer be employed. He or she can not only advise how to achieve lighting effects but can install it safely. Always ensure that lights and electrical fittings used outside are intended for that specific purpose.

Lighting styles (some illustrated below)

Japanese lanterns were traditionally carved

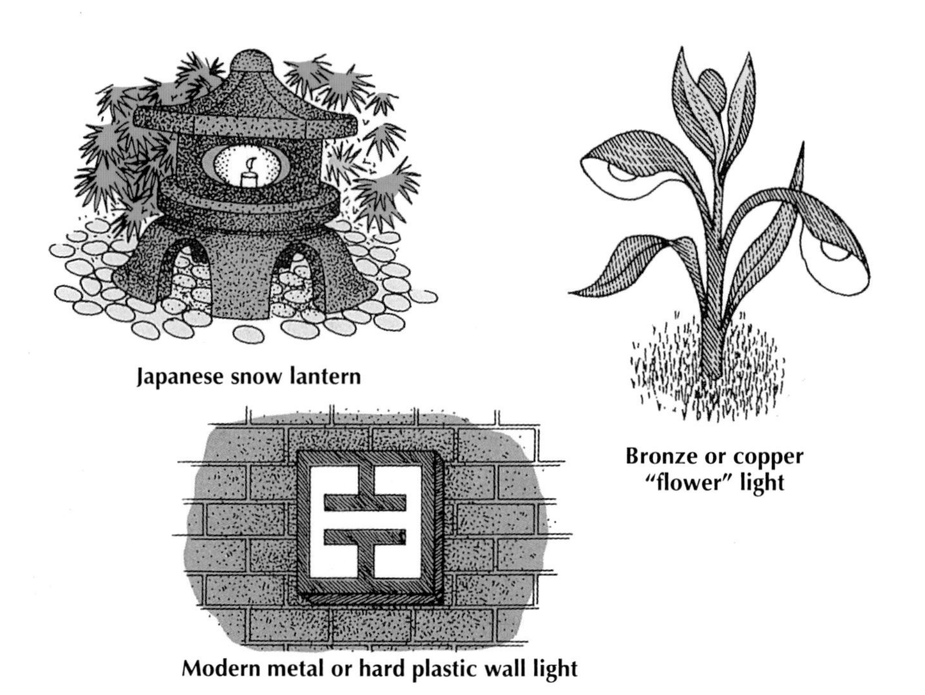

Japanese snow lantern

Bronze or copper "flower" light

Modern metal or hard plastic wall light

from stone in a variety of styles. Modern editions are available in reconstituted stone.

Metal "flower" and "plant" lamps are eye-catching, probably more so in the day than at night. Mostly made of anodized bronze or copper, they are very popular in the US.

Enamelled coloured lights of modern design look best associated with modern architecture.

Chinese lanterns are very cheery with inherent party qualities. If, as is traditional, they are made of paper, it would be safer to use them with electric lights than candles, because the lightweight lamps are easily rocked by breezes and may catch fire.

A fountain is even more spectacular when illuminated at night. The water droplets reflect the rays of the lamps in the pool beneath.

Mushroom lights are useful for illuminating paths and borders where the effect of the light is wanted without a view of the source, which could be distracting. Mushroom lights are mostly made from coated or enamelled steel or aluminium and are available in a range of colours. Bollard lamps in a variety of styles and materials are also useful for general illumination and for lighting a driveway or path, when they can be positioned as a series. Coated metal bollard lamps are available which have a modern look.

Recessed lights are useful for illuminating steps, paths and adjacent architecture. They are available in various sizes but the most commonly used type is the size of a brick: 215 x 65 mm (9 x 2¾ in). The lamp is built in flush with the wall. A special hood is available to direct the light downward, and can be painted the same colour as the wall.

Festive lighting

Fairy lights can be an enchanting addition to garden illumination. Normally woven in and out of the branches of trees, they make a wonderful spectacle, especially when reflected in snow.

Giant candles light the garden effectively for parties and barbecues. These range from glass-filled cylindrical "candles" to large wax and wicker ones. A candle can also be placed in a jar suspended from a branch, but always make sure there is a heat-deflecting plate included to reduce rising heat damage to the tree.

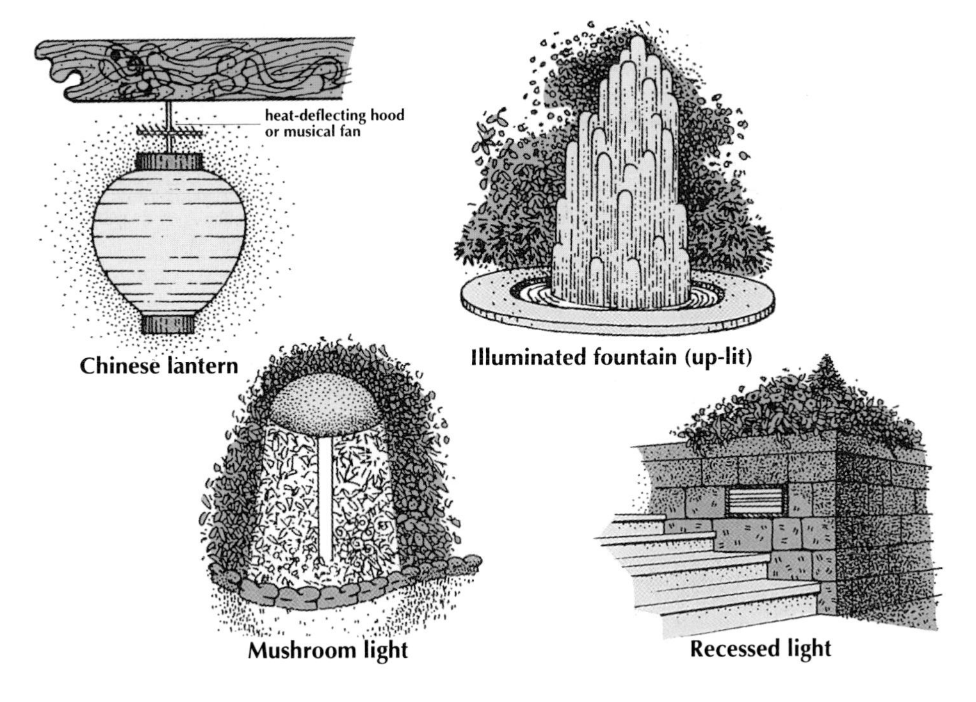

Chinese lantern

Illuminated fountain (up-lit)

Mushroom light

Recessed light

Low maintenance by design

An important part of good garden design is a fair calculation of the time required for maintenance. No garden, however delightful initially, will continue to be so if it is not properly maintained, so a compromise must be reached at the design stage between what is desired in the garden and what can reasonably be maintained.

Maintenance can be reduced in two ways: firstly by incorporating labour-saving devices into the fabric of the garden construction; secondly by using efficient techniques during the day-to-day maintenance procedures.

"Designed in" maintenance devices

Tree guards Plastic tree guards are useful to protect the tree from bark-eating rodents and, depending on the design, to protect the tree from cold winds in its early years. Flexible tree guards are available in the form of square or round plastic tubes of various heights, or as spirals which are wound around the tree stem. Tree ties should be checked regularly to ensure they are neither too loose nor too tight.

Paving surfaces

These should be designed to be easily cleaned by brushing or washing off. If the surface is too rough, detritus will become trapped in the surface holes and hollows; too smooth and the paved surface will become slippery in wet or icy conditions. If necessary, try test-brushing a sample at the stockist.

Mowing edges

Where grass grows directly against a wall or steps, cutting is difficult and abrasions may be caused to hands or knuckles when using shears or mowers. Equipment and machinery can also be damaged. A good cutting edge has its upper surface set just below that of the adjacent grass

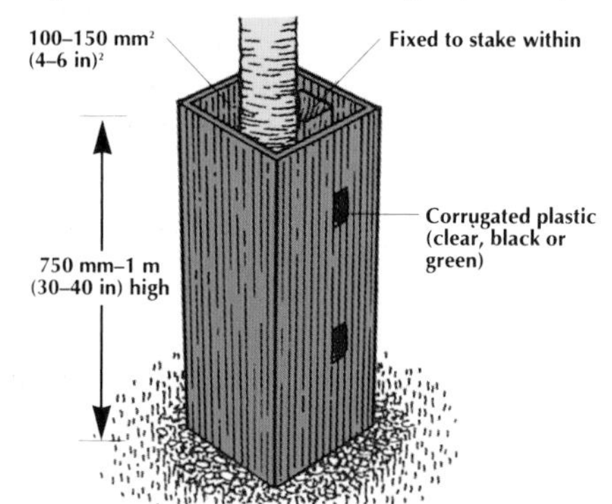

Box-type tree guard

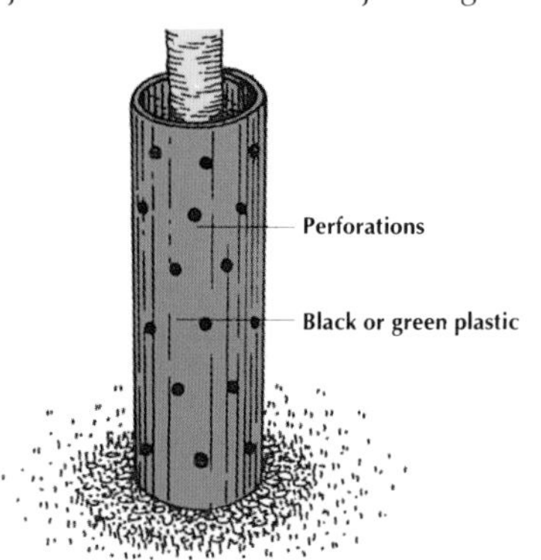

Split-tube tree guard

Evenly surfaced textured paving

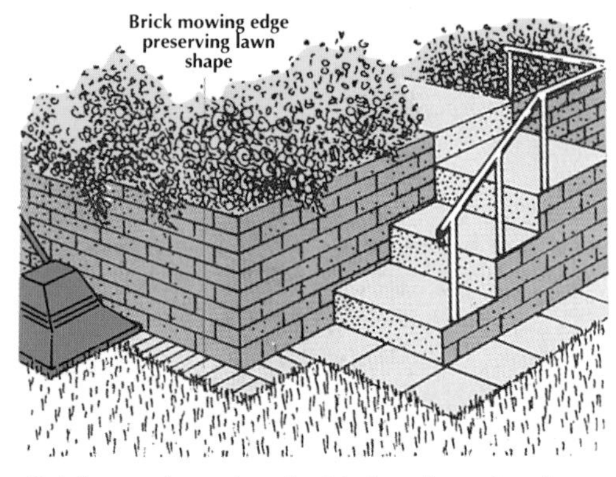

Brick mowing edges just below lawn level

turf, so that no contact damage is inflicted on or by mower blades. The mowing edge itself can be of practically any flat material. Brick, concrete or stone are all suitable but the choice should be influenced by materials in adjacent constructions.

Laying the mowing edge on a bed of mortar ensures that it is stable and remains level or at least even (if on a slope). For low walls up to 900 mm (3 ft) high, a 100–150 mm (4–6 in) wide mowing edge is appropriate. Above this height, a 225 mm (9 in) wide edge is more accommodating to mowing equipment.

Lawn edging

Some lawns need to be physically contained to preserve their shape. This is particularly important in a formal layout. If a mowing edge is not wanted but the shape of the lawn is still to be preserved, use a timber or steel edge set just below the level of the turf.

Where paths cross lawns, lay them so that the upper surface is at or just below that of adjacent turf levels. Where a bed or border abuts a path, ensure that the soil level is below that of the path. This will discourage soil migration onto the path itself by acting as a mini retaining wall.

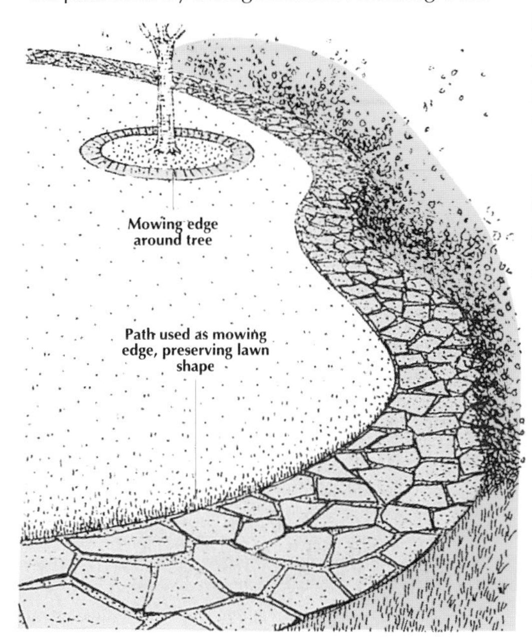

Mowing edge preserves lawn shape

Mulching

This helps to suppress weed growth and reduces the need for watering. Mulches are useful for most plant situations and can be applied around shrubs, borders, vegetables and fruit. Where trees are planted in areas of long grass a proprietary flexible mulch (polythene, PVC or natural fibre and bitumen felts) is effective. Bitumen and natural fibre felts break down after a few years, so do not have to be lifted.

Organic or gravel mulches conserve moisture, making plants grow more healthily and inhibiting weed growth. Not all plants like mulches immediately around them, however. Those with bulbs or rhizomes, such as irises, need to be sun-ripened, as do the soft stems of some herbaceous plants. Mulches should be applied at a minimum depth of 75 mm (3 in) and then left on the soil surface, not dug in. In open areas where the mulch becomes a ground cover in its own right, gravel, pebbles or stone can be used.

Weed growth can be inhibited by placing polythene sheets or a geotextile membrane beneath the mulch. The latter is self-draining, while polythene may need to be punctured to provide drainage holes. Save time on maintenance, sowing, planting and lifting by choosing permanent plants, such as shrubs, trees and perennials, rather than annuals or bedding plants. When slopes are steep or inaccessible to mowing equipment or regular cultivation, use a vigorous ground-cover plant instead.

Good nurseries will give advice based upon precise information that they have regarding site, soil and aspect. On embankments, ground-cover plants should be planted a little more closely than they would be on a level site. This helps to ensure that they establish quickly and spread, in spite of the slope's drier and more inhospitable environment.

Irrigation systems

One of the necessary but potentially most labour-intensive maintenance operations is watering. In hot summers, pots and containers especially need to be watered usually once a day and pots and containers sometimes twice.

Mulching and incorporating organic materials into the soil is always helpful in retaining water. However, in areas of low rainfall or where hot dry summers are the norm, it is worth investigating the possibility of having an

Low maintenance by design 2

irrigation system installed and, the larger the garden, the more labour-saving it will be. There is a choice of types ranging from simple tap-operated DIY kits to sophisticated timed multi-systems that must be designed and installed by professionals. Irrigation systems operate more efficiently and cost-effectively at night, when the water is absorbed into the soil and taken up by the plant with least water loss through evaporation.

The "pop-up" watering head illustrated below (a) is for planted and grassed areas. An alternative is the looped, leaking pipe system (b), which may be unsophisticated but is much less wasteful than the sprinkler as a means of irrigation. If a conventional hose is your preferred method for watering, save time by fitting a winding reel, either wall-mounted or mobile. This is quick to use and helps to prevent the hose from twisting.

Sloping areas

When a grass embankment slopes downward to finish at a fence or wall, conventional mowing is often impossible (see examples, bottom) Lengthy cutting sessions with the shears or strimmers may then be needed. As a more workable alternative, it is better to create a level area at the bottom of the slope that is wide enough to accommodate mowers. In conjunction with this, place a mowing edge against the fence or wall.

Strimmers are easy to use for cutting grass in awkward places, as are some hover mowers, but both the operator and any young trees and shrubs incorporated in the lawn need to be protected. Goggles or a face mask should be worn to protect the operator from flying stems, gravel or soil, and trees benefit from having a durable plastic guard at their bases to protect the stems from strimmer laceration or bruising.

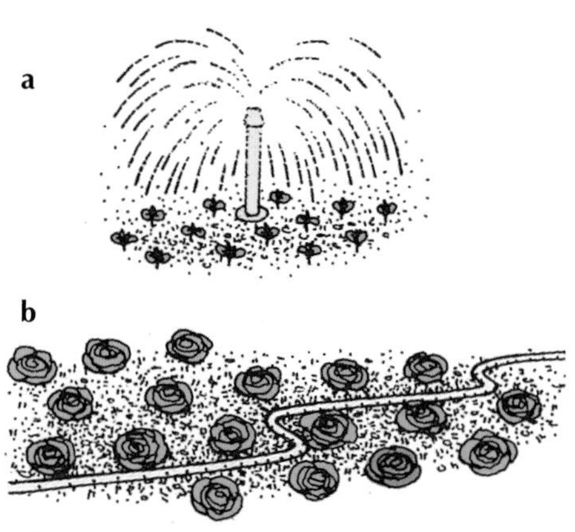

(a) "Pop up" watering system
(b) Leaky pipe

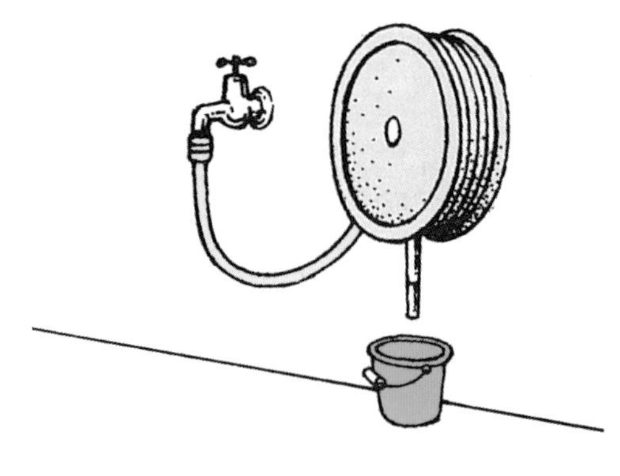

Conventional hose with reel

Grass sloping down to fence or wall

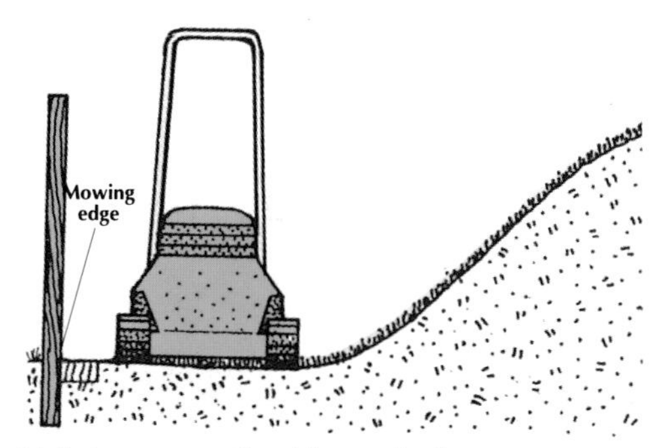

Maintenance path with gentle slope

Structures
The maintenance of all structures must form part of the programme. Structures of stone, concrete and brick will call for the least attention, apart from cleaning.

Timber structures and fences need to be checked regularly for signs of rot or deterioration and dealt with appropriately. Practically all soft woods can be pre-treated with a suitable wood preservative but are then guaranteed only for a finite period of time, typically 12 to 15 years. The life of many garden structures should exceed this, so they will almost certainly need a "follow up" treatment with preservative. Alternatively, use the initially more expensive hardwoods, but only those obtained from renewable sources.

Stained preservatives applied to wood are longer-lasting and far less time-consuming and costly to apply than paint. Paint must be re-applied on more a regular basis, especially on hardwoods, and removing any climbing plants from the structure can be awkward.

Access
For garden machinery access, make sure the plan takes account of the type and size of equipment and machinery necessary to maintain the garden and allow adequate access. Where new gardens are concerned this may include larger construction plant or machinery. The need for access points can be easily underestimated or even overlooked during the planning stage.

Chemical herbicides
Garden chemicals can be dangerous to humans, animals and plants. Their degree of effectiveness under the right conditions, however, is unquestionable. Some herbicides prevent weed germination while others kill growing weeds.

Always seek expert advice about the particular type to use in a given situation and follow to the letter the manufacturers' instructions on mixing, application and storage; and unless you are totally familiar with their effects.

Awkward areas and embankments planted with vigorous ground cover plants, not grass

Timber structures should be stained with preservative, or cell-cured, not painted

Safety in the garden

Safety in the garden must be included in the original list of requirements as a priority. Safety procedures must be observed not only during the maintenance and day-to-day use of the garden, but also during its construction. Machinery and mechanical plant should always be made safe and used only in accordance with recognized procedures: hands, feet, eyes and ears should be protected by suitable clothing.

Fires should be sited in open areas and never left unattended. Trenches should be supported from within and covered after the working day. Tidiness is important: many accidents occur when materials or tools are left lying about after hours. Children are particularly at risk here.

Where possible, fence off work areas whether you are doing the work yourself or engaging the services of a contractor. The immediate area of operations is then made secure and the inevitable disruption or mess contained. Skips and any materials left on public roads must be well signposted and lit.

Using the garden safely

When in use, a garden must always be a safe place: paving should not be uneven or slippery; steps should be convenient and safe to climb; structures should be soundly built and well founded so that they do not blow over or collapse under the weight of plants or snow. There are many potentially dangerous situations: slippery slopes or ramps, pot holes in the lawns or paving, or insecure fences which could allow children or pets to slip out, but there are less obvious hazards too. Projecting hanging baskets and window boxes pose a danger to passers-by, who can collide with them – or they may even fall to the ground if inadequately fixed. Windows or doors opening outward onto adjacent pathways can also injure passers-by. Avoid this by placing a border next to the house equal in width to the opened window or door.

Dangerous plants

Many popular plants have thorns or sharp-edged leaves, poisonous fruits, seeds, flowers, stems or roots, or may cause skin or eye irritation. For gardens which are to be used by young children and pets, check for any potentially hazardous plants at the planning stage and exclude them. Consider all the features on the requirements list to see if they might be dangerous.

Water in the garden

Water is one of the most obvious dangers in a garden and should be incorporated with the utmost care. Young children and elderly people are particularly at risk. Safety fences, high enough to prevent anyone from falling in, must not be positioned too near the edge of a pool, or they may prevent someone who has fallen in the water from getting out. Internal pool slopes steeper than 20 degrees are dangerous, especially when the pool has a smooth line, again because it makes the pool difficult to climb out of. Underwater steps sloping back into the water are a safer option, but if in doubt, postpone constructing the pool until children are older.

Safety as a priority

Always employ a qualified person to carry out electrical installations and use a circuit breaker on all exterior electrically powered tools. Always put tools and machinery away securely: never leave them lying around the garden.

Gardening clubs and colleges of agriculture often run courses in garden safety and it would be advisable to enroll for one of these before starting the garden construction. Learning first aid to deal with anything from stings to electric shocks and deep cuts should be as much of a priority as acquiring garden maintenance skills.

Garden chemicals

Chemical herbicides must be used strictly in accordance with the manufacturer's instructions and stored securely. If misused they can cause poisoning through skin- or eye-contact, by ingestion or inhalation, depending on the type. Some cause irreversible damage to the respiratory system and internal organs: these are potential killers and must be handled with great care. Never use herbicides unless you are totally familiar with their application and effects. Climatic conditions are an important factor, as is the time lapse necessary before entering an area after herbicidal application – both for animals and humans. Protective clothing and a face mask must be worn when such chemicals are used.

Various publications deal with the use of herbicides and the need for secure storage: they are essential reading. A safer alternative would be to use more natural methods of weed control, which are becoming increasingly available.

Implementing the plan

On completion of the garden design, work out a strategy for its implementation. From the start, some idea as to the degree of involvement of the owner and designer will have been agreed according to ability, commitment and available time. Some sections of a garden's implementation, such as planting out, might be enjoyable and these are most likely to be carried out by the owner; other tasks may involve skilled labour and specialized equipment and may be best left to contractors.

Choose only those nurseries, suppliers or contractors who are known or recommended to you. Obtain references for contractors and follow them up. Check whether your contractor is a member of a recognized professional trade body: such organizations supply lists of their members.

Organizing the work

Creating a garden on your own means that the pace can be set according to the time and money available. Part of the strategy, then, is to know the scope of your own ability and then to obtain estimates from a professional for the remainder of the work.

You will need to draw up a timetable of tasks, some to be carried out by yourself, others by the contractor. The result will probably show a series of overlapping phases, for logistical, constructional and horticultural reasons.

Estimates and contracts

Estimates should always be sought from suppliers and contractors before orders are placed or instructions given. Obtain several estimates and, in the case of a professional contractor, a quotation if possible.

A quotation differs from an estimate in that it sets out a mutually agreed fixed price. An estimate can rise, indeed it is more likely to rise than to fall. Contractors' estimates can vary according to instructions to include labour only, or labour and materials. Ensure that everyone asked to quote or estimate is given the same information and requirement details. Each estimate will then be based on the same work.

If appropriate, obtain in writing a commencement and finishing date for the contract (weather permitting). At the same time agree the payment terms and the timing of payments. Alterations made to the plan during the contract period will have cost implications. These should be agreed before the event and not afterwards, since misunderstandings of this nature can easily lead to dispute.

Reputable nurseries, suppliers and contractors will usually guarantee their plants, products and services for up to one year. This assumes that materials and plants are installed properly, used only for their intended purpose and have been maintained conscientiously.

Sequence of action

A logical sequence of events for the realization of a garden would be as follows:

1 **Complete garden plan** to detail.
2 **Prepare a work schedule** taking into account normal seasonal variations.
3 **Order construction materials** and plants, requesting delivery dates appropriate to the timetable and season. Some may have to be ordered months ahead – for more unusual plants, this can take up to a year.
4 **Clear the garden** of unwanted materials, weeds and plants.
5 **Carry out major ground contouring,** taking care not to mix sub-soil and top-soil together.
6 **Install underground service lines,** pipes and drains, removing excess materials from the garden to use for infilling elsewhere. Excavate for ponds. Lay foundations and bases, erect fences and so on. Line out, finish and fill ponds.
7 **Construct all vertical elements,** such as steps, walls and pergolas, followed by the hard horizontal elements, such as patios and paths.
8 **Finalize soil contouring** and bring to adjacent path and patio levels. Cultivate areas to be planted, importing additional or exporting surplus top-soil as required. Incorporate organic materials and fertilizers if and when appropriate.
9 **Implement the planting plan** and mulch on completion. Plant the trees in the proposed grassed areas. Finish planting around pools.
10 **Finely cultivate the areas to be grassed,** incorporating organic matter, fertilizer and surface drainage material appropriate to soil type and intended use, for example ornamental sward or hard-wearing grass for a games area.
11 **Turf or seed** the areas to be grassed.
12 **Make final checks** and any final adjustment.
14 **Work out** a maintenance schedule.
15 **Enjoy the garden** and watch it develop.

Index 1

Index 2/Acknowledgements

Acknowledgements

Editors: Alex Bennion, Diane Pengelly
Executive Art Editor: Mark Richardson
Designer: Victoria Harvey, Town Group Consultancy
Artists: Ken O'Brien, Andrew MacDonald, Maltings Partnership

The designer and owner of the garden featured on the front cover is Penny Sinclair.

THE R.H.S ENCYCLOPEDIA OF PRACTICAL GARDENING

EDITOR-IN-CHIEF: CHRISTOPHER BRICKELL

A complete range of titles in this series is available from all good bookshops or by mail order direct from the publisher. Payment can be made by credit card or cheque/postal order in the following ways:

BY PHONE Phone through your order on our special credit card hotline on 01903 828503; speak to our customer services team during office hours (9am to 5pm) or leave a message on the answer machine, quoting your full credit card number plus expiry date and your full name, address and contact telephone number.

BY POST Simply fill out the order form below (it can be photocopied) and send together with your payment to LITTLEHAMPTON BOOK SERVICES, FARADAY CLOSE, DURRINGTON, WORTHING, WEST SUSSEX BN13 3RB

ISBN	TITLE	PRICE	QUANTITY	TOTAL
1 84000 160 7	Garden Planning	£8.99		
1 84000 159 3	Water Gardening	£8.99		
1 84000 157 7	Garden Structures	£8.99		
1 84000 151 8	Pruning	£8.99		
1 84000 156 9	Plant Propagation	£8.99		
1 84000 153 4	Growing Fruit	£8.99		
1 84000 152 6	Growing Vegetables	£8.99		
1 84000 154 2	Growing Under Glass	£8.99		
1 84000 158 5	Organic Gardening	£8.99		
1 84000 155 0	Garden Pests and Diseases	£8.99		
			Postage & Packing	£2.50
			Grand Total	

Name...(BLOCK CAPITALS)
Address..
....Postcode......................

I enclose a cheque/postal order for £..................... made payable to Octopus Publishing Group Ltd.
or:
please debit my: Access ❑ Visa ❑ AmEx ❑ Diners ❑ account
by £......................... Expiry date..................

Account number ❑❑❑❑❑❑❑❑❑❑❑❑❑❑❑❑

Signature................................

Whilst every effort is made to keep our prices low, the publisher reserves the right to increase the price at short notice. Your order will be dispatched within 28 days, subject to availability. £2.50 p&p applies to UK only. Please call 01903 828503 for details of export p&p.

Registered office: 2-4 Heron Quays, London, E14 4JP Registered in England no 3597451

This form may be photocopied.